FUNDAMENTALS OF MEASUREMENT:

TECHNIQUES AND PRACTICES

FUNDAMENTALS OF MEASUREMENT:

TECHNIQUES AND PRACTICES

Second Edition

N. M. DOWNIE

Professor of Psychology
Purdue University

NEW YORK
OXFORD UNIVERSITY PRESS
LONDON   TORONTO
1967

Third printing, 1968

PREFACE TO THE SECOND EDITION

Almost ten years have passed since the first edition of *Fundamentals of Measurement* was written. This new edition has the same purposes as the earlier one and contains the same basic material. In a decade many advances are made in test development, and frequent changes in test usage occur. New tests appear and old ones slowly disappear. Much research is directed toward the uses to which tests are put, especially in attempts to improve the prediction of human behavior. It is these changes, innovations, and results of research that have been incorporated in this second edition.

The audience for whom the book was written remains the same, the schoolteacher and counselor. An attempt has been made to make it especially meaningful to individuals in those occupations.

N. M. D.

Lafayette, Indiana
June 1966

PREFACE

This book in elementary educational psychological measurement results from teaching classes of students both in psychology and in education. The emphasis in this volume is on the general principles of educational and psychological measurement. This book does not contain, chapter after chapter, a discussion of all the various standardized tests in any one area. A few tests are cited as examples of a group. Neither does the book contain, chapter after chapter, such titles as measurement in biology, evaluation in high-school mathematics, measurement in elementary school mathematics, until all the school subjects have been covered. It is felt that there are general principles of measurement and evaluation which are basic to, and almost the same in, evaluation in all areas of human learning.

It seems that this emphasis on principles is the soundest approach to educational and psychological measurement. The writer feels that students get lost in the maze of detail about tests and research studies pertaining to tests. The common question is, what am I supposed to know about all of this? The unhealthy situation of having to learn a vast number of facts confronts students. As educators, we know that such learning is inefficient and in the long run wasteful.

This book is not an attempt to impress colleagues and others with the writer's erudition. There are plenty of such scholarly tomes in this area now. It is hoped that this book will be of most use to the classroom teacher and others who use tests dealing with individuals extending from the kindergarten through the university. As a result of having read and studied it, a teacher should be able to make better tests, do a better job in evaluating and grading students, and have an understanding of the use and interpretation of standardized tests. Aiding the classroom instructor and the counselor is the chief purpose of this book.

The writer feels that what is covered in this volume must be supplemented with practice. An elementary measurement course should have a laboratory as an integral part of it. Two hours of lecture-discussion and two hours of laboratory work per week for a semester would be a good arrangement. If a situation such as this is not possible, some of the regularly scheduled class periods should be used for these laboratory sessions. At the beginning of the course these work periods could be devoted to developing competence in elementary statistics. Later, time could be spent on item writing. Then a collection of the more widely used standardized tests should be purchased in such areas as intelligence, reading, mechanical ability, interests, and adjustment. These would be administered, scored, discussed, and evaluated by members of the class. There is no better way to learn about the contents, uses, and misuses of standardized tests than by spending the time taking them.

A rather long chapter on elementary statistics appears early in this book rather than at the end of the volume, or, as in some texts, not at all. It is inconceivable to the writer how anyone can work intelligently and successfully in this area without an understanding of the basic statistical principles and manipulations. Enough time should be spent on this material to assure an adequate understanding on the part of the students.

The book is basically made up of three parts. Part I is concerned with elementary statistics, scores, reliability, and validity. Part II is entirely devoted to the construction and use of achievement tests. Part III includes chapters covering the appraisal of intelligence, special abilities, adjustment, interest, attitudes, and teaching. The material can be covered adequately in a one-semester course.

The writer acknowledges the contribution of his teachers and of the writers of all the texts and articles on measurement that he has ever read. But he takes sole responsibility of everything included herein. The writer acknowledges with thanks the permissions to quote references and to use illustrations granted by various authors and publishers. The majority of the clerical work was ably carried on by Virginia De Young. Many of the drawings were made by the writer's wife.

N. M. D.

Lafayette, Indiana
August 1957

CONTENTS

ix

TABLES AND FIGURES

PART I

STATISTICS, SCORES, THEORY, AND
GENERAL USES OF TESTS

INTRODUCTION: PHILOSOPHY AND PSYCHOLOGICAL PRINCIPLES UNDERLYING EVALUATION AND MEASUREMENT

In this chapter we shall examine both the philosophy and the underlying psychology of measurement and evaluation and some of the basic terms used. Let us begin by considering the words *measurement* and *evaluation* to differentiate between them. MEASUREMENT, as the word is used in daily living, implies the assignment of an exact and quantitative number to an object, such as 2 pounds, 3 yards, 4 amperes, or 50 miles per hour. The early workers in psychometry were basically concerned with trying to measure and describe man as the physical scientist described inanimate objects. "Reaction time," "mental age," "words per minute," and "per cent correct" became part of the working vocabulary of educational and psychological measurement. But these quantitative terms are by themselves of limited use. After measurements are made, they have to be made meaningful by relating them to other variables or studying them statistically or comparatively. Suppose that a student obtains a raw score of 77 on a plane geometry test and that his instructor turns this into a letter grade of "B." Placing this "B" upon the boy's performance is evaluation. EVALUATION, then, in this context of educational and psychological measurement, consists of placing a value on something, on the basis of standards that have been set up.

Today the words *measurement* and *evaluation* are used loosely and frequently interchangeably, for after all there is little that can be learned from raw measurements as they stand after being made. Another word, *appraisal,* is also used more or less as a synonym for *evaluation.*

Evaluation also has a more restricted use, as shown by the Evaluation Movement of the 1930's and early 1940's. Up to that time, a large part of the measurement activities in schools was concerned with a student's score on a test that mostly measured facts in a course of study. But in the 1930's, emphases were directed to all the objectives of American education—to developing good mental health, for example—and attempts were made to measure attainment of each of these objectives. To do this, new instruments had to be developed, and because of the different nature of the trait or skill measured, these instruments were less precise and less objective than the earlier tests. The use of these new appraisal techniques was referred to as EVALUATION.

Now let us look at a set of assumptions that was drawn up by the Evaluation Staff of the Eight-Year Study (8). These assumptions give a good idea of what is involved in basic educational measurement and evaluation. They can be summarized as follows:

1. Education is a process, the chief goal of which is to bring about changes in human behavior.
2. The sort of behavioral changes that the school attempts to bring about constitute its objectives.
3. Evaluation consists of finding out the extent to which each and every one of these objectives has been attained.
4. Human behavior is so complex that it cannot be described or summarized in a single score.
5. The manner in which an individual organizes his behavior patterns is an important aspect to be appraised. Information gathered as a result of measurement or evaluation activities must be interpreted as a part of the whole. Interpretation of small bits of behavior as they stand alone is of little real meaning.
6. The techniques of measurement and evaluation are not limited to the usual paper-and-pencil tests. Any bit of valid evidence that helps a teacher or counselor in better understanding a student and that leads to helping the student understand himself better

is to be considered worth while. Attempts should be made to obtain all such evidence by any means that seems to work.

7. The nature of the measurement and appraisal techniques used influences the type of learning that goes on in a classroom. If students are constantly evaluated on knowledge of subject-matter content, they will tend to study this alone. Teachers will also concentrate their teaching efforts upon this. A wide range of evaluation activities covering various objectives of a course will lead to varied learning and teaching experiences within a course.

8. The development of any evaluation program is the responsibility of the teachers, the school administrators, the pupils, and, in some respects, the parents. Maximum value can be derived from the most democratic approach, and this involves the participation of all concerned.

From the above, we can infer that evaluation should be comprehensive enough to cover all aspects of an individual's growth and adjustment. All data obtained should be put together to give a total picture of the individual. Many different types of evaluative devices must be constantly in use to carry on all the different types of appraisals needed for the understanding of the individual. And, finally, it must be re-emphasized that the *type* of evaluation practiced affects both learning and teaching.

THE PURPOSES OF EVALUATION

At this point we shall briefly list the purposes of measurement and evaluation. Each of these points will be discussed in greater detail in the various chapters that follow. In the list below the purposes are arranged in a random order, but some of these aims are obviously much more important than others.

1. To provide information for effective educational and vocational counseling.
2. To provide information for grading students, for promoting students, and for making meaningful reports to parents.
3. To discover problems or difficulties associated with learning.
4. To evaluate the student's capacity to learn.

5. To appraise the effectiveness of a teaching method or methods.
6. To select students for various curricula or for admission to college or university or to some other educational, vocational, industrial, or military program.
7. To evaluate the effectiveness of the teaching in a single course or of a single teacher.
8. To appraise the effectiveness of the entire educational institution and to point up how certain of its aspects might be improved.

If we wanted to generalize, we could summarize all the above by saying that the main purpose of all evaluative activities is to promote and to improve learning. Examination of each of the 8 purposes above, one at a time, will lead to this conclusion. The first should be considered in particular. Some writers have claimed that the chief purpose of all evaluation is to provide information for effective counseling. But, if we follow through with this idea, a student who is well adjusted emotionally and who has educational and vocational goals that are most realistic for him will probably do better in school than a student who has not had the experience of counseling. This individual whose problems have been minimized should then, on the basis of what we know about learning, learn better.

THE PHILOSOPHY OF EVALUATION

As workers or future workers in American personnel work, we all, presumably, subscribe to a democratic philosophy of living. One aspect of democracy is a concern for the worth and integrity of every individual. Our evaluation activities should be consistent with this democratic philosophy.

We might illustrate this point by taking any elementary-school classroom. In this classroom of from 30 to 40 students we will find a range of differences in mental ability covering 4 or 5 years. A typical fourth-grade class is apt to have children whose mental ages range from $7\frac{1}{2}$ to $12\frac{1}{2}$ or beyond, with a mean of 10. An examination of the records of those at the bottom of this distribution shows us that they are the children who are usually receiving the failing or low grades, the "F's" and the "D's." Day after day, month after month, year after year, they are constantly reminded of their inability to keep up with the rest of the class. Usually this slowness is caused by no fault for which they are directly responsible. It is important that we examine how the individuals feel about their constant failure. We might try to examine what happens to their sense of worth and well-being. The teacher behavior exemplified by these grading practices is inconsistent both with our democratic philosophy and with everyday life. An adult who finds himself in such an intolerable situation, being a free agent, can pull up stakes and move to other situations where he can find activities more commensurate with his abilities and that will result in feelings of gratification and success. Laws prevent students from doing this.

Psychologists are generally agreed that all individuals need success experiences in order to carry on normal living. If individuals do not get these experiences in one way, they will attempt to do so in another. Many children cannot get them by answering the teacher's questions, so they turn to other types of behavior, frequently undesirable. The trouble-maker, the child who talks back to the teacher, the child who starts something when the teacher's back is turned—each may be doing these things to make himself appear wonderful in the eyes of his classmates. These trouble-makers are often poor students. Delinquent behavior, such as stealing, can, in some cases, also be related to this lack of school success. Many youths steal not because of a physical need for material things but because stealing builds them up in the eyes of their peers. The school is sometimes accused of contributing to poor mental health and to delinquency. Some of our testing activities may be very directly related to these charges.

The solution to this problem would seem to be that the teacher be aware of individual differences and, more than that, that he be flexible enough and willing to do something about such differences. The current school population is so heterogeneous that the individual achievement in any given class will vary widely. The writer contends that, unless students do have success experiences, there is very little motivation in the classroom. An analogy is in order here. Suppose that you, the reader, decided to become a skilled trackman. Every morning you appeared at the track and every morning you had for a partner a man who won the 100-meter dash in the

Olympics. Just how long do you feel that you would keep getting up early to practice against this competition? A much healthier situation would be for you to appear with a stop watch, time yourself today and on future days, to see how much improvement you are making. The first part of this analogy illustrates measurement by holding all individuals up to a high standard—a standard beyond the realm of possible achievement for many. The second part illustrates self-evaluation—the individual comparing his progress against his own ability. If the individual sees that he is improving, he will be motivated to keep on with his practice.

Troyer (9) has summarized evaluation activities as follows: First, as we have already mentioned, the major purpose of evaluation is to improve learning. Secondly, evaluation should be done *with* rather than *to* an individual. The teacher should help the student become adept in identifying his own strengths and weaknesses. Thirdly, progress should be evaluated on the basis of an individual's ability to learn. This third activity—along with making certain that those of limited ability are rewarded for doing well what they are capable of doing—will also take care of some of the brighter students. Under current classroom procedures, which are geared to the level of the average, some of these boys and girls in the top of the distribution develop habits of academic laziness from which they sometimes never recover. They are never really stimulated. Frequently, they are bright enough to do an adequate job on most of our tests with a minimum of effort.

In the chapters that follow, one evaluation technique after another will be discussed. These techniques have no built-in safeguards to control their use and misuse. It is up to the teacher and the school groups to decide how these instruments should be used, and the writer feels that the philosophy of their usage should conform as much as possible to that described above. The writer is aware that what has just been said can all be shoved aside as being theoretical and impractical. But he does not believe this is necessarily so. He feels that good teachers respect the personalities of their students and do their best to help each student to develop within the limit of his abilities. A plea is made here that teachers try to evaluate in this manner.

Dressel (4), in discussing the future of testing, listed a group of basic assumptions or principles which are in line with what is being stressed here. Reworded and in a shortened form these are:

1. In a democracy each individual should receive that education that most fully allows him to develop his potential.
2. In a democracy each individual should be so placed that he contributes to society and receives personal satisfaction in so doing.
3. Fullest development of the individual requires recognition of his essential individuality along with some rational appraisal by himself and others.
4. The judgments required in assessing an individual's potential are complex in their composition, difficult to make, and filled with error.
5. Such error can be reduced but never eliminated. Hence any evaluation can never be considered final.
6. Composite assessment by a group of individuals is much less likely to be in error than assessment made by a single person.
7. The efforts of a conscientious group of individuals to develop more reliable and valid appraisal methods lead to the clarification of the criteria for judgment and reduce the error and resulting wrongs.
8. In a democracy every form of appraisal will have critics, which is a spur to change and improvement.

THE PSYCHOLOGY OF EVALUATION

For evaluation activities to be most effective, they should consist of the best possible techniques, used in accordance with what we know to be the best and most effective psychological principles. We shall now consider some of these principles of psychology; they are basic to sound evaluation procedures.

First, for many years readiness has been recognized as a very important prerequisite for learning. A baby cannot be taught to walk until he is ready for walking. This means that not until his muscles and nervous system have matured and developed to the state where these activities can be coordinated into the complex skill that we know of as walking can the child learn to walk. So it goes for talking, reading, and much of our complex and cognitive learning. In order to teach a child to read, he has to have reached a certain stage of mental and physical development. In the same manner, evaluation is most successful when the student is ready for it. A student is ready when he understands and accepts the values and objectives involved. When the student sees that basically all evaluation is to help him, then the problem of getting the student motivated for testing disappears to a great extent.

Secondly, it has long been known that people tend to carry on those activities which have success associated with their results. This has been known as Thorndike's *Law of Effect*. Students in any classroom soon come to realize that certain types of behavior are associated with success—in this case, high marks on a test or grades in a course. Thus, if a certain teacher uses tests that demand rote memory, the students will become memorizers. If a test, on the other hand, requires students to apply principles, interpret data, or solve problems, the students will study with the idea of becoming best fitted to do well on these types of test items. In the long run, the type of evaluation device used determines, to a great extent, the type of learning activity in which students will engage in the classroom. If only one objective is evaluated on certain course tests, then both the teacher and students in that class have really only one objective. Lip service may be given to others, but unless these objectives are appraised, they mean little to either teacher or student.

Thirdly, early experiments in human learning showed that individuals learn better when they are constantly appraised in a meaningful manner as to how well they are doing. Quite a while ago, Book and Norvell (2) set up an experiment requiring individuals to cross out the letter *e* from pages of print. One group was told about its scores, how well it was doing, and was encouraged to do better. The other group was just given the task to be performed. As time went on, the experimental group did better than the group made up of individuals who were told nothing. At a certain point in the experiment, the treatment given the 2 groups was reversed and very shortly so was the performance of each group.

In an experiment related to a course in educational psychology, Little (7) divided a series of class sections into 3 groups. The first group took all its examinations on a cash-registerlike machine. The items were on a roll. One item was turned up, read, and answered. If the item was responded to correctly, a bell rang, and the student went on to the next item. If the response was incorrect, the student kept at it until he obtained the correct answer. The second group had its papers scored as soon as they were finished, by taking them to the back of the room. This group learned results very soon after completing the tests, but there was no activity here in correcting the wrong answers. The members of the third group, the real control group, were informed of their results the next day when the class met again. At the end of the quarter, all 3 groups took the same final examination, which consisted of both objective and essay test items. The median score of the group which used the machines was highest, that of the group which learned of its results the same day second, and the control group attained the lowest median score.

Other workers have also demonstrated the effect of immediate knowledge of results on learning. Guilford (6) related how the training of aerial gunners in World War II was ineffective until a system of communications was rigged up that told the trainee immediately after firing how far he was from the target and in which direction he erred. Angell (1), using a punch-card device, showed the effect of immediate knowledge of results upon grades in chemistry. This will be discussed later in detail in the chapter on scoring devices.

The machines that have been used in research are usually too expensive to be used in the typical public-school or university class. But the least thing that an instructor can do is to return papers promptly. The latest should be what is the earliest in many cases, the next day. The longer the papers or test results are withheld, the less interest the examinees have in them and the less use the papers are as learning devices. It might be added that this concept of the effect of the immediate knowledge of results on learning is one of the basic principles underlying programmed learning. These early machines constructed by Little and Pressey were the ancestors of the complex programmed-learning machines of today.

The fourth psychological aspect of evaluation to be discussed is motivation. The motivation of students is one of the most important —and sometimes the most difficult to handle—of all problems related to evaluation. In later chapters, frequent mention will be made of

motivation as it is applied to different evaluation devices. It is re-
dundant for us to say that a person's performance on a test is directly
related to his motivation. Research has shown that when a student
is really motivated, performance is much closer to his real top performance than when motivation is lacking. In experiments, the use
of rewards, such as candy bars or money, has produced significant
differences in performance. Also, when doing well on a test is of
great importance to an individual—such as determination of admission to a fraternity—performance is high. Fatigue, minor illnesses,
and feelings of distress have been shown to have no slowing-down
effect on individuals when they are strongly motivated to do well
on a test. In World War II many draftees took their induction tests
in a very indifferent manner. A few months later some of these men
found that, because of their low test scores, such opportunities as
going to technical schools or applying for officers' training, were
closed to them. Some men applied for a retest. Quite a few increased
their scores considerably on the second taking of the tests. This time
they had something to gain as a result of a high performance.
Actually, in this situation, the chief factor that had undergone any
real change was motivation.

In dealing with public-school students, motivation seems to be
related to the socio-economic status of the individual. Children from
middle-class homes, in the long run, are more strongly motivated
than those from lower-class homes. It is part of the culture of the
middle-class child to try to do his best when confronted with a piece
of paper with questions on it. Success is the constant aim of the
child, his parents, and all his friends. Performance on these tests is
of much less concern to the child from the lower-class home and to
his parents. This will be discussed at greater length in a later
chapter.

A fifth psychological factor or principle that has implications in
testing is that learning is most efficient when there is activity on the
part of the learner. In a rather old but relevant study, Curtis and
Woods (3) showed the effects of varying amounts of student activity
in the evaluation process upon learning. Over a period of years, the
effects of common methods of grading examination papers were
studied in high-school science classes. Four methods were used:

1. Teacher read the correct answer while each student corrected his own paper. Discussion followed.
2. Teacher marked wrong responses, but wrote nothing else upon the paper. Papers were then returned and discussed item by item.
3. Teacher wrote in all corrections, and papers were returned and treated as in 2 above.
4. Teacher wrote in all corrections, but when papers were returned, only specific questions asked by the students were discussed.

In each case, these tests, which were of the objective type and were made up of 100 items, were repeated on the next day and again 6 weeks later without any previous notice. A consistent pattern of merit for the 4 methods was obtained. The method in which the teacher was least active proved to be the best. Methods 2 and 3 were of about equal merit, and method 4, in which student activity was at a minimum, was poorest of all.

Promptly the question arises as to how we can prevent cheating in situations like this where student participation is desired. If tests are used as they should be—that is, used to improve learning—in the long run, we should expect a de-emphasis of grades. When school administrators, teachers, and students come to see that tests have their greatest value in diagnostic work and counseling, and when teachers can develop some other better motivators for classroom learning, then students will be less concerned about grades and more interested in their own performances that led up to those grades. Cheating on self-correcting examinations would be of little value except from the point of view of the real information that a student keeps from himself because of cheating. Grades are not analogous to paychecks—nor should they be. The sooner educators get around to realizing the real value of scores, the sounder will be our evaluation programs.

The machine and punch-board methods mentioned above could also be repeated here, because much student activity is involved in each of them. At this point we might summarize by saying that, when test results are placed on answer sheets and run through a scoring machine, neither teacher nor student learns anything about how the student behaved on the test. All that is at hand is a total score that the machine operator wrote or the machine printed on the answer sheet. When the teacher hand-grades the papers, he at least can get some idea as to where the strong and weak parts of the class are. And when the student grades his own paper, he becomes involved, learning takes place, and, psychologically, the soundest method is being used.

SOME COMMON TERMS *

In studying a new subject such as educational measurement, the reader must, as soon as possible, learn the exact meaning of a few special words that appear throughout the book. All tests and evaluation devices can be placed into one of 2 categories: group or individual. Individual tests can be administered to only one person at a time. The early successful attempts at making appraisals were practically all of this type. However, not much real progress was made until group tests became available, because of the basic inefficiency of the individual approach. At the present time, individual tests are used mostly with young children, the mentally retarded, and in such situations requiring much clinical information as dealing with adjustment problems. As far as the teacher goes, there is practically no job that cannot be done as well or better with group tests than with an individual test. Group tests are frequently divided into two types, *verbal* and *nonverbal.* Nonverbal tests use figures, forms, and pictures instead of words. Intelligence tests given to kindergarten children and first graders are of this type. In structure, these tests are similar to those used with older individuals and supposedly measure the same thing. Some individual tests are called *performance tests.* Here the examinee is confronted with a task that is usually performed with his hands. Some of the tests used in measuring the intelligence of young children are of this type, as are many of the tests used by industry and the U.S. Armed Forces in selecting individuals for different types of training. As opposed to performance tests we have the very familiar *paper-and-pencil tests.*

Tests are said to be OBJECTIVE or SUBJECTIVE. An *objective test* is one on which the same results are produced regardless of who scores it. If errors are made, they are brought about by carelessness

* The Glossary contains a comprehensive list of measurement terms.

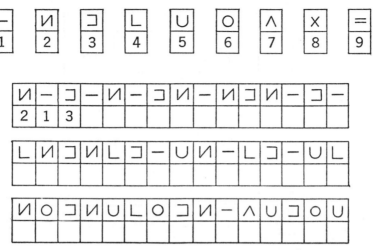

Fig. 1:1. EXAMPLE OF A NONVERBAL TEST. ITEMS FROM THE *Revised Beta Examination* *

and inaccuracy on the part of the scorer, not the examinee. On *subjective tests* results emerge that, in many cases, reflect the emphases, values, and idiosyncrasies of the scorer. The essay examination with which we have long been familiar is an example of a subjective test. Many of the newer evaluation instruments will also have to be placed in this category when classified.

Tests are also grouped into two other categories, SPEED and POWER. A *speed test* is of such a nature that, given enough time, every individual could answer every item correctly. The items are all very easy, and the purpose of the test is to see how fast an individual really is. Such tests are widely used as tests of clerical ability. A *power test* is so made that the examinee has a chance to try himself out to see exactly what he can do when it comes to ability and achievement. Such an intelligence test as the *Ohio State Psychological Examination* † has no time limit. Examinees are encouraged to work at it until all items are answered. Most of our tests fall actually into neither the "speed" nor the "power" categories. They might best be called *time-limit tests*. These are chiefly

* Used by permission of the Psychological Corporation, Copyright 1935.
† Published by the Ohio State University Research Foundation.

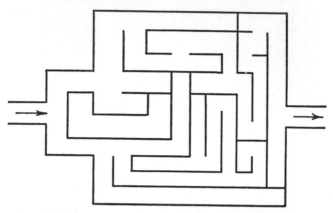

Fig 1:2. EXAMPLE OF A PERFORMANCE TEST. PART OF A MAZE

power tests, because the items are so arranged that, in the time allotted for taking, most people reach a level that is very close to their capacity. Tests which contain items measuring an assortment of things and in which the items are arranged in order of difficulty are called *spiral-omnibus tests*. Tests that are made up of only one type of item arranged in order of difficulty are referred to as *spiral tests*. As will be seen, many of our older intelligence tests are of the spiral-omnibus type. In dealing with intelligence, we frequently encounter the term *low-ceiling*. This means that for some of the individuals taking the test, the test was too easy and did not allow them an opportunity to reveal their capacities. When test results show a grouping of scores near the maximum possible score, a test with a low ceiling was used.

Many tests are labeled *standardized test*. This means that they have been given to appropriate groups, and, as a result of this, norms are available. The opposite of the standardized test is the *teacher-made test*. Usually, the standardized test contains well-made items and has been subjected to all that modern test-construction practice demands. The norms, as will be shown in a later chapter, may be of little use to the individual school or teacher. The teacher-made tests should at least do a good job of measuring the objectives of the individual instructor and what he has taught. A well-constructed teacher-made test is as good as or superior to a purchased test when it comes to evaluating student achievement in a given classroom.

Two terms that we have seen before and that, for some unknown reason, always seem to be mixed up in the minds of readers are *validity* and *reliability*. A whole chapter will be devoted to them. For now, a simple definition of each will suffice. An evaluation instrument is VALID when it does what it is supposed to do. A test that really measures fifth-grade arithmetic or the ability necessary to assemble small objects in a factory is said to be "valid" for each of these purposes. VALIDITY might be referred to as truthfulness. RELIABILITY, on the other hand, is simply defined as "consistency." An evaluation instrument which produces results that are similar from application to application is a RELIABLE one.

Many of our modern evaluation instruments are described as PROJECTIVE. Such instruments should not be called "tests" because test items are usually thought of as having a right and wrong answer. Probably the most widely used projective instrument is the *Rorschach* or inkblot technique in which an individual tells what he sees in cards each of which contains a large inkblot figure. A *projective technique* is best thought of as a disguised situation in which the examinee has an opportunity to reveal unwittingly things about himself when he responds to the various items. His own feelings and attitudes may be obtained from his over-all responses. Projectives are the tools of the skilled clinical psychologist, and the average classroom teacher will find little need for them.

In modern measurement, the term *factor* is frequently encountered. Many of our currently used ability and personality inventories are based upon what is known as a FACTOR ANALYSIS. Factors are theoretical variables derived from a rather complex statistical analysis of related data. These variables are given names by psychologists, with the result that we describe mental ability as being made up of a "verbal factor," a "spatial factor," and others. One outcome of this factor approach is to produce results that are broken down into a series of subscores rather than a single score that represents test performance. It must be noted, though, that we have other tests from which subscores are obtained that are not the results of factor analyses.

TESTING TODAY

Today testing is big business, and it is becoming more so daily in spite of all its critics. With more and more children entering our schools and colleges every year, testing can go in only one direction. To give some idea of the vastness of the enterprise, a glimpse of the annual report of the President of the Educational Testing Service (5) will suffice. In this report the various testing programs provided by this agency are listed. On the first page of this listing it is shown that over one million students took the *Preliminary Scholastic Aptitude Test* and that close to 1,800,000 took one or more parts of the *College Boards* during the previous year. The number of students tested by this organization runs into millions annually. This organization, in addition, sells many tests outright to schools and colleges which do their own administering and scoring. And this is *only one test publisher.* Combine with this the numbers from the other publishers and add to that the countless numbers used by our schools and universities, industry, and the Armed Services, and the results, if obtainable, would verge upon the astronomical. Such an interprise merits serious study of its aims, techniques, and results. It is hoped that this book will give some understanding of what this is all about.

TYPES OF CHARACTERISTICS EVALUATED

It is customary to organize a book such as this on the basis of the type of abilities or characteristics measured. Usually, our measurement and evaluation activities can be classified into 5 major areas. The first of these is *achievement.* This is concerned with measurement of the outcomes of our educational instruction. In a more limited sense, achievement covers the appraisal of attainment of subject matter in the elementary grades or in specific high-school or university courses. Perhaps the majority of our evaluation and measurement activities are in this area.

The second area is *intelligence,* or general *mental ability,* as some prefer to call it. This is one area in which the major emphasis is on measurement rather than on evaluation. Closely associated with this general ability is our third grouping, which we shall call *special abilities.* In this category appear mechanical, clerical, musical, and artistic ability. The fourth major category consists of the large area of *personality* or *adjustment.* In this area we shall find that we tend to rely less upon measurement devices and much more upon evaluation techniques. Finally appear *interests* and *attitudes.* Along with these five areas we will pay some attention to the evaluation of background or environment and to teacher evaluation. The area of physical abilities is not included in this book because it is usually well treated in physical-education courses.

REFERENCES

1. Angell, G. W. The effect of immediate knowledge of quiz results on final examination scores in freshman chemistry. *J.ed. Res.,* 1949, 42, 391-4.
2. Book, W. F., and Norvell, L. The will to learn: an experimental study of incentives in learning. *Pedagogical Seminary,* 1922, 29, 305-62.
3. Curtis, F. D., and Woods, G. G. A study of the relative teaching value of four common classroom practices in correcting examination papers. *School Review,* 1929, 37, 615-23.
4. Dressel, P. L. Role of external testing programs in education in the *University of Kansas Conference on External Testing Programs.* Kansas Studies in Education, Vol. 14, No. 2. Lawrence, Kansas: University of Kansas, 1964.
5. Educational Testing Service. *Annual report of the president to the board of trustees,* 1963-64. Princeton, N.J.: Educational Testing Service, 1965.
6. Guilford, J. P. Lessons from aviation psychology. *Amer. Psychologist,* 1948, 3, 1-11.
7. Little, J. K. Results of the use of machines for testing an drill upon learning in educational psychology. *J. exper. Educ.,* 1934, 3, 45-9.
8. Smith, E. R., and Tyler, R. W. *Appraising and recording student progress.* New York: Harper, 1942.
9. Troyer, M. E. *Accuracy and validity in evaluation are not enough.* The J. R. Street Lecture for 1947. Syracuse, N. Y.: Syracuse University Press, 1947.

CHAPTER 2

STATISTICS

After a teacher administers a test and grades the papers, he has a series of scores called raw scores which in themselves have very little meaning. A student makes a score of 49 on a 64-item test in plane geometry. This score of 49 tells us the number of items that he has responded to correctly or his score after a correction formula has been applied. Whether it is good or bad, high or low, we do not know. The purpose of this chapter and the next is to show how we can make scores meaningful. This treatment of measurement data is called STATISTICS. Here we shall have only an introduction to some of the more widely used statistics.

FREQUENCY DISTRIBUTIONS

Suppose that a teacher gives a test and obtains the following 40 scores:

Table 2:1. SCORES OBTAINED ON A PHYSICS TEST

50	34	32	30	28	26	22	18
44	33	31	29	27	25	21	17
39	33	30	29	27	24	21	16
38	32	30	28	26	24	19	12
37	32	30	28	26	23	19	10

As can be seen, these scores are arranged from high to low. The first thing that we shall do is to set up a FREQUENCY DISTRIBUTION. This is easily accomplished in the following steps:

20

1. Determine the range. The range is defined as the high score minus the low score plus 1. For the above data we have (50 − 10) + 1 which is 41.
2. Decide upon the size for the interval. Customarily we have between 10 and 20 intervals in a frequency distribution. By a trial-and-error process we can arrive at an appropriate size for the class interval. Ten goes into our range of 41 approximately 4 times and 20 approximately 2 times. Hence 2, 3, or 4 would be an appropriate size for the class interval. Suppose that for our problem we decide upon 3 and then we write $i = 3$.
3. Set up the frequency distribution with the low scores at the bottom. Many follow the practice of starting the bottom interval as a multiple of the class interval. Since for these data our lowest score is 10, the bottom interval would be 9-11.
4. After the distribution has been set up, the scores are tallied in and the tallies for each interval are summarized. This entire process is illustrated in Table 2:2.

Table 2:2. SETTING UP A FREQUENCY DISTRIBUTION

			f
48-50	1		1
45-47			0
42-44	1		1
39-41	1		1
36-38	11		2
33-35	111		3
30-32	~~1111~~	111	8
27-29	~~1111~~	11	7
24-26	~~1111~~	1	6
21-23	1111		4
18-20	111		3
15-17	11		2
12-14	1		1
9-11	1		1
			$N = 40$

In the frequency table it will be noted that the symbol f is placed at the head of the summarized column. This stands for frequency and N is the number of cases.

In using numbers in statistics we usually assume that each number is a point on a continuum. Such as this:

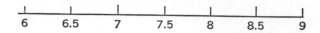

The number 7 in the above is said to have a lower limit of 6.5 and an upper limit of 7.4999. We round the latter and say that it has an upper limit of 7.5. The number 7, then, is thought of as covering that segment of the continuum from 6.5 to 7.5. To go back to our frequency distribution, the bottom interval has a lower limit of 8.5 and an upper limit of 11.5. When the former is subtracted from the latter we obtain a value of 3, which is the size of our class interval.

Each of the intervals in our distribution has a midpoint that is half the distance between the upper and lower limits or the lower limit plus one half the size of the class interval. The midpoint of the bottom interval of our data, then, is 8.5 plus 1.5, which gives us a value of 10. It should be noted that, when the size taken for the interval is an odd number, the midpoints will all be whole numbers and that, when an even number is taken for the size of the interval, all the midpoints are decimals.

We shall find that the midpoints become important in our statistical manipulations. For example, we first make an assumption that, for any given interval, the average of all the scores in that interval would be equal to the midpoint. The interval 30-32 has a frequency of 8. If these scores are averaged and our assumption above is met, the average of these scores should be 31, the midpoint of the interval. It should be obvious that this rarely happens. Sometimes, the average of our scores is below the midpoint of the interval and sometimes above it. For the data at hand, the average of the 8 scores is 30.875. In the long run, discrepancies tend to cancel out. Slight differences in our results come about from these variations and we label these discrepancies as resulting from errors of grouping. If two teachers each take the same set of data and one uses an interval of 3 and the other an interval of 4, there will be minor differences in the results. Or if one starts with the bottom interval as 9-11 and the other as 10-12, both using an interval of 3, there will again be slight differences in the results. Both differences are brought about by the errors of grouping.

Graphs

In educational measurement, two types of graphs are most useful. The first of these is the FREQUENCY POLYGON. The other is the OGIVE, which will be discussed later. The construction of a frequency polygon will be illustrated using the data in Table 2:2. The general rules for the construction of a frequency polygon may be summarized as follows:

1. The ratio of the vertical axis (Y-axis) to the horizontal axis should be approximately as 2 is to 3. If the vertical axis is 6 inches, the base should be 9 inches.
2. The frequencies (f) are placed on the Y-axis and the scores on the X-axis. Both are adequately labeled.
3. In plotting the frequencies, place the point representing each frequency above the midpoint of its interval on the X-axis. This is in keeping with our earlier assumptions that the average of all scores in any given interval is equal to the midpoint of that interval.
4. These points are connected by using a ruler.

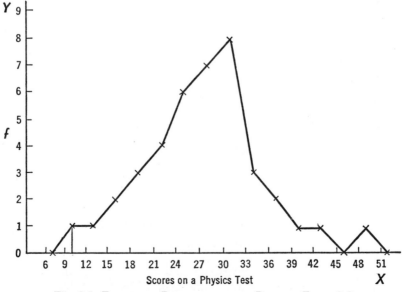

Fig. 2:1. FREQUENCY POLYGON FOR THE DATA IN TABLE 2:2

Note that, rather than leave the graph suspended above the X-axis, we anchored it at the lower end by drawing a line down to the midpoint of the next lower interval and giving it a frequency of zero. The same process is repeated at the top of the distribution.

Frequency polygons are very useful when we wish to portray graphically the results of two or more groups on any given test. One group can be shown in one color, another in a different color or different types of lines can be used for each group. If the numbers in the various groups are quite different in size, the frequencies of each group are changed to proportions or percentages and these proportions or percentages appear along the Y-axis instead of frequencies.

AVERAGES

The Mean

Next we shall take up averages or measures of central tendency. These statistics show us the score or point about which our scores tend to pile up or center. The first one of these, the MEAN, has long been familiar as the arithmetic average. This is our most commonly used measure of central tendency. It is defined as the sum of the scores divided by the number of cases. Symbolically it can be written as follows:

$$\overline{X} = \frac{X_1 + X_2 + X_3 + X_4 + \cdots X_n}{N}$$

$$\overline{X} = \frac{\Sigma X}{N}$$

where

$\overline{X}$ = mean

X_1 = 1st score, X_2 = 2d score, etc.

N = number of cases

Σ = (capital sigma) summation of

X = any raw score

When the data are grouped we find the mean as follows, using the data from Table 2:2 which are recopied here in Table 2:3.

Table 2:3. COMPUTATION OF MEASURES OF CENTRAL TENDENCY

	f	x'	fx'	
48-50	1	7	7	
45-47	0	6	0	
42-44	1	5	5	
39-41	1	4	4	
36-38	2	3	6	
33-35	3	2	6	
30-32	8	1	8	
				(+36)
27-29	7	0	0	

←————————————17

24-26	6	-1	-6	
21-23	4	-2	-8	
18-20	3	-3	-9	
15-17	2	-4	-8	
12-14	1	-5	-5	
9-11	1	-6	-6	
				(−42)

$$N = 40 \qquad \Sigma = -6$$

1. We take an interval and use the midpoint of that interval as the arbitrary reference point. Actually, it makes no difference which interval is used, but it will be noted that work is kept at a minimum when an interval near the center of the distribution is taken. In the illustration, 28, the midpoint of the interval 27-29, is taken as the arbitrary reference point.

2. Next we set up a second column and label it x', deviation from this arbitrary reference point. Since the interval 27-29 was taken as the interval containing our reference point, there is no deviation and a 0 is placed opposite this interval in the x' column. The interval 30-32 deviates one interval from the arbitrary reference point and a 1 is entered for this interval in the x' column. This is continued upward until all intervals are assigned a value. Note that any interval that has a 0 frequency is given an x' value and that all such values below the starting point are negative. Some individuals take the bottom interval as their arbitrary origin. This results in all positive values, but larger numbers appear in the calculations.

3. The next column, labeled fx', is obtained by multiplying the row values in the two columns to the left. Then these products are

summed and the total written at the bottom of the column. It is best to add the positive values, then the negative ones, and then combine these results.

4. To find the mean we use the following equation:

Mean is equal to the midpoint of the interval containing the assumed mean plus the correction term.

In symbols:

$$\overline{X} = M' + \left(\frac{\Sigma fx'}{N}\right) i$$

where M' is the arbitrary reference point, i the size of the class interval, and the other symbols are as previously used.

$$\overline{X} = 28 + \left(\frac{-6}{40}\right) 3$$

$$\overline{X} = 28 + (-.45)$$

$$\overline{X} = 27.55 = 27.6$$

It might be noted here that when these 40 scores are summed and averaged, the mean is 27.5. The difference between this and that obtained above is brought about by the error of grouping.

The Median

The second measure of central tendency that we shall take up is the MEDIAN (Mdn). The median is defined as a *point* in a distribution that has an equal number of cases on both sides of it. It is the midpoint of a distribution. Consider the following simple illustrations:

$$17, 18, 20, 21, 22, 24, 28$$

The median in the above series is 21, for 21 has 3 scores on each side of it.

$$17, 18, 20, 21, 22, 23, 28, 29$$

The median this time is 21.5 for 21.5 is the point in our distribution which has 4 scores on each side of it.

For ungrouped data, the median can be obtained by counting from one end or the other of a distribution and finding the midpoint of the distribution.

For grouped data we go through the following steps (see Table 2:3):

1. Divide N by 2. In this case $40 \div 2 = 20$.
2. Starting from the bottom begin to count up 20 cases. In the problem at hand we can count up 17 cases which brings us to the top of the interval 24-26. If we add in the frequency of the next interval we would have 24 cases, which would be too many. So we write down the upper limit of the interval 24-26 and then we have to interpolate.
3. The upper limit of the interval last reached and the frequency of which was entirely used is 26.5. Up to this point we have a cumulative frequency of 17. We need 3 more cases $\left(\dfrac{N}{2} - 17\right)$. There are 7 cases in the next interval and we assume that they are spread equally throughout that interval. We need 3 of them. Hence, we will go $\dfrac{3}{7}$'s of the distance through this interval of 3.

In brief:

$$Mdn = 26.5 + \frac{3}{7}(3)$$

$$Mdn = 26.5 + 1.3$$

$$Mdn = 27.8$$

The median can always be checked by repeating the process starting at the top. This time we count down and we can use 16 cases which brings us to the top of the interval 27-29. We need 4 more cases out of the 7 in this interval. Hence

$$Mdn = 29.5 - \frac{4}{7}(3)$$

$$= 29.5 - \frac{12}{7}$$

$$= 29.5 - 1.7$$

$$Mdn = 27.8$$

Note this time when we interpolate we place a minus sign in front of our term so that we continue going down.

The Mode

A third measure of central tendency which is used very infrequently is the MODE (*Mo*). For ungrouped data, the mode is defined as that score which occurs most frequently. For grouped data it is the midpoint of the interval containing the largest number of cases. For our problem, the mode is 31.

When to Use Mean, Median, and Mode

At this point, the student probably wonders when each of these three statistics should be used. In references to the mean and median, we say that we use the mean when our data form a normal or bell-shaped distribution. If our data depart from this and are skewed, we use the median.

Suppose that 10 people make the following contributions to an organization:

$$\$.25, .25, .50, .50, .50, 1.00, 1.00, 1.00, 1.00, 20.00$$

The mean for these values is $2.60 and the median is approximately $.75. To use the mean in this case would give a very erroneous picture of the "average" contribution. It should be noticed that the mean is of such a nature that every score in a distribution affects it. If one or two scores in a distribution are away out from the center, then the mean is pulled out in the direction of these deviate scores. In the computation of the median, however, these extreme scores are counted over, and it makes no difference how far out they are from the center. So unless we really want to distort the picture, the data should be examined and the correct statistic used.

Usually if our data are fairly normal and if further computations are to be made—and they usually are—the mean should be used in preference to the median. Also of these three measures the mean is the most reliable. By this we mean that from sample to sample it will tend to be more similar. From our data we obtained a mode of 31. A change in the position of just 1 frequency might drop the mode to 28. Hence the mode tends to jump around. It is only used when we need a rapidly computed measure of central tendency.

Skewed Distributions

In the paragraphs above we referred to *skewness*. We might look at this concept further, since skewed distributions are by no means rare in educational work. Suppose a teacher gives a test that was very easy. A majority of the students received high scores. A graph of this distribution of scores would take the shape of Figure 2:2.

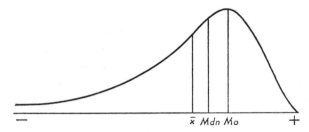

Fig. 2:2. A NEGATIVELY-SKEWED DISTRIBUTION

We describe this as a "negatively-skewed distribution." It is the tail of the distribution that determines the sign of the skewness. A line has its negative end at the left and its positive end at the right. Hence this distribution is negatively skewed and of the 3 measures of central tendency the mean is lowest in numerical value and the mode highest.

If a test was extremely difficult, we would have a pile up at the other end of distribution and our curve would be described as "positively skewed." This is shown in Figure 2:3.

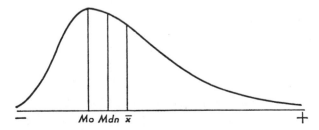

Fig. 2:3. A POSITIVELY-SKEWED DISTRIBUTION

The properties and nature of the bell-shaped or normal curve will be described later.

MEASURES OF VARIABILITY

If we have two groups of scores, A and B, each with a mean of 72, it is still impossible for us to say much about these distributions except that they have the same mean. It is possible that distribution A has a high score of 78 and a low score of 66. Distribution B might have a high score of 112 and a low score of 32. Then we see that we have two very different groups. It should be apparent, then, that if we are going to describe a distribution, we need not only a measure of central tendency but also a MEASURE OF VARIATION about this center. When the mean is used as a measure of central tendency, the statistic usually employed to measure variability is called the standard deviation or sigma and its symbol is s. We shall consider this statistic next.

Standard Deviation

First, for a simple illustration, let us take these 5 scores: 10, 8, 6, 4, 2, and find the mean and standard deviation. We can set our data up as shown in Table 2:4.

Table 2:4. COMPUTATION OF STANDARD DEVIATION

(1)	(2)	(3)
X	x	x^2
10	4	16
8	2	4
6	0	0
4	-2	4
2	-4	16
$\Sigma X = 30$		$\Sigma = 40$
$N = 5$		

$$s = \sqrt{\frac{\Sigma x^2}{N}}$$

$$\overline{X} = \frac{\Sigma X}{N} = \frac{30}{5} = 6 \qquad s = \sqrt{\frac{40}{5}} = \sqrt{8} = 2.8$$

1. The first step is to find the mean which is equal to the sum of the scores divided by N. $\bar{X}$ equals 6.
2. The second column is obtained by getting the deviation of each score from the mean. We always use the symbol x for this. Each score is taken separately and subtracted from the mean or vice versa.
3. The third column is obtained by squaring each value in the second column and this column is summed, giving a value of 40. We refer to this as the "sum of the squares."
4. The standard deviation is obtained by dividing this sum of squares by N and taking the square root of this quotient:

$$s = \sqrt{\frac{\Sigma x^2}{N}} = \sqrt{\frac{40}{5}} = \sqrt{8} = 2.8$$

Next we shall compute the standard deviation for the problem on which we have been working previously in this chapter. The data are again reproduced in Table 2:5. We add one more column

Table 2:5. Computation of Standard Deviation for Grouped Data

Scores	f	x'	fx'	fx'^2
48-50	1	7	7	49
45-47	0	6	0	0
42-44	1	5	5	25
39-41	1	4	4	16
36-38	2	3	6	18
33-35	3	2	6	12
30-32	8	1	8	8
27-29	7	0	0	0
24-26	6	−1	−6	6
21-23	4	−2	−8	16
18-20	3	−3	−9	27
15-17	2	−4	−8	32
12-14	1	−5	−5	25
9-11	1	−6	−6	36
	$N = 40$		$\Sigma = -6$	$\Sigma = 270$

(fx'^2), which is the product of the 2 previous columns, and sum it. For these data Σx^2 is obtained by the formula

$$\Sigma x^2 = i^2 \left[\Sigma f x'^2 - \frac{(\Sigma f x')^2}{N} \right]$$

$$\Sigma x^2 = 3^2 \left[270 - \frac{(-6)^2}{40} \right]$$

$$\Sigma x^2 = 9 \left[270 - \frac{36}{40} \right]$$

$$= 9(270 - .9)$$

$$= 9(269.1)$$

$$= 2421.9$$

The formula for standard deviation

$$s = \sqrt{\frac{\Sigma x^2}{N}}$$

$$s = \sqrt{\frac{2421.9}{40}}$$

$$s = \sqrt{60.55}$$

$$s = 7.8$$

As mentioned previously, the mean is used as a measure of central tendency when the data at hand tend to form a normal distribution. The concept of standard deviation is tied in with the normal curve. When our data are normal, or approximately that, the following relationships as shown in Figure 2:4 always hold.

1. If we take the mean and measure off on the base line 1 standard deviation in each direction, we cut off approximately 68 per cent of the area or 68 per cent of the cases. That is, between the points 19.8 and 35.4 we would expect to find 68 per cent of our cases.

2. If we take the mean and measure off 2 standard deviations on each side of it, we would include approximately 95 per cent of

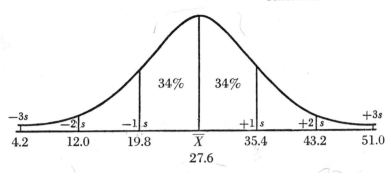

34%   34%

−3s   +3s

−2 s   −1 s   +1 s   +2 s

4.2   12.0   19.8 $\overline{X}$ 35.4   43.2   51.0

27.6

Fig. 2:4. THE NORMAL CURVE

the cases. Between 12.0 and 43.2, then, we would expect to find
95 per cent of the cases.
3. And, finally, 3 standard deviations on each side of the mean will
   include practically all of the cases (99.74 per cent to be precise).
   These values in our distribution are 4.2 and 51.0.

These relationships between standard deviation units and the normal curve are very important in statistics. Standard deviation units
are usually expressed in z-scores or standard scores that are obtained
by the following formula:

$$z = \frac{X - \overline{X}}{s}$$

Examination of this formula reveals that a z-score is actually the
number of standard deviation units a raw score is above or below
the mean. Referring to Figure 2:4 we see that a value of 35.4 is one
standard deviation above the mean. This distance above the mean,
when divided by a standard deviation of 7.8, results in a standard
score of 1.

Table 2.6 contains an abbreviated table that gives the areas cut off
by various standard deviation units taken from the mean. Notice that
a standard score of 1.00 cuts off .341 of the area of the curve when
measured from the mean and that a z-score of 2.00 includes .477 of
the area when so taken. Doubling each of these proportions and
changing each to a percentage result in the percentages of the area
noted when Figure 2:4 was discussed.

Table 2:6. Areas under the Normal Curve at Various Standard Deviation Units from the Mean

z Standard Score (1)	Area from Mean to z (2)	(1)	(2)
.00	.000	1.70	.455
.05	.020	1.75	.460
.10	.040	1.80	.464
.15	.060	1.85	.465
.20	.080	1.90	.471
.25	.099	1.95	.474
.30	.118	1.96	.475
.35	.134	2.00	.477
.40	.155	2.05	.479
.45	.174	2.10	.482
.50	.192	2.15	.484
.55	.209	2.20	.486
.60	.226	2.25	.488
.65	.242	2.30	.489
.70	.258	2.35	.491
.75	.273	2.40	.492
.80	.288	2.45	.493
.85	.302	2.50	.4938
.90	.316	2.55	.4946
.95	.329	2.58	.4951
1.00	.341	2.60	.4953
1.05	.353	2.65	.4960
1.10	.364	2.70	.4965
1.15	.374	2.75	.4970
1.20	.385	2.80	.4974
1.25	.394	2.85	.4978
1.30	.403	2.90	.4981
1.35	.412	2.95	.4984
1.40	.419	3.00	.4987
1.45	.426	3.10	.4990
1.50	.433	3.20	.4993
1.55	.439	3.30	.4995
1.60	.445	3.50	.4997
1.65	.450	3.70	.4999

When we talk about area under the curve, we assume that our cases are equally distributed over the area and, if we cut off a surface that includes 34 per cent of the area, it follows that 34 per cent of the cases have been included. Theoretically the tails of the normal curve never touch the base line. Note from Table 2:6 that, for a

z-score of 3.70, .4999 of the area has been included between the mean and that point. Also note that all z-scores in the table are positive. Negative standard scores cut off equivalent distances on the other side of the mean. Two particular z-scores, 1.96 and 2.58, have also been included in this table. When the area cut off by these scores is doubled or when each is taken on both sides of the mean, 95 and 99 per cent respectively of the area of the curve has been taken into account. These two standard scores are very important in sampling statistics and will be further discussed there.

Quartile Deviation

When the median is used as the measure of central tendency, we usually use with it the QUARTILE DEVIATION (Q), sometimes called the semi-interquartile range. Q is defined as one half the distance between the 2 quartile points, Q_1 and Q_3 or $Q = \dfrac{Q_3 - Q_1}{2}$.

To obtain this statistic we must first obtain the 2 quartile points. Q_1 is defined as that point in a distribution below which fall 25 per cent of the cases, and Q_3 as that point below which fall 75 per cent of the cases. The calculation of Q_1 is similar to that of the median, except that this time instead of dividing by 2 to see how many cases fall on each side of the midpoint, we divide by 4 or take 25 per cent of N. To go back to our original problem, we divide our N of 40 by 4 and obtain 10. Q_1 then will be that point which has 10 cases below it. Starting from the bottom, we begin counting up, and we can go up to the bottom of the interval 21-23. Up to this point we have accumulated 7 cases. We now need 3 more of the cases in this interval, or we must go three-quarters of the way through the interval.

$$Q_1 = 20.5 + \frac{3}{4}(3)$$
$$Q_1 = 20.5 + 2.25$$
$$Q_1 = 22.75$$

In a similar fashion, starting from the top and coming down 10 cases, we have

$$Q_3 = 32.5 - \frac{2}{8} \ (3)$$

$$Q_3 = 32.5 - .75$$

$$Q_3 = 31.75$$

Then substituting in the formula for the quartile deviation we obtain:

$$Q = \frac{Q_3 - Q_1}{2}$$

$$Q = \frac{31.75 - 22.75}{2}$$

$$Q = \frac{9}{2} = 4.5$$

The interpretation of the quartile deviation follows along that of the standard deviation. In a normal distribution, if we take the median and measure off 1 quartile deviation on each side of it, we shall cut off 50 per cent of the area or 50 per cent of the cases. If we measure off 4 quartile deviations on each side of the median, we shall include practically all our cases. The quartile deviation is thus always smaller than the standard deviation. For our data with a median of 27.8, we would expect to find 50 per cent of the frequencies between 23.3 and 32.3. An inspection of the data will show this to be approximately so.

CENTILES OR PERCENTILES

A centile point or percentile point is defined as that point in a distribution below which fall a certain per cent of the cases. For example, the 77th centile point, written C_{77} or P_{77}, is that point below which lie 77 per cent of the cases. So far we have computed the median which is C_{50} and Q_1 and Q_3 which are the equivalents of C_{25} and C_{75}, respectively. Since we already have learned how to find these 3 points, we should now be able to find any centile point. For example, if we wanted to find C_{40}, we should take 40 per

cent of N, which is 16, and start up from the bottom of the distribution to find that point with 16 cases below it.

$$C_{40} = 23.5 + \frac{5}{6}(3)$$

$$C_{40} = 23.5 + 2.5$$

$$C_{40} = 26$$

In a similar fashion if we wished to find C_{67}, we should take 67
per cent of N and work up from the bottom of the frequency distribution. However, if the number of cases is large, it would be more
efficient to take 33 per cent of N and start down from the top.
Thirty-three per cent of N is 13.2; so we are looking for the point
with 26.8 cases below it and 13.2 cases above it.

$$C_{67} = 32.5 - \frac{5.2}{8}(3)$$

$$C_{67} = 32.5 - 1.95$$

$$C_{67} = 30.6$$

To compute all the centile points in the above fashion would be
a tedious process. Fortunately we can obtain them rapidly by constructing an S-shaped or ogive curve on a large piece of graph
paper. Ogive curves are constructed as follows (Table 2:7).

1. Obtain the cumulative frequencies by starting at the bottom. How
   many frequencies are below the upper limit of the bottom interval (9-11)? The answer is 1. How many below the upper limit
   of the second interval (12-14)? The answer is 2. This interval
   then has a cumulative frequency of 2. In this fashion the cumulative frequency for each interval is computed.
2. Each of these cumulative frequencies is changed to cumulative
   proportions or percentages. The easiest way to do this is to obtain
   a constant multiplier by dividing 100 by N and multiplying
   each cumulative frequency by this constant. In this case we have
   $100 \div 40$, which is 2.5. Each of our cf's is then multiplied by

Table 2:7. OBTAINING CUMULATIVE FREQUENCIES
AND CUMULATIVE PERCENTAGES

Scores	f	cf	cP
48-50	1	40	100.0
45-47	0	39	97.5
42-44	1	39	97.5
39-41	1	38	95.0
36-38	2	37	92.5
33-35	3	35	87.5
30-32	8	32	80.0
27-29	7	24	60.0
24-26	6	17	42.5
21-23	4	11	27.5
18-20	3	7	17.5
15-17	2	4	10.0
12-14	1	2	5.0
9-11	1	1	2.5

$$N = 40$$

this constant and the last column, cP (cumulative percentage), in our table is obtained.

3. Set up a graph using the same proportions as were used for the frequency polygon. On the Y-axis is placed the cumulative percentage values and on the X-axis the scores. The points corresponding to our cumulative percentages this time appear above the points representing the upper limits of each interval.

4. A smoothed curve is drawn in such a fashion that about half the points are above it and half below it.

5. To obtain the various centile points, draw a line from the desired point on the Y-axis until it reaches the curve. Drop a perpendicular from this point on the curve to the X-axis. The point where this line intercepts the X-axis is the desired centile point. In Figure 2:5 to find C_{50}, a line is drawn across and down. On the X-axis we read 28. C_{50} is then 28. In a similar fashion Q_1, or C_{25}, is found to be approximately 23. In order to obtain accuracy with this process, the graph should be plotted to an appropriate scale on large graph paper.

The use of these centile points will be discussed in the chapter on scores and grades (Chapter 3).

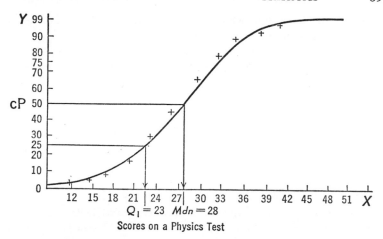

Fig. 2:5. Ogive Curve for the Data in Table 2:7

CORRELATION

In a discussion of either reliability or validity, it is almost impossible to avoid using CORRELATION COEFFICIENTS. Since these are important statistics in measurement work, we shall now devote quite a bit of space to them.

Correlation Coefficients

A correlation coefficient is an index which shows the relationship between two variables. Perfect relationship is assigned a value of 1. Suppose 6 individuals take 2 tests and we summarize their ranks on the 2 tests as follows:

Student	Test A	Test B
1	1	1
2	2	2
3	3	3
4	4	4
5	5	5
6	6	6

We would have here an example of a perfect positive relationship. The individual who scores highest on Test A also scores highest on

Test *B*. The individual who is second highest on Test *A* is second highest on Test *B*, and so on right down the list.

Now suppose that we have the following situation showing the ranks of the same 6 individuals on 2 more tests:

Student	Test *C*	Test *D*
1	1	6
2	2	5
3	3	4
4	4	3
5	5	2
6	6	1

This time we have an example of a perfect negative relationship. The individual who scored highest on Test *C* scored lowest on Test *D* and the individual who scored lowest on Test *C* scored highest on Test *D*, etc.

In actual practice we never run into perfect relationships. The measured relationship comes somewhere in between. We can picture the correlation coefficient then as being a continuum which extends from −1 through 0 to +1 as this:

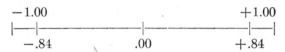

It follows that, as far as the size of a correlation coefficient goes, one of −.84 is just as large as one of +.84. The only difference here is the sign which shows that we have an inverse relationship between the variables in the case with the negative coefficient. The absence of relationship is denoted by a correlation coefficient of .00.

In the typical process for computing a correlation coefficient we assume that there is a straight line or linear relationship between 2 variables (Figure 2:6)—that is, as one increases or decreases, the other increases or decreases proportionately.

In some cases as shown in Figure 2:7, as one variable increases, the other variable also increases for a part of the range. After a certain point is reached, however, a reverse relationship begins. As the first variable continues to increase, the second begins to decrease. We call this type of relationship CURVILINEAR. An example of this is found when we study such things as running ability and

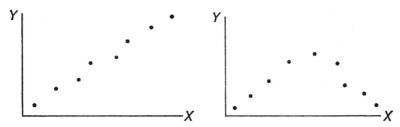

Fig. 2:6. A Linear Relationship   Fig. 2:7. A Curvilinear Relationship

correlate this with age. As a child grows older, he runs faster up to a certain point in his development and then, as he becomes older, he slows up. There are many situations in education where curvilinear relationships prevail. If a teacher has evidence that the relationship between 2 variables is not linear, then the techniques described below should not be used. A statistics book should be consulted and the statistic known as the *correlation ratio* applied.

Pearson Product-Moment Correlation Coefficient

The most commonly used correlation coefficient is the Pearson Product-Moment Correlation Coefficient. The symbol for it is r. The basic formula for r is

$$r = \frac{\Sigma xy}{\sqrt{\Sigma x^2 \Sigma y^2}}$$

where x and y are deviations of each score from its respective mean. If a calculating machine is available either of the following formulas may be used:

$$r = \frac{\Sigma XY - \dfrac{(\Sigma X)(\Sigma Y)}{N}}{\sqrt{\left[\Sigma X^2 - \dfrac{(\Sigma X)^2}{N}\right]\left[\Sigma Y^2 - \dfrac{(\Sigma Y)^2}{N}\right]}}$$

or

$$r = \frac{N\Sigma XY - (\Sigma X)(\Sigma Y)}{\sqrt{[N\Sigma X^2 - (\Sigma X)^2][N\Sigma Y^2 - (\Sigma Y)^2]}}$$

where X and Y are the raw scores for each variable and N is the number of pairs of individuals.

In Table 2:8 are presented 2 sets of scores for 35 students. Test X is one form (A) of a clerical test and Test Y is an equivalent form (B) of the same test. We shall now proceed to calculate r using the second of the above machine formulas.

Table 2:8. COMPUTATION OF A CORRELATION COEFFICIENT

1 Ind.	2 Test X (A)	3 Test Y (B)	4 $X - 20$ (X')	5 $Y - 20$ (Y')	6 X'^2	7 Y'^2	8 $X'Y'$
1	61	62	41	42	1681	1764	1722
2	54	58	34	38	1156	1444	1292
3	54	53	34	33	1156	1089	1122
4	52	56	32	36	1024	1296	1152
5	51	50	31	30	961	900	930
6	49	52	29	32	841	1024	928
7	48	46	28	26	784	676	728
8	48	47	28	27	784	729	756
9	48	50	28	30	784	900	840
10	48	48	28	28	784	784	784
11	47	48	27	28	729	784	756
12	47	46	27	26	729	676	702
13	46	47	26	27	676	729	702
14	46	44	26	24	676	576	624
15	45	47	25	27	625	729	675
16	45	42	25	22	625	484	550
17	44	46	24	26	576	676	624
18	43	40	23	20	529	400	460
19	42	44	22	24	484	576	528
20	41	40	21	20	441	400	420
21	41	41	21	21	441	441	441
22	40	42	20	22	400	484	440
23	40	38	20	18	400	324	360
24	39	39	19	19	361	361	361
25	39	40	19	20	361	400	380
26	38	37	18	17	324	289	306
27	37	39	17	19	289	361	306
28	37	40	17	20	289	400	340
29	36	32	16	12	256	144	192
30	33	34	13	14	169	196	182
31	32	29	12	9	144	81	108
32	29	30	9	10	81	100	90
33	25	28	5	8	25	64	40
34	24	29	4	9	16	81	36
35	21	16	1	−4	1	16	−4
			$\Sigma = 770$	780	19,602	20,378	19,873

In order to make our work easier, the first thing to do is to reduce all the scores in the X column by a constant of 20. Notice now that column 4 is headed $X - 20$ (or X'). In a similar fashion the Y variable has had each score reduced by 20. Column 5 then is headed $Y - 20$ (or Y'). This process of subtracting a score from each score in a distribution is called coding and will in no way affect our results. Constants may be added to each score in a distribution, or each score in a distribution may be multiplied by or divided by the same constant and the size of the correlation coefficient remains the same.

In column 6 we have the square of each coded score on Test X (column 4) and in column 7 we have the square of each coded score on Test Y (column 5)*. Column 8, which we call the cross-products, is the result of multiplying each coded X score by its corresponding coded Y score. The last five columns are summed and we are ready for substituting into the formula. This time we shall write the formula using X' and Y' to denote the fact that these are coded values and not the original raw scores.

$$r = \frac{N\Sigma X'Y' - (\Sigma X')(\Sigma Y')}{\sqrt{[N\Sigma X'^2 - (\Sigma X')^2][N\Sigma Y'^2 - (\Sigma Y')^2]}}$$

$$= \frac{(35)19{,}873 - (770)(780)}{\sqrt{[(35)19{,}602 - (770)^2][(35)20{,}378 - (780)^2]}}$$

$$= \frac{695{,}555 - 600{,}600}{\sqrt{(93{,}170)(104{,}830)}}$$

$$= \frac{94{,}955}{98{,}829}$$

$$= .96$$

If we become proficient in the operation of a calculating machine, we do not have to write all the values for each step as shown in Table 2:8. These values are accumulated in the machine and the sums read from the machines when finished.

Another method for computing r is the scattergram method. When

---

* The use of the table of squares in Table 2:9 will greatly facilitate the work at this point.

Table 2:9. SQUARES OF NUMBERS 1 THROUGH 99

N	N²	N	N²	N	N²
1	1	34	1156	67	4489
2	4	35	1225	68	4624
3	9	36	1296	69	4761
4	16	37	1369	70	4900
5	25	38	1444	71	5041
6	36	39	1521	72	5184
7	49	40	1600	73	5329
8	64	41	1681	74	5476
9	81	42	1764	75	5625
10	100	43	1849	76	5776
11	121	44	1936	77	5929
12	144	45	2025	78	6084
13	169	46	2116	79	6241
14	196	47	2209	80	6400
15	225	48	2304	81	6561
16	256	49	2401	82	6724
17	289	50	2500	83	6889
18	324	51	2601	84	7056
19	361	52	2704	85	7225
20	400	53	2809	86	7396
21	441	54	2916	87	7569
22	484	55	3025	88	7744
23	529	56	3136	89	7921
24	576	57	3249	90	8100
25	625	58	3364	91	8281
26	676	59	3481	92	8464
27	729	60	3600	93	8649
28	784	61	3721	94	8836
29	841	62	3844	95	9025
30	900	63	3969	96	9216
31	961	64	4096	97	9409
32	1024	65	4225	98	9604
33	1089	66	4356	99	9801
				100	10000

no calculating machine is available, this is an easier method than that above. Again, we shall use the data in Table 2:8, and our work will be done in the scattergram that is shown in Table 2:10. The steps for this process are outlined below.

1. Take the first column of scores (A-scores), determine the range, an appropriate interval size, and set up the steps for the frequency distribution on the vertical axis. For our data the range is 41. An appropriate interval size would be 4. On the vertical

axis we begin our frequency distribution with the bottom interval being 20-23.

2. Repeat this process for the B-scores and set up the frequency
   distribution on the horizontal axis. The intervals are written
   across the top of the scattergram. This time we have a range
   of 46. An appropriate interval size for this is again 4. So, starting at the left at the top of the scattergram, we set up our distribution with the first interval being 16-19.

3. Next we plot our score on the scattergram. This is done pair
   by pair. The first pair is $A = 61$, $B = 62$. We go up the vertical
   axis until we come to the interval containing 61; next we go
   across the horizontal axis until we come to the interval containing 62 and in that cell we place a tally. Then we take the next
   pair. We go up to the interval 52-55 and across to the interval
   56-59 and place the second tally. This process is continued
   until all pairs of scores are plotted.

4. At the bottom of the scattergram notice fx, frequency of B-scores.
   We complete this row by adding the tallies in each column and
   we do the same for the fy column by adding the tallies in each
   row. The sum of the fy column should equal the sum of the fx
   column. Even if it does, it does not mean that no mistakes have
   been made. The work is best verified by replotting the scores.

5. The next three rows at the bottom, x', fx', and fx'^2 are already
   familiar from our previous work on means and standard deviations. In this work we are assuming the mean to be at the bottom
   of the distribution in the interval 16-19. Hence, the first x' cell
   has a value of 0, the second 1, etc. The fx' row is obtained by
   multiplying each value in the fx row by its corresponding value
   in the x' row. And the fx'^2 row by multiplying each cell in the x'
   row by its corresponding cell in the fx' row.

6. In a similar fashion the y', fy', and fy'^2 values are obtained.

7. Next sum the fx', fx'^2, fy', and fy'^2 rows and columns.

8. Next go to the column headed $x' y'$, the product of the deviations
   from the two arbitrary reference points. This is how the values in
   this column are obtained. First go to the row 60-61. In this row
   there is 1 tally that is 11 units from the arbitrary reference point
   for X and 10 units from the arbitrary reference point for Y. That
   is $x' = 11$ and $y' = 10$ and the product, $x' y'$ is 110, which is

CLASS INTERVALS — Y AXIS Form A

CLASS INTERVALS — X AXIS Form B

$\bar{X} = 17.5 + \left(\dfrac{219}{35}\right)4$

$= 17.5 + 25.0$

$= 42.5$

$\bar{Y} = 21.5 + \left(\dfrac{182}{35}\right)4$

$= 21.5 + 20.8$

$= 42.3$

$s_x = \sqrt{\dfrac{\Sigma x^2}{N}} = \sqrt{\dfrac{2891.2}{35}} = \sqrt{82.60} = 9.1$

$s_y = \sqrt{\dfrac{\Sigma y^2}{N}} = \sqrt{\dfrac{2585.6}{35}} = \sqrt{73.87} = 8.6$

$\Sigma x^2 = i^2 \left[\Sigma f_x'^2 - \dfrac{(\Sigma f_x')^2}{N} \right]$

$= 4^2 \left[1551. - \dfrac{219^2}{35} \right]$

$= 16\,(180.7) = 2891.2$

$219 = N$

$1551 = \Sigma x'^2$

$219 = \Sigma x'$

$35 = N$

$\Sigma y^2 = 4^2 \left[1108 - \dfrac{182^2}{35} \right]$

$= 4^2\,(161.6) = 16(161.6)$

$= 2585.6$

Table 2:10. COMPUTATION OF A CORRELATION COEFFICIENT BY THE SCATTERGRAM METHOD

entered in the x' y' column. Since there are no frequencies in the next row 0 is placed in the x' y' column. In the next row there are 3 tallies. We find the x' y' value of each and then sum these. The first is 72 (9 × 8), the second 80 (10 × 8), and the third 80 (10 × 8). Summed they equal 232. This technique is followed until all x' y' values are obtained and then the column is summed.

9. The Pearson r is then obtained by the use of the following formula:

$$r = \frac{\Sigma x'y' - \dfrac{(\Sigma fx')\,(\Sigma fy')}{N}}{\sqrt{\left[\Sigma fx'^2 - \dfrac{(\Sigma fx')^2}{N}\right]\left[\Sigma fy'^2 - \dfrac{(\Sigma fy')^2}{N}\right]}}$$

$$r = \frac{1302 - \dfrac{(219)(182)}{35}}{\sqrt{\left[1551 - \dfrac{(219)^2}{35}\right]\left[1108 - \dfrac{(182)^2}{35}\right]}}$$

$$= \frac{1302 - 1138.8}{\sqrt{[1551 - 1370.3][1108 - 946.4]}} = \frac{163.2}{\sqrt{(180.7)(161.6)}}$$

$$= \frac{163.2}{170.9}$$

$$= .955$$

The discrepancy between this value of r and the one obtained by the machine formula is brought about by the error of grouping.

The scattergram method has the advantage of showing immediately after the scores have been plotted the sign and the approximate size of the coefficient. If the tallies tend to fall along a straight line that extends from the lower left to the upper right of the scatter-plot, we have a high, positive relationship. If the tallies fall along a line from the upper left to the lower right, we have a high, negative relationship. As the relationship between the two variables decreases, the tallies spread out more and more from these lines until, when the relationship is zero, they are scattered all over it. Also an inspection of the scattergram will reveal a curvilinear relationship, when present. The means and standard deviations for each variable can be computed directly from data on the scattergram.

Correlation Coefficients and the Range

One of the major determinants of the magnitude of a correlation coefficient is the range of talent in the sample. For example, if one studied the correlation between intelligence test scores and grades made in graduate school, he would find that the r is usually quite low. However, if one took children in grades 2-6 and correlated their intelligence test scores with grades, a moderate correlation ($\pm$ .50) would be obtained. Graduate students are a select group and tend to be much more similar in respect to intelligence test scores than do individuals spread through grades 2-6. Similarly, if one took boys in grade 3 and correlated measures of their height and weight, a low correlation coefficient would be obtained. Taking boys in grades 2-7 and running a correlation between the same 2 variables would probably result in a much larger coefficient. It follows that it is important to know about the variability of a group when one evaluates correlation coefficients. A moderate coefficient obtained from a fairly homogeneous group may be just as meaningful as a very high one derived from a group with a wide range of talent.

Spearman Rank-Order Correlation Coefficient

Next we will take up another correlation method which is useful when the number of pairs is small, less than 30. This method is called the Spearman Rank-Order Method and its symbol is rho (p). We shall demonstrate this by taking the 20 pairs of values shown in Table 2:11.

To compute rho we go through the following steps:

1. Rank the scores on the first test (column 1) and write these values in column 3. The score of 61, which is the highest score, has a rank of 1. There are two 54's and these occupy the second and third place in our ranks. Rather than give one a rank of 2 and the other a rank of 3, we average their ranks and give each the average rank. In this case $2 + 3 = 5$ divided by 2 gives 2.5. Thus the second and third scores each have a rank of 2.5. We continue then until all scores are ranked.

Table 2:11. Computation of Spearman Rank-Order Correlation
Coefficient

	1	2	3	4	5	6
Student	X	Y	R_X	R_Y	D	D^2
1	61	184	1	3.5	2.5	6.25
2	54	197	2.5	2	.5	.25
3	54	143	2.5	10	7.5	56.25
4	52	184	4	3.5	.5	.25
5	50	206	5	1	4	16
6	48	182	6	5	1	1
7	47	124	7	16	9	81
8	46	142	8	11	3	9
9	40	168	9.5	7	2.5	6.25
10	40	147	9.5	9	.5	.25
11	39	136	11	14.5	3.5	12.25
12	38	140	12	13	1	1
13	37	174	13	6	7	49
14	36	102	14	18.5	4.5	20.25
15	30	141	15	12	3	9
16	28	136	16	14.5	1.5	2.25
17	27	154	17	8	9	81
18	22	111	18	17	1	1
19	20	98	19	20	1	1
20	18	102	20	18.5	1.5	2.25

$\Sigma = 355.50$

2. Do the same for the scores on the second test and place their ranks in column 4.

3. Obtain the difference for each pair of ranks in columns 3 and 4. Since these are to be squared in the next step, negative signs may be disregarded.

4. Square each of these differences.

5. Sum this column.

6. Solve for rho as follows:

$$\text{rho} = 1 - \frac{6\Sigma D^2}{N(N^2 - 1)}$$

$$= 1 - \frac{6(355.50)}{20(400 - 1)}$$

$$= 1 - \frac{2133}{7980}$$

$$= 1 - .267$$

$$= .733$$

It should be apparent now that if N is large we would spend a considerable amount of time in setting up the ranks. For all practical purposes this Spearman rho is considered equivalent to the Pearson r and is interpreted in the same way as it is.

SAMPLING

The statistics that we have considered so far—mean, median, standard deviation, correlation coefficients, etc.—are known as DESCRIPTIVE STATISTICS because they can be used in describing the characteristics of a sample. Modern statistics goes far beyond this into another area that is called SAMPLING STATISTICS. In sampling statistics, 2 major operations can be performed. First, we can make inferences on the basis of the sample values that we have at hand. The aim of most research is not to find out some information about a small group. We hope that we can, on the basis of our sample, make statements about all such situations as those with which we are concerned. For example, if we are carrying on research with reading disabilities of a group of fifth graders or studying the mental ability of a group of 12-year-olds, our research has real value when we can go beyond our samples and make inferential statements about the reading disabilities of all fifth graders or the mental ability of all 12-year-olds.

Secondly, by the use of sampling statistics we can test differences between two groups. Suppose that we match 2 groups of sixth graders, one of which, called the experimental group, is taught by a new technique whereas the second, called the control group, is taught by a conventional method. At the end of the year, both groups are given the same test and our means and standard deviations computed. There is a difference between our 2 mean scores on this final examination. The question before us is whether this difference is a real difference that would hold up again and again or whether it is merely a chance difference. We can answer this question by making a test using sampling statistics to see what the probability is of these differences being real or significant.

Standard Error

In order to understand what STANDARD ERROR is, suppose that we start with a population made up of all seventh-grade students in any given state. Note that in statistics, *population* (or *universe* as it is sometimes called) is an arbitrarily defined group with which we are concerned at the moment. Let us now suppose that a random sample of 30 is drawn from our population. A RANDOM SAMPLE is one set up in such a way that every individual in the population has an equal chance of being drawn. Each individual in our sample is given an intelligence test and the mean and standard deviation computed. Let us suppose that we know that in the population the mean intelligence test score is 100 with a standard deviation of 15. We find that the mean of our sample is 97 with a standard deviation of 12. Suppose now that we draw another random sample of 30 and administer the same intelligence test. This time we find that the mean is 103 and the standard deviation is 17. Suppose that we were to continue this process for 498 more times until we had 500 samples. If we computed the mean of these 500 means, we would have a value very similar to our population mean of 100. If we computed the standard deviation of these 500 means about this population or grand mean, we would call this value the STANDARD ERROR OF THE MEAN. A standard error, then, is the standard deviation of a group of sample values about the population value. Suppose that in this case we found the standard error of the mean to be 3. Since the standard error is a standard deviation, we can say that we would expect to find two thirds of our sample means in the band 97-103— that is, the population mean plus and minus 1 standard error.

In actual practice, we don't have population means or population standard deviations. We estimate the size of the standard error of the mean by use of the formula

$$s_{\overline{X}} = \frac{s}{\sqrt{N-1}}$$

where s is standard deviation of the sample and N is the number of cases. Suppose that we calculated the mean and standard deviation for a set of data and find them to be 76 and 14 respectively where N is 50. Then

$$s_{\overline{X}} = \frac{14}{\sqrt{49}} = \frac{14}{7} = 2$$

Interpreting this standard error as a standard deviation, we can say that the chances are 2 out of 3 (68 in 100) that the population mean lies within the band 74-78 (76 ± 2), the sample mean plus or minus 1 standard error of the mean. We could go further and say that the chances are 95 in 100 that the population mean is within the band 72-80 (76 ± 2($s_{\bar{X}}$)).

All statistics have standard errors. Some of the commonly used ones are listed below. For others and for detailed information on this topic the student should consult an elementary statistics book.

Mean

$$s_{\bar{X}} = \sqrt{\frac{s}{N-1}}$$

Median

$$s_{Mdn} = \frac{1.253s}{\sqrt{N}}$$

Proportion

$$s_p = \sqrt{\frac{pq}{N}} \qquad \begin{array}{l} p = \text{Proportion} \\ q = 1 - p \end{array}$$

Standard Deviation

$$s_s = \frac{s}{\sqrt{2N}}$$

Score (Standard Error of Measurement)

$$s_{Meas.} = s\sqrt{1-r}$$

(This statistic is discussed in the section on reliability.)

Tests of Differences

Next we shall take up the second use of sampling statistics, namely testing differences. Suppose for an illustration that we have been interested in a new method in teaching reading. In a large school system we set up our experimental group of 100 children and apply our new technique to them for one year. We also have a control group that is taught by the technique usually used in this school system. At the end of the year, we give each child the same reading test and then compute means and standard deviations for each group. These are

Experimental Group	Control Group
$\overline{X}_1 = 66$	$\overline{X}_2 = 63$
$s_1 = 8$	$s_2 = 7$
$N_1 = 101$	$N_2 = 101$

When we make a statistical test of this nature, we start out by setting up a *null hypothesis*. In this case we state either that there is no difference between these two means or that the two means are the same. The procedure is as follows:

1. Calculate the standard error of the first mean:

$$s_{\overline{X}_1} = \frac{8}{\sqrt{100}} = \frac{8}{10} = .8$$

2. Calculate the standard error for the second mean:

$$s_{\overline{X}_2} = \frac{7}{\sqrt{100}} = .7$$

3. Compute the standard error of the difference between the two means:

$$s_{\overline{X}_1 - \overline{X}_2} = \sqrt{s_{\overline{X}_1}^2 + s_{\overline{X}_2}^2}$$
$$= \sqrt{.8^2 + .7^2}$$
$$= \sqrt{.64 + .49}$$
$$= \sqrt{1.13}$$
$$= 1.06$$

4. Compute t, where t is defined as the difference between the means divided by the standard error of the difference between the means. Some writers use Critical Ratio (CR) instead of t when dealing with large samples, reserving the use of t for small samples.

$$t = \frac{\overline{X}_1 - \overline{X}_2}{s_{\overline{X}_1 - \overline{X}_2}}$$

$$t = \frac{66 - 63}{1.06}$$

$$t = \frac{3}{1.06}$$

$$t = 2.83$$

We use this t in deciding what to do with our hypothesis. The discussion that follows is based upon large samples. When samples are very small, the student should consult a table found in the appendix of a statistics book because, as the number of cases decreases, larger t's are required to reject hypotheses. In reference to our original null hypothesis, 3 things may happen as a result of applying our t value:

1. We may reject the null hypothesis at the 1-per-cent level. This means that the chances are 99 in 100 that there is a real or significant difference between these two means. When N is large, any t value of 2.58 or larger allows us to reject the null hypothesis at the 1-per-cent level. Hence, for our problem with a t of 2.83, we can state that the chances are 99 in 100 that this difference between the means is a true or real difference and not a chance difference. Of course, it is possible that we have at hand that 1 chance in 100 when this difference is a chance difference. There is no way of telling this. A well-planned piece of research should be run at least twice.

2. We may reject the null hypothesis at the 5-per-cent level. This means that the chances are 95 in 100 that this difference between the means is a true difference. With a large sample, a t of between 1.96 and 2.58 constitutes the 5-per-cent level. Since we now have 5 chances in 100 or 1 in 20 of being wrong, this is not so good a test as the first one. In most scientific research workers don't go beyond this. At the 10- or 25-per-cent level the chances are too great of being wrong. In fact, some workers only use the 1-per-cent level.

3. We may let the null hypothesis stand. This is the case for

large samples when the t value is less than 1.96. The above may be summarized:

Null hypothesis stands		Reject 5% level		Reject 1% level
Size of t	1.96		2.58	

Negative t's are interpreted in the same way.

The reader should notice that in no case above did we conclude that the 2 means were the same. We either said that there was no difference between the 2 means, or we made a probability statement about their being the same.

The formula used above for computing the standard error of the difference between 2 means is to be used only when the data are not correlated. For example, if we took a sample, tested each individual, then treated each individual in some fashion, and again tested the same individuals, we would have correlated data. Two groups using brothers and sisters measured with intelligence tests would produce correlated data. When correlation does exist between the 2 sets of measurements, our formula becomes:

$$s_{\bar{X}_1 - \bar{X}_2} = \sqrt{s_{\bar{X}_1}{}^2 + s_{\bar{X}_2}{}^2 - 2r_{12}s_{\bar{X}_1}s_{\bar{X}_2}}$$

where

$s_{\bar{X}_1}$ = standard error of first mean,

$s_{\bar{X}_2}$ = standard error of second mean,

r_{12} = correlation coefficient between the two variables.

Actually this is the basic formula, the one used previously being a special case obtained when $r = 0$.

The above process for testing the difference can be generalized for testing the differences between proportion, percentages, medians, etc. Correlation coefficients present a special case beyond the scope of this discussion.

EXERCISES

1. The following raw scores were obtained by administering an intelligence test:

63	70	44	28	43	38	42	36
40	42	48	32	58	63	29	29
38	36	54	38	22	28	37	39
42	50	36	37	24	46	39	41
40	46	34	44	28	42	41	40

(a) Set up a frequency distribution using an interval of 5. Let your bottom interval be 20-24.

(b) Set up another distribution also with an interval of 5. This time let your bottom interval be 22-26.

(c) Draw a frequency polygon for the frequency distribution set up in (a) above.

(d) For these data, using the first frequency distribution, calculate each of the following:

     (1) Mean   (4) Standard Deviation
     (2) Median   (5) Quartile Deviation
     (3) Mode   (6) C_{77}; C_{17}; C_{30}

(e) Construct an ogive curve for these data and read the decile points. (The first of these is equal to C_{10}; etc.)

2. Two groups of college freshmen were given a test of mental ability. The results are shown below:

College A	f	College B	f
160-169	1	150-159	2
150-159	6	140-149	0
140-149	12	130-139	4
130-139	22	120-129	7
120-129	26	110-119	13
110-119	46	100-109	23
100-109	38	90-99	19
90-99	22	80-89	12
80-89	15	70-79	9
70-79	10	60-69	7
60-69	0	50-59	4
50-59	2		
	$N = 200$		$N = 100$

(a) Set up a frequency polygon for both of these sets of data, using the same graph.

(b) Compute the mean and standard deviation for both distributions.

(c) By means of a *t* test, test these 2 means to see if the difference between them is significant.

3. Fifty students took an intelligence test and a reading test. Their raw scores occur below.

Student	Intelligence	Reading	Student	Intelligence	Reading
1	72	90	26	39	62
2	68	78	27	38	59
3	64	88	28	38	58
4	63	74	29	37	50
5	58	70	30	37	44
6	55	74	31	37	58
7	54	73	32	36	57
8	53	84	33	34	51
9	49	86	34	34	49
10	48	79	35	34	56
11	48	72	36	33	40
12	47	62	37	32	50
13	47	73	38	32	56
14	46	60	39	31	44
15	45	61	40	30	42
16	43	77	41	30	48
17	42	59	42	30	38
18	42	64	43	29	30
19	42	61	44	27	36
20	41	61	45	26	38
21	40	57	46	25	37
22	40	63	47	24	38
23	40	68	48	22	31
24	39	65	49	21	40
25	39	62	50	19	29

(a) Using the Rank-Order technique, compute the correlation co-efficient between these scores. Use only the first 25 pairs.

(b) Using the entire 50 pairs, calculate the Pearson *r*.

(c) Calculate the mean and standard deviation of each.

REFERENCES

To enlarge upon any topic in this chapter, the student is referred to any elementary statistics text. Among some of the newer ones are the following:

1. Downie, N. M., and Heath, R. W. *Basic statistical methods.* 2nd ed. New York: Harper and Row, 1965.
2. Guilford, J. P. *Fundamental statistics in psychology and education.* 4th ed. New York: McGraw-Hill, 1965.
3. McNemar, Q. *Psychological statistics.* 3rd ed. New York: Wiley, 1962.
4. Peatman, J. B. *Introduction to applied statistics.* New York: Harper and Row, 1963.
5. Senders, Virginia. *Measurement and statistics: A basic text emphasizing behavioral science applications.* New York: Oxford University Press, 1958.

CHAPTER 3

SCORES, GRADES, AND NORMS

In this chapter we will, first, give consideration to the various types of scores that are used in educational measurement; secondly, to the problem of changing test scores to grades; and, thirdly, to the types and uses of norms.

SCORES

After a test has been administered and graded, a score is obtained. This unit is referred to as a *raw score*, which is in itself of little or no use. To say that an individual has a score of 42 on a geography test, a score of 86 on a spelling test, and a score of 23 in arithmetic is practically meaningless. In order for values such as these to have meaning, an individual's performance has to be compared with that of a group, either his own or, on a standardized test, a group similar to his upon whom the test was developed. Many teachers in the past and some teachers of today solved this problem by expressing all test scores in per cents, 100 representing perfect performance. Such percentage scores are limited in what they reveal. A score of 65 per cent on one test may be equivalent to a score of 80 per cent on an easier test. These scores will be discussed further in the section on grading. Over the last 60 years many different types of scores have been developed and most of them used, at least to a limited extent. The student who is interested in a classification

59

and description of the different types of scores is referred to Lyman (11). Fortunately not all of these scores have become popular and it is possible to pick a certain few that are extensively used. These are the ones that will be discussed here. Of these, the most important and the ones that will probably be encountered more and more frequently in future tests work are standard scores. It is with these that we shall start the discussion of test scores.

Standard Scores

STANDARD SCORES are units based upon the number of standard deviations a given score is from the mean. The formula for a standard score is

$$z = \frac{X - \overline{X}}{s} = \frac{x}{s}$$

where

z = standard score

X = any raw score

x = deviation of score from the mean

$\overline{X}$ = mean of the distribution

s = standard deviation of the distribution

Suppose for an example we have the following raw scores in a distribution whose mean is 80 and standard deviation is 10.

X	z-score
80	.00
90	1.00
70	−1.00
100	2.00
110	3.00
60	−2.00
50	−3.00
65	−1.50

When standard scores are computed, it should be noted that the z-score equal to the mean is zero. The z-score equivalent to a raw score 1 standard deviation above the mean is $+1.00$, equivalent to a raw score of 2 standard deviations above the mean, +2.00. We could describe a distribution of z-scores by saying that they have a mean of 0 and a standard deviation of 1. Hence if we understand standard deviations, we can easily understand standard scores. If we look at Figure 3:1, which shows a distribution of standard scores, we note that a standard score of +1, since it is a standard deviation, has between it and the mean 34 per cent of the cases. It is the equivalent of the 84th centile. These relationships are always the same with standard scores for any distribution. We also notice from Figure 3:1 that a standard score unit of 1 taken at any place in the distribution always includes the same number of raw score units, in this case 10. There are no variations here as are found with centile units. These scores can then be manipulated numerically.

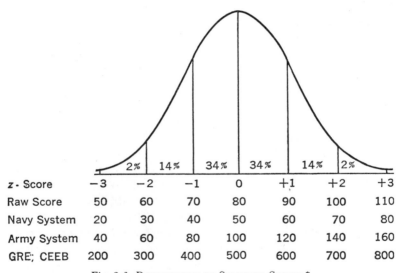

	2%	14%	34%	34%	14%	2%	
z - Score	−3	−2	−1	0	+1	+2	+3
Raw Score	50	60	70	80	90	100	110
Navy System	20	30	40	50	60	70	80
Army System	40	60	80	100	120	140	160
GRE; CEEB	200	300	400	500	600	700	800

Fig. 3:1. DISTRIBUTION OF STANDARD SCORES *

TRANSFORMATION OF z-SCORES. Standard scores of the type discussed so far have two disadvantages in that half of them are negative and that they tend to run to 2-point decimals. To eliminate these

* Based upon Bulletin 48, Psychological Corporation (14).

defects, which make computations slow and cumbersome, various systems have been devised. For example, the tests used by the U.S. Army in World War II had a mean of 100 and a standard deviation of 20. The U.S. Navy tests had a mean of 50 and a standard deviation of 10. Currently, the tests of the College Entrance Examination Board and the *Graduate Record Examination* have a mean of 500 and a standard deviation of 100. To change z-scores to any of these systems is very simple. For example, to translate z-scores to the system used by the U.S. Army, we take the z-score already obtained, multiply it by 20, and add it to 100. Or starting from the beginning:

$$\left(\frac{X - \overline{X}}{s}\right) 20 + 100$$

Some of these transformed scores are shown in Figure 3:1. On an Army test an examinee obtained a score of about 40 for writing his name on his paper—the bottom score—and the top score was 160. Actually on the *U.S. Army General Classification Test* a score of 42 was used as the lower limit of the distribution.

It should be emphasized that the above z-scores and the transformations thereof have not been normalized. If these were based on a positively skewed distribution of scores (obtained from a difficult test), then the distribution of z-scores or of transformed scores is still skewed positively. Such transformations as these are said to be linear. It is possible to normalize a distribution of scores on the basis of the normal curve. Examples of these are found in normalized percentiles, and McCall's T-scores (12). For the construction and use of these, the student should consult a statistics book or the reference cited. Anastasi (2) notes that when the original distribution of scores approaches a normal curve, the linearly derived standard scores are very similar to those obtained by the normalizing processes and can be interpreted as the latter.

In recent years stanines (standard nines) have been introduced into the reporting of test results in the schools (5, 6). These statistics were developed and used extensively by the Air Force in World War II. In its simplest form a stanine scale is a 9-point scale with a mean of 5 and a standard deviation of 2. The percentages of cases included in each stanine are shown as follows:

Stanine	Percentage of cases	
9	4	High
8	7	
7	12	} Above average (19%)
6	17	
5	20	} Average (54%)
4	17	
3	12	
2	7	} Below average (19%)
1	4	Low

The distribution of stanines is based upon the distribution of the normal curve. A distribution like stanines has the advantage in this day of punch cards of requiring only one column on the card to represent a score. For some individuals such a grouping of scores is too coarse, but for many practical and statistical purposes, stanines have proved quite successful. Certain modifications have been made to the usual stanine distribution such as giving each stanine a plus and minus value, 5+, 5, 5—. In this way 27 scores are used to do the work of the original nine. Also 0 and 10 have been added to the extremes of the distribution to include the bottom and top 1 per cent of the cases respectively. Such a modification would be desirable mostly when the number of cases is large. Cattell (4) has a scale of scores with these extra units that he calls stens (standard tens). Using this system the percentage of cases in each sten score is as follows:

Sten	1	2	3	4	5	6	7	8	9	10
Percentage	2	5	9	15	19	19	15	9	5	2

Whatever advantages are claimed for this scale are negated by the fact that they require two columns on an IBM card.

Guilford (7) has used with his personality inventories such as the *Guilford-Zimmerman Temperament Survey* a C-score that is similar to both of the preceding. This score contains 11 units as follows:

C	0	1	2	3	4	5	6	7	8	9	10
	Lowest										
%	1%	3	7	12	17	20	17	12	7	3	1

Guilford notes that it might be a good idea to have the *C*-scale go from 1 to 11 to avoid having to tell an individual that he has a score of 0 on a test.

Another type of standard score is found on the *Wechsler-Bellevue* and other intelligence tests (20). Here the scores are called IQ's, but actually they are standard scores with a mean of 100 and a standard deviation of about 15. The subtests of the Wechsler also are expressed in standard scores, each having a mean of 10 and a standard deviation of 3. The *Wechsler Intelligence Scale for Children* (*WISC*) is also expressed in these deviation IQ's.

Standard scores are most useful because they are equal units of measurement and their interpretation is always the same. They represent common basic units and the performance of an individual on several tests can be compared when reduced to this type of unit. Suppose we have the following data, the scores of 4 students on 5 tests:

	A	B	C	D	$\overline{X}$	s
Hist.	40	50	30	58	40	10
Geog.	25	40	40	42	30	5
Arith.	42	70	48	76	60	8
Spell.	80	68	102	148	100	20
Read.	60	70	85	105	70	15

If we transform each of these to standard scores with a mean of 50 and a standard deviation of 10 based upon the appropriate mean and standard deviation, we obtain:

	A	B	C	D
Hist.	50	60	40	68
Geog.	40	70	70	74
Arith.	28	62	35	70
Spell.	40	34	51	74
Read.	43	50	60	73
Average	40.2	55.2	51.2	71.8

Since the mean of the above standard scores is 50 for all with a standard deviation of 10, the above data are now in a form to compare performances among the 4 students as well as to compare the performance of each student on the 5 different tests. Notice also that the 5 standard scores have been averaged for each student.

Such situations as this are really only made meaningful when reduced to standard scores.

Centiles or Percentiles and Centile Ranks

A centile score is defined as a point below which fall a certain
percentage of the cases in the group upon which the test was normed.
For example, an individual at C_{13} on an intelligence test is at a point
below which 13 per cent of the norm group scored. The computation
of centiles was described in Chapter 2, where it was also shown
how centiles can be obtained from an ogive curve.

Centiles are widely used, chiefly because they are so easy to interpret. To the uninformed they seem to be like per cents and hence
can be used meaningfully. Many scores dealing with adult performance on intelligence, aptitude, interest, and adjustment tests and
inventories are expressed in centiles.

However, in spite of the above they suffer from a serious limitation
in that they are not equal units of measurement. Remembering the
definition of a centile as a point below which a certain per cent of
the cases fall, by taking successive tens, we could build up a centile
distribution such as the following:

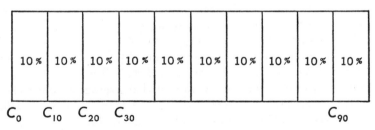

Fig. 3:2. RECTANGULAR DISTRIBUTION OF CENTILES

That is, 10 per cent of the cases would fall between the bottom score
and C_{10}. Between this point and C_{20}, another 10 per cent would fall.
And so on we could repeat this process until a rectangular distribution as in Figure 3:2 is set up.

In actual practice in educational and psychological measurement
our distributions tend to follow the normal curve. When centiles

are actually computed, results similar to Figure 3:3 are obtained.

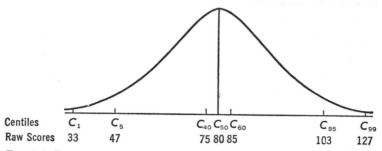

Centiles	C_1	C_5		$C_{40} C_{50} C_{60}$		C_{95}	C_{99}
Raw Scores	33	47		75 80 85		103	127

Fig. 3:3. RELATION BETWEEN CENTILE SCORES AND NORMALLY DISTRIBUTED RAW SCORES

Notice in this figure that a difference in 10 centile points near the center of the distribution, between C_{50} and C_{60} is equal to a difference in raw score units of only 5. Small differences near the center of the distribution are greatly magnified. Now take 2 other centile differences in the tail of the distribution. The centile points C_{95} and C_{99} have a difference of only 4, but in terms of raw scores this difference is 24. It should be apparent from this that, first, stated differences in centiles between differences near the center of a distribution are of no meaning or importance. To talk about one individual at C_{52} in our distribution shown in Figure 3:3 as being different or even higher than an individual at C_{48} in the same distribution is without meaning. Secondly, centiles should not be treated arithmetically since their size varies so greatly depending upon the part of the distribution in which they are found. When we have our results in terms of centiles and wish to find an average or to correlate our data, we should use our raw scores for this. Finally, centile units based on different tests standardized on different normative groups are not comparable.

On many tests scores are reported in centile ranks. For example, a person with a centile rank of 33 has a score that is higher than 33 per cent of those individuals upon whom the test was normed, an individual at the 99 centile rank has a raw score exceeding 99 per cent of the individuals in the norm group. Each centile rank has a corresponding point in the test score distribution known as the centile point.

Some test results are also presented in deciles (D) where D_1 is equal to C_{10}, D_2 to C_{20}, etc. In Chapter 2 the derivation of centiles was given and at that time quartile points were also mentioned. These have some use in test work in situations where we talk about an individual being in the top quarter, or bottom quarter, etc.

Grade-placement Norms

Scores on achievement tests used in the elementary grades are frequently expressed in GRADE-PLACEMENT NORMS. A typical child, normal as far as advancement through school is concerned, just entering fifth grade should have a grade placement of 5.0. If an achievement test was administered at this time, all scores could be compared against this 5.0. He might have such scores as 4.9 in arithmetic, 5.2 in spelling, 5.1 in history. These would indicate about normal performance. These scores when used as above give a meaningful picture of a child's status in the school subjects.

Grade-placement norms are obtained by administering a test or battery of tests to a representative group of third-, fourth-, fifth-, and sixth-grade students at about the same time of the year. A plan could be set up so that on October 1 in selected schools all over the United States a certain test is administered. A mean for each of the 4 grades would be computed and a graph set up with the line connecting these 4 points. If the tests were well made, this line would tend to be a straight line and to be fairly steep. By interpolation, values corresponding to a fraction of a grade may be obtained. By extrapolation it would be possible to read grade-placement scores as high as 10 or 11 or down to 1 or 2.

EVALUATION OF GRADE-PLACEMENT NORMS. To their credit, it can be said that these scores are easy to understand. Teachers, parents, and pupils have no difficulty with them. They are not difficult to obtain and are as useful as any of the devices used in the elementary school. However, they are far from perfect. First, they are based upon an assumption of equal growth in all subjects throughout the year. The year is divided into 10 parts, or 9 parts and 1 to include all the summer vacation. Human learning does not conform to this neat plan. For some individuals, growth is slow or nonexistent and, then all of a sudden, because of maturational factors or insights, more growth takes place in 1 week than had occurred in all the past 6 months. In some periods, especially over the summer holiday, individuals lose in their ability to do school work in certain school areas. Then growth in vocabulary and language usage is going on all the time.

The technique of extrapolating described above is also open to question. What does it mean when a fifth grader achieves a grade placement of 10 or 11 in a school subject? Does this mean that the fifth grader is performing at the tenth-grade level? In some areas, geography for example, there is usually no tenth-grade level. For most individuals, when a child scores high like this, it merely means that the child has had very good instruction in that area and this, combined with perhaps high academic ability, permits him to answer correctly a much larger number of items than would be expected. Thus he has a much higher score and a higher grade placement and, instead of knowing anything about tenth-grade geography, knows very much about fifth-grade geography.

Elementary-school teachers often make the mistake of regarding these grade-placement scores as standards. A fifth-grade teacher at the end of the year might expect each child to be up to 5-10 or 6-1 in all subjects. At least that might be the teacher's goal. Such an approach is unrealistic. These grade-placement scores are norms based upon averages. In a typical grade at any given time, a teacher might expect half his class to be above the average for the class at that time and the other half below. It would be the very exceptional class that would be entirely above or at the norm for its own grade group.

Educational Age

It is possible, on the basis of an achievement-test battery, to arrive at a score called an educational age (EA). This is similar to the idea of mental age discussed below in this chapter. If a single test, such as reading, is used, it is possible to have a reading age, or an arithmetic age. Educational age has been divided by chronological age to obtain an educational quotient, EQ. These quotients suffer from the severe limitation that they are specific to only one test. Since all achievement tests are based upon different and unequal units of measurements, there is no way of comparing educational quotients.

Mental Ages and IQ's

For many years some psychologists have used the concept of mental age in reporting scores made on intelligence tests. This, however, has always been a rather cumbersome procedure and the majority of test builders have avoided the use of age scales by constructing point scales. Basically, on point scales each item, when responded to correctly, results in a score of 1 being added to an individual's total score.

Binet, in the second edition of his intelligence test (1908), introduced the concept of mental age. L. M. Terman (17) used mental ages in reporting scores on the *Stanford Revision of the Binet-Simon Intelligence Scale*. This test is made up of a group of tests, each for a specific age level. Suppose that we take a year which is covered by 6 items. Each item is then worth 2 months. An individual's score on the test is the sum of the number of months obtained by adding up the value of all those items to which he responded correctly. A mental age of 8 means that the individual who attains this score has the same measured ability as the typical or average 8-year-old child. Mental ages are written as 10-8, which is read as 10 years and 8 months.

In 1912, Stern introduced the concept of intelligence quotient or IQ. This was first put to practical use by Terman in his 1916 edition of the *Stanford-Binet*. IQ is defined as the quotient that results when the mental age in months is divided by the chronological age in months and the result multiplied by 100.

$$IQ = \frac{MA}{CA} \times 100$$

This quotient would be very useful if individuals constantly increased in mental age as they grew older. Actually this is not so. According to Terman and Merrill (18), the increase in mental age begins to slow down typically at age 13 and stops by the age of 16. It can be seen that the use of the above formula with a constantly increasing denominator and a constant numerator would give a bizarre picture of an adult's mental ability. Terman and Merrill state that, during the chronological ages of 13 to 16, for every 3-month increase in chronological age there is only a 2-month increase in mental age. Mental growth ceases for the typical individual at 16, but because of the actual deceleration of mental growth between 13 and 16, the value used in the IQ formula for all individuals 16 and over is 15. The IQ of an 18-year-old boy with a mental age of 16 would be:

$$IQ = \frac{16 \times 12}{15 \times 12}(100) = \frac{192}{180}(100) = 107$$

For individuals whose ages are between 13 and 16, adjustments in chronological age are made on the basis of this 2-month increase in mental age *versus* 3-month increase in chronological age.

It should be interpolated here that psychologists are by no means in accord that mental growth ceases at age 16. Some place it at 18 and some in the early 20's (20). Others have maintained that it never ceases.

An IQ is a measure of the rate of intellectual development. From it a teacher can get an indication of the speed with which a child will learn in the classroom. Research has shown that a child's IQ over the years tends to be fairly constant. This is especially so if only measures from ages 5 or 6 and up are used. Early measures of intelligence have been shown to be very unreliable (2). We must also always keep in mind that there are other factors which are associated with success in school, chief of which is interest or motivation. Hence, when looking at an IQ and making a prediction or an observation, any teacher must also consider these other factors. The average IQ is taken to be 100 and the average spread about this mean on the *Stanford-Binet* is 16. There are on this test, rather wide differences in spread of scores, with the standard deviation ranging from 12 at one age level to 20 at another. Other tests would have different standard deviations.

Probably the death blow was administered to age scales when the 1960 revision of the *Stanford-Binet, Form L-M,* appeared (19). Here for the first time standard scores are presented for use with this test (13). These new *Stanford-Binet* standard scores are deviation IQ's with a mean of 100 and a standard deviation of 16. In the earlier forms of this battery there was considerable variability of the standard deviation of scores for the different age levels. This variability led to complications in studying a child's mental growth from year to year, in comparing scores, or in fact in doing anything with the scores statistically. These deviation scores facilitate the comparison of performance over a period of years or among children.

While IQ's were deeply rooted in American psychology and education, there have always been individuals who have strongly opposed their use. Among the issues raised by these opponents was one that an IQ was meaningless when applied to adults. Secondly there was considerable variation obtained with different tests. Old studies like that of Sangren (15) have pointed this out. In that study a range of 15-61 in IQ points with a mean of 32 was found for a group of first graders who had been given 6 different intelligence tests. The obtained IQ's of one child ranged from 104 to 165. IQ's were very variable and unreliable labels to put on a child, as some teachers and others at that time were wont to do. There was not uncommon belief back in those remote days of testing that an IQ of any child was a constant, that it was reliably measured, and that, once obtained for a child, an IQ became one of his unchanging characteristics similar to his eye color.

Summary of Scores

It is important that great concern be given to test scores because these scores have to convey meaning to the student, the teacher, parents, the guidance counselor, and to other school personnel. Scores must be easily interpreted and understood by those who are going to use them. Hence it follows that scores must be statistically sound, but expressed in as simple a form as possible to make for easy and rapid comprehension on the part of all users. All scores that we have so far discussed satisfy these criteria.

On the preceding pages we have evaluated the most frequently encountered scores. Many more kinds that exist have not been mentioned. Many of these others have no real advantages over those that have been discussed. What is needed is not more scores, but greater agreement upon which scores to use and then concentration on this selected few in all of our test work. Of the various scores evaluated, standard scores are by far superior to all others for reasons already pointed out. In order to bring about some conformity in score usage, it is proposed that standard scores with a mean of 50 and a standard deviation of 10 be the ones used in test work when two-digit scores are desired, and stanines when scores of a one-digit number are desired.

While centiles are very useful in building profiles to present test results to students in counseling and to parents, similar profiles can be made using standard scores. However, centile scores and centile ranks are readily comprehended by those individuals who know little or no statistics because of the close resemblance of centiles to percentages, statistics which these individuals have been using all their lives. This argument is steadily losing validity as an examination of the mathematical curricula in the public schools reveals that quite a lot of statistics is being taught in high school, and in some places even earlier. Grade-placement scores also have their advantage in being very useful in describing to parents a child's achievement. It is felt that when such placement norms are used they should be translated into standard scores before being entered into the school records.

GRADES AND GRADING OF OBJECTIVE TESTS*

One of the major purposes of achievement testing is to place a value or grade upon a student's performance. We shall attempt in the paragraphs that follow to offer some suggestions on grading. The giving of grades is actually one of the most difficult aspects of teaching. Of course, here we are referring to reliable and fair grades. Over the years much has appeared in educational literature on the subject of grading. One of the best summaries and discussions on the subject appears in the small volume by Wrinkle (21).

In discussing grading practices, we shall divide the discussion into two parts, the first on assigning grades to a single test and the second to the computation of a final grade for a course.

Grades for a Single Test

Some teachers feel that this problem is solved by constructing

* The grading of essay tests is discussed in Chapter 9.

all tests so that they can be graded on a basis of 100 per cent. This is supposed to represent a perfect paper. In reality it merely means that the student who obtains this grade answered all the questions correctly in one teacher's opinion. Another grade, usually 70 or 65, is set up as the lowest passing score. All this is very arbitrary. In some classes all may pass; in another all may fail. There is apparently no reason either for selecting the passing point as 65 or 70, except it has been there so long traditionally. Every once in a while, the New York State Regents has to lower its passing mark from 65 to 60 or 58 because of the unusual number of failures brought about by a difficult test.

As opposed to this arbitrary percentage system, there is the other method of grading in which the class sets the pace and the mean or average score is based upon those taking the test. It might be mentioned here that the writer has never noted students slowing up or behaving in any other way to keep the average from being too high. American students do not behave that way. Usually when a paper-and-pencil test is put before them, they attempt to turn in a creditable performance.

The mean is first computed and then the standard deviation. With a class of about 30, the writer usually spreads the papers out from high to low (see Table 3:1). The mean gets a grade of "C." Then gaps are looked for in the distribution. It is rather amazing how these so frequently and conveniently appear. In Table 3:1 are reported the scores of undergraduates on an hour test in educational measurement. A mean of 80 and a standard deviation of 11.3 were obtained in the usual fashion. The writer very arbitrarily drew lines breaking up the distribution into the letter grades as shown. This system of changing scores to grades seems to work as well as any.

When a large number of cases is available in a class that is very heterogeneous in its make-up, grading on the curve can be accomplished. Grading on the curve is based entirely upon the mean and measured standard deviation units from it. Take the mean and add to it ½ a standard deviation and subtract from it ½ a standard deviation. This band gives the raw scores which receive a grade of "C." Take the point which is ½ sigma unit above the mean and add to it 1 sigma. This band cuts off the "B" grades. All scores above this receive an "A." Next take the point which is ½ standard deviation below the mean and subtract from this 1 standard deviation. This band contains all grades of "D." Scores falling below this bottom of this band receive an "F." This is illustrated in Figure 3:4, using the data in Table 3:1.

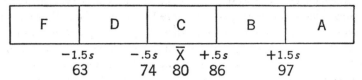

F	D	C	B	A

$-1.5s$ $-.5s$ $\overline{X}$ $+.5s$ $+1.5s$
63   74 80 86   97

Fig. 3:4. GRADING ON THE CURVE USING THE DATA IN TABLE 3:1

Note that for the data in Table 3:1 this method produces the same number of "D's" and "F's" as obtained earlier but only 1 "A" instead of the 6 obtained by the other method. This latter seems to be more judicious and sensible. Instead of calculating means and standard deviations, many who use this system determine the letter grades by using one of the following groups of percentages or other similar ones:

A	B	C	D	F
7	24	38	24	7
5	20	50	20	5
10	20	40	20	10

It should also be noticed that, when we grade on the curve, there is always a certain percentage of "A's" and a similar percentage of failures. The writer has had some classes in which he felt that a dozen out of 30 deserved "A's" and other classes in which no one deserved an "A." He has not hesitated in grading in line with this. Grading on the curve, as noted above, is justified only in *very large mixed* classes. At the university level this would be the case in large freshman lecture classes in chemistry, psychology, or history. As a student progresses through high school or the university he becomes a member of a more and more select group. Grading on a curve becomes ridiculous in such groups. A third-year high-school French class is made up of those who have survived the hurdles which existed as French I and French II. Graduate students in a university offer an even more extreme example of the results of educational selection and attrition. Grading becomes an even more difficult problem at this level.

Table 3:1. Scores on an Educational Measurement Test

(1) Ind	(2) X	(3) x	(4) Standard Score
1	98	18	66
2	96	16	64
3	96	16	64
4	94	14	62
5	94	14	62
6	93	13	61

_____ A

7	91	11	60
8	89	9	58
9	88	8	57
10	86	6	55
11	85	5	54
12	85	5	54

_____ B

13	83	3	C+	53
14	82	2		52
15	82	2		52
16	81	1		51
17	81	1		51

$\bar{X} = 80$ _____ C

18	78	− 2	48
19	77	− 3	47
20	77	− 3	47
21	75	− 5	46

_____ C−

22	72	− 8	43
23	71	− 9	42
24	70	−10	41
25	67	−13	39
26	65	−15	37
27	65	−15	37
28	64	−16	36

_____ D

| 29 | 62 | −18 | 34 |
| 30 | 62 | −18 | 34 |

_____ F

$N = 30$ 2409

$\bar{X} = 80$
$s = 11.3$

A problem associated with grading at the college level is that, while students have become a much more select group, the college faculty continues to pass out grades paying no attention to this. An extreme example of this is illustrated by a class of very superior students who have been selected for a class or program on the basis of high achievement in the past. It is not unusual to find in classes like this that after the first test the distribution of grades in this class resembles that of a class made up of unselected students. The average students in this group of high achievers, or those near the mean of the test, receive C's because traditionally in the minds of faculty members average students receive C's. The ability of the group has nothing to do with this grading, and it not even being considered. Aiken (1) reported that in a woman's college where the mean score on the verbal part of the *Scholastic Aptitude Test* of the College Boards rose 43 points over a 3-year period and the means on the mathematical part of the same test rose 31 points, there was no significant change in the average grade received by the freshmen in that school. Because the abilities of students are increasing, the standards of college work, and high school work, to a certain extent, are rising.

Combining Test Scores

In the fourth column of Table 3:1 will be found the standard scores of each student on this test. These were obtained by taking each raw score, subtracting it from the mean or the mean from it, dividing this deviation (x) by the standard deviation, multiplying this standard score by 10, and adding this product to 50.

$$\text{Standard Score} = \left(\frac{X - \overline{X}}{s}\right) 10 + 50$$

$$\begin{array}{c} \text{For Student No. 1} \\ \text{in Table 3:1.} \end{array} = \left(\frac{98 - 80}{11.3}\right) 10 + 50$$

$$= 66$$

If a teacher wants all his tests to be of equal value in the final grade, scores on each test should be changed to some type of standard score

(16, 8). Suppose that a second test given to the 30 students shown in Table 3:1 had a mean of 42 and a standard deviation of 7, and that a third examination had a mean of 52 and a standard deviation of 8. If a student's raw scores for these three tests were added to make a total score and his grade based upon this total score, this first test with a mean of 80 and standard deviation of 11.3 would count more in the final grade than the other two. However, if a student's raw score on each of these tests was changed to some type of standard score and these three standard scores were averaged, each test would be contributing equally to the final grade. If a teacher wants the last test, perhaps a final examination, to count twice as much as each of the others, all that he has to do is to enter the standard score for the final twice into his computations and in this case divide the sum by 4. The computation of these standard scores can be done in less than 5 minutes after scores have been set up as in Table 3:1 and after the teacher has computed a set once or twice.

Final Grades

Computing final grades is a more complicated process than the above. Students should know in advance, long in advance, at the beginning of the course, just what factors are going to make up the final grade. Some teachers work this out with the students as a joint problem. Usually each teacher has several tests which take up an entire period, a final examination, several to many short quizzes, laboratory grades, reports on readings or special projects, and evaluations of other assorted academic activities. Usually it is not a good idea to put too much weight on the final test. Frequently, because of the way these are administered, the students find it impossible to do adequate reviewing when three or four finals covering a semester's or a year's work are given in one day. This doesn't mean that finals are of no use. If their nature is changed so that they are such that the student has to organize, summarize, and apply what he has learned, they then become learning sessions, not the end of a night of wild cramming. Placing too much weight on the final is poor measurement practice too. All year or all semester a teacher has had an opportunity to observe and collect data on a student. The average of all these samples of behavior should be a much more reliable measure of what an individual knows or does not know, can or cannot do, than any short final examination.

A decision is arrived at. The hour examinations will count 60 per cent, the final 10 per cent, quizzes 10 per cent, and laboratory grades a certain per cent. In order to make these grades reliable and have the guesswork taken from them they should all be expressed as standard scores. Then, after reducing all to this common denominator, they can be weighted in accordance with the predetermined system.

In making grades we must take into account only those factors that show evidence of attainment of the objectives of the course (see Chapter 6). Sometimes such variables as attendance, attitude, and effort get involved in final grades. A student is penalized because of too many absences, because of doing things differently from the methods studied in class (even though correct), or because of any or many of the thousand and one other things that are found in student-teacher relations. A grade in history should reflect the amount of achievement toward the objectives of the history course— and only this. If only one mark is given it should measure academic attainment. These other variables must be evaluated under their own specific categories dealing with social and personal adjustment. Many schools make this possible with the "multi-trait" report cards now in use.

After a score has been obtained to represent the semester's or year's achievement of a student, this must then be converted to a letter grade or whatever other system the school uses. This is done in a manner similar to that described earlier for a single test.

NORMS

All standardized tests contain in their manuals norms of one type or another. These norms are usually of a type called national. If these norms are obtained carefully they may be of some value in evaluating scores of individuals in a given school. Good norms are based upon a representative and random sampling of the population upon which they are based. Large numbers do not make norms acceptable. For example, norms based upon 100,000 students in a large urban center probably would make good norms for use in that city but would be of little value or useless in many other places. Some testmakers try to get a representative sample of the entire country. This is a tremendous undertaking and has never worked out too well.

Tests today are frequently accompanied by regional norms and norms for different types of schools, private and public. Length of school year, type of student in the school, geographic location of the school, and other factors all seem to be related to scores achieved on tests. While regional norms are more useful than national norms, many schools and colleges operate on their own norms constructed locally on their own populations. Rather than national norms, a university may use local norms for its freshman test scores. A city or county school system sets up local norms for the standardized achievement tests that they use. Any individual can set up norms for the local situation after several hundred students have taken a test. These norms can at least be tentative ones and revised later when more data are available. From this short discussion on norms then, it should be apparent that the more specific the norms, the more useful they are. Local norms should be set up for standardized tests used in the school. Sometime when a school sytem is made up of schools containing very dissimilar groups, it is imperative that various types of local norms be set up on the basis of such variables as economic status of parents, type of curriculum in which enrolled, sex, or other pertinent variables.

In summary, probably the best norms for achievement tests are local norms. Such norms may also prove useful for intelligence tests and tests of special abilities. Before the norms provided with tests are used, the user should examine them closely to learn all that he can about the norm group. Well-made norms will describe in detail the population group or groups upon which they were established. The methods of obtaining the samples used in setting up the norms should also be described in detail. The age of the norms should also be examined, for norms, especially those provided with achievement tests, may get out of date in several years because of curriculum changes, changes in the make-up of the student body, differences in motivation, and the possible effects of different teaching methods. Finally, the user of norms should be on the alert for norms based upon small samples such as are occasionally found in the manuals of some personality and interest inventories. These may be useless because of their unreliability. An important task of the test user then is to evaluate the norms accompanying a test to see if they are actually suited to those he is testing. If he finds that they are not, his job then is to set up local norms and to keep them up to date over the years. Any person familiar with the essentials of statistics and who has taken a course similar to the one for which this book was written should be able to do this.

REFERENCES

1. Aiken, L. R., Jr. Grading behavior of a college faculty. *Educ. psychol. Measmt.*, 1963, 23, 319-22.
2. Anastasi, A. *Psychological testing.* 2nd ed. New York: Macmillan, 1961.
3. Cattell, P. *Measuring intelligence of infants and young children.* New York: Psychological Corporation, 1940.
4. Cattell, R. B. *Handbook for the IPAT High School Personality Questionnaire.* Champaign, Ill.: Institute for Personality and Ability Testing, 1958.
5. Durost, W. N. *The characteristics, use, and computation of stanines.* Test Service Notebook, No. 23. New York: Harcourt, Brace & World, 1959.
6. Durost, W. N. *The use of local stanines in reporting test results in a large cosmopolitan school system.* 16th Yearbook, National Council on Measurement Used in Education, 1959.
7. Guilford, J. P. *Fundamental statistics in psychology and education.* 4th ed. New York: McGraw-Hill, 1965.
8. Lacey, O. L. How fair are your grades? *AAUP Bulletin*, 1960, 46, 281-3.
9. Lavin, D. E. *The prediction of academic performance.* New York: Russell Sage Foundation, 1965.
10. Lindquist, E. F. *Educational measurement.* Washington, D.C.: American Council on Education, 1951.
11. Lyman, H. B. *Test scores and what they mean.* Englewood Cliffs, N. J.: Prentice-Hall, 1963.
12. McCall, W. A. *How to measure in education.* New York: Macmillan, 1922.

13. Pinneau, S. R. *Changes in intelligence quotient: infancy to maturity.* Boston: Houghton Mifflin, 1961.
14. Psychological Corporation. *Methods of expressing test scores.* Bulletin 48. New York: Psychological Corporation, 1955.
15. Sangren, P. V. Comparative validity of primary intelligence tests. *J. appl. Psychol.*, 1929, 13, 394-412.
16. Smith, O. J. M. Grading without guesswork. *Educ. psychol. Measmt.*, 1953, 13, 367-90.
17. Terman, L. M. *The measurement of intelligence.* Boston: Houghton Mifflin, 1916.
18. Terman, L. M., and Merrill, M. A. *Measuring intelligence.* Boston: Houghton Mifflin, 1937.
19. Terman, L. M., and Merrill, M. A. *Stanford-Binet intelligence scale: manual for the third revision. Form L-M.* Boston: Houghton Mifflin, 1960.
20. Wechsler, D. *The measurement of adult intelligence.* Baltimore: Williams and Wilkins, 1944.
21. Wrinkle, W. L. *Improving marking and reporting practices in elementary and secondary schools.* New York: Rinehart, 1947.

CHAPTER 4

RELIABILITY AND VALIDITY

$\bigcirc$ ne of the main reasons for testing is to be able on the basis of one or more scores to make a statement about some trait or traits of an individual. If our measurements are reliable, we can make our statements with confidence. But we must also be sure that our measurement tests are valid.

RELIABILITY

One of the important characteristics of any measurement or evaluation device is how reliably it measures. In the simplest of nontechnical language, *reliability* means *consistency*. If we give a child an intelligence test and we obtain a raw score of 86, we would expect to find that, if we retested him two weeks later with the same or with an equivalent test, his score is somewhere near 86.

In modern test theory reliability is described as follows: Every obtained score is thought of as being made up of 2 parts, a component which is called the *true score* and a second part called the *error score*. In symbols we would write this

$$X_t = X_\infty + X_e$$

where

$$X_t = \text{obtained score}$$
$$X_\infty = \text{true score}$$
$$X_e = \text{error score.}$$

The error part of the score is that which is attributable to such factors as temporary characteristics of an individual: health, fatigue, emotional upset, differences in motivation, etc. The mean error score is assumed to be zero. Hence

$$\overline{X}_t = \overline{X}_\infty + \overline{X}_e$$

where

$$\overline{X}_t = \text{obtained mean}$$

$$\overline{X}_\infty = \text{true mean}$$

$$\overline{X}_e = \text{error mean}$$

or $\overline{X}_t = \overline{X}_\infty$. These error scores then tend to cancel out and the obtained mean equals the true mean.

The variance of any test can be written:

$$s_t^2 = s_\infty^2 + s_e^2$$

and dividing each term by s_t^2 where

$$1 = \frac{s_t^2}{s_t^2} = \frac{s_\infty^2}{s_t^2} + \frac{s_e^2}{s_t^2}$$

where

$$s_t^2 = \text{variance of the test}$$

$$s_\infty^2 = \text{true variance}$$

$$s_e^2 = \text{error variance.}$$

Reliability is defined as that part of the variance which is true variance.

$$r_{tt} = \frac{s_\infty^2}{s_t^2} \quad \text{or}$$

$$r_{tt} = 1 - \frac{s_e^2}{s_t^2}$$

where

r_{tt} = reliability of test and other terms are defined as above.

The above equation for reliability shows that as the error variance increases, reliability decreases. Error variance to a certain extent can be controlled, as we shall see, and reliability raised.

Correlation Coefficients

In discussing reliability, two concepts are used: correlation coefficients and the standard error of measurement. The correlation approach will be taken up first. There are several ways of estimating the reliability coefficient of a test, but this discussion will be limited to 4. More detailed information on the materials of this chapter may be found in Helmstadter (7) and Lindquist (10).

1. TEST–RETEST METHOD. In this method a given test, A, is administered on a certain day and a week later the same test is read-ministered to the same individuals. A correlation coefficient is computed on the basis of the 2 sets of scores for each individual. It should be apparent that the length of time between the 2 test administrations has considerable effect on the size of this reliability coefficient. In general, the greater the time, the lower the reliability coefficient. If the time between the 2 test administrations is very short, individuals tend to remember their first response to an item and mark it in the same manner on the second test. Individuals change sometimes considerably between the 2 administrations. There are learning, maturation, differences in physical and emotional health, etc., to be considered. Because of these elements, which affect the reliability coefficient, it is the opinion of some test experts that this method should not be used with the usual paper-and-pencil test. Some refer to this type of coefficient as a COEFFICIENT OF STABILITY.

2. EQUIVALENT FORMS. This type of reliability coefficient, also called the parallel form method, consists of administering form A of a certain test first and following it with form B on the second administration of the same individuals. A correlation between the 2 sets of scores produces this time a reliability coefficient called a COEFFICIENT OF EQUIVALENCE.

The chief problem with this procedure is in setting up 2 or more equivalent forms of the same test. Two tests are said to be equivalent when they have equal means and standard deviations. They should be made up of the same number of similar items, measuring similar things. Both should produce similar coefficients when correlated with an outside criterion. Two equivalent tests of spatial ability should correlate equally with grades in engineering drawing, the outside criterion. Sometimes equivalent forms are constructed by making one very long test and then, on the basis of an item analysis, assigning items of equal value and merit to each form. This is the procedure which Terman followed in making Forms L and M of the 1937 *Revision of the Stanford-Binet.*

This method eliminates some of the disadvantages of the test-retest method, but some factors, such as changes which take place within and to an individual, are still present. However, this is a widely used technique, and there are certain types of tests, such as speed tests, where this is the only legitimate technique to be used.

3. SPLIT-HALVES. This type of coefficient, which is called a CO-EFFICIENT OF INTERNAL CONSISTENCY, consists of dividing a test into 2 parts and obtaining a correlation between scores on the 2 parts. The usual procedure is to obtain for each paper an odd score, the number of odd items answered correctly, and an even score. The type of split made is not particularly important unless one makes a first-half–second-half split. This is not recommended because on many tests the first half is quite dissimilar to the second in content, difficulty, and hence in the number of items answered.

The correlation obtained by this method is actually the correlation between 2 tests each of which is one half the length of the original test. The size of a reliability coefficient is directly related to the length of a test. At this point we make a correction by using the Spearman-Brown formula. Suppose that on a 100-item test, a reliability coefficient of .82 was obtained as a result of a split using the odd-even method. We correct this as follows

$$r_{tt} = \frac{2r_{oe}}{1 + r_{oe}}$$

where

r_{tt} = the reliability of the original test

r_{oe} = the reliability based on the split-half technique

$$r_{tt} = \frac{2(.82)}{1 + .82} = \frac{1.64}{1.82}$$

$$= .90.$$

The Spearman-Brown formula can be written in a general fashion as

$$r_{tt} = \frac{Nr}{1 + (N - 1)r}$$

where

N = the number of times the length of the test is to be increased or decreased

r = reliability of original test.

We could use this formula if we had a long test, say, of 150 items that took two hours to administer. The idea is to cut this long test to 75 items so that it can be administered in half the time. To find what the reliability of the shortened test would be, we enter the Spearman-Brown formula in this case with $N = \frac{1}{2}$. Or we could reverse this. Suppose we had a 20-item test of certain reliability. How long should it be to have a reliability of .90? This time the Spearman-Brown formula can be solved with N as the unknown.

This type of reliability coefficient should not be used with a test that is basically a speed test. A real speed test is one which is made up of very easy items and, given enough time, there is no reason why most individuals would not get them all correct. The *Minnesota Clerical Test* is an example of this. When odd and even scores are computed on a speed test, the two scores tend to be very similar and the obtained reliability coefficient would tend to be close to 1 or perfect. Most of our tests are not of this nature. Although timed, they are basically power tests, and results will not be so severely affected when the split-half technique is used with them.

4. KUDER-RICHARDSON FORMULAS. Other measures of internal consistency are obtained by use of formulas developed by Kuder and Richardson (9). These should be applied to tests which are not speed tests and on which all items have been attempted. In the previous method we obtained a correlation coefficient on the basis of one specific type of split. These formulas result in a coefficient that is an average based upon all possible splits. Here only one Kuder-Richardson formula, Number 20, will be discussed.

$$r_{tt} = \frac{k}{k - 1}\left[1 - \frac{\Sigma pq}{s_t{}^2}\right]$$

where

k = number of items

p = proportion of individuals responding to each item correctly

$q = 1 - p$

s_t^2 = standard deviation squared or variance of the total test scores.

Suppose that we have a test of 60 items, we could set up a work sheet like this:

Item No.	p	q	pq
1	.50	.50	.2500
2	.80	.20	.1600
3	.75	.25	.1875
4	.20	.80	.1600
—	—	—	—
—	—	—	—
—	—	—	—
—	—	—	—
60			
			$\Sigma pq =$

The variance of the test is obtained by using the method presented in Chapter 2 for obtaining standard deviations. This Kuder-Richardson method is particularly useful when an item analysis has been made and the p-values (difficulty values) for each item are available.

Factors Affecting Reliability

Four factors that affect the reliability of a test will be considered next.

1. LENGTH OF TEST. The length of a test has already been discussed in reference to the use of the Spearman-Brown formula with the split-half technique. Many tests present a total test score and several or many subtest scores. The reliability of the total score may be high. Some subtests are based on 8 or 10 items. When reliabilities for these subtests are reported in test manuals, the coefficients usually tend to be quite a bit lower than the coefficient of the total test. It is not unusual for a total test score to have a reliability coefficient above .90 and the reliabilities of the subtests in

the .60's, .70's, or .80's. When this is so, we should be cautious in our use of subtest scores. If the manual presents no reliability data on subtests, the best procedure is to ignore the scores on them and use only total scores.

2. RANGE OF TALENT. The variability of the group affects the size of the correlation coefficient. A wide range results in high coefficients and a restricted range in low ones. Hence, to interpret a coefficient we need a measure of the variability of the group. A correlation of .70 from a restricted group may be just as good as one of .90 from a group with greater range.

This effect of range may be illustrated by the following data from the *Test Service Bulletin No. 44*, (13) of the Psychological Corporation which shows the scores and ranks of 20 students on 2 forms of an arithmetic test. An inspection of Table 4:1 shows that the shifts in rank from the first to the second test are relatively small and the computed correlation would be rather high.

Table 4:1. RAW SCORES AND RANKS OF STUDENTS ON TWO FORMS
OF AN ARITHMETIC TEST *

Student	Form X		Form Y	
	Score	Rank	Score	Rank
A	90	1	88	2
B	87	2	89	1
C	83	3	76	5
D	78	4	77	4
E	72	5	80	3
F	70	6	65	7
G	68	7	64	8
H	65	8	67	6
I	60	9	53	10
J	54	10	57	9
K	51	11	49	11
L	47	12	45	14
M	46	13	48	12
N	43	14	47	13
O	39	15	44	15
P	38	16	42	16
Q	32	17	39	17
R	30	18	34	20
S	29	19	37	18
T	25	20	36	19

* From *Test Service Bulletin No. 44*, The Psychological Corporation, 1952.

If, however, we take only the first 5 individuals and examine their positions, we see that the shifts in ranks are the same as before, but the importance of the shifts has been greatly exaggerated. In the large group, student C's shift in rank from third to fifth place represented only a 10-per-cent shift (2 places out of 20). In the smaller group the same shift represents a 40-per-cent shift (2 places out of 5). In the large group this change of from third to fifth rank for student C leaves him still in the top part of the distribution. In the smaller group he has dropped from the middle of the distribution to the bottom. A coefficient based on these 5 cases would be low. It is not the size of the group which affects the size of reliability coefficient, but this range. Taking five other cases A, E, J, O, and T, who rank from first to twentieth, would produce a coefficient as large as that based on all 20 students.

3. ABILITY LEVEL OF SUBJECTS. There are certain tests that are used through a rather long age or educational range. Sometimes, one of these tests will have high reliability for older students and low reliability for the younger ones. Lack of understanding and guessing on the part of the younger subjects results in scores that are less reliable than those of the maturer individuals. Some authors try to do too much with one test.

4. TESTING CONDITIONS. By now it should be apparent to the reader that differences in the administration of a test will present difference in scores. An arithmetic test in a classroom is one thing; in a gymnasium (12), it is something else. The manner and attitude of the examiner will influence scores. Differences in instructions and the number of practice items may affect scores. Then on highly speeded tests there is the problem of timing. On all tests the difficult problem of getting individuals motivated is always present. Finally, here also must be repeated the length of the interval between the two administrations of the test.

It should be emphasized that reliability is not something that we buy when we buy a test. A manual may state that a test has a reliability coefficient of .92. This reliability coefficient was obtained when that test was administered to a certain group of individuals under certain conditions. When we duplicate those two conditions, we will probably have a similarly high reliability coefficient. If we use the tests in different situations, it is up to each test user to demonstrate that it has reliability. Reliability is relative to a specific situation or situations.

SCORER RELIABILITY. So far we have been concerned with reliability of test scores. Another type of reliability is scorer reliability. This is very important in such areas as grading essay tests, scoring Binet or Wechsler intelligence tests (individual tests), and in many projective devices. This type of reliability will be discussed in the chapter on essay tests. At this point, it should be mentioned that such an index merely tells us how consistent the scorers or readers were. We still need to go beyond this and get a real measure of how reliably the test is measuring. This requires the use of one of the methods discussed on pages 84-87.

Standard Error of Measurement

Earlier in this chapter we defined reliability as

$$r_{tt} = 1 - \frac{s_e^2}{s_t^2}$$

which reads that the reliability of a measuring instrument is equal to unity minus that part of the variance which is error variance. If we solve this equation for s_e, we have the standard error of measurement.

$$r_{tt} = 1 - \frac{s_e^2}{s_t^2}$$

$$r_{tt}s_t^2 = s_t^2 - s_e^2$$

$$s_e^2 = s_t^2 - r_{tt}s_t^2$$

$$s_e^2 = s_t^2(1 - r_{tt})$$

$$s_e = s_t\sqrt{1 - r_{tt}}$$

that is, the standard error of measurement is equal to the standard deviation of the test multiplied by the square root of 1 minus the reliability coefficient.

Suppose that on a test, which produces a certain reliability and standard deviation in a given situation, the standard error of measurement is found to be 3. Since standard errors are standard deviations, we can say that the chances are 2 out of 3 that an individual's obtained score is within 3 units of his true score. The smaller the size of this standard error, the more confidence we can place in our obtained scores. The standard error of measurement obtained by the above formula gives us an estimation of the variation we might expect if it were possible to test and test over and over again the same individual with the same test. We would theoretically obtain a different score each time. The mean of all these scores would be our best estimate of the true score and the standard deviation of these scores about this mean would be the standard error of measurement.

This statistic is an absolute term for the expression of consistency, whereas correlation coefficients, when so used, are *relative* terms. It has been shown that the standard error of measurement tends to stay the same regardless of the spread of talent sampled. This is a tremendous advantage over reliability coefficients which we saw to be greatly affected by range of abilities in the sample. Hence, we can use this statistic when we apply the same test to new groups, even when the new groups differ considerably in variability on the trait sampled.

Several writers have demonstrated that the standard error of measurement tends to be constant throughout the range. Lord (11) showed that the standard error of measurement was equal to .432 $\sqrt{k}$ where k is the number of items. Swineford (19) developed that this standard error was equal to .435 $\sqrt{k}$.

Using this information Saupe (18) developed a formula for estimating Kuder-Richardson formula No. 20:

$$r_{tt} = \frac{k}{k-1} \left[1 - \frac{.19k}{s_t{}^2} \right]$$

where all symbols are as previously defined.

Evaluation of Reliability Coefficients

The question frequently arises as to what is an acceptable reliability coefficient. In the past, writers had a series of values for different types of tests below which reliability coefficients were no longer acceptable. At the present time we are inclined to be not quite so dogmatic. It is expected that well-constructed achievement and aptitude tests will have reliability coefficients above .90. Coefficients for adjustment inventories tend to run a bit lower, in the .80's. As far as the ordinary classroom test is concerned, its reliability is much lower than any of the above values. An r of .50 might be typical. But rather than state that the reliability coefficient has to be so high for such a type of test, it is better to be more practical and, if the coefficient is useful for a specific situation, to use the test.

VALIDITY

Different test theorists and test users have proposed various definitions of validity. An early, and still useful, one is that a test is valid to the extent that it measures what it was built to measure. Over the years various types of validity were described and a diversity of names applied to the different types. To a certain extent this lead to confusion. A committee of the American Educational Research Association and one of the American Psychological Association (1), which have overlapping membership, set up standards related to test construction and usage. In these publications an attempt was made to standardize the nomenclature and concepts of validity.

In discussing validity, members of these committees looked upon it as the extent to which a test is capable of achieving certain purposes. It was stated that tests are used to make three different types of judgments, and for each of these a distinct type of study is necessary to establish validity. The following three aims of testing were described: (1) the test user wishes to know how well a student will perform in types of situations that the test situation is said to represent; (2) the test user wishes to predict a subject's future performance or standing on a variable that is different from the one measured by the test; and (3) the test user wishes to infer the extent to which a subject possesses some theoretical trait or construct assumed to be reflected by performance on the test.

A different type of validity data is necessary to demonstrate that a test can serve each of the above-mentioned functions. Three types of validity are distinguished, one for each of the functions: content, criterion-related, and construct, respectively. Any single test may have any or all of the types of validity. A mathematics test may be used to measure an individual's standing at a particular time in mathematics, this test being a sample of a universe of all such mathematics tests. Secondly, the test may be used to predict behavior, such as how well the subjects will do in a mathematics course or in an engineering curriculum, the latter two items being the criteria predicted by the test. Finally, scores on this test might be used as the means of making an inference about intellectual ability. In the material that follows, we shall discuss these three types of validity separately.

Content Validity

Another name for this type of validity when applied to achievement tests is curricular validity. In Chapter 6, on the general principles of constructing tests, we will show that, by using a table of specifications in constructing a test, a teacher can cover both the objectives of his material for which the test is to be used and the subject matter of the course. A test so made is valid then because it adequately covers both the content and the objectives of a course or unit.

In the construction of a new standard high-school biology test, the authors would proceed something like this. A copy of each of the more widely used high-school biology texts would be obtained and analyzed for content. Various outlines of biology curricula would be obtained from state departments of education and these studied. A list of the objectives of high-school biology would be drawn up and these sent to a group of experts—high-school and university biologists —to be rated or ranked as to their importance. In the above ways the authors could obtain a consensus on both the objectives and subject matter of high-school biology and then construct a valid test. At the present time, most of our achievement tests are validated by this method.

Criterion-Related Validity

In obtaining evidence of this type of validity, tests are given and the test scores correlated with data collected at a future date. For example, an entering freshman class of a college is given a new test of academic ability. At the end of the first semester, grades on this test are correlated with each student's average grades for the semester. In this case, these first-semester grades are called the CRITERION. Grades then become a very commonly used CRITERION MEASURE. An analysis of the research on the relationship between intelligence scores and grades over the years shows a validity coefficient usually falling within the range of .40-.60, with a median value of approximately .50. A thoughtful examination of this situation reveals that the predictor variable—the test—has high reliability. What can be said of the reliability of the college grades? Grades are influenced by all sorts of other variables, such as motivation, luck, getting along with the instructor, absences, etc., so that they tend to be both unreliable and invalid to a certain extent. In the majority of predictive validity coefficients this contamination of the criterion tends to lower them.

We might look at another example. Suppose that a test of manual and finger dexterity is being constructed to select women for jobs of assembling small parts in a television factory. This time the test is given to all applicants as they are hired and the results filed. Later, after several months, daily production figures for each operator are obtained and correlated with the original test scores. Here again the criterion—daily production—suffers from unreliability because of such factors as differences in motivation, the speed of different machines, light, noise, temperature, and other factors. Instead of production figures, another criterion—foreman's or supervisor's ratings—might be used. The results would be about the same as ratings too suffer from unreliability because of inadequate knowledge of those being rated, bias, etc. In a similar fashion, attitude, adjustment, and interest inventories are validated. With achievement tests the problem is in finding adequate criteria. In a course in social studies we find such objectives as preparation for citizenship in our democratic society. It would take years to obtain data on how effective the students tested were as citizens. The criteria in our academic areas are, in most cases, remote in time and so complex that the collection of data about them becomes almost impossible. Hence, achievement tests are validated by using content validity.

In most of the criterion-related situations there is a connotation of the future. However, this need not be so as sometimes criterion data are collected at the time the tests are administered. Tests used to separate different vocational groups, different students into different curriculums, or the psychologically disturbed from the normal, each of these is studied against a contemporary criterion. This is sometimes referred to as concurrent validity.

Construct Validity

This type of validity is evaluated by investigating the psychological qualities that a test measures. By this is meant the degree to which certain exploratory concepts or constructs are responsible for performance on a certain test. Studies of construct validity basically are attempts to evaluate the theory underlying the test. In establishing construct validity, the following steps are carried out. First, the investigator sets up hypotheses about the test he is using. In the case of a test of study-habit skills a hypothesis might be set up that differences in academic ability are related to different study-habit skills, other things equal. Second, he collects data to test his hypothesis. Finally, in the light of the data collected, he makes an inference as to whether or not his data can explain the students' behavior on the test. In the example cited here, if the original hypothesis is sound, and if the items on the test of study-habit skills differentiate between good and poor students, construct validity has been demonstrated.

Another way of showing construct validity is to correlate a new test with other tests. Tests of a certain type should correlate higher with other tests of the same type than they do with tests of another variety. That is, a test of spatial ability would be expected to correlate higher with other tests of spatial ability than with a vocabulary test. Correlation studies may be made of test data by using a method known as factor analysis. An application of this methodology results in concepts known as factors and a test may be shown to be valid because of its correlation with these factors or factor. For example, Thurstone (21) demonstrated that by the factorial method mental ability could be reduced to a group of factors bearing such labels as "verbal," "numerical," "spatial," "reasoning," and the like.

A test that correlated with any of these factors would be said to have factorial validity, a type of construct validity.

The differences among the types of validity are not clear-cut. Content and criterion-related validity might be thought of as special aspects of construct validity. For work in the classroom, where the major emphasis is on achievement, content validity is of greatest importance. As was noted, the test builders use subject-matter experts to assure that the test has content validity. A teacher in selecting a test for his use examines it to see how well it fits his purposes. That is, he attempts to determine how well it measures the content and the stated objectives of his course. When a similar achievement test is used as a part of a test battery devised for use in selecting students for a school or program, it is later related to the student's success (the criterion) and is thus shown to have or not to have criterion-related validity. And finally an achievement test may be administered and the results used to cast light on construct validity. The question of whether or not a certain test of chemistry measures an ability to apply information rather than to recall facts or of whether or not the chemistry test reflects reading or numerical abilities to a certain degree—all such questions are related to construct validity.

Face Validity

This term is used frequently to describe a test. This merely means that the test appears to the individual taking the test to be valid for the purpose for which he is taking it. An intelligence test used in hiring industrial workers that uses terms and situations related to factory work appears to be more justified to the job applicant than does a test made up of the usual academic items. Face validity merely means that the test items seem valid. Whether a test is valid or not has to be established in one of the 3 ways described above.

Restriction of Range and Validity

Since validity coefficients are, like reliability coefficients, correlation coefficients, they are similarly affected by the range of talent being measured. Thorndike (20) reports a study carried on in the AAF Aviation Psychology Program in World War II in which a special group of trainees were admitted to pilot training regardless of their scores on the selection tests. In the past, using selected individuals, validity coefficients between certain tests and the criterion of pass–fail in training were very low. Some validity coefficients were: for a mechanical interests test, .03; for a general information test, .20; for a complex coordination test, −.03. These same coefficients for the unselected group became: mechanical interests, .44; general information, .46; and complex coordination, .40. It would appear from this that an inspection of the range of scores used when validity coefficients are mentioned is in order.

What is an acceptable validity coefficient? We have previously noted that for certain reasons validity coefficients never are very high. Their median value as reported in research tends to run about .50. Many times they are much lower than this. Sometimes they go as low as .10. Coefficients in the .20's and .30's are not rare. The best answer to our original question is that any validity coefficient with which we can predict better than by chance is an acceptable one. Even a coefficient of .10 becomes useful when used in dealing with large numbers of individuals.

Response Set

A variable that greatly affects validity is the response set of individuals. Cronbach (2, 3) was one of the first to point this out. He defined a response set as any tendency causing an individual consistently to give different responses to test items than one would if the content of the item were presented in some other form. Cronbach noted that response sets were present in situations where individuals had to answer an item on a continuum from "strongly agree" to "strongly disagree." These words mean different things to different people, and individuals differ in the frequency of their use of each term. Also it is easier to be agreeable than disagreeable. If items have more than one correct answer, some individuals are willing to quit after finding one correct response. Others are satisfied on finding two answers, whereas others persist and work each item for all that it is worth. Gambling on taking chances on items also allows for individual differences in test behavior. The tendency to mark items "true" on a true-false test would be another example of response set.

Since Cronbach's earlier work, considerable research has been carried out on response sets. In general, the findings of these studies point first to the idea that response sets are consistent and tend to be present whenever an individual takes a test. Secondly, response set is most prominent in unstructured and ambiguous situations. With a free-response test, such as an essay test, each student establishes his goal and responds to the test with this in mind. All students taking the same test behave differently, each responding in his own way, with opportunities for each individual's response set and style to run rampant. The results of such tests are often meaningless especially when one is interested in comparing the achievement of students. To the extent that response sets are acting, they contribute to the ambiguity of test scores. Finally, the difficulty of the test is related to the occurrence of response sets, the more difficult the item, the greater the opportunity for response sets to operate.

Cronbach stated that the effects of response set could be eliminated by having each individual answer every item on a test and to use only single-response multiple-choice items. This latter has been demonstrated to be true in an experiment performed by Rapaport and Berg (15), in which they administered 2 forms of an achievement test to a group of 284 college students. These tests were 4-response, 70-item, general information tests. Forty of the items were very difficult; 30 were easy; all were selected from a popular encyclopedia. The 40 difficult items were of such a nature that only by chance would a student choose the correct answer. The correct answer to each of these was rotated on each test. By chance alone, it was hypothesized that each individual would select 10 options at each of 4 positions. The results did not disprove this hypothesis.

Later research has confirmed Cronbach's original ideas. Another type of test item, the forced-choice item was developed and used in an attempt to control response set. This has not been as successful as was originally hoped. The use of such items will be dicussed later in the chapter on personality evaluation. In addition to using single-response multiple-choice items or paired-comparison ones, it has been suggested that response set may be controlled or minimized by adapting the difficulty level of the test to the examinees, by structuring the test to guide the student as he responds, and by making the student "test-wise" through informing him that correction formulas will or will not be used in scoring the tests or that, if true-false items are used, the number of items with true responses is equal to that with false. Finally some attempts have been made to correct the effects of response set by the use of specific formulas. This has not been very successful.

Rorer (16) and Rorer and Goldberg (17) have cast some doubt on the importance of response sets, especially as related to the problem of acquiescence when a subject is responding to a personality inventory. As a result of his research using one of these inventories, Rorer concluded that there is no evidence that acquiescence response style is an important contributor to personality test scores. In these articles Rorer distinguishes between response set and response style, style being used to refer to a manner of responding such as has been used in this chapter for set. Rorer used the term set to refer to the criterion by which an examinee evaluates item content when choosing his answers. An example of set is social desirability. When this is operating, the examinee is responding to that part of the item that he feels to be most socially desirable rather than to the whole item, as the authors intended him to do. So in the end, instead of having a valid score, the score reflects the social desirability. It will probably be a long time before the last word has been said on response set and response style.

Use of Validity Coefficients in Prediction

For individual prediction of one variable from another, a regression line is first determined from the data at hand. Suppose that a correlation coefficient has been computed either by the scatterplot method or by the raw score formula between scores on a test, the predictor, and a chosen criterion measure. When a Pearson r is used, a condition of a linear relationship between the two variables correlated is assumed to be present and the relationship between the two may then be set up in terms of a straight line. Such a line is called a regression line, the equation for which is:

$$Y' = a + bX$$

where

Y' = predicted value of Y

b = the slope of the regression line

$$= \frac{\Sigma XY - \dfrac{(\Sigma X)(\Sigma Y)}{N}}{\Sigma X^2 - \dfrac{(\Sigma X)^2}{N}} = \frac{\Sigma xy}{\Sigma x^2}$$

a = the Y intercept, the point at which the line crosses the Y axis.

Suppose that for a fictional problem we take values from the solution carried out in determining the correlation coefficient and insert them into the above equations solving for both a and b. The equation would be then written like this, using our obtained a and b values:

$$Y' = .82 + 1.05 X$$

This is read that the predicted value of Y is equal to .82 plus 1.05 times an individual's X score. For example, when $X = 0$, the predicted value of Y is .82, when $X = 10$, Y' is 11.3, when $X = 20$, Y' is 21.8, and so on for any value of X. In Figure 4:1 this line has been drawn. Since 2 points determine a straight line, any 2 sets of points obtained from the equation may be used in making the graph. For example, the points $X = 0$, $Y' = .82$ and $X = 20$, $Y' = 21.8$ are plotted, the points connected, and the straight line for $Y' = .82 + 1.05 X$ is the result.

Suppose that we have 30 individuals with a score of 20, $X = 20$. The predicted Y score for each of these would be 21.8. When the obtained Y scores are examined for these 30 individuals, it will be found that they vary considerably and that this 21.8, the predicted Y score, is actually the mean of these scores. The obtained scores (Y's) are normally distributed about this mean and the standard deviation of this distribution of obtained scores about the regression line is referred to as the standard error of estimate or the standard error of prediction. This statistic can be obtained by the formula

$$s_{yx} = s_y\sqrt{1 - r_{xy}^2}$$

where

s_{yx} = standard error of estimate in predicting Y from X

s_y = standard deviation of the predicted variable

r_{xy} = the validity coefficient.

This is a standard deviation and is interpreted as such. Suppose that for our above illustration we find that the standard error of estimate is 3. This is interpreted by saying that when $X = 30$, the chances are 2 out of 3 that the Y score will fall in the band 32.0, the value obtained from drawing a line up to the regression line from 30 and then over to the Y axis, plus or minus 3 or 29.0-35.0. This line has been drawn in Figure 4:1. On this figure a line 3 units distant from the regression line on each side of it and parallel to it has been drawn. Between these 2 parallel lines we can expect to find two-thirds of the Y scores. Since the standard error of estimate is a constant throughout the range, it is possible to do this and the same probability statement may be made for all values of X.

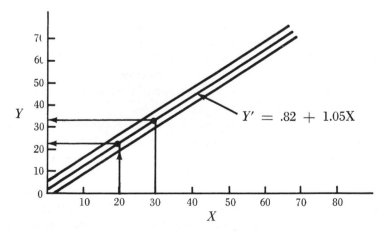

Fig. 4:1. SHOWING THE REGRESSION LINE FOR PREDICTING Y from X

The equation for the regression line may also be stated as follows:

$$Y' = r_{yx} \frac{s_y}{s_x} (X - \overline{X}) + \overline{Y}$$

where

Y' = predicted value of Y

r_{yx} = validity coefficient, correlation between y and x

s_y = standard deviation of predicted variable

s_x = standard deviation of predictor variable

$\overline{Y}$ = mean of predicted variable

$\overline{X}$ = mean of predictor variable

X = obtained score on the predictor variable.

The interested student is referred to Downie and Heath (4) or Guilford (6) for further discussion of regression.

Another statistic used in predicting is E, the index of forecasting efficiency

$$E = 100(1 - \sqrt{1 - r^2_{xy}})$$

when all terms are as previously defined. Earlier in this chapter it was noted that the median validity coefficient was .50. When this is applied to the above equation an E equal to approximately 13 per cent is obtained—that is, when a validity coefficient of .50 is at hand, we can predict with this 13 per cent better than if the correlation between the two variables were zero.

This is a rather dismal picture, but actually our tests are very useful in spite of such low efficiency. The above prediction equations were, it may be recalled, for individual prediction. Given a certain score on one variable, what is the exact predicted score on the other variable? We usually are not concerned with such precision. Rather than predict that a certain student will be at the 92d percentile in his high-school class, we are more concerned with predictions of success or failure—or broad areas of success—such as top 10 per cent. Also much prediction work is concerned with extremes in a distribution.

Thus tests that do not predict with accuracy whether a student will be in the 50th or 60th centile will do a good job in predicting that very few of the high scorers will be in the low centile points or vice versa.

We see that prediction becomes more useful when applied to groups rather than individuals. On the basis of previous experience with tests, expectancy tables are developed. The following fictitious data show scores on a mechanical aptitude test and percentages of trainees successfully completing a program:

Scores	Per Cent Successful
76+	92
66-75	80
56-65	70
36-55	30
less 35	10

From the above an individual with a score of 78 on this test has a good chance of completing the training program. An individual with a score of 32 would be a very poor risk. For a good, detailed discussion of such tables, the reader is referred to *Test Service Bulletin No. 45* of the Psychological Corporation (14).

It might be added finally that prediction is made more efficient by using more than one predictor variable. In the above discussion we talked about predicting freshman grades on the basis of intelligence test scores. It is possible by means of a multiple regression equation to predict freshman grades on the basis of high-school rank, an intelligence test score, a mathematics and an English achievement test score, and the results of an interest inventory. By using all these variables, we find that the size of the multiple correlation coefficient goes up, the standard error of estimate decreases, and prediction becomes more efficient (6).

Validity, In Summary

To end our discussion certain aspects of validity must be emphasized. First of all, validity in a test is not in itself enough. Associated with validity, we must have reliability, the two being an inseparable pair. It must also be stressed that validity is something that is specific. No test has validity per se. A test is valid when it is used under certain conditions with certain subjects. Under different conditions with different subjects, the same test may or may not be valid. It is up to the user of any test to demonstrate that the test has validity for the situation in which he is using it. The vagaries of tests as predictors are well demonstrated in a study by Jones and Siegal (8) in which they used high school rank, scores on the *American Council on Education Psychological Examination* (A.C.E.), and scores on both the *Cooperative English Test* and the *Cooperative Mathematics Test* as predictors of academic achievement for students entering one university from 15 different high schools. With the students from one high school, high school rank was the only variable that predicted academic success. With students from another high school, scores on the A.C.E. were the chief predictors. With students from other high schools scores from all 3 tests plus high school rank were important predictors. The point is that, until one analyzes his own data, he does not know whether he has an effective predictor or not, or in other words, a valid test for what he is trying to do.

Much has been written recently on the subject of validity and a study of these outpourings tends to leave the reader confused. One writer (5), has gone as far as to question whether or not validity is necessary. Instead of the conventional validity studies, he suggests that criteria be set up to describe the goodness of standardized tests. Among these he would have: (1) the importance of the abilities required by the test; (2) the meaningfulness of test scores based upon the reliability of the test, operational definitions of the measurement procedures, knowledge of the relationship of the scores to other measures, and the appropriateness of the norms; and (3) the practicality or convenience of the test in use. Some of Ebel's ideas are aspects of construct validity and others are points that an intelligent user of a test looks for when he uses or proposes to use a test. In spite of the confusion, measures of and information about validity are very important to the teacher and the counselor, and every effort must be made to demonstrate a test's validity when it is being used.

EXERCISES

1. Below are the scores of 20 students on a 15-item test.

	1	2	3	4	5	6	7	8	9	10	11	12	13	14	15	Score
Students																
A	+	+	+	0	+	+	0	0	+	0	+	0	0	0	0	7
B	+	+	+	+	+	0	+	+	+	0	+	+	0	0	+	11
C	+	0	0	+	0	0	+	+	0	+	+	+	+	0	0	8
D	+	0	+	+	+	+	+	+	+	+	+	+	+	+	+	14
E	+	+	+	+	+	+	+	+	+	+	+	+	+	+	0	14
F	0	+	0	0	+	0	+	0	+	+	0	0	0	0	0	5
G	+	0	+	+	0	+	0	+	+	0	+	+	+	+	0	10
H	+	+	+	+	0	0	+	+	0	+	+	+	0	0	+	10
I	0	+	+	+	+	+	0	0	0	0	0	0	0	0	0	5
J	+	+	0	0	0	+	+	+	0	0	0	+	0	+	0	7
K	+	0	+	0	+	0	+	+	0	+	0	+	+	0	0	8
L	+	+	+	+	+	+	+	+	+	0	+	+	0	0	+	12
M	+	+	+	0	+	+	0	0	+	+	+	+	0	+	0	10
N	+	+	+	0	+	+	0	0	+	+	0	+	0	+	0	9
O	+	+	+	+	0	+	+	+	0	+	0	+	0	0	0	9
P	+	+	+	+	+	0	+	+	+	+	+	0	0	+	0	11
Q	0	+	+	+	0	+	+	+	0	+	0	+	0	0	0	8
R	+	+	+	+	+	0	0	0	+	0	+	0	0	0	+	8
S	+	+	+	+	+	0	+	0	0	+	0	+	0	+	0	9
T	0	+	+	+	+	0	+	0	+	+	+	0	+	0	0	9
Number Correct	16	16	17	14	14	11	14	12	12	13	12	14	6	8	5	

(a) Using the above data, compute the reliability coefficient of this test using the Kuder-Richardson formula given in the chapter.

(b) Suppose that this test were lengthened to a test of 60 similar, well-made items. What would the new reliability coefficient be?

(c) Suppose that this test were cut to 10 items. Estimate the new reliability coefficient.

(d) Compute the standard error of measurement for this test.

(e) How do you interpret this standard error of measurement?

2. Given the following data for variables X and Y:

$$\Sigma X = 900 \qquad \Sigma Y = 1600$$
$$\Sigma X^2 = 29360 \qquad \Sigma Y^2 = 86000$$
$$\Sigma XY = 44620$$
$$N = 40 \qquad r = .61$$

(a) Set up the regression equation for predicting Y from X.

(b) From this equation determine several sets of points and plot the regression line.

(c) Calculate the standard error of estimate when predicting Y from X with these data.

(d) Interpret this standard error of estimate using an X of 40.

REFERENCES

1. American Psychological Association. *Standards for educational and psychological tests and manuals.* Washington, D. C.: American Psychological Association, 1966.

2. Cronbach, L. J. Response sets. *Educ. psychol. Measmt.*, 1946, 6, 475-93.

3. Cronbach, L. J. Further evidence of response sets and test design. *Educ. psychol. Measmt.*, 1950, 10, 3-31.

4. Downie, N. M., and Heath, R. W. *Basic statistical methods.* 2nd ed. New York: Harper and Row, 1965.

5. Ebel, R. E. Must all tests be valid? *Amer. Psychologist*, 1961, 26, 640-47.

6. Guilford, J. P. *Fundamental statistics in psychology and education.* 4th ed. New York: McGraw-Hill, 1965.

7. Helmstadter, G. C. *Principles of psychological measurement.* New York: Appleton-Century-Crofts, 1964.

8. Jones, R. L., and Siegal, L. The individual high school as a predictor of college academic performance. *Educ. psychol. Measmt.*, 1962, 22, 785-9.

9. Kuder, G. F., and Richardson, M. W. The theory of the estimation of test reliability. *Psychometrika*, 1937, 2, 135-8.

10. Lindquist, E. F. *Educational measurement.* Washington, D. C.: American Council on Education, 1950. Chapters 15 and 16.

11. Lord, F. M. Tests of the same length do have the same standard error of measurement. *Educ. psychol. Measmt.,* 1959, 19, 233-9.

12. Phares, E. J., and Rotter, J. B. An effect of the situation on psychological testing. *J. consulting Psych.,* 1956, 20, 291-3.

13. Psychological Corporation. *Reliability and Confidence.* Test Service Bulletin No. 44. New York, 1952.

14. Psychological Corporation. *Better than chance.* Test Service Bulletin No. 45. New York, 1953.

15. Rapaport, G. M. and Berg, I. Response sets in multiple-choice tests. *Educ. psychol. Measmt.,* 1955, 15, 58-62.

16. Rorer, L. G. The great response style myth. *Psychol. Bull.,* 1965, 63, 129-56.

17. Rorer, L. G., and Goldberg, L. R. Acquiescence on the *MMPI. Educ. psychol. Measmt.,* 1965, 25, 801-17.

18. Saupe, J. L. Some useful estimates of the KR formula #20 reliability coefficient. *Educ. psychol. Measmt.,* 1961, 21, 63-71.

19. Swineford, F. Not. on "Tests of the same length do have the same standard error of measurement." *Educ. psychol. Measmt.,* 1959, 19, 241-2.

20. Thorndike, R. L. *Personnel selection.* New York: Wiley, 1949.

21. Thurstone, L. L. *Primary mental abilities.* Chicago: University of Chicago Press, 1938.

CHAPTER 5

THE SELECTION, ADMINISTRATION,
AND SCORING OF STANDARDIZED TESTS

In selecting standardized tests, we should consider 3 things: validity, reliability, and practicality. Chapter 4 was devoted to a discussion of reliability and validity, so here we need only emphasize again that, if a test is to have value, it must produce valid and reliable results. But, in addition to these 2 important criteria, when selecting tests, we must also consider practical characteristics.

SELECTION OF TESTS

In the first part of this chapter, we shall discuss the practical characteristics of standardized tests. Although these will not be taken up in order of importance, each characteristic merits careful consideration before a test is selected.

Time Needed for Administration

The purchaser of a standardized test should carefully investigate the time needed for administration to make certain that the daily routine of the entire school will not be upset by the testing program. Many tests are so constructed that they can be administered in a 30- to 45-minute period. Some are so made that they can be conveniently cut into 2 parts and given on 2 consecutive days at the same period. In considering the time question, we must remember that, frequently, considerably more time is needed to administer the test than the specified time limit. Time is needed to get the group settled, to pass out the test papers and other necessary materials, to read directions, to complete practice items, and, after the time limit is up, to collect the materials. We should be very generous in our time estimate.

Ease of Administration

The ease with which a test is administered should be considered from the point of view of the administrator. Does a single individual have to administer all the tests or are they of such a nature that the classroom teacher can help out? A test that requires special skills and learnings for giving has limited use in a school testing program. The directions should be evaluated as to their simplicity, yet clearness.

Ease of Scoring

Exactly how a test is to be scored should be decided before it is purchased. Any testing program that is dependent upon the classroom teachers for scoring the papers is off to a bad start. Most teachers feel that they have enough to do in keeping up with their own work and resent having to grade extra papers. It also stands to reason that one or two counselors in a school should not have to grade all tests administered. This problem can be solved in various ways. First, full-time clerical help can be engaged to score and record tests. A few schools have tried using part-time student help. This is a bad practice, especially in small schools where everyone knows everyone else. However, there is no reason why selected senior-high-school students cannot be used in the scoring of elementary-school papers. Secondly, papers can be sent to a scoring center to be machine-scored. Large urban school systems have their own scoring machines. In some counties, various schools have joined together to rent a scoring machine that is used cooperatively. If schools get together like this and coordinate some of their testing, a scoring machine and operator can be kept busy during the entire school year. Thirdly, self-scoring examination booklets or answer sheets can be purchased. These cost a bit more than regular answer sheets, but the time saved is well worth the extra money. Some of these scoring devices will be discussed below. Fourth or fifth graders are mature enough to use answer sheets.

Costs

In these days, tests are relatively expensive. Their prices, like those of other commodities, seem always to be rising. It is important to have an up-to-date catalogue at hand when ordering tests. The chief way to keep testing costs down is to purchase tests with reusable test booklets. Then each time the test is given all we need to reorder is more answer sheets. Also, the testing program should be staggered so that several groups taking the same test can take it at different times. Determine the maximum number of individuals who will take any given test at any one time and then order that number of test booklets plus a few others. It is also worth the time spent to review the research on tests as frequently as possible, because many times a short inexpensive test will do a given job just as adequately—even better—than one that costs much more.

Availability of Alternate Forms

It is frequently desirable to have 2 or more parallel forms of the same test on hand. Sometimes a test is given at the beginning of the year or term and another at the end of the year or term to measure progress made during the period. It is better to use a parallel form of the test the second time. Then, too, we may sometimes feel that an intelligence-test score is too low or too high. The administration of a parallel form of the same test will serve as a check upon the first score.

It is also useful to have tests that are available at different levels—that is, tests with primary, elementary, intermediate, and higher forms. There are 2 reasons for this. First, frequently, individuals who do very well on a test should never have been given that form of the test in the first place; it was too easy for them. They had no opportunity with such a test to reach their limit. Others may have been so slow or are such poor readers that their score was affected in the other direction. A lower level test would be useful with this group. To use the same test at different levels throughout a school system has the additional advantage of conformity. If tests are similar in content and structure at the different levels, then there is some justification in comparing the scores that a student made at different levels. It must be stressed that scores obtained on different tests, even if given the same label, such as IQ, should not be treated as being measures of the same thing or as being equal. The authors of a series of tests for different educational levels are more apt to have tests approximately the same at the different levels.

Ease of Interpretation

A test that is most useful for educational and vocational work is one that does not require the completion of 3 extra graduate courses in order to understand it. Some of the tools of the clinical psychologist, such as projective techniques, are of this nature. If tests are to be used in an elementary school, they should be of such a nature that all teachers, at least after one or more training meetings, understand what the test measures, what the scores mean, and how the teacher can make most use of these scores. The same is true in the secondary school. And, in addition, it follows that when test results are used in counseling, results should be reported in such a way that they can be easily understood by the counselee.

Norms

As was discussed in Chapter 3, in many cases, the best type of test norms is a local norm based upon individuals in our own school system. This is particularly true of achievement tests and, to some extent, of intelligence tests. Yet there are times when norms supplied by the test publisher are useful and sometimes necessary. Norms should be based upon representative samples. Large samples in themselves are not enough. Norms, to be useful, should be based upon students found in similar communities or in the same parts of the country or in the same type of school as the students upon whom they are to be used. In looking at norms that come with interest inventories, we do well to consider the number of different occupational groups for which norms are available and also the size of the sample upon which these different occupational norms are based. Sometimes the number of cases used in these groups is very small. Such norms have little use.

Other Information about Tests

Before we purchase any test, it is a good idea to write to the major test publishers and obtain their catalogues. A list of these publishers is found in Appendix A. Sample tests and manuals can be obtained for prices listed in each catalogue. It is worth spending a few dollars for a collection of sample tests if none is available about the school. The manuals should be examined carefully. The answers to many of the points raised in this chapter frequently will be found here. For most of the newer tests, manuals are adequate and honest in presenting the information needed by a test purchaser and test user.

Information of a less biased nature than that found in test manuals is obtained by referring to the publications of O. K. Buros. In 1938 he published the first in a series of *Mental Measurements Yearbooks*. Despite the name of yearbook, these amounted to occasional publications, the fifth and sixth being published in 1959 (6) and 1965 (7). In searching for information about tests, usually only the most recent of these volumes need to be consulted as most tests in current use undergo frequent revisions. However, if one wishes information on an older test, the earlier volumes are useful.

In Buros' *Yearbooks* we find critical reviews of tests. Usually a brief summary of the test, content, level, cost, and forms is given first, followed by reviews written by several individuals who are supposedly competent to evaluate the test. These reviewers may be either persons who have had experience using the test or persons who are specialists in the area covered by the test. The test evaluations are arranged alphabetically by type. The last part of the *Yearbook* is devoted to an abstracting of articles and books about tests written in the period since the last issuance of the yearbook.

Buros (5) published a book entitled *Tests in Print* which serves as an index to the various yearbooks. All tests currently available are listed and references made to the various editions of the yearbook in which they are reviewed. About the last quarter of the volume contains information on out-of-print tests. Buros has also printed the technical recommendations for the use of psychological tests published by the American Psychological Association (2) and similar recommendations for the use of achievement tests published by the American Educational Research Association (1). Finally, there is a complete test publishers directory and index. Distributors of tests in the major countries of the world are also listed.

Information about tests is also to be found in periodic issues of the *Review of Educational Research*. About every 3 years, an issue appears that covers all the research or work done with achievement tests or intelligence tests or personality tests since the preceding review that covered the same topic. Also, the journal *Educational and Psychological Measurement* is devoted to advances in test construction, information on the use of tests, reviews of new tests and books on testing, and similar topics.

Another publication devoted completely to measurement is the *Journal of Educational Measurement,* the official publication of the National Council of Measurement in Education. In this periodical are published, in addition to the proceedings of the annual meeting of the council, articles on research in measurement and reports on the use of tests mostly in an educational setting. The *American Educational Research Journal* also contains articles on tests, test usage, test concepts, and reports of research in which tests were used. Many other educational and psychological journals frequently carry articles on test usage and reviews of new tests.

It is a good idea for a test-user to build and use an evaluation sheet that has spaces to jot down notes on most of the matters discussed so far in this chapter. An example of such a Test Appraisal Form appears on page 114.

THE ADMINISTRATION OF STANDARDIZED TESTS

After a standardized test has been selected we must give attention to several matters before it can be administered successfully.

Following Directions

Probably the most important aspect of test administration is making sure that the directions stated in the manual are followed exactly. We should keep in mind that the test was standardized on the basis of these directions. Therefore, if the directions say to read aloud to the examinees and to see that all work the sample items correctly and understand what they are to do, that is exactly what the examiner must do. When a test is timed, a good stop watch or timer should be available, the time of starting written on the board or a piece of paper, and the greatest care taken to end the test at the exact second. On some tests, such as the *Minnesota Clerical Test,* which is a highly speeded test of determining whether pairs of numbers and names are

Fig. 5:1. Test Appraisal Form *

I. Name of test_____

Author_____ Publisher_____

Date of issue_____ Forms available_____

Levels for which constructed_____

Purpose of the test_____

_____

Make-up of the test—types of items and content—subtests_____

_____

_____

II. *Validity*

Indices	No. & Types of Subjects	Criterion	Comments
_____	_____	_____	_____
_____	_____	_____	_____
_____	_____	_____	_____
_____	_____	_____	_____
_____	_____	_____	_____

III. *Reliability*

Indices	No. & Types of Subjects	Method Used	Comments
_____	_____	_____	_____
_____	_____	_____	_____
_____	_____	_____	_____
_____	_____	_____	_____

IV. *Norms*

Reported for what ages, grades, sex, etc.?_____

_____

How reported? IQ's, MA's, %iles, etc._____

_____

Adequacy of the norms and sampling?_____

_____

V. *Practicality*

Costs?_____ Are answer sheets available?_____ Cost?_____

Time required to administer?_____ Time required to score?_____

How scored?_____

What training is necessary to administer and interpret the test?_____

_____

Evaluation of the manual_____

_____

VI. On the back of this sheet record your general evaluation of the test and any comments you wish to make. Evaluations of others may also be included here.

* Adapted from a form used at Evaluation Services Center, Syracuse University.

similar or not, quite a few items can be covered in a few extra seconds. Once the test has started no questions should be answered about the test items or what is to be done. It is assumed that everyone knows what to do before he starts.

It is a good idea to have a few extra pencils handy because some student always breaks his point. Frequently, too, especially if the test is a long one, lasting all morning or all afternoon, some student will become ill. The best practice is to excuse the student and either let him finish the test later or give him another form. If tests are being administered to large groups, proctors are needed. One individual can handle 25 or 30 students adequately, but for each additional 25 or 30 an additional proctor should be available to aid in handing out and collecting material, to answer questions and help out when the students are doing the practice items, and to carry on the usual observational routine once the test has started. It is most important, especially when answer sheets have been used, to see that all test booklets are returned. This can be accomplished by numbering answer book and answer sheets. Then if a test booklet disappears, it can be traced. Standing at the door and collecting an answer sheet and test booklet from each individual as he passes out of the testing room is also recommended. If scratch paper was passed out, it is important that this be collected also.

Where to Give Tests

The next matter to be discussed is where to give the test. Research has shown that children do best when tested in familiar surroundings. It would appear that they should be examined in small groups, in their own rooms and by their own teacher. When we deal with older students, the practice frequently is to give the tests in the high-school auditorium or in some large hall on the campus. Lapboards are passed out to be used as desks. The problems of seating and of proctoring increase tremendously with this procedure. The directions have to be read over a public-address system. Many individual problems go unattended because of the size of the operation. The writer, who has administered tests to several thousands at once, feels that this is an undesirable situation which should be avoided whenever possible. It goes without saying that such factors as temperature, lighting, humidity, and freedom from distracting noises should always be considered when selecting a testing room or hall. In parts of the United States, especially in the summer, air-conditioned rooms should be used whenever available.

Who Should Administer Tests

Standardized group tests can be given by any competent teacher. The person in charge of the testing should see that all test administrators get together before the testing period. Then he should go over the test with them, especially the directions, and offer suggestions to cover points where he feels that there may be difficulties. Actually the requirements for an examiner are that he be interested in what is going on, that he be a good oral reader, that he familiarize himself with the test directions ahead of time, and that he keep time accurately. One good way to become familiar with a test is to administer it to oneself. There is, however, a group of individual tests that should be administered only by a trained psychologist. The writer has in mind here such intelligence tests as the Stanford-Binet and the Wechsler scales and adjustment and personality instruments of a projective type. Students to whom such tests need be administered should be referred to the school psychologist or to a clinic that has personnel trained for such testing. Save for these exceptions, there are few instruments and tests in this area that the teacher cannot learn to administer.

The test administrator should appear friendly to the group at the beginning of the testing period. This attitude, as compared to that typified by the old Army sergeant, is apt to produce better scores. Start with a smile, perhaps tell an appropriate joke. Do anything to relieve the tension. To most individuals all testing situations are threats. Some students are so scared that they may be unable to function. A pleasant attitude on the part of the examiner should be a prerequisite.

When to Give Tests

Because many tests are administered as part of the school routine or on an individual basis by the counselor, they present no special problems as to time of administering. In the early days of World War II a not atypical picture was for a draftee to arrive at an induction center during the middle of the night after a long train trip frequently without adequate sleep or meals. There had been weeks of mental uncertainty and confusion before this for him. The draftee and his group were given a physical examination, perhaps medical "shots," and then tested. Many universities treat their freshmen almost as badly. The usual picture is to incorporate the freshman testing program into the hectic orientation-week schedule. No freshman is at his intellectual best during orientation week. Many suffer from various degrees of homesickness. Some are confused by the new and large world into which they are now plunged more or less upon their own. New friends are being made, and none of the old overseers is around to tell what to do. This is a period of complicated adaptations and not the best time for testing. Furthermore, if the tests are to be used in counseling freshmen, they should be administered ahead of time so that the results are available for use during orientation week. Some schools now ask many of their freshmen to come to the campus during the summer to take the tests. An alternative is to administer the tests in the high schools before the end of the spring term. Colleges and universities could make arrangements to have this done by a competent person in the high schools.

In the public schools, tests should be administered during that time of the year when greatest use can be made of the results. This means that many tests should be administered in the fall rather than in the spring, as is now the practice. Tests used in counseling should be so administered. And the achievement tests used in the elementary school can be turned into useful diagnostic instruments for both teacher and students when given at the beginning of the school year. (This will be discussed in detail in Chapter 11.) Concerning the time of day when tests should be administered in the elementary school, morning is best. A long test should be broken into 2 or 3 pieces and administered on consecutive mornings. This practice is followed with some of the standardized tests. In the junior and senior high school, tests used in counseling can be administered as a part of the orientation course or program.

Motivation of Examinees

A very important problem in test administration is how to motivate the examinees to the point where each will turn in a paper that is a good measure of himself. The writer feels that this very frequently does not happen. Some of our boys and girls are much more strongly motivated in a testing situation than are others. Socio-economic status or class has something to do with this. Children from most middle-class homes live in a world in which everyone is strongly motivated. Father is struggling to get ahead in business, industry, or profession. Mother frequently is doing the same thing. The dominating philosophy of the home is to succeed. Children from the beginning are encouraged to do well in school. The parents frequently, from the time of a child's birth, plan his education. They often help him or try to help him with his school work. The day's happenings in school are discussed at home. Special awards are given for good report cards. A child from such a background tends to turn in a creditable performance. Children from lower-class homes frequently have parents who see little value in school. They left as soon as the law would allow. Such children are seldom offered encouragement. Frequently, a child may be derided for being interested in books and such. A child from this background takes the test in his stride, treating it as just another of those things to be endured since he has to go to school. However, there are students from lower-class homes who are aware that the main factor in social mobility in the United States today is education and behave as strongly motivated individuals. Some upper-class children also may not be strongly motivated in testing situations. After all, they have arrived.

Some individuals get so strongly motivated at times that they perform miserably or not at all. When examinations mean much to an individual, such as passing or failing a course, getting a scholarship, or passing the final examination for the master's degree or doctorate, many individuals get so emotionally wrought up that they can do nothing. They "blank out." Even if this does not happen, their performance is handicapped by their aroused emotional state. As opposed to this, there are individuals who make no effort to do well on a test. A freshman might get the idea that if he does well on his orientation tests, the instructors will expect much from him later on.

When students feel that something worth while comes from these standardized tests, they are apt to be more strongly motivated in taking them. But when a student sees a need for something and when the satisfaction of that need is important to him, he will participate actively and enthusiastically. We should try to sell our testing programs to the students and to show each student how he might benefit, thereby getting him ready for the test. After all, test results are to be used.

SCORING THE OBJECTIVE TEST

Once administered, tests may be scored by any one of a number of methods.

By Strip Key

Of the various techniques used in the scoring of objective tests the oldest is probably the strip key. This is a strip of paper listing the correct answers, which is to be laid alongside the student's answers, which usually are in the test booklet. This type of key can be used very efficiently when a group of scorers is available. Suppose a 5-page test is to be scored. The first person will take the key for page 1, score the page, then turn the test to page 2, and then pass it on to the second person. This process is continued until all 5 pages are scored. The sixth person then sums up the scores and records the sum or sums in the appropriate spaces in the test booklet. Frequently, it is more efficient to mark and count errors and to subtract the sum of these from the test or subtest totals to obtain the score, rather than obtaining the number-right score for each page.

By Scoring Stencils

A second scoring device involves the use of scoring stencils. These are usually supplied when answer sheets are purchased. The stencil is placed over the answer sheet, and the number of correct marks as seen through the holes is counted. Of course, there is more to this than just summing the number of holes in which correct answers appear. The sheets must be scanned to see if there are 2 or more answers to any one item. These will not be visible when the usual opaque scoring stencil is used. If a correction formula is applied in obtaining the final scores, the number of wrongs have to be counted also. Omits are usually disregarded, but these do have to be looked for when summing the number wrong. This stencil device is rather slow and hard on the eyes.

By Carbons

A third device is the self-scoring test that uses carbons. Such tests as the consumable forms of *Henmon-Nelson Test of Mental Ability** are built around this device. In this test, the test booklet consists of 2 pages, fastened securely together. The items are printed on the front and back sides. The student answers each item by placing an "X" in one of a series of boxes like this for the answer he feels to be correct. These boxes are in the right hand margin, and the test appears like any other test in make-up. A strip of carbon paper, however, lies under the boxes, and hence the student's responses are printed on the inside. On the inside there is only one box for each item. This is for the correct answer. To obtain a score all that one does is open the test booklet and add up the number of these little squares that contain marks.

A similar device was developed by the California Test Bureau and is known as *Scoreze*. On this the student uses an answer sheet similar to the regular scoring-machine answer sheet. A piece of red carbon is beneath this, and the correct responses appear as red marks in circles on the inside sheet. Scores are obtained as with the Clapp-Young device.

The Houghton Mifflin tests which use the Clapp-Young device are relatively inexpensive tests. *Scoreze* answer sheets cost about 3 cents more than the regular answer sheets and can be used with quite a few of the tests of this publisher. It would seem that, in small schools where scoring is a problem and no machines are available, these tests which use such carbon devices should be widely used. They are cheap and certainly worth the few additional cents, considering all the time saved in scoring when compared with hand-scoring.

By Pinpricks

A fourth device was developed by Toops for use with the *Ohio State Psychological Examination*. Students are supplied with answer sheets which have series of little boxes with circles in the center. The student inserts a pin into the circle corresponding to his choice

* Published by Houghton Mifflin, Boston.

of the correct answer. The answer sheet lines up alongside the test booklet, and in some of the tests which use this device the pages of the test booklet get smaller and smaller, as the student works his way through the test, to avoid the pinpricks on preceding pages. It is necessary to supply a thick piece of corrugated cardboard or some other heavy material to place under the answer sheet to make the pin enter the answer sheet easier. On the *Ohio State* examination, the answer sheets are opened and items with pinholes appearing in the correct space are counted to obtain the score. On some of the other tests, circles are present and the appearance of a pinhole in a circle constitutes a score of 1.

This device of Toop's was purchased by Science Research Associates and is used as an alternate type of scoring on many of their tests. They usually offer machine-scored answer sheets as the other choice. With such tests as the *Kuder Preference Record,* where test scoring by the students themselves seems logical, the pin-punch method is strongly recommended. However, these test booklets are relatively expensive, and the initial capital outlay is apt to be high. The necessary separate answer sheets cost a little more than 10 cents per student.

By Punchboard

Another rather ingenious self-scoring device that appeared on the market a few years ago was the *Troyer-Angell Self-scorer* * (10). This consisted of a punchboard into which the student poked with his pencil the hole corresponding to his choice of the correct answer. The board was set up with 5 holes after each item number. If a red disk appeared upon punching, this signified that the item was answered correctly. If a white spot appeared, the student was wrong and took another punch. This was continued until the student obtained the red disk or the correct answer. This technique was similar to the cash-registerlike machine developed by Pressey and his students previously at the Ohio State University (Chapter 1).

The research performed with this punchboard, and also the research conducted with Pressey and Little's machines, has shown that,

* Issued by Science Research Associates, but no longer available.

when students take all their examinations over a quarter or a semester on these devices, they make better grades on a conventional final examination than do students who do not use the machines. This is true in carefully controlled experiments in which other related variables are controlled by matching or statistical techniques. Angell (3) showed significantly higher results with the use of the *SRA Self-scorer* in freshman chemistry classes at Syracuse University, and Fields showed this to be true in psychology courses (10).

With devices such as this, learning takes place during the testing. We have here a good example of the effect of the immediate knowledge of results upon learning. People learn better when they know how they are doing, the type of error being made, and the direction of the error.

By IBM Machines

A sixth scoring device is the International Business Machines (IBM) test-scoring machine. This requires special answer sheets and pencils that contain a compound mixed with the graphite to make the graphite a conductor of electricity. Schools usually send their answer sheets to be scored at a scoring center at a university or test bureau. Only a large school system would find it economically feasible to maintain its own machine. A scoring stencil similar to the one used for hand-scoring is put into the IBM machine. This makes it possible for a mark in the correct place on the answer sheet to make contact with the electrical counter and contribute to the total score. The pressing of a button at the top of the machine causes the machine to score the sheet. The operator reads a dial and records the score on the test sheet. Again answer sheets have to be scanned for double markings. Also sometimes the student's marks are not heavy enough to be recorded accurately by the machine. Such sheets have to be scored by hand or gone over and heavier marks made. Also the answer sheets should be spot-checked by doing a few by hand to see if the machine is working correctly. Such machines as these get out of working order very easily. When a correction formula is to be applied, the machine can take care of this by the use of the appropriate stencils, and the operator's turn of another dial. A score, such as the number rights minus the number wrongs divided by 4, can easily be obtained. This type of machine is most useful in item-

BE SURE YOUR MARKS ARE HEAVY AND BLACK.
ERASE COMPLETELY ANY ANSWER YOU WISH TO CHANGE.

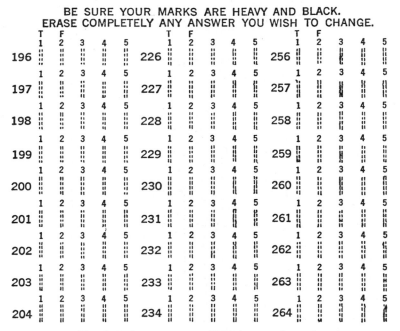

Fig. 5:2. SECTION OF AN IBM ANSWER SHEET *

analysis work because some models have a built-in item-counter. After running the papers through the machine separately and pressing a lever as each is inserted, the machine will print a record of the number of correct responses to each item.

By Electronic Computers

A seventh scoring device, the newest, is the electronic test-scoring machine. Pioneer work with such machines was done by Lindquist (9) at the University of Iowa, and such tests as the *Iowa Tests of Basic Skills* were among the first to be scored by this method. Users of this test sent their answer sheets to Iowa City, where they were scored and the results returned to the user. The advantage of these machines is the speed with which they score tests of varying degrees of complexity, print profiles, and compute test statis-

* Reproduced by permission of the International Business Machines Co.

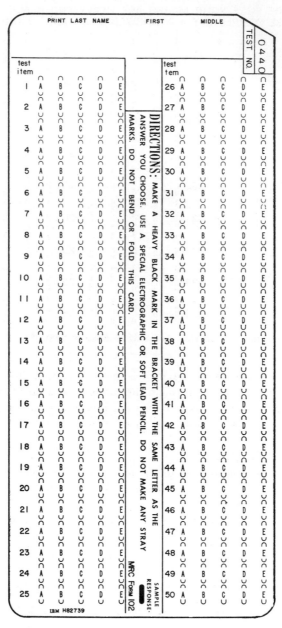

Fig. 5:3. Type of Card Used for Responses That Are to Be Scored by a Computer

tics, such as item analysis data and reliability coefficients and the like. In the past the scoring of such tests as the *Strong Vocational Interest Blank* was a laborious task by any method. There were 50 or more keys for this scale. Since the answer sheet used had places for responses on both sides, one sheet had to go through an IBM scoring machine 100 or more times for a complete scoring. When *Strong* answer sheets were hand scored, this was done for only what seemed to be the few most relevant scales. With the electronic scoring machines, *Strong* answer sheets are scored rapidly for all keys, profile sheets are printed, and the completed results returned to the user for a small fee.

Weisbrodt *et al.* (11) described the use of a computer for scoring tests on a university campus. The student places his responses on a card similar to the one shown in Figure 5:3 and these cards are fed through a computer for scoring. As a result a print-out is made of the number of rights, wrongs, and omits for each student. The mean and the standard deviation of the test are also determined, each score changed to a standard score with a mean of 50 and a standard deviation of 10, and a frequency distribution of scores made. This machine is capable of processing papers of 100 items each at the rate of 110 per minute.

So successful was the Iowa scoring center, that very soon after its establishment all testing agencies had such facilities and made them available to the users of their tests, or in some cases for any tests that had to be scored. Much of the drudgery associated with test scoring and test analysis has been completely abolished and many new possibilities for research with tests opened up through the use of these electronic test-scoring machines. So great has been the interest in and the use of computers that two of the 4 annual issues of the journal *Educational and Psychological Measurement* have a special section devoted to articles on the application of computers to test analysis and research.

ADMINISTERING THE TOTAL TESTING PROGRAM

It would probably be desirable at this point for us to make an overview of an entire testing program for the public schools from kindergarten through twelfth grade. We might look upon this as a sort of minimum testing program that should be established in all schools.

In kindergarten, toward the end of the year, a reading readiness test would be in order. This is about the only testing that is feasible at this level unless there happens to be someone available capable of giving *Stanford-Binet.*

Starting in first grade, an intelligence test would be desirable. However, in some schools this is postponed until third grade, when it is more convenient to administer a verbal type of test than the nonverbal form, which must be used with first graders because of their limited reading skill. After third grade another test should be given in fifth grade as a check on previous ones. Intelligence tests should be administered at the transition points in the school system. If the system has a junior high school then tests could be given at the end of sixth grade or at the beginning of seventh grade. This would be followed with another test at the end of ninth grade or the beginning of tenth grade. It is also recommended that a test be administered at the beginning of twelfth grade for counseling purposes.

Standardized achievement tests should be used when teachers need them. Little is to be gained by forcing teachers to use these tests when actually they see no need for them. When tests of this nature are used, it is recommended that they be given early in the fall of the year for maximum usage. Interest inventories can be used annually or when necessary for counseling from late in junior high school on up through the twelfth year. Tests of special abilities and personality inventories are best used on an individual basis for curriculum selection or vocational counseling. It should be emphasized again that fall is the best time of the year to carry on testing programs. The results can then be put to all sorts of uses which help both student and teacher. When administered late in the spring, many test results are filed and that is the end—a big waste of time and money. Bauernfeind (4) considers the school testing program in great detail.

External Testing Programs

Testing programs established and administered by an outside agency are in this category. Usually the results obtained with these tests are not used by the schools themselves but by an institution such as a college, university, or an agency concerned with scholarships. While the number of external testing programs is large, especially at the university level, four major ones have an impact upon the public schools. These are the *National Merit Scholarship Qualifying Test (NMSQT)*, *College Entrance Examination Board (CEEB)*, *American College Testing Program (ACT)*, and *Preliminary Scholastic Aptitude Test (PSAT)*. Of these the *CEEB* and *ACT* are college entrance batteries. The *CEEB* consists of two main parts, the *Scholastic Aptitude Test (SAT)* and the achievement tests that cover the basic high school subjects. The *ACT* actually is a measure of an individual's entire educational development and is made up of four tests covering English usage, mathematics usage, social studies reading, and natural science reading. Even though this battery is constructed as an achievement test, it does indirectly give a measurement of intellectual ability. The *NMSQT* is similar in content to the *ACT* and the *PSAT* is a form of the *SAT* of the College Boards, giving, like it, a measure of both verbal and numerical ability. These latter two batteries are essentially college scholarship tests.

That such external testing programs have an effect upon the schools is not doubted. This has lead to various articles and conferences on the topic (8, 12). The major concern has been the effect that such testing has upon the over-all school program. In brief, such programs are charged with being too time-consuming for the students and sometimes for the staff also. It is felt that too many students take them and also that students take too many of them. In some places, a student may find himself taking all four batteries mentioned above and perhaps others too. Students are required to pay before they can take any of them, and in some cases this can be a considerable expense. Perhaps one of the most serious concerns is related to the effect on the school program. It is argued that such programs may lead to an almost complete standardization of the high school program by dictating what will be taught and how. Having students do well on these batteries could become the major goal of high school education. A teacher or school might not dare try out any new ideas in teaching because of the possible effects on the students' test scores. Another important charge is that these tests build up pressures that have a bad effect on students and parents. Since such batteries are used by colleges for selection and admission and since colleges are becoming increasingly more selective, the pressure to do well on these tests is constantly increasing so that the student may get into the college of his choice, or for some students into any college at all.

That there is truth in these charges no one denies. Suggested solutions vary; one would have test makers themselves get together and consolidate their efforts to see if one battery could not be built to serve the purpose of all four, another would have the school officials select those students who will take the tests. In some schools any student with the slightest intention of going to college takes the *NMSQT*, whereas only the top 2 per cent get by the first scholarship screening test. Some schools require students to participate in programs just for the practice. Womer (12) suggested two categories of possible solutions. In the first he offers three possible things to do: (1) the elimination of all external testing programs; (2) the setting up of a single national program; and (3) a reduction to two of the number of such programs: one of the educational development type, as exemplified by the *ACT* and the *NMSQT*, and one of the separate intelligence and achievement type, such as the *CEEB* and *PSAT*. In his second category he offers 8 possible solutions to some of the problems caused by these programs. First, he suggested that equivalency tables be established so that a high school could offer to colleges and scholarship agencies a score for any student on that particular battery used in a certain school. Second, he asked that the communication between parents, students, and counselors be improved and that the whole procedure of college admission be explained and that it be understood that more than tests scores were considered in admitting students to college. Third, he recommended that all of these tests be administered on Saturady to avoid loss of school time. Fourth, he advocated that the publicity associated with becoming a semifinalist or a winner should be reduced, the idea being that the less the publicity, the less the competition and associated undesirable effects. Fifth, he proposed appropriate conferences between high school and college personnel to discuss the problems associated with external testing programs and college admission. Sixth, he suggested that the number of students allowed to take the *NMSQT* be limited to the top 10 per cent of the senior class, as this is the usual source of winners. Seventh, he proposed that schools take a strong stand against coaching for these tests. In this way the effects on the curriculum and on what is taught will be alleviated. Finally he advocated that the *SAT* part of the *CEEB* be administered in June of the students' junior year. This would serve two purposes by (1) eliminating the need for a *PSAT* and (2) making it possible to supply *SAT* scores to colleges much earlier than at present. Finally, the achievement part of the *CEEB* would be given to high school seniors at the end of the senior year, the results to be used in guidance and placement activities in college and not for admission. Each of these suggestions has merit, but also arguments against it. But each one should be considered in an attempt to aid in the control of what is becoming an increasingly more bothersome problem in secondary education.

REFERENCES

1. American Educational Research Association, Committee on Test Standards. *Technical recommendations for achievement tests.* Washington, D. C.: National Education Association, 1955.
2. American Psychological Association. *Technical recommendaions for psychological tests and diagnostic techniques.* Washington, D. C.: American Psychological Association, 1954.
3. Angell, G. W. The effect of immediate knowledge of quiz results on final examination scores in freshman chemistry. *J. ed. Res.*, 1949, 42, 391-4.
4. Bauernfeind, R. N. *Building a school testing program.* Boston: Houghton Mifflin, 1963.
5. Buros, O. K. *Tests in print.* Highland Park, N. J.: The Gryphon Press, 1961.
6. Buros, O. K. *The fifth mental measurements yearbook.* Highland Park, N. J.: The Gryphon Press, 1959.
7. Buros, O. K. *The sixth mental measurements yearbook.* Highland Park, N. J.: The Gryphon Press, 1965.

8. Dressel, P. L. The role of external testing programs in education. In *Testing Programs in Education, the University of Kansas Conference on External Testing Programs.* Kansas Studies in Education, Vol. 14, No. 2. Lawrence, Kansas: University of Kansas, 1964.

9. Lindquist, E. F. The Iowa electronic test scoring machines. In *Proceedings, 1953, Invitational Conference on Testing Problems.* Princeton, N. J.: Educational Testing Service, 1954.

10. Troyer, M. E., and Angell, G. W. *Manual for the SRA self-scorer.* Chicago: Science Research Associates, 1949.

11. Weisbrodt, J., *et al.* Use of IBM 1401 and 7090 computers in a university testing service. *Educ. psychol. Measmt.,* 1964, 24, 659-62.

12. Womer, F. B. Pros and cons of external testing programs. *North Central Association Quarterly,* 1961, 36, 201-10.

PART II

——

ACHIEVEMENT TESTS

ACHIEVEMENT TESTS—THEIR NATURE,
USES, AND GENERAL DIRECTIONS
FOR CONSTRUCTION

Any test that measures the attainments or accomplishments of an individual after a period of training or learning is called an ACHIEVEMENT TEST. Achievement tests do not necessarily have to be associated with classroom situations. Industry uses them in hiring and placing new employees. Colleges and universities use them in selecting new students, and the Armed Forces use them in classifying and assigning personnel.

Of all the different types of examinations the achievement test is used most frequently. If we were to add up the numbers used annually in our schools and colleges, by our many testing services, and by industry and the Armed Services, the total would run into many millions. Since this is the most widely used type of test, we will devote considerable space to it.

HISTORY OF ACHIEVEMENT TESTING

In the early universities, and up to the nineteenth century, examinations were usually oral (15). In this country, when enrollments were small, the final examinations of eighth graders were used as a community social event in which everyone turned out to hear the "scholars" put through their paces. As compulsory attendance laws were introduced, this practice of oral examinations became impossible. In the 1840's Horace Mann, who was then secretary of the Massachusetts Board of Education, wrote enthusiastically of written examinations that were in use in Boston. Others became interested, for these seemed to work, to be efficient, and to bring needed conformity—at least up to minimum standards—in the schools of the various cities and states. The use of written examinations soon spread. In 1865, the New York State Regents' Examinations were instituted. These still exist, though in modified form and covering far fewer areas than did the original tests. At the present time, most states no longer have statewide examinations.

In 1897 we have an important milestone in educational measurement with the work of Joseph Meyer Rice. Rice was concerned with achievement in spelling as related to the amount of time given to spelling instruction. Having constructed spelling tests and administered them in various large cities, he found that the amount of time spent in teaching spelling had no effect upon achievement. In the light of our present-day knowledge of educational research, his study is full of flaws. But it was the *first* time in history that an attempt was made to study large numbers of individuals with the same test.

The first decade of the twentieth century saw the real beginning of the modern testing movement. In 1900, the *College Entrance Examinations* (or "College Boards" as they are called) were begun. These are still widely used across the nation in the selection of students, especially for private colleges and universities. In the first few years of the century, E. L. Thorndike began to write and to attract students to Columbia University. It was at this time that he laid down his famous dicta that "If a thing exists, it exists in some amount. If it exists in some amount, it can be measured." Thorndike and his students began constructing standardized tests and scales in the various school areas. These were readily accepted by educators because of the demonstrated unreliability of the tests then in use (see Chapter 9). By the early 1920's a teacher could buy standardized achievement tests in practically all elementary- and high-school subject-matter areas.

Granted that these tests were improvements over earlier methods, they were still far from perfect. If we were to analyze them, we would notice that they were almost entirely concerned with knowledge of facts. Hence the question shortly arose whether knowledge of facts was the main and only purpose of American education. Research by Tyler (18), Greene (11), and others also demonstrated that this emphasis on the testing of knowledge of facts was rather pointless. Tyler readministered final examinations in September to students who had completed a course the previous spring and had taken no further work in that area. Later, at regular intervals, he readministered tests to the same students. All this demonstrated that, as time went on, students performed worse and worse on the factual parts of these tests. On certain other parts that were concerned with the application of principles to new situations and the drawing of conclusions the students tended to improve as time went on.

No one argues that students shouldn't know facts. We cannot think in a vacuum. But a lot more attention should be paid to some of the objectives of education that, in the long run, are equally or more important.

In the 1930's, we had what is known as the Eight-Year Study (1). This was, in brief, a study of the university and college achievements of matched students from 2 different types of schools—"traditional" and "progressive." The Eight-Year Study is important in measurement because it was concerned with all the objectives of education, and attempts were made to set up tests to evaluate achievement toward the attainment of each objective (16). This work was done under the direction of R. W. Tyler. We shall discuss some of these different and newer types of tests in the chapters that follow.

In the 1930's also, educators began writing about *evaluation*. The evaluators used as their starting point the objectives of education. Various groups and committees spent considerable time in drawing up and describing the desired outcomes of education, as will be seen below. It was soon noticed that many of these objectives could not be measured with the usual objective achievement test. More subjective techniques were developed to appraise achievement in such areas as appreciations, attitudes, and adjustment. The emphasis on all these objectives constituted the *evaluation movement*.

Also in the 1930's, the Cooperative Test Service of the American Council on Education was publishing well-made achievement tests in most of the high-school subjects and in some major basic university areas. Emphasis was placed on careful item construction, and an attempt made to cover the major objectives of courses. In 1938, O. K. Buros began publishing his reviews of tests with his first *Mental Measurements Yearbook* (7). To date, as noted earlier, five additional volumes have been published in this series. In 1941 appeared the first volume of *Educational and Psychological Measurement* which over the years under the able editorship of G. F. Kuder has been the leading journal devoted to both test theory and usage. In 1964 appeared the first issue of the *Journal of Educational Measurement*, the official publication of the National Council on Measurements in Education. This periodical is completely devoted to articles on test development, theory, and usage mostly in an educational setting.

In the early 1950's the growing use and misuse of tests created much concern among the professional test people. A result of this was the appointment of a committee by the American Psychological Association and another by the American Educational Research Association to attempt to set up rules, procedures, criteria, and the like related to the construction and use of educational and psychological tests. In 1954 and 1955 each of these organizations issued a small volume, the 1954 one being entitled *Technical Recommendations for Psychological Tests and Diagnostic Techniques* and the 1955 publication called *Technical Recommendations for Achievement Tests*. For a decade these volumes served as useful guidelines for the builders, sellers, and users of tests. In 1966 was published another volume prepared by a joint committee from these two organizations and members from the National Council on Measurements in Education. This new booklet, entitled *Standards for Educational and Psychological Tests and Manuals,* updates and revises the standards believed essential or desirable for the consideration of those who construct, sell, and use tests.

THE USES OF ACHIEVEMENT TESTS

We began this chapter with a brief mention of some of the uses of achievement tests. Now we shall consider these in detail.

1. Establishing Grades

This has been and probably will be the use to which the majority of achievement tests are put. Scores on these tests become in many schools the single basis of promotions. Also these same grades become the means of selecting students for honors and awards.

2. Diagnosis

Here the concern is with the student's strong and weak points as revealed by examinations. Achievement tests can be used at the beginning of a course or at the beginning of a year in the elementary school to find out where each student stands in the various academic areas. Should the fourth-grade teacher go ahead and teach fourth-grade arithmetic? Or would it be better to see what his boys and girls know about arithmetic and use this as a base for his teaching? The results of standardized achievement tests used in the fall of the year can be used for this. On any test, if a student goes over his test himself and studies and summarizes those parts that he missed, it has been shown that learning has been enhanced. One series of achievement tests, the *California Achievement Tests* (8), has a page on which all items are classified as to the area that each measures. On this page the student encircles the items missed; then and there he has some evidence of where he needs improvement.

3. Sectioning

In many schools and colleges, students are put into English, mathematics, and some science courses on the basis of their scores on achievement tests given in these areas at the beginning of the year. In the area of freshman English at the university level, for example, we find 3 possible places for the entering students: in a zero-credit course, which is a review of basic rules and concepts; in the regular freshman English course; and in an advanced English course, which usually is in writing and literature. His achievement-test score determines where the student will be placed. In some schools, because of high achievement-test scores, a student may be allowed to skip the regular course and take more advanced work. In the lower grades, reading readiness and intelligence tests are more apt to be used for sectioning than are achievement tests.

4. Motivation

Some teachers use the first 10 minutes of class to test students on the work contained in the new assignment. Such a practice seems hardly justified. If this is the only way that a teacher can get students interested in the work at hand, perhaps the teacher is in the wrong type of work. Tests do motivate, and they can be used as motivation when given their proper emphasis. They should cause the student to reflect, to tie things together, and to see the subject matter or areas as a whole. If tests motivate in this way, they are desirable.

5. Evaluation of Teaching

A teacher can use achievement tests to see for himself how effectively he is doing, what is getting across and what is not. Notice here that the emphasis is on the teacher using tests for this purpose. When a principal or other administrator evaluates a teacher's work on the basis of the scores made by his students, this is a misuse of these tests. There are too many variables associated with student achievement to hold any teacher responsible for them all.

6. Counseling

In counseling we have a most important use of these tests. "Should I study engineering when I go to college?" "How about medicine or law?" Questions such as these are partially answered by administering to the student interested in engineering, for example, achievement tests in mathematics and science or by using grades in these areas, which, of course, are based on earlier tests. Outside school we have similar uses of these tests. Suppose that an individual who has worked as a baker is out of work and appears at one of the branch offices of a state employment agency. The interviewer might refer to a volume entitled *Oral Trade Tests*. This contains a series of very short tests in many areas and is used to find out whether an individual knows anything about the area in which he claims to have worked. The items tend to be rather technical, but basic.

GENERAL DIRECTIONS OF TEST CONSTRUCTION

In this chapter on achievement testing, we will give attention to certain rules and principles that must be considered, regardless of the type of evaluation or measurement instrument being constructed. Our starting point in making an evaluation instrument is to determine specifically what we are going to measure. This means that we must determine the objectives of the course or, if we are making a more comprehensive type of test, the objectives of the entire year or curriculum.

General Objectives

There are, for the most part, two types of objectives: general and specific. As we read the current and past educational literature we notice that much time has been spent in attempting to formulate a list of useful and attainable objectives of American education. These objectives are of the type called GENERAL OBJECTIVES. Quite a few years ago, a group set forth what were known as the 7 cardinal principles of education (19).

These objectives were:

1. to promote good health,
2. to teach command of the fundamental processes,
3. to provide for worthy home membership,
4. to aid in the selection of a vocation,
5. to offer civic education,
6. to assure of worthy use of leisure time,
7. to promote ethical character.

In the Eight-Year Study (1), we find this list of objectives:

1. the development of effective methods of thinking;
2. the cultivation of useful work habits and study skills;
3. the inculcation of social attitudes;
4. the acquisition of a wide range of significant interests;
5. the development of increased appreciation of music, art, literature, and other esthetic experiences;
6. the development of social sensitivity;
7. the development of better personal-social adjustment;
8. the acquisition of important information;
9. the development of good physical health;
10. the development of a consistent philosophy of life.

A more recent set of objectives may be taken from the *Report of the President's Commission on Higher Education* (13). Here we find:

1. to develop a code of behavior on ethical principles consistent with democratic ideals;
2. to participate actively as an informed and responsible citizen in solving the social, economic, and political problems of one's community, state, and nation;
3. to recognize the interdependence of different peoples and one's responsibility for fostering international understanding and peace;
4. to understand the common phenomena in one's physical environment and to understand and use the scientific method;
5. to understand the ideas of others and to express one's own effectively;
6. to attain a satisfactory emotional and social adjustment;
7. to maintain and improve one's health and the health of the community;
8. to understand and enjoy literature, art, music, and other cultural activities and to participate in some form of creative activity;
9. to acquire the knowledge and attitudes basic to a satisfying family life;
10. to choose a socially useful and personally satisfying vocation that will permit one to use to the full his particular interests and abilities;
11. to acquire and use the skills and habits involved in critical and constructive thinking.

Specific Objectives

If we examine carefully the 3 listings above, we notice that the objectives are very broad. That they are desirable all would agree. But they are so broad that neither what aspects of the curriculum should be evaluated to measure each objective nor what type of evaluation device should be used is clear. Hence, we are forced on to consider the next type of objective, which we can classify as SPECIFIC OBJECTIVES.

A group of objectives that appeared in a report of the American Council on Education (2) contained not only a listing of very broad educational objectives but also more than 200 specific objectives that were defined in terms of both student behavior and subject matter. The several hundred objectives were classified into ten major outcomes of education. This classification of educational objectives was an antecedent of the now much referred to *Taxonomy of Educational Objectives, Handbook 1: The Cognitive Domain* (6). This small volume was the result of the joint efforts over a period of years of a group of university examiners who attempted to organize and systematize educational objectives and the measurement that followed. In this work an effort was made to arrange behavior from simple to complex and to separate it into areas, or domains as they were called. There were three of the latter: cognitive, affective, and psychomotor. The first of these is the concern of this chapter, the second was reported on by Krathwohl (12), and to date very little has been done with the third as not much is concerned with the manipulative skills in high schools and colleges. The affective domain covers attitudes, appreciations, interests, values, and general psychological adjustment.

The work of this committee resulted in a classification of the cognitive educational objectives into 6 major categories:

1.00 Knowledge
2.00 Comprehension
3.00 Application
4.00 Analysis
5.00 Synthesis
6.00 Evaluation

Some of these are broken down into subsections as follows:

1.00 Knowledge
  1.10 Knowledge of Specifics
    1.11 Knowledge of Terminology
    1.12 Knowledge of Specific Facts.

Under every heading, both major and minor, there is a definition and a discussion of the meaning of each followed by illustrations of the type of educational objective included in the category. At the end of each of the sections, for example, 1.00 *Knowledge,* there is an excellent presentation of types of test items that can be used to measure achievement of the various parts of each objective. While these are mostly objective test items, they are highly complex and make excellent examples of the use of objective test items to measure more than the recall of simple factual information.

The major categories were arranged from the more simple to the more complex. Within each of these the arrangement of the objectives is also from the relatively simple and concrete to the more complex and abstract. This is illustrated in the *Knowledge* category where on one end is found such an objective as to define technical terms by giving their properties, attributes, or relationships and on the other end an objective requiring the understanding of the interrelations of chemical principles and theories.

Building a Table of Specifications for a Test

A teacher might proceed somewhat like this: First, he states the objectives of his course or grade. These should be as specific as possible.

Next, he attempts to define each objective in terms of student behavior. For example, a common objective of teachers is to teach students to think. But this is difficult to evaluate. The teacher must first decide exactly what students do when they think. What does he mean when he uses *think* as an objective? Since there are various types of thinking, he might have several descriptions of student behavior that demonstrate how students think. Suppose, in this case, that he is interested in how students evaluate new material or data. In carrying on a type of thinking called "critical," he might decide that students learn how to recognize trends in data, become aware of the limitations of the data, and learn finally how to draw logical conclusions from the data.

Finally, after he has decided what the students must do in order to typify the objective, the teacher looks for situations in which he feels the students will have a chance to show whether or not they have attained the objective in question. These situations comprise the test items. As will be seen later, some of these may be quite simple and others, of necessity, must be quite complex.

So the classroom teacher must first set up the objective he and the pupils are striving to attain. Suppose that the teacher is making a test to cover the unit on weather in a high-school general-science course. He should start out by making a list of objectives, all of which pertain to the unit, like this:

1. Knowledge of facts and principles
2. Applications
3. Development of the scientific method
4. Etc.

A worksheet, such as that below, could be set up. In the left-hand column a brief outline of the course or unit is developed. As an item

Fig. 6:1. WORKSHEET FOR TEST CONSTRUCTION

Topical Objectives	Objectives			
	1. Knowledge of facts and principles	2. Applications	3. Development of the scientific method	4. Etc.
A. Weather 1. Formation of rain, snow, dew, frost	(1) (18)	(5)	(12)	
2. Thunder and lightning	(4)	(2)		(14)
3. Formation of storms	(3)		(16)	
4. Etc.				

is written, it is given a number, and this number is put in the most appropriate cell of the worksheet. Suppose that the first item the teacher writes is a very specific one on the formation of dew. He inserts a (1) in the upper left-hand cell under "Objectives." His second item measures the second point in the topical outline and is an application item. He places a (2) in the appropriate cell. In such fashion, each item as it is written is studied, classified, and put in the appropriate space. Remmers (14) referred to such a worksheet as a "table of specifications."

There are several advantages to the use of such a worksheet. First of all, it assures the validity of the test. An achievement test such as this is valid when it adequately measures both the content and the objective of a course. It provides an adequate sampling of the entire course. That part which the teacher likes best is treated like the rest of the material when it comes to testing. Also a test so constructed can no longer be put into that group which is criticized as being 98-per-cent factual. When a test is so made, a student no longer feels that a good share of his studying was a waste of time because there were no test items covering most of what he studied.

Secondly, various topics can be weighted with reference to the amount of time that has been spent on each. Obviously, a topic that took 3 weeks to cover should have more items than one that took only 3 days.

Thirdly, the examination can be put together by objectives and a diagnostic instrument as well as an achievement test made. Part I of the test could include all factual items, Part II application items, etc. This is the procedure followed with our newer standardized achievement tests. However, if all types of items are used to measure each objective, we might do better to arrange the items by type or at least by type under each objective.

Difficulty of Items

In writing test items, we should strive for a wide range of difficulty if we wish to distinguish good students from poor ones. On the test there should be a few very easy items, a few very difficult ones. When we are finished, the average difficulty of all items should be about 50 per cent (see Chapter 10 on item analysis). A wide range of difficulty assures us of a wide range of scores. For example, consider a 70-item test on which scores of 67-68 receive an "A," 65-66, a "B," 63-64, a "C," 61-62, a "D," and the remaining scores an "F." Here we have a difference of only 4 points between an "A" and a "D." From what we know about students' scores, we are aware that all are unreliable to a certain extent. Each score is merely a sample of a given student's behavior at the time of testing. If he is tested again and our test is reliable, we don't expect him to achieve the same score but some score close to the first one. Hence, any student's grade might shift considerably because of chance errors if the test is repeated. It would be far more desirable in a test of 70 items to have a range of from 15 to 65 in a group of 100 or more students.

Length of Test

The test should be of such a length that, in most cases, practically all the students have an opportunity to finish in the allotted time. This statement is qualified because in certain test situations, such as typing, shorthand, and calculation, speed of performance is an object of the measurement. When a large part of the examinees do not finish a test, the value of the examination is reduced to a certain extent. Whenever certain students are unable to complete a test, the question arises whether an unsatisfactory score indicates lack of achievement in the subject matter or slow reading. Consequently, the test should be of such length that all students have a chance to reach each item on the test. Whether they can answer each one or not is another question.

Test Directions

At the beginning of every examination, or at the beginning of each part when there are subtests, the student should be told very precisely what he is supposed to do, how he is supposed to do it, and, finally, where to do it. If the test is of a new type, this is of most importance. In many cases it pays to have a good illustration with the correct answer or answers worked out. Best results are obtained when the test-maker takes nothing for granted.

Correction for Guessing

Many people feel that, if correction formulas for guessing are to be applied, the students should be so informed in the directions. The use of these formulas is a controversial issue among the experts in test construction. The basic formula used is

$$\text{Score} = \text{No. Right} - \frac{\text{No. Wrong}}{N-1} \quad \text{or} \quad \text{Score} = R - \frac{W}{N-1}$$

where N is the number of possible answers. When true-false items are used this formula reduces to

Score = Rights — Wrongs.

These formulas are based on the assumption that when a student misses an item this error is the result of blind chance or guessing. No account is taken of the fact that many students miss items because of misinformation. Also for most students, there are few items about which he knows nothing if he has been halfway attentive in class. Consider a multiple-choice item with 5 responses, the answer to which the student is not sure of. Here is what he does. First, he notices that the first and fifth responses are silly. Next, he eliminates the third one on cues. He is left with the second and fourth. Then he guesses. There is no formula in existence that will cover this type of behavior and also take into account errors based upon misinformation.

Telling students that a correction formula will be applied has different effects on different individuals. Some people will take a chance on anything. They ignore the statement. Others become so cautious that only that of which they are very sure gets on the answer sheet. Validity is affected by these differences in behavior.

As far as the classroom teacher goes, he can minimize this whole problem by using types of items that minimize the opportunity to guess. In other words, don't use simple true-false items. Or he can give the students adequate time so that they do not have to do a lot of wild guessing as the end of the period draws near. Or he can ask students not to guess wildly and help in their conforming to this by not counting items omitted as wrong items. Correcting each student's score by the use of one of the correction formulas is a lot of work and the results seldom justify the work. Of course, if a teacher uses a test that is scored by a correction formula and also uses the norms that come with the test, he has no choice.

General Points

It goes without saying that test items should be written in clear, concise, and grammatical English. The language should be adapted to the level of the individuals being tested. This can be achieved by checking the words used in the test against such word lists as that of Thorndike and Lorge (17) or using one of the newer word-count techniques as described by Flesch (9) or Forbes and Cottle (10). Ambiguity must be ruled out of test items. One way to do this is to avoid qualitative terms, such as *some, always, large, short,* etc. Because these mean different things to different people, they have no place in test items.

Items should be written daily if possible. There is no better time to write items about a piece of subject matter than immediately after the class period covering that subject has ended. Of course, many times this is impossible, but a teacher can at least make notes on ideas for items. Having students write items has its merits as learning situations for the students. But such items must be edited carefully and cautiously before they are ever used. Students know very little about item-writing and their emphasis is placed too much on the trivial and highly factual.

Finally, it should be pointed out that there is no rule that says we should always use the same type of test item. It is a good idea to be flexible and to use the type that best measures the objective at hand. Some items are much better than others when applied to the evaluation of certain objectives. Also a test made up of different types of items is more interesting to the examinee. But no matter what the type of item selected, it should be of such a nature that experts in an area would agree upon the answer chosen as correct. There is little justification for the use on an achievement test of items with controversial responses. They belong on an attitude test.

EXERCISE

1. Set up a table of specifications as illustrated on p. 143 for a test to cover a unit of work in a subject you teach or plan to teach.

REFERENCES

1. Aiken, W. M. *The story of the Eight Year Study.* New York: Harper, 1942.
2. American Council on Education. *A design for general education.* Washington, D. C.: The Council, 1944.

3. American Educational Research Association, Committee on Test Standards. *Technical recommendations for achievement tests.* Washington, D. C.: National Education Association, 1955.

4. American Psychological Association. *Standards for educational and psychological tests and manuals.* Washington, D. C.: American Psychological Association, 1966.

5. American Psychological Association. *Technical recommendations for psychological tests and diagnostic techniques.* Washington, D. C.: American Psychological Association, 1954.

6. Bloom, B. S., ed. *Taxonomy of educational objectives. Handbook 1: The cognitive domain.* New York: David McKay, 1956.

7. Buros, O. K. *Mental measurements yearbooks* (1938, 1940, 1949, 1953, 1959, 1965). 1965 ed., Highland Park, N. J.: The Gryphon Press.

8. California Test Bureau. *California Achievement Tests.* Los Angeles, 1957.

9. Flesch, R. F. *How to test readability.* New York: Harper, 1951.

10. Forbes, F. W., and Cottle, W. C. A new method for determining readability of standardized tests. *J. appl. Psychol.,* 1953, 37, 185-90.

11. Greene, E. B. The retention of information obtained in college courses. *J. educ. Res.,* 1931, 24, 262-73.

12. Krathwohl, D. R., et al. *Taxonomy of educational objectives. Handbook 2: The affective domain.* New York: David McKay, 1964.

13. President's Commission on Higher Education. *Establishing the goals.* Vol. 1. Washington, D. C.: Government Printing Office, 1947.

14. Remmers, H. H., and Gage, N. L. *Educational measurement and evaluation.* Rev. ed. New York: Harper, 1955.

15. Scates, D. E. Fifty years of objective measurement and research in education. *J. educ. Res.,* 1947, 41, 241-64.

16. Smith, E. R., and Tyler, R. W. *Appraising and recording student progress.* New York: Harper, 1942.

17. Thorndike, E. L., and Lorge, I. *The teacher's wordbook of 30,000 words.* New York: Teachers College, Columbia University, 1944.

18. Tyler, R. W. *Constructing achievement tests.* Columbus, O.: Ohio State University, 1934.

19. U. S. Department of Interior, Bureau of Education. *Cardinal principles of education.* Bulletin 38, 1918.

CHAPTER 7

MULTIPLE-CHOICE ITEMS

Of the various types of objective-test items, the multiple-choice form is the most popular today. An examination of the newer standardized tests reveals that the multiple-choice type of item is used almost exclusively. What are the reasons for this? First, this type of test item is adaptable to many different types of situations (see below). It can be used to measure almost all the desired outcomes of education, including the so-called "higher mental processes." Secondly, multiple-choice items keep guessing to a minimum, especially in comparison with the true-false type. The more possible responses, the more difficult guessing becomes. Thirdly, with this type of item, machine or other forms of answer sheets can always be used.

ONE-ANSWER MULTIPLE-CHOICE ITEM

The typical multiple-choice item consists of an introductory statement or questions (the stem) and several statements listed beneath it, which complete the stem. One of these statements is the correct or best answer and the others, which are incorrect, are called *distractors* or *decoys*.

The multiple-choice item may be written as a statement:

The value obtained by adding all the scores in a distribution and dividing by the number of scores is called the

    A. median   + C. mean
    B. mode   D. sigma

or as a question:

Which of the following is obtained by adding all the scores in a distribution and dividing by the number of cases?

A. median   + C. mean
B. mode   D. sigma

Any statement can be put in one or the other of the above forms. The correct answer and the distractors should come at the end of the statement or question so that, on the completion of the reading, the examinee has the answer right in front of him. If the answer is put in the beginning of the statement, the whole statement has to be read and then the examinee has to go back and select the correct answer. If space is not important, it is better to put the correct answer and distractors in tabular form beneath the item as above rather than to run them together at the end of the item.

At the present time, most multiple-choice items are of the one-answer type. Some teachers do make multiple-choice items with directions to select all the correct responses. In our previous discussion of validity (p. 97), we pointed out that such a practice made it possible for "response set" to be a factor contributing to an individual's score. These items with more than one correct answer lead to problems of scoring, of the use of answer sheets, and of item analysis. Their use is not recommended.

Examples of One-answer Items

Below are a series of multiple-choice items, each with one correct answer. These cover various subject-matter areas and would appear on different tests. The correct answers are marked +.

1. Insects always have
   A. four wings   C. four legs
   B. chewing mouth parts   + D. jointed appendages
2. If the President and the Vice President of the United States were to die, they would be succeeded by
   + A. the Speaker of the House   C. the Secretary of State
   B. the Chief Justice   D. the presiding officer
       of the Supreme Court   of the Senate
                                         E. none of the above

3. While listening to a radio program originating in Chicago, a man heard a clock strike 8. On looking at his watch, he saw that it was 6 o'clock. How many degrees west of Chicago was he?

    A. 15
    + B. 30
    C. 45

    D. None; he was east of Chicago

4. An intelligence test is said to be reliable when it

    A. measures what it is supposed to measure
    + B. measures consistently whatever it measures

    C. measures objectively
    D. does all the above

5. Which would you use to determine the chief exports of Chile?

    + A. A geography
    B. An atlas

    C. A dictionary
    D. A history book

6. In mammals, the nervous tissue and sense organs develop from an embryonic germ layer known as the

    + A. ectoderm
    B. endoderm
    C. metaderm

    D. mesoderm
    E. neuroderm

7. Which of the following words is spelled incorrectly?

    A. analysis
    B. supersede
    C. separate

    + D. synthisis
    E. reminiscence

8. How many syllables are there in the word *geography?*

    A. 2
    B. 3

    + C. 4
    D. 5

Questions 9, 10, and 11 refer to this diagram:

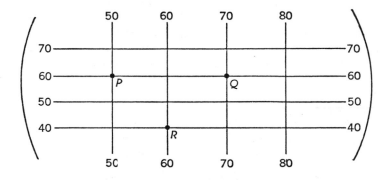

9. The latitude of point *P* on the chart above is
   + A. 60° north   D. 60° east
     B. 60° west   E. 50° east
     C. 60° south
10. At which point would the sun first appear in the morning?
    A. *P*   D. Impossible to tell as
   + B. *Q*   more data are needed.
    C. *R*
11. What part of the world would you say was located by the above scale?
    A. Eastern United States   D. Central Africa
    B. Western Europe   + E. Asiatic Russia
       (France)
    C. Brazil
12. A woman having just purchased a new hat that she really did not need reasons that her husband would have spent the money if she had not. Such reasoning is an example of
    A. infantile behavior   D. an illusion
    B. compensation   + E. rationalization
    C. projection

Uses for One-answer Items

Mosier and others (8) made a listing of the various kinds of questions that can be adapted to the multiple-choice form. In the pages that follow, this listing* is reprinted with examples taken from various areas of instruction.

1. Definition
   (1) Which type of neuron carries impulses from the central nervous system to a gland?
       + A. motor   C. connective
         B. sensory   D. afferent
   (2) Secretions of the ductless glands are called
         A. juices   + C. hormones
         B. regulators   D. enzymes
2. Purpose
   (1) Vitamin C is added to diets to prevent
         A. beri-beri   C. sterility
         B. cretinism   + D. scurvy

* Used by permission of G. F. Kuder.

(2) When the early explorers went westward from Europe, they were chiefly searching for

   A. gold

+ B. a direct route to the Indies

   C. living space for the habitants of overpopulated Europe

   D. an answer to the question as to the shape of the earth

3. *Cause*

(1) Which gland when it malfunctions causes cretinism?

   A. parathyroid   + C. thyroid

   B. adrenal   D. pituitary

(2) Burning fuel with a limited supply of oxygen causes an increased production of

   A. H_2O + C. CO

   B. CO_2 D. HCO_3

4. *Effect* (the reverse of the above)

(1) When a large glass jar is inverted over a burning candle, the lighted candle

   A. increases in bright-   C. remains the same
       ness

+ B. dies down and goes
     out

(2) A pathological condition in the Islands of Langerhans leads to

   A. scurvy   C. gigantism

+ B. diabetes   D. myxoedema

5. *Association* (What tends to occur with?)

(1) As a rainstorm approaches an area,

   A. temperature rises

+ B. barometric pressure falls

   C. winds blow from the east

   D. electrical activity increases

6. *Recognition of error*

(1) In which of the following has a mistake been made?

   A. $24 - 12 = 12$ C. $24 \div -2 = -12$

   B. $24 \times 0 = 0$ + D. $24 - (-12) = 12$

(2) A student found the mean and standard deviation of a set of 300 test scores to be 80 and 4 respectively. He concluded that

   A. his group was fairly homogeneous

      B. two thirds of his scores would lie between 76 and 84
+ C. practically all of his scores fell between 68 and 88
      D. the quartile deviation would be less than four

7. *Identification of error* (What type of error is this? What principle is violated?)

  (1) A student reads a thermometer and records a reading of 80°F. Later he records a reading of 40°F. He concluded that the first temperature was twice as warm as the second. Which of the following is most probably the cause of the error?

      A. He was confusing the Fahrenheit scale with the Centigrade scale.
      B. He assumed that degrees on the Fahrenheit scale are equal units of measurement, which they are not.
+ C. He overlooked the fact that 0° on this scale is not absolute zero.
      D. Actually he was correct, as the first reading denotes a condition twice as warm as the second.

8. *Evaluation*

  (1) Which of the following instruments or techniques in the long run would produce the highest reliability coefficients?

      A. Rorschach technique
      C. Bell Adjustment Inventory
+ B. Wechsler-Bellevue
      D. Guess-who technique

  (2) Which of these lengths is the smallest?

+ A. 2⅙ inches
      C. ⅞ inches
      B. ⅓ foot
      D. 1/12 yard

9. *Differences*

  (1) The basic difference between a dictatorship and a democracy is that in the dictatorship

      A. a king rules
+ B. little attention is paid to the rights of individuals
      C. public officials are not elected
      D. economic affairs take precedence over everything else

10. *Similarity*

  (1) One tenth of 1 per cent (.1%) is the same as

      A. .1
      + C. .001
      B. .01
      D. none of these

(2) *Harper's Magazine* is most similar to
    A. *The Saturday Review*   C. *The Reporter*
   + B. *The Atlantic Monthly*   D. *The New Republic*

11. *Rearrangement*

(1) Between the Revolutionary War and World War II, the USA was engaged in five other wars that occurred in the following order:
    A. Mexican, Spanish, 1812, Civil, World War I
   + B. 1812, Mexican, Civil, Spanish, World War I
    C. 1812, Mexican, Civil, World War I, Spanish
    D. Mexican, 1812, Civil, Spanish, World War I

(2) The parts of a reflex arc in the order that a stimulus would traverse it are
    A. motor neuron, connecting neuron, sensory neuron
   + B. sensory neuron, connecting neuron, motor neuron
    C. efferent neuron, connecting neuron, afferent neuron
    D. sense organ, connecting neuron, motor neuron

12. *Incomplete arrangement*

(1) Given the series 18, 6, 12, 4, 8, which number comes next?
    A. 2   + C. 2⅔
    B. 2⅓   D. 4

(2) The parts of the pistil of a flower are ovule, ovary, style, and
    A. anther   C. pollen
    B. filament   + D. stigma

13. *Common principles*

(1) Which of the following does not belong?
    A. hydrogen   C. oxygen
   + B. crypton   D. nitrogen

(2) Ink-blots, finger-paintings, drawings, writings are all similar in that they
    A. can be used with children equally well
    B. are all relatively easy to interpret after training
   + C. can be classified as projectives
    D. all possess the above three characteristics

14. *Controversial subjects* (Although not everyone agrees ——, those who support it do so mostly because ——.)

(1) Paper-and-pencil personality inventories have been widely criticized for many years; yet they are still used by many personnel workers. Most of these workers would agree that these inventories are

    A. most useful in diagnosing
    B. more valid than projectives
    C. honestly completed by students
 + D. useful as screening devices

Directions for Writing One-answer Items

Multiple-choice items are not easy to write. Skill in item-writing is important. It is far easier to write items measuring facts than it is to write items that measure applications, reasoning, and appreciations. Adkins (1) stated that experienced item-writers feel that the construction of from 5 to 15 acceptable multiple-choice items is a good day's work. Adkins here was writing for those who construct our Federal Civil Service Examinations. Contrast this with the teacher who thinks little about making 4 complete tests in one evening. Good test-making takes time. The following suggestions should be helpful to any item-writer.

1. Use plausible or logical distractors. Each decoy should by its content or nature be such that it appears to have something to do with the question. Unrelated distractors appear silly to a thoughtful examinee. As the number of possible answers is cut down, the item loses some of its value. The following item illustrates the use of implausible distractors:

The most important factor in New York City's development as an important seat of commerce is its
    A. large foreign-born population
 + B. excellent harbor facilities
    C. scenic setting, worth visiting
    D. population of industrious citizens

The item above becomes an easy one because of the poor distractors.

A good way to obtain plausible distractors in some areas is to study the errors that students make and to use these as distractors. In the following, each of the distractors is the result of the misuse of a geometric formula:

Given a circle with diameter equal to 12, the area of this circle is approximately
    A. 19 (using πr)   + C. 113 (using πr^2)
    B. 38 (using πd)   D. 453 (using πd^2)

The above is preferable to inserting in A., B., and D. random numbers that are in no way related to the problem.

Here is another example from elementary statistics.

In a sample with $N = 25$, the sum of the squares ($\sum x^2$) is 180. The standard deviation is
   A. 13.4 (not dividing by N)
   B. 8.5 (taking square root incorrectly)
   C. 7.2 (not taking the square root)
  +D. 2.7 (correct answer. Divided 180 by 25 and took square root)

2. Make certain that the stem consists of a statement or an idea, not just a single word. For example, this item is poorly made:

Charles Darwin
   A. applied the mutation theory to development
 + B. wrote the *Origin of Species*
   C. first observed the fertilization of an ovum
   D. discovered the phagocytic functions of leucocytes

The item as it stands is really an example of a simple true-and-false item. Multiple-choice items made in this fashion will usually be limited to the measurement of factual information.

3. Place all common elements in the stem of the item. This adds simplicity and compactness to the item. Do not write such items as this:

One of the major functions of the adrenal gland is
 + A. to regulate the amount of sugars in the blood
   B. to regulate the amount of proteins sent to body cells
   C. to regulate the secretion of wastes
   D. to regulate the secretion of insulin

By putting all common elements in the stem, we have:

One of the major functions of the adrenal glands is to regulate the
 + A. amount of sugars in the blood
   B. amount of proteins sent to the body cells
   C. secretion of wastes
   D. secretion of insulin

4. When dealing with items that have numerical answers, arrange the answers in order from large to small or vice versa.

Given a triangle with a base of 8 inches and altitude of 4 inches, the area of this triangle is

A. 4	C. 32
+ B. 16	D. 80

The same rule should be applied to dates in history and also in making a list of centuries.

5. Avoid the use of cues that reveal the correct answers. Sometimes such items as the following get into tests:

A biologist who specializes in the study of the relationships of an organism to its environment is known as an

+ A. ecologist	C. ethnologist
B. structuralist	D. taxonomist

The appearance of the word *an* in the stem rules out the B. and D. responses as possible answers. This situation can be remedied by using the combination *a(an)* at the end of the stem or by having all distractors begin with a vowel.

Frequently words appear in the stem that give away the answer or require no mental effort at all to get the correct answer:

The *Strong Vocational Interests Blank* is used to measure

A. aptitudes	C. achievement
+ B. interests	D. adjustment

Item-writers often tend to make the correct response much longer than the others. The alert student becomes aware of this and, when in doubt about the correct response, selects the longest. "Teachers and professors are wordy individuals and require a lot of words to make an exact statement," he argues. This difficulty is easy to control if we just watch our responses as we write them.

An item-writer has to be careful that one item does not contain the answer to another item. Many times, as he nears the end of a test, a student finds an answer to one of the earlier items that he had passed over because of uncertainty. A construction of a table of specifications as discussed in Chapter 6 will tend to eliminate this kind of cue.

The item-writer should carefully examine each distractor to see that each makes a good, complete sentence when attached to the stem.

Sometimes because of differences in grammatical construction some distractors make better sentences than others. The good English is more representative of the usage of the item-writer than the poor English and hence serves as a cue to the correct answer. The item below illustrates this point:

A test is said to be valid when
+ A. it does what it says it does.
B. including only multiple-choice items.
C. reliability is important too.
D. to score it one is objective.

6. Make each item completely independent of every other item. Suppose that in arithmetic we have two successive items, the first of which requires the correct solution for the area of a certain type of figure. The second item asks the student to compute the cost of laying a certain type of floor covering over the first area at so much per square foot. If the answer to the first item is incorrect, it then becomes impossible to solve the second correctly. A student knows how to compute correctly the cost of the floor covering, but, perhaps, because of a simple arithmetic mistake in the first item, he gets no credit on the second. Such groupings of items lower the validity of a test.

7. Eliminate all unrelated details from an item. For example, suppose that an item-writer wanted to construct an item for the computation of the area of a triangle and gave data such as these: base 19.96 inches, altitude 7.97 inches. The purpose of the item is to see if a student knows how to compute the area of a triangle. This can be as validly measured by using such data as 20 and 8 instead of the above. This is not a suggestion that test-writers should overlook accuracy. The objective here is merely to find out if a student can compute the area of a triangle, not how well he can manipulate 9's.

Sometimes much irrelevant material, which has really nothing to do with the answer, appears in the stem.

Singapore, a large and beautiful city founded by the British several hundred years ago and long noted for its export of rubber and tin, is located . . . etc.

The purpose of the above item is to locate Singapore. The Chamber of Commerce propaganda has nothing to do with the item and should be left out.

8. Be sure that the distractors and the correct response possess homogeneity—that is, they should be fairly similar in content or in location. The following item lacks homogeneity and as a result is very easy.

London is closest to
+ A. Paris   C. Hong Kong
  B. Singapore   D. Rome

Changing this as follows makes it a better item:

London is closest to
+ A. Paris   C. Geneva
  B. Berlin   D. Prague

In the following item about the eye, other sense organs are brought in:

The part of the eye that is sensitive to light waves is called the
+ A. retina   D. iris
  B. cochlea   E. stapes
  C. septum

This item is improved by using only parts of the eye:

The part of the eye which is sensitive to light waves is called the
+ A. retina   D. iris
  B. lens   E. fovea centralis
  C. choroid layer

9. Use "*none of the above*" as a distractor or as a correct answer. This is particularly useful in vocabulary, spelling, or mathematics tests. For example, an item from a spelling test in which the student is looking for a misspelled word might read:

Which of the following words is misspelled?
  A. illicit   C. illegal
  B. illusion   + D. none of the above

An example in mathematics:

Given $p = vgt^2$, $t =$

+ A. $\sqrt{\dfrac{p}{vg}}$

B. $p\sqrt{vg}$

C. $\dfrac{p}{vg}$

D. none of the above

When "none of the above" is used, it should appear as the correct answer every fourth or fifth time.

The use of "*all the above*" creates problems and is not so useful as "none of the above." When items are constructed so that "all the above" is the correct answer, an alert student can obtain the correct answer on only partial information. He might recognize the A. response as correct, and then he spots the D. response as correct. Why go further? Since two responses are correct, then "all the above" is the correct answer. Good, well-disguised, "all the above" items are difficult to make.

Sometimes one runs into "only A. and C. of the above" as the F. response, "only A. and D. of the above" as the G. response, etc., until all combinations are used up. The writer fails to see the value of such items and feels that their construction should be discouraged. And there is the other situation in which we find the A., B., and C. responses all correct, D. is "none of the above," and E. is "all the above," the correct answer. The D. response makes the correct answer absurd.

10. If it is impossible to obtain more than 3 plausible responses, don't waste time trying to invent some others. The chances are good that no student will select them. Suppose that in a physics situation we are comparing two forces, X and Y. X is greater than Y, smaller than Y, or equal to Y. It can't be anything else, hence the item-writer should stop at that point.

11. In general, avoid negative statements, but if the word *not* does appear in the stem or question, underline it to draw the student's attention to it.

12. If the student is to write the letter corresponding to his choice of the correct answer on an answer sheet or in the test booklet, instruct him in the directions to use capital letters. Items should be

constructed with capital letters as in all the examples in this chapter. These are much easier to grade. Capital letters do not look alike as frequently as do lower case a's and d's or c's and e's, and leave no question as to what the student wrote. If standard answer sheets are used, the above makes no difference. Letters are better than numbers especially in mathematic items, and they cannot be so easily changed as numbers can by unscrupulous students. A 1 can very conveniently change into a 4.

13. Rotate the position of the correct answer. This can be done easily by using a tally sheet to keep track of the position of the correct response as items are written. Some item-writers feel that when the correct response occupies the first position the item becomes very easy. This is not so. And when a test-maker runs to C. and D. responses, the student may spot the habit. When he is uncertain of the answer to some item, he will mark it C. or D.

14. Avoid items in which the distractors overlap.

1. If in a normal curve, one measures off 1 standard deviation on each side of the mean, what per cent of the area would be cut off?

   A. 32   D. More than 75
   B. 50   E. 95
+ C. 68

The D. and E. distractors cause trouble because of overlap. Since the C. response includes both A. and B., it might be argued that all are correct. Instructions to select the *"best"* answer will take care of this, but nothing except careful item-writing will solve the D. and E. problem.

Adkins (1) concludes her section on item-writing with a check list and says that one should be able to answer "yes" to each item on the check list for each item written. A modified form of her list appears below.

1. Is the item as a whole realistic and practical?
2. Is each item independent of every other item?
3. Is the item as a whole specific?
4. Is the central problem clear?

5. Is the problem stated accurately?
6. Is the problem stated briefly but completely?
7. Is each distractor important and plausible rather than obvious?
8. Are all irrelevant and extraneous cues eliminated?
9. Are the distractors and correct response homogeneous?

SPECIFIC MULTIPLE-CHOICE ITEMS

The above directions were written for multiple-choice items in general. We will now consider some specific types of multiple-choice items.

1. Best-answer Type

More and more in recent years, the best-answer type of multiple-choice item has been used because the choice of the correct response requires the student to do some thinking. Each response has to be evaluated carefully, for the well-written best-answer item has shades of truth in all its responses, although one is "more truthful" than the others. Rote memory can be ruled out with items such as this. Best-answer items are difficult to make, but all test-makers should attempt to have some on their achievement tests. Examples of best-answer items follow.

1. The most important and basic cause of the Civil War was the
    A. publication of *Uncle Tom's Cabin*
    B. election of Lincoln
    C. writings of Garrison and other Northerners
    + D. issue of the freedom of each state to control its destiny
2. The parent of the child having a temper tantrum should
    A. spank the child
    B. put him to bed without a meal
    C. give him a piece of candy to stop crying
    + D. ignore the child
3. The major purpose of evaluation is to
    A. provide information for grading
    + B. improve learning
    C. make sectioning of students possible
    D. gather data for effective counseling

4. The most important difference between teacher-made tests and standardized tests is that the
   A. latter are printed
+ B. latter have norms
   C. former are usually essay tests
   D. former cover specific objectives

2. Worst-answer Type

In this type of item we have the reverse of the above. Here we find that 3 or 4 of the responses are good or equally relevant and the other has little or nothing to do with the item. When items of this type are used, they should be separated from the others and prefaced with very specific directions. Usually, these items are easy to make, because it is often easier to make 3 or 4 true statements than the same numbers of false ones. Such items also encourage thinking, since the student has to evaluate carefully each response before deciding which to mark.

Examples of worst-answer multiple-choice items follow.

Directions: Remember in these items to pick out the response that is not true or that is the worst answer.

1. Reliability of intelligence tests can be determined by correlating scores
   A. based on the odd-numbered items against those based on the even-numbered items
   B. obtained from two forms of the same test administered to the same individuals
   C. obtained by administering the test to the same group of individuals twice
+ D. on the test with a criterion such as grades
2. Intelligence tests are used in the public schools in
   A. sectioning students   C. counseling students
+ B. promoting students   D. predicting achievement
3. A student went to the campus health center complaining of being tired, run down, and subject to frequent colds. He was advised to
   A. exercise in fresh air
+ B. include more carbohydrates in his diet
   C. purchase and take a certain type of vitamin pill
   D. include more meat, especially liver, in his diet

4. The following are fundamental life processes found only in animals.
+ A. photosynthesis   C. circulation
   B. respiration   D. digestion

5. The following are examples of standard scores.
   A. Wechsler IQ's   + C. Stanford-Binet IQ's
   B. Army General Classification   D. *T*-scores
      Test Scores   E. stanines

3. Some Simpler Types

ANALOGIES. In certain areas of learning, knowledges of relationships, such as those of similarities of structures or functions, can be evaluated by the use of analogy items. Usually these items are set up in groups like the following with no directions other than a statement to the student to select that which best completes the analogy.

Examples in science:

tibia : fibula :: radius : [(A) femur, (B) humerus, (C) clavicle, (D) *ulna*]

[(A) gills, (B) *trachea*, (C) spiracles, (D) pores] : insect:: lungs : snake

Examples in social studies:

mayor : city :: [(A) sheriff, (B) *governor*, (C) capitol, (D) president] : state

Japanese Current : Japan :: Gulf Stream : [(A) New England, (B) Labrador, (C) Gulf States, (D) *England*]

SELECTING THE MOST INCLUSIVE TERM. With this type of item, the directions tell the student to examine each of the following series of terms, names, concepts, etc., and to select the one which includes all the others. These items are usually administered in groups, such as the following.

(A) iron, (B) copper, (C) *element*, (D) gold, (E) silver
(A) ward, (B) *county*, (C) precinct, (D) town

SELECTING THE MOST DISSIMILAR TERM. This type is very similar to the above except that this time the student is told to examine each of the following series and to underline the one he feels is different from all the others.

(A) snake, (B) turtle, (C) lizard, (D) *salamander*, (E) crocodile

(A) sulphur, (B) iron, (C) *steel*, (D) carbon, (E) aluminum

These three types can be constructed fairly easily in most areas of learning. They are severely limited, though, by the fact that about all we can do with them is to measure the simpler outcomes of learning—the recall of factual information.

EXERCISES

1. Using Mosier's classification system, construct at least one multiple-choice item representing each type for a unit of a course included in your specialty.
2. Construct 5 best-answer, multiple-choice items for another unit.
3. Construct 5 worst-answer, multiple-choice items for another unit.
4. Obtain an older standardized test and classify the objectives measured. Do the same for a current test and compare the results.
5. Classify the items of both the tests mentioned in Exercise 4 according to Mosier's system.

REFERENCES

The following books and any other books on educational measurement contain illustrations of multiple-choice items and offer suggestions for their construction.

1. Adkins, D. C., *et al. Construction and analysis of achievement tests.* Washington, D. C.: Government Printing Office, 1947.
2. Bloom, B. S., ed. *Taxonomy of educational objectives. Handbook I: The cognitive domain.* New York: David McKay, 1956.
3. Ebel, R. L. *Measuring educational achievement.* Englewood Cliffs, N. J.; Prentice Hall, 1965.
4. Educational Testing Service. *Multiple-choice questions: A close look.* Princeton, N. J.: Educational Testing Service, 1963.
5. Green, J. A. *Teacher-made tests.* New York: Harper and Row, 1963.
6. Lindquist, E. F. *Educational measurement.* Washington, D. C.: American Council on Education, 1951.
7. Micheels, W. J., and Karnes, M. R. *Measuring educational achievement.* New York: McGraw-Hill, 1950.
8. Mosier, C. I., *et al.* Suggestions for the construction of multiple-choice items. *Educ. psychol. Measmt.*, 1945, 5, 261-71.

9. National Council for the Social Studies. 35th Yearbook. *Evaluation in social studies.* Washington, D. C.: The Council, 1965.
10. National Council of Teachers of Mathematics. 26th Yearbook. *Evaluation in mathematics.* Washington, D. C.: The Council, 1961.
11. Remmers, H. H., *et al. A practical introduction to measurement and evaluation.* New York: Harper and Row, 1960.
12. Wood, Dorothy A. *Test construction: development and interpretation of achievement tests.* Columbus, O.: Merrill, 1960.
13. Wrightstone, J. W., *et al. Evaluation in modern education.* New York: American Book, 1956.

CHAPTER 8

OTHER TYPES OF OBJECTIVE-TEST ITEMS

In this chapter we shall discuss the true-false, completion, matching, arrangement, and application and interpretation types of test items. While none of these is as widely used on standardized tests as the multiple-choice item, each has possibilities for the classroom teacher. As was pointed out in the previous chapter, standardized tests today are made up almost exclusively of multiple-choice items.

TRUE–FALSE ITEMS

A very common type of test item used by the classroom teacher is the 2-response or ordinary true-false item. The reason for its popularity has been of interest to the writer, as he has always felt that the true-false item is about the poorest and least useful of all the various objective-test types. One reason for its popularity is that true-false items are apparently easy to make. They do not require the time and thought involved in the construction of multiple-choice items. Another reason is that the true-false item provides for very extensive sampling in a given period of time. In some areas, social sciences, for example, it is not unusual for students to respond to 150 to 200 items in a classroom period.

One major disadvantage or limitation of true-false items is that they are frequently ambiguous. A good student sees something in the item that the poor student does not; thus the former misses the item. Items that cause such results lower the usefulness of any test.

Another disadvantage is that this type of item tends to be very easy. It is not unusual for a teacher to find, after studying a test made up of 100 true-false items, that 20 or 30 of these items were responded to correctly or almost correctly by everyone. All that these easy items contributed to the test was to raise every student's raw score 20 or 30 points. A third disadvantage is that guessing is encouraged and favored. Obviously, with only 2 possibilities the odds are much more in a student's favor than on a 4- or 5-response multiple-choice item. There is justification for the use of correction formulas (Chapter 6) when this type of item is used. And, finally, because of the way in which the typical item is constructed, true-false items usually measure only one objective of education: knowledge of facts and principles. Because of the simple nature of true-false items, it is difficult to be other than factual.

Types of True–False Items

True–false items may fall into one of the following four groups.

1. SIMPLE TWO-RESPONSE ITEMS. This is the commonest type of true-false items.

Directions: Consider each of the following items and if it is true place a circle about the "T" (or "Yes" or "+") and if it is false, place a circle about the "F" (or "No" or "−").

Ⓣ F 1. A valid test measures what it is supposed to measure.

ⓉF 2. The mean is the most reliable measure of central tendency.

Yes Ⓝⓞ 3. One standard deviation measured off on each side of the mean cuts off inclusively 50 per cent of the area.

Yes Ⓝⓞ 4. A correlation coefficient is basically a measure of cause and effect.

⊕ − 5. A correlation coefficient of +.80 is of the same magnitude as one of −.80.

+ ⊖ 6. Percentiles scores, like any other type of test scores, are justifiably averaged.

The answers to these can be placed in the right-hand margin if it is so desired. When the student has to write his responses on an answer sheet or before the item, he should be told in the directions to mark the item "T," if it is true, and "O," if false. When a teacher uses "F" or "—" for false, these can be easily changed by the unscrupulous student after the papers have been returned to a "T" or to a "+." No question arises when the first system is used.

2. THREE-RESPONSE ITEMS. The form of these items is similar to the two-response item, but the student responds on a 3- (or 5-) point scale. Many times, items as they stand are neither true nor false. On these items the student is given a chance to note that sufficient evidence or data have not been presented to make it possible to mark the item either "true" or "false." So the directions inform the student that he is to mark the item "True," if true, "False," if false, and "can't tell" (CT), if there is not enough evidence to mark it either true or false.

T   (CT)   F   1. A validity coefficient of .20 is of no value in predicting academic success.

(T)   CT   F   2. Reliability of our commonly used intelligence tests tends to be about .90.

Yes   (?)   No   3. Two boys have IQ's of 120 and 110 respectively. The former boy will do the better school work.

Yes   ?   (No)   4. Reliability of a speed test may be computed by the split-halves method.

This method of response can be elaborated into a 5-point scale, such as the following:

1. Always true—true without exception.
2. Probably true.
3. Insufficient evidence or data to draw any conclusion about the statement.
4. Probably false.
5. Always false—false without exception.

As we shall see later, this type of response is used on some of our newer type test items.

3. CORRECTION-TYPE ITEMS. In this type, the directions read as follows: "*Directions:* If the item is true, mark it '*true.*' If it is false, correct it by writing in the space provided the word or words you would substitute for the underlined word or words to make the statement true." It is necessary to underline words or phrases in order to

prevent individuals from inserting or removing *nots,* which is the easiest way of correcting a false statement. This type of true-false item controls guessing and is desirable at least from that point of view.

1. The most easterly of the Great Lakes is Lake Ontario.	1. ___T___
2. A Great Lakes freighter leaving Duluth would most probably be loaded with wheat.	2. iron ore
3. The Soo Canal connects Lake Erie and Lake Ontario.	3. Welland
4. The largest Midwestern city is located on Lake Erie.	4. Michigan
5. All these lakes eventually connect with the Atlantic Ocean by way of the St. Lawrence River.	5. ___T___

Sometimes instead of being asked to answer in the above manner, the student is given a space in which to tell or to explain why the item is false. Another possible way of working the item is to ask the student to underline the words which he believes make the statement false.

4. CLUSTER-TYPE ITEMS. In the cluster-type true-false item, the directions tell the student to select and mark all statements that are true. This type is similar to the poorly made, low-level, multiple-choice items illustrated and discussed in the previous chapter.

1. Hurricanes
    - __X__ 1. form in the Caribbean area.
    - _____ 2. are most common in early summer.
    - _____ 3. typically enter the United States in the Louisiana-Texas area of the Gulf States.
    - __X__ 4. are intense low pressure storms.
    - _____ 5. when passing over land are known as tornadoes.
    - __X__ 6. consist typically of heavy wind and torrential rain.
2. World War I
    - __X__ 1. led up to the founding of the League of Nations.
    - _____ 2. resulted in Germany's being divided into 2 parts.
    - __X__ 3. had origins similar to those of World War II.
    - _____ 4. resulted in the establishment of Israel as an independent nation.
    - __X__ 5. was the only war in which extensive use was made of poisonous gases.

Directions for Writing True–False Items

1. Write each item so that it contains only one idea. Confusion results when two or more ideas, some true, some false, appear in the same item.

> Red blood cells carry oxygen; whereas white blood cells transport carbon dioxide.

The above item is best made into two separate items, the first concerning the function of red blood cells, the second, white blood cells.

> World War II, which started in 1940, was the direct result of Hitler's aggressive policies.

> Reliability is frequently computed by correlating the scores on odd-numbered items with those obtained on even-numbered items, but the technique can be used only with speed tests.

Both of the above items as they stand are good examples of *what not to do.*

2. Do not lift items directly from the text. Sometimes slight changes such as inserting a *not* are made. This in no way improves the item. Items should at least be stated in a fashion in which the examinee has not seen them before.

3. Take great care to avoid the use of certain words that make it possible for the student to respond correctly to the item even when he knows nothing about the material. The word *always* calls for a "false" response, *sometimes* or *usually* a "true" response, *never* a false response, etc. If the test-writer is careful to distribute words of this nature equally among true and false items, this problem is eliminated. Another factor to be considered here is the length of the item. Unless the item-writer is careful, long, involved statements will tend to be true. A wise student will soon become aware of this and mark long items "true" even when he knows nothing about the subject.

4. Be certain that the language is exact and expressed in numerical terms when necessary.

> It is a *short* distance from Chicago to Detroit.

Short means what? In a superjet, this distance seems trivial. If one were to creep or walk the distance, it would seem endless. Qualitative words mean so many different things to different people that they must not be used. Usually we don't know the frame of reference from which an individual responds to qualitative words. Such words as *large* and *small, many* and *few, more* and *less* have no place in true-false items.

5. Don't emphasize the trivial. If the type of examination has anything to do with the type of learning that takes place—and it does—this is one way to encourage rather useless learning.

Charles Darwin was born Feb. 12, 1809.
Right: Charles Darwin was born early in the nineteenth century.

6. Avoid parenthetical phrases or clauses that have little to do with the central idea of the item.

Gregor Mendel, a prominent French biologist, first stated the principle of the inheritance of dominant and recessive traits.

The insertion of "a prominent French biologist" in the above is considered by many to be a trick. A well-constructed test is not an arena for the teacher to try to outwit his students.

7. Avoid negative statements. After an examinee has read several *nots* and *nevers* in a series of clauses, he becomes confused. He has heard that two negatives make a positive, so he tries to evaluate the statement from this point of view and then to decide whether it is true or false.

8. Attribute to someone statements that reflect attitudes, basic philosophies, schools of thought, etc., otherwise there is no scorable answer.

All dreams are expressions of our repressed desires and frustrations.
Right: According to Freud, all dreams are expressions of our repressed desires and frustrations.

9. Have, in the long run, an equal number of true and false statements. These should be arranged so that there is no particular pattern of response.

10. Use more than 2 responses or have the students correct items they consider to be false.

RECALL OR COMPLETION ITEMS

In this type of objective-test item the student supplies information asked for by the question or needed by the statement. The 2 types of items previously discussed, multiple-choice and true-false, are usually classified as RECOGNITION items, and the task of the examinee is to respond to and evaluate given material.

Types of Recall Items

Recall items may be in any one of a variety of forms.

1. SHORT-ANSWER ITEMS. The simplest recall item is the question or statement that demands a short answer to be written in given spaces.

1. What season of the year begins on the twenty-
   first of June in Australia?   1. _____
2. A major export of Australia is   2. _____
3. What mammal almost ruined agriculture in
   Australia and now has been almost eliminated?   3. _____
4. Central and northern Australia is best de-
   scribed as being mostly   4. _____
5. What is the capital of Australia?   5. _____
6. The Australian settlers came mostly from   6. _____

2. LISTING ITEMS. These are very similar to the above and are frequently found on the so-called "essay tests" of some instructors.

A. List 5 digestive enzymes and note in the second space the type of food each works on.

    1. _____   1. _____
    2. _____   2. _____
    3. _____   3. _____
    4. _____   4. _____
    5. _____   5. _____

B. In the spaces below, list the parts of the pistil of a flower.

    1. _____
    2. _____
    3. _____

4. _____

5. _____

C. List in order the types of neurons over which a nerve impulse travels in a simple reflex arc.

1. _____

2. _____

3. _____

3. COMPLETION ITEMS. These are very similar to short-answer items except that the student has to write the word or words which have been omitted from statements. In the sample below the same items are used as in the short-answer item above.

1. In Australia, June twenty-first is at the beginning of _____.   1. _____

2. A major export of Australia is _____.   2. _____

3. Extensive damage to Australian crops in the past has been caused by the _____.   3. _____

4. A term that adequately describes central and northern Australia is _____.   4. _____

5. The capital of Australia is _____.   5. _____

6. Australia was settled chiefly by emigrants from _____.   6. _____

4. ANALOGY ITEMS. These can be constructed similarly to those mentioned on p. 165 in the previous chapter.

Radius : ulna :: tibia : _____
$SD : \bar{X} ::$ _____ : median
cilia : paramecium :: _____ : earthworm

5. PROBLEMS. Problems may be considered as a type of recall item. Data are presented and the student manipulates these to obtain an answer.

A child of 7 years, 7 months has a Stanford-Binet mental age of 8 years and 2 months. Calculate his IQ.
Given a circle with a diameter of 14 inches, find the area of this circle.

6. IDENTIFICATION ITEMS. This type requires the student to label parts of a diagram of a plant or animal, to identify a group of

formulas, to write an important title of a book after each name in a list of authors, or to locate places.

Below are some formulas used in elementary statistics. In the space at the right, write the name of the statistic obtained when each is used:

1. $\dfrac{x}{s}$ 1. _____

2. $\dfrac{\Sigma X}{N}$ 2. _____

3. $\sqrt{\dfrac{\Sigma x^2}{N-1}}$ 3. _____

4. $\dfrac{Q_3 - Q_1}{2}$ 4. _____

5. $\dfrac{\Sigma x^2}{N-1}$ 5. _____

6. $\dfrac{\Sigma xy}{\sqrt{\Sigma x^2 \Sigma y^2}}$ 6. _____

In the space at the immediate right, write the name of the author of each book given and in the second right-hand space identify the nationality of the author:

1. *Tom Jones*   1. _____   1. _____

2. *Walden*   2. _____   2. _____

3. *Pride and Prejudice*   3. _____   3. _____

4. *Moll Flanders*   4. _____   4. _____

5. *Joseph and His Brothers*   5. _____   5. _____

6. *Candide*   6. _____   6. _____

7. *War and Peace*   7. _____   7. _____

Directions for Writing Recall and Completion Items

1. Omit only key words and only one or two of these. Completion items can reach such absurdities as _____ causes _____ and _____! Only the instructor knows the correct answer to this. The writer has known one university instructor who used such items and argued that since students were taking his course they should know what he was talking about.

2. Repeat blank or blanks at the end of the statement. This is simply a matter of efficiency. When so placed, the student can complete the statement on finishing the reading. If the blanks appear at

the beginning of the statement, he has to read to the end, go back to the beginning, and sometimes go through the entire statement again.

3. Provide answer sheets or spaces in the margins of the test book-let for the written answer. Papers with the answers written in the blanks as the blanks appear in the context require considerable time to be scored.

4. Try to have items that have only one correct response. This is often impossible and leads to the major problem in the use of completion items—the subjectivity of grading. Such considerations as the following arise: Are all synonyms to be considered in grading? Are all synonyms equally acceptable? If so, does the teacher accept them? The English language is a rich language. This results in varieties of terms appearing in many completion items. Teachers would differ in their acceptance of some of these words. Hence, the same student would get different scores on the same test, if graded by different teachers. Associated with the matter of synonyms is what to do about misspelled words. Suppose that a student puts the correct word into an item blank on a chemistry test. The word is *oxygen*, but he spells it *oxijin*. He knows his chemistry, not his spelling. If the teacher marks the item as wrong, the validity of the test is low-ered because the test is a test to measure knowledge of chemistry. Should the teacher allow half credit? Or should he allow full credit? Correct spelling is the responsibility of all teachers. But if the teacher deducts credit for incorrect spelling, the validity of the test as a test of special subject matter is lowered. One solution to this is to give two grades, in this case, one for chemistry and one in the spelling of chemical terms.

5. Finally, follow here many of the other rules already discussed for true-false items—that is, don't lift items directly from the text; be brief, be clear; use quantitative terms, if possible; etc. These rules apply equally well to recall or completion test items.

MATCHING ITEM

The matching item in its typical form contains a series of statements in one column to be associated with another series in a second column. For example:

1. *Directions:* For each item in the left-hand column locate in the second column the individual identified with it and place the appropriate letter in front of each term in the first column.

(D)	1. Discovered the cell	(A)	Brown
(A)	2. Discovered the cell nucleus	(B)	Schwann
(C)	3. Fertilization	(C)	Hertwig
(H)	4. Laws of heredity	(D)	Hooke
(I)	5. Acquired characteristics	(E)	Cuvier
(B)	6. Cell theory	(F)	C. Darwin
(N)	7. Filial regression	(G)	Haeckel
(K)	8. Spermatozoa	(H)	Mendel
(G)	9. Recapitulation	(I)	Lamarck
(L)	10. Mutations	(J)	Harvey
		(K)	Leeuwenhoek
		(L)	Muller
		(M)	T. Huxley
		(N)	Galton

2. Select from the column at the right the term that identifies each formula and place the capital letter corresponding to your choice in the appropriate space.

B.   1. $\dfrac{x}{s}$ A. Spearman rho

G.   2. $\dfrac{\Sigma X}{N}$ B. standard score

F.   3. $\sqrt{\dfrac{\Sigma x^2}{N}}$ C. quartile deviation

C.   4. $\dfrac{Q_3 - Q_1}{2}$ D. Pearson r

H.   5. $\dfrac{\Sigma x^2}{N}$ E. interquartile range

D.   6. $\dfrac{\Sigma xy}{\sqrt{\Sigma x^2 \Sigma y^2}}$ F. standard deviation

       G. mean

       H. variance

3. In the space to the extreme left of the title of each book write the *capital* letter corresponding to the name of the author and in the next space write the *small* letter corresponding to his nationality.

G.	a.	1. *Tom Jones*	
E.	b.	2. *Walden*	
J.	a.	3. *Pride and Prejudice*	
B.	a.	4. *Moll Flanders*	
K.	c.	5. *Joseph and His Brothers*	
I.	d.	6. *Candide*	
F.	g.	7. *War and Peace*	
A.	a.	8. *Nicholas Nickleby*	

A. Dickens   a. English
B. Defoe   b. American
C. Dostoevski c. German
D. Thackeray d. French
E. Thoreau   e. Italian
F. Tolstoy   f. Swiss
G. Fielding g. Russian
H. Emerson   h. Canadian
I. Voltaire
J. Austen
K. Mann
L. H. James

From the above it should be noted that matching items can be used very effectively to cover a large amount of related factual material rapidly.

Directions for Constructing Matching Items

1. Place the ·larger parts of the lists in the left-hand column. Reduce the responses in the right-hand column to one or two words. (See example 1 on page 178.)

2. Limit the number of entries to about 10. If situations arise where 20 or 30 entries must be considered, construct 2 or 3 matching items. When long lists have to be matched, the student wastes too much time trying to find the correct response.

3. Don't break items by the bottom of the page. The complete item should all be on the same page.

4. Have a longer list in the right-hand column than in the left-hand column. Or put fewer entries in the left-hand column and state in the directions that these may be used more than once. When there are an equal number of terms in each column it is possible for the student, after responding to some, to complete his task by elimination and guessing.

5. Strive for homogeneity. It is very important with this type of item. In the item on page 178, all the right-hand parts were names of biologists who worked in the area of cellular theory and develop-

ment. No attempt was made to cover the entire history of biology or of science. The following item does not possess homogeneity:

——— 1. *Origin of Species*	(A)	digests starch
——— 2. saliva	(B)	emotions
——— 3. hereditary	(C)	lean meat
——— 4. diabetes	(D)	Charles Darwin
——— 5. vision	(E)	retina
——— 6. balance	(F)	insulin
——— 7. adrenalin	(G)	semicircular canals
——— 8. protein	(H)	leg bone
——— 9. femur	(I)	nucleus
——— 10. controls cell activity	(J)	gene
	(K)	arm bone

It covers the whole subject matter of biology. It is spread so thin that it has become easy. Look at it. *Origin of Species* is the only book title; it must be associated with "Charles Darwin," the only name. The uniqueness of each part makes the item a lot easier than it would be if the item possessed homogeneity.

6. If it is possible, for each correct response in the right-hand column have 2 or 3 other responses that are similar in certain ways and make good distractors. This is rather difficult to do, but, if done, the matching item is comparable to a well-made series of multiple-choice items which have been telescoped into the matching exercise.

ARRANGEMENT ITEMS

In history, science, and some mathematics courses, such as plane geometry, a list of facts or steps may be presented for the student to arrange in either logical or chronological order.

Answer the following items by placing a (1) in front of that which came first or appeared earliest; (2) for the second; and (3) for the third.

1.   2   Vesalius
     1   Galen
     3   Harvey
2.   1   Settling of Jamestown
     2   Plymouth Colony
     3   New Amsterdam

3. <u>3</u> Pearl Harbor
    <u>1</u> Hitler's invasion of Poland
    <u>2</u> Hitler's invasion of Belgium and France

Such items are most easily scored by giving a point or two for the correct solution of each group and making no attempt to give partial credit. When the items are longer, like these two below, it is hardly fair to treat them on an all or none basis.

4. <u>3</u> Battle of Lexington
    <u>6</u> Valley Forge
    <u>4</u> Declaration of Independence
    <u>9</u> Inauguration of Washington
    <u>1</u> Stamp Act
    <u>7</u> Arnold's betrayal
    <u>8</u> Battle of Yorktown
    <u>5</u> Battle of Saratoga
    <u>2</u> Boston Tea Party

5. Below are the steps that one goes through in computing a mean by the group method. Place a (1) in front of the first step and continue until all are numbered.

<u>3</u> Set up the frequency distribution
<u>5</u> Assume the mean to be in one of the intervals
<u>8</u> Use the equation

$$\bar{X} = M' + \frac{\Sigma f x'}{N}(i)$$

<u>2</u> Decide upon the size of the interval to use
<u>6</u> Set up an x' column
<u>4</u> Tally the scores
<u>1</u> Determine the range
<u>7</u> Find each fx' and their sum

With either of these two examples it is best to follow some plan, such as suggested by Remmers and Gage (10). These writers propose that, when more than 4 parts are to be arranged, first the sum of squared differences between correct and worse answers be obtained as follows:

Correct response	1	2	3	4	5	6
Worst order	6	5	4	3	2	1
Difference	5	3	1	1	3	5
Difference squared	25	9	1	1	9	25

In this case, the sum of the squares is 70. Suppose that a student arranged his responses 1, 5, 3, 2, 4, 6. The sum of his squared deviations from the correct order is 14. This sum can next be subtracted from the sum of the squares for the worst possible score, which in this case is 70. The higher this remainder the better the answer.

Cureton (3) developed a table that is entered with the sum of the deviations of a student's response from the key and the score is obtained from this table. The reader who plans to use arrangement items would find it worth his while to consult this article as the use of this table would save considerable time in the grading of these items.

APPLICATION AND INTERPRETATION ITEMS

As was noted in Chapter 6, one of the high points in the history of achievement testing was the Eight-Year Study (1) and the ensuing emphasis on attempting to evaluate all the objectives of education. The evaluation activities of this experiment have been recorded by Smith and Tyler (12), and the reader who wants more discussion about these evaluation methods than we give here is referred to that volume. Briefly, Tyler and his associates constructed tests that attempted to evaluate application of principles in science and in social science, application of the principles of logical reasoning, beliefs on social issues, interpretation of data, appreciation of literature, interests, personal and social adjustment, and ability to evaluate assumptions and proofs. Gradually, as the years go by, more and more of these attempts to measure the higher mental processes have appeared in the schools. In some of the training programs of the Armed Forces, examinations are administered which are made up almost entirely of these newer type items. In addition to the work of Smith and Tyler, the interested reader is also referred to Part I of the Forty-fifth Yearbook of the National Society for the Study of Education, *The Measurement of Understanding* (9). In this book he will find a chapter devoted to the problem of measuring understanding in each of the major subtest areas of the high-school curriculum, including the vocational subjects. It is a fruitful source of ideas for item-writing. An invaluable source of ideas and models for thought-provoking items is the *Taxonomy of Educational Objectives* (2).

More specifically the Twenty-sixth Yearbook of the National Council of Teachers of Mathematics (8) includes interpretation, application, and other varieties of evaluative items particularly adapted to mathematics. The Thirty-fifth Yearbook of the National Council for the Social Studies (7) has chapters on the evaluation of critical thinking in the social studies, the evaluation of basic skills in that area, the measurement of non-cognitive objectives in the social studies, and related topics. Either or both of these books would be valuable for any high school teacher even if he does not teach either of these areas specifically because of the illustrations that are applicable to other subjects.

Interpretation-of-data Items

The new type item will be illustrated first by an interpretation-of-data test item. The writer has found this type very useful in his own classes and feels that it should be much more widely used. In this type of item, data are presented to the student, who responds to the data on the basis of what he knows about the subject. These data may come from any source and can be in the form of verbal descriptions, maps, charts, graphs, tables of statistics, results of experiments, case studies, etc. The only criterion to be applied to the data is that the data be new to the student. It must be something that he has never seen before, something which has not been used in class. Most teachers have access to such data in their professional journals or in other textbooks not available to the student.

After the data, which are new, relevant, and practical, have been selected, test items are written. The items can be either in the true-false or multiple-choice form. Here is a situation in which 5-response true-false items can be easily used. Sometimes ideas for items can be obtained by merely including the data in an examination that is currently being administered and to ask each student to draw 5 conclusions from the data. Thirty students will provide 150 conclusions representing all shades of correctness from "absolutely true" to "absolutely false" and including some that are irrelevant. Fifteen or twenty of these of varying shades of truth are selected, and the item is made. Figure 8:1 illustrates one of these interpretation-of-data items that was constructed for a course in educational measurement. Here we have the profiles of three students, *A*, *B*, and *C* on 5 achievement tests and one intelligence test. Note that the items are to be interpreted in the light of the above data and what the student knows about such materials—that is, using the course content. Many such items using multiple-choice forms are found on standardized reading tests and tests covering the objectives of general education.

If multiple-choice items are used, scoring presents no special problem. But if 5-choice true-false responses are used, special considerations have to be taken. Suppose that an item is keyed "true." One student marks it "probably true," a second student marks it "probably false." There is no question that the first response is much better than the second. Notice in Figure 8:1 that the "true" response is marked (1), the "probably true" response (2), etc. In the situation at hand, the first student who marked "probably true" deviated by 1 unit (2 minus 1) and the second student by 3 (4 minus 1) from the correct response. To grade these, place the key in front of the student's response and mark each response on the basis of how far it deviates from the keyed response. These deviations are then summed and usually subtracted from an arbitrary constant. This is done to prevent having negative values for the interpretation item. For example, in the problem in Figure 8:1 a constant of 35 could be used, and the sum of each student's deviations subtracted from this. A few individuals might still end up with negative scores. These can be given a score of zero for the item. In dealing with younger children, a 3-point scale, such as T (true), CT (can't tell), and F (false), should be used instead of the one just described.

Each student can, when the papers are returned, set up a chart similar to the one shown in Figure 8:2, which has been adapted from Smith and Tyler(12). The student takes his responses and tallies them against the key. For example, suppose that for the first item the student marked "true" (1), but the item was keyed "probably true" (2). A tally mark is then placed in cell 2 in the scattergram. The student's response to the second item was, let us say, "insufficient data" (3), but the item was keyed "false" (5). This time a tally is placed in cell 15. In this fashion the student tallies all his responses against the key. If the number of items is small, this scatterplot could be kept and future item responses plotted on it to have a more reliable measure of behavior.

From this scattergram, various subscores can be obtained. Cells

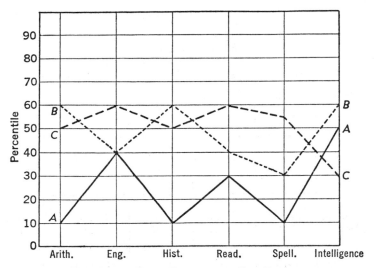

PROFILES OF THREE PUPILS ON A TEST BATTERY

Consider each of the following items in the light of the above data and of what you know of educational measurement and mark each one according to the following scale:

Data   (1) sufficient to make the statement true.

alone   (2) sufficient to indicate that the statement is probably true.

are   (3) not sufficient to indicate whether there is any degree of truth or falsity in the statement.

         (4) sufficient to indicate that the statement is probably false.

         (5) sufficient to make the statement false.

( ) 1. Pupil A is about normal intelligence.

( ) 2. If pupil C were to apply himself more, his grades would be better.

( ) 3. Pupil B is twice as bright as pupil C.

( ) 4. Pupil B is retarded in school.

( ) 5. Pupil C could be classified as an overachiever.

( ) 6. Pupil A has a score of 40 in English.

( ) 7. Of the 3 students, only B is working up to his ability.

( ) 8. If pupil B were motivated, he would do better work.

( ) 9. Arithmetic is the hardest subject in this class.

( ) 10. Pupil A would profit by remedial work in reading.

Fig. 8:1. INTERPRETATION-OF-DATA ITEM

1, 7, 13, 19, and 25 represent perfect agreement with the key. The percentage of the total number of tallies falling in these 5 cells could be obtained and the result called an ACCURACY SCORE. Cells 2, 3, 8, 18, 23, and 24 represent going beyond the data. For example, a tally

Key

Student Responses	1 True	2 Probably True	3 Insufficient Data	4 Probably False	5 False
1 True	Accurate 1	① Beyond Data 2	Beyond Data 3	Crude Error 4	Crude Error 5
2 Probably True	Caution 6	Accurate 7	Beyond Data 8	Crude Error 9	Crude Error 10
3 Insufficient Data	Caution 11	Caution 12	Accurate 13	Caution 14	① Caution 15
4 Probably False	Crude Error 16	Crude Error 17	Beyond Data 18	Accurate 19	Caution 20
5 False	Crude Error 21	Crude Error 22	Beyond Data 23	Beyond Data 24	Accurate 25

Fig. 8:2. Summary of Interpretation-of-Data Test Items *

in cell 2 means that a student has taken an item keyed "probably true" and decided that it was true. The percentage of the total numbers in these cells would give a "going beyond the data" score. Cells 6, 11, 12, 14, 15, and 20 represent the opposite of the above—that is, not going so far as the data allow or using caution. In the same manner as above, a "caution" score can be computed. The other 8 cells labeled "crude error" show the number of "true" or "probably true" items marked "false" or "probably false" or vice versa. A "crude error" score can also be computed as described above.

Once again it should be stated that the student does this plotting. Here he has a chance to enter into the evaluative process and to learn

* Adapted from chart appearing on page 54, *Appraising and Recording Student Progress.* Used by permission of the publishers, Harper and Brothers, Copyright 1942.

a bit about his own thinking process. This is true of many of the evaluative devices used in the Eight-Year Study.

Application of Principles Item

A second example of these newer type items is the application of principle item illustrated below by a part of P.E.A. Test 1.31. In this type of item, data are presented to the student, and he has to make a decision or to draw a conclusion that he thinks is most reasonable in the light of his knowledge about the situation and that is most consistent with the facts as given. Usually 3 conclusions or decisions are presented below the original data. These are followed by 10 or more so-called "reasons." The examinee goes through these and marks those which explain or support the conclusion that he checked.

In setting up these exercises, criteria similar to those used in selecting interpretation-of-data items are used. Smith and Tyler (12) list the specific criteria to be met in constructing these items as: (1) newness to the student; (2) similarity to a life-like situation; (3) significance of problem to daily living; and (4) appropriate vocabulary level.

The "reasons," which make up a large part of the item, consist of, along with a number of correct statements, statements of the following types:

1. False statements given as if they were true facts or correct principles. (See reason 1 in sample item.)

2. Irrelevant reasons. True statements are noted which are in no way related to the problem. (See reason 9.)

3. False analogies. Relating by analogy the phenomenon with some other to which it is not related.

4. Popular misconceptions. Here common beliefs with no factual basis are used.

5. Citation of unreliable authorities. Using statements which begin with "People say . . .", "They say . . .", etc.

6. Ridicule. The reasons start out like this. "It is ridiculous to think . . ." (See reason 2.)

7. Assuming the conclusion. (See reason 5.)

8. Teleology. This assumes that all living and nonliving things are purposive and rational. (See reason 10.)

These reasons are of the sort that students offer when they respond to such material as presented here when the material is given in essay or free-response form.

Items, such as P.E.A. item 1.31, are scored by computing the number of correct or appropriate reasons checked by the student and changing these into a percentage of the possible number of correct ones. Perhaps more important than the score is the analysis of the types of reasons selected by the examinee in justifying the conclusion that he drew. Concern here is with the number and type of different kinds of erroneous reasons selected. In other words, we are investigating the student's thinking, both from the viewpoint of accuracy and from the number and type of errors made. It might also be added that, for more reliable scores, a test should be made up of a series of these application items when we are attempting to appraise this objective of how individuals carry on critical thinking.

Below is an item that is one part of P.E.A. Test 1.31, *Applications of Principles in Chemistry.*

A motorist on a trip in the West had his tires checked to 25 pounds on the edge of Death Valley Desert at about 2:00 p.m. That night he stayed in a tourists' camp nearby. He remarked the next morning that he had been uncomfortably cold during the night. What happened to the tires on his car during the night?

Directions: Choose the conclusion which you believe is most consistent with the facts given above and most reasonable in the light of whatever knowledge you may have, and mark the appropriate space on the Answer Sheet under Problem IV.

Conclusions
   A. The tires on the car were flatter.
   B. One of the tires—an old, thin one—blew out.
   C. No change was observed in his tires.

Directions: Choose the reasons you would use to explain or support your conclusion and fill in the appropriate spaces on your Answer Sheet.

Reasons
   1. As temperature decreases, the pressure exerted and the volume occupied by a confined body of air increase.

2. It is ridiculous to think that tires do not become flatter on cold nights.
3. Just as a warm piece of metal cools on a cake of ice, so a warm body of confined air decreases in volume when the temperature is lowered.
4. Tire manufacturers say that tires are flatter in cold weather than in hot weather.
5. Tires on automobiles are flatter on cold days than on hot days.
6. When temperature decreases, the pressure of a confined body of air decreases.
7. The pressure exerted and the volume occupied by a confined body of air remain constant as the temperature of the air changes.
8. As the pressure of air in an expansible container decreases, the volume of the air decreases.
9. Cold air is heavier than warm air.
10. Air adjusts itself to a lower temperature by contracting.
11. If a tire becomes "soft," it is due to a leak in the tube.

A third type of item to be illustrated is that called the *Nature of Proof* (P.E.A. Test 5.2). In our society individuals are constantly being confronted with so-called "proofs"—why they should do or believe various things. The radio, television, newspapers, and magazines, especially in their advertising, are forever suggesting that people believe this, buy that, vote for this candidate, continue to smoke a certain cigarette, trade cars, and do many other things. How do our students react to these "proofs"?

With this picture of American life in front of them, the research workers in the Eight-Year Study described the types of behavior involved in reacting to these "proofs" (12). Analyses showed that these behaviors included the disposition to analyze proofs critically; the recognition of basic assumptions upon which a conclusion depends; and an awareness of the need for more data before any conclusion can be drawn.

With this type of item, a problem, similar to those used in the other examples in this section, is set up and completed by a conclusion. This is followed by a series of statements, each of which is to be evaluated as shown in the item below. Responses can be analyzed

from the viewpoint of accuracy—that is, agreement with the key—
and analyzed diagnostically into the types of errors made.

This item is one of a series that make up P.E.A. Test 5.2, *The Nature of Proof.*

Are you learning to recognize and evaluate assumptions? It is an established fact that a small piece of magnesium will ignite and burn with a bright light in an atmosphere of chlorine gas, leaving white ashes. Bill knew this fact. He secured some chemicals, which when mixed together and heated, gave off a colored gas. He collected some of this gas in a bottle. The chemistry teacher gave him a small piece of magnesium. Bill put it in the bottle of colored gas. The magnesium ignited, burned with a bright light, and left white ashes. *Bill told his friends that his results conclusively proved that the colored gas was chlorine.*

Part 1. Directions: Read each statement below. Is the statement a FACT, or is it an ASSUMPTION? Place a check mark in the appropriate column before the statement. If you think the statement is neither a fact nor an assumption, place your check mark in the column headed "neither."

Part 2. Directions: Read over again *only* those statements which you have marked as ASSUMPTIONS. Place a check mark on the blanks *after* those ASSUMPTIONS which *you must accept as true* and which are *absolutely necessary* in proving that the gas was chlorine.

List of Statements

Fact	Assumption	Neither		
———	———	———	*a.* If he repeated the experiment in exactly the same way he would get exactly the same result.	———
———	———	———	*b.* The material the chemistry teacher gave him was magnesium.	———
———	———	———	*c.* That chlorine gas is the only gas in which magnesium will ignite, burn with	

List of Statements (Cont.)

Fact   Assumption   Neither

————   ————   ————

a bright light, leaving white ashes.   ————

————   ————   ————   *d.* Bill mixed and heated some chemicals which gave off a colored gas.   ————

————   ————   ————   *e.* It is an established fact that a small piece of magnesium will ignite and burn with a bright light in an atmosphere of chlorine gas, leaving white ashes.   ————

————   ————   ————   *f.* That it is possible to collect chlorine gas in a bottle.   ————

————   ————   ————   *g.* Bill collected some of the colored gas in a bottle.   ————

————   ————   ————   *h.* That the presence of the colored gas in the bottle was the only cause of the magnesium igniting, burning with a bright light, and leaving white ashes.   ————

————   ————   ————   *i.* Bill put a small piece of magnesium in the bottle.   ————

————   ————   ————   *j.* That no other gas was present in the bottle or collected in the bottle but the colored gas.   ————

————   ————   ————   *k.* That chlorine gas could result from mixing and heating the chemicals he used.   ————

————   ————   ————   *l.* That he (Bill) had sufficient knowledge of chemistry to conduct an experiment and to interpret the results.   ————

————   ————   ————   *m.* The colored gas must be chlorine.   ————

List of Statements (Cont.)

Fact   Assumption Neither

———   ———   ———   *n.* That the magnesium ignited, burned with a bright
light, and left white ashes.   ———

———   ———   ———   *o.* That no other gas has
properties quite similar to
chlorine.   ———

———   ———   ———   *p.* That chlorine is a colored
gas.   ———

Are you learning how to develop a logical proof? When arguments for or against some proposition are presented in newspapers, magazines, speeches, or textbooks, we often feel that the
discussion could have been made more logical. Authors sometimes
put in statements that are really unnecessary to prove their point;
at other times they leave out important arguments; on still other
occasions they arrange their statements in such poor order that
the conclusion does not seem to be based on or to grow out of the
arguments.

Part 3. Directions: Suppose *you* were describing this experiment
in order to prove that chlorine gas was collected. What are *all* of
the *absolutely necessary* steps in the complete development of
the proof? Use as many of the statements above as are *necessary*
and place the letters of these statements in their proper order on
the line below. Do not use any unnecessary statements.

*Are you learning to support your own conclusions with sound
arguments?*

Part 4. Directions: In Part 3 of this test you presented a logically
developed proof which reached the conclusion that the colored
gas Bill made must be chlorine. You may or may not believe
that it has been adequately proved that the colored gas must be
chlorine. Check the statement which best represents your own
personal opinion as to the nature of the gas:

——— *a.* I believe that the colored gas Bill made was chlorine.

——— *b.* I do not believe that the colored gas Bill made was
chlorine.

——— *c.* I do not believe that it has been adequately proved that
the colored gas Bill made was chlorine.

Write out the reasons you have to support your opinion.

Are you learning to judge the reasonableness of assumptions, accepting only those which are more or less true and relevant?

Part 5. Directions: Whether you agree with the conclusion or not, you do have some opinion regarding each single statement given in the List of Statements. Place the letter of each statement on the appropriate line below.

(Place the letters of the statements here.)

1. I accept because they are true, or probably true, or more true than false, these statements: _____
2. I reject because they are false, or probably false, or more false than true, these statements: _____
3. I am undecided about these statements: _____

EXERCISES

1. For a unit of work in your subject-matter area, construct 10 correction-type true-false items.
2. Change the above items to completion items.
3. Try reviewing the important facts of this unit by a well-made matching exercise.
4. Construct an arrangement item of at least 6 parts in your teaching area.
5. Obtain data in your teaching area and set up an interpretation-of-data problem-type item using a 5-response true-false scale.
6. For another set of data, set up the items in multiple-choice form.

REFERENCES

Some of the references listed below that are not specifically referred to in the chapter are listed as sources of ideas on item writing.
1. Aiken, W. M. *The story of the Eight-Year Study.* New York: Harper, 1942.
2. Bloom, B. S., ed. *Taxonomy of educational objectives. Handbook I: The cognitive domain.* New York: David McKay, 1956.
3. Cureton, E. E. The rearrangement item. *Educ. psychol. Measmt.*, 1960, 20, 31-6.

4. Ebel, R. L. *Measuring educational achievement.* Englewood Cliffs, N. J.: Prentice-Hall, 1965.
5. Green, J. A. *Teacher-made tests.* New York: Harper and Row, 1963.
6. Lindquist, E. F. *Educational measurement.* Washington, D. C.: American Council on Education, 1951. Chapter 7.
7. National Council for the Social Studies. 35th Yearbook. *Evaluation in social studies.* Washington, D. C.: The Council, 1965.
8. National Council of Teachers of Mathematics. 26th Yearbook. *Evaluation in mathematics. Washington,* D. C.: The Council, 1961.
9. National Society for the Study of Education. 45th Yearbook, Part 1. *The measurement of understanding.* Chicago: University of Chicago Press, 1946.
10. Remmers, H. H., and Gage, N. L. *Educational measurement.* Rev. ed. New York: Harper, 1955.
11. Remmers, H. H., *et al. A practical introduction to measurement and evaluation.* New York: Harper and Row, 1960.
12. Smith, E. R., and Tyler, R. W. *Appraising and recording student progress.* New York: Harper, 1942.
13. Wood, Dorothy A. *Test construction: Development and interpretation of achievement tests.* Columbus, O.: Merrill, 1960.
14. Wrightstone, J. W. *Evaluation in modern education.* New York: American Book, 1956.

THE ESSAY TEST

For many years after the introduction of written examinations, practically all tests were of the so-called "essay" type. In the first decade of this century some rumblings were heard which foreboded that all was not well.

RELIABILITY AND VALIDITY OF THE ESSAY TEST

In 1908, Max Meyer (12) at the University of Missouri, after studying the grades handed out by a large group of instructors over a 5-year period, showed such results as 55 per cent of the students getting an "A" in a certain philosophy course and only 1 per cent in an English course, 28 per cent failures in English II, none in Latin I. Studies at other universities showed this to be the usual pattern rather than the exception.

Reliability of the Essay Test

Early in the second decade of this century, Starch and Elliott (18) performed one of the most famous pieces of pioneering work in educational research. They took two English themes of equal merit and had them graded by 142 English teachers on the basis of 100 per cent. Grades on the first paper ranged between 50 and 98 with a median of 80.2 and on the second paper between 64 and 99 with a median of 88.2. The variability of the two sets of grades was about the same.

These results were not too unexpected for, after all, English composition is a rather subjective subject. Later, Starch and Elliott (17) sent a plane geometry paper to 138 geometry teachers for grading. This time the grades ranged between 28 and 95 with a rather normal spread throughout the range. Geometry had been considered to be an objective subject. These findings were rather amazing to early educators. Results similar to Starch and Elliott's have been confirmed over and over again in later years. One of these later studies was carried out by Falls (9) who asked 100 English teachers to grade a paper written by a high-school senior and to estimate the grade level at which they thought the writer of the essay to be. This essay, incidentally, was selected by a committee as being a first-class piece of work, and the writer of the essay, interested in journalism, was a correspondent for a large metropolitan daily. Grades on this paper ranged from 60 to 98, and the writer of the paper was said to be at levels ranging from fifth grade to a junior in college.

Other studies have been concerned with the different scores obtained when the same examiner regrades a paper. Any teacher can perform this experiment. Read the papers the first time, putting no grades on the papers but recording them on a separate sheet of paper. A week or a month later, again grade the papers. Compute a correlation coefficient between the two sets of grades. Unless the teacher is very unusual, there will not be a high correlation between the two sets of scores. James (11) selected 4 compositions judged of equal merit and reproduced 2 of them in good handwriting and 2 in poor. Forty-three English teachers graded the papers for him. Two months later the same themes were presented to the same English teachers but with the handwriting reversed. The 2 that had been in good penmanship were now in bad writing and vice versa. This time there was a difference of about 8 points or one letter grade in favor of the good writing. The writer once knew a rather unambitious student who took a summer-school course requiring a large number of abstracts of research articles to be handed in weekly. This student borrowed a complete collection of these abstracts from a student who had taken the course the previous summer. All were in longhand and each had been graded. The contribution of the second student was merely to type each one before handing it in. These were returned consistently graded one letter higher than the handwritten version.

Ashburn (3) has stated that the passing or failing of about 40 per cent of students depends not on what they know or don't know but upon *who* reads their papers. Also the passing or failing of 10 per cent of the papers depends on *when* the papers are read. Consider the situation of the teacher who takes a stack of papers home and starts reading them after dinner. At seven o'clock he is relatively fresh and the papers receive his critical attention. At midnight he is still reading papers. It has been a long day and a longer evening. Now many things slip by which earlier in the evening would have caused credit to be deducted. Scores then tend to rise as time passes. Where a paper lands in a pile also has an effect upon its grade. For example, consider the paper of the "C" student which follows that of an "A" student. Another "C" student is luckier and his paper follows that of an illiterate "F" student. The first student's "C" may turn into a "D" and the second student's into a "B."

Diederich (5) has shown that many of the so-called "values" of the essay test can be discredited by a judicious selection of papers. Essay tests in English are frequently claimed to measure growth and progress between the first of the semester and the end. Diederich claims that by the appropriate selection of papers and topics he can show as much gain between papers written before lunch and those written after lunch as between the beginning and end of the semester. After all, it is traditional for teachers to grade the first theme severely and to ease up as the semester goes on. Diederich also feels that teachers get accustomed to students' styles as the year goes on and tend to become more lenient.

That the situation has not changed over the years has been demonstrated by Anderson (2) who administered Forms A and B, level 3, of the essay test of *Sequential Tests of Educational Progress* to 55 eighth-grade students on four different testing occasions. Students wrote the Form A essay in the morning and B in the afternoon. At weekly intervals for the next 3 weeks the students wrote essays on the same 2 topics. In all each student wrote 8 essays, four on each form, on 4 different testing occasions. These 440 essays were graded by 3 experienced readers on 4 different marking occasions over intervals of approximately one week. Both students and readers were paid for their time, and it was also noted that the 3 readers were interested in the project. Anderson analyzed his data using an F-test (a test of significance) and found that the F value for readers, for tests, for testing occasions, and the interaction between readers and marking occasions were all significant beyond the 1 per cent level. This significant difference among markers or readers again illustrated what had already been shown many times previously, the difference between the two essays showed the unrepresentative character of a single essay, and the difference between testing occasions demonstrated the fluctuation in the function underlying composition ability. The significant interaction of markers by marking occasions was evidence that the grading standards of some readers fluctuate from time to time more than do the standards of others. Individual analyses were also made of the 8 essays written by each of the 55 students. Of these, 39 or 71 per cent showed significant differences in the compositions written from occasion to occasion, and 78 per cent demonstrated significant marker or reader variability.

In another study conducted by the Educational Testing Service (7), 300 essays written by college students were rated by 53 outstanding representatives in 6 different fields on a scale from 1 to 9. It was found that all essays received at least 5 of the 9 possible ratings, 34 per cent received all 9 ratings, 23 per cent received 7, and 5 per cent received 6.

In another study carried on at Educational Testing Service (6) a sample of students from institutions that used the College Board examinations wrote two 40-minute and three 20-minute essays. Each essay was rapidly read by 5 readers who scored it on a 3-point scale. In the end the 5 papers written by each student were read by 5 different sets of 5 readers and the scores from all these readers were summed. To establish consistency among the readers in reading, all markers of papers scored sets of sample essays on all 5 topics several times during the first two days of scoring and noted where their grades stood on a distribution of grades for each test. The reading reliability for each essay, that is agreement among readers, fell between .74 and .78. When each essay was treated as one item on a 5-item test, a reliability coefficient for the total test was .84. Similar results were reported by Sale (14) who showed that by a systematic approach the reliability coefficients associated with the English tests of the College Boards would be in the .70's and .80's.

A summary of the reader reliability of essay tests was made by

Vernon and Millican (19). They noted first that inexperienced readers are more reliable than experienced ones because the former tend to mark on the basis of mechanics and details, whereas the more experienced readers tend to base their evaluations on such aspects of a theme as style, thought content, and the like. Thus the former produce more reliable results. Second, they noted that highly trained markers are much more reliable than the untrained. Third, it was found that long responses are more reliable than short ones. Fourth, they observed that there was a positive relationship between the specificity or precision of the marking criteria used and the reliability of the marking. Fifth, a positive relationship between the amount of structure in the question and the reliability of the readers was found. Sixth, they stated that the greater the variability found in the samples of essay writers, the higher the reliability; and, last, they stated that familiarity with the writer of an essay leads to greater reliability than does unfamiliarity.

All of the above remarks are actually concerned with the reliability of the reader, marker, or grader of the essay test. Nothing had been said about the reliability of the essay test itself because very little research has been done on this topic. In one of the few articles on this problem Cureton (4) stated that to obtain an estimate of the reliability of an essay test, or of any subjective test such as most of our projective instruments, two equivalent forms of the test are necessary at the start and that these must be administered to the subjects at an optimal time interval. Each reader must read all of the answers to a given question on both forms A and B. When these conditions are met, and then only, the correlation between grades obtained with form A and those obtained with form B may be considered as an estimate of the reliability of the subjective test.

In summary, reliability of the essay test seems not to have increased greatly in the 60 years covered by this summarized research. That essay questions can be read reliably is no longer a question to be debated. We have studies that repeatedly show this, especially work done with the College Boards. A basic reason for a large part of the unreliability is that the typical reader of essay tests considers himself a final authority and grades his papers absolutely. He feels no need of any statistician or psychologist to help him do a job that he knows he is doing well.

Validity of the Essay Test

In Chapter 4 it was shown that achievement tests are validated by the so-called "content method." That is, a test is valid because it adequately covers the subject matter and the objectives of a course or unit of a course. Objective test items allow for very extensive sampling, and hence this type of validity is assured. But the typical essay test is limited to 5 or 6 questions for an hour examination. Obviously, much of the content has to be omitted. Many times after taking such a test, students remark about the great waste of their study time because so large a share of the course was not covered by the essay questions. The writer has seen essay tests the questions of which were based on obscure footnotes and even on the preface of one of the books read in the course. Validity then tends to be low because of poor sampling.

Secondly, validity is lowered because of the situations that arise in which an individual is given credit for saying something even if he has nothing to say. A student reaches an item about which he knows very little. He, however, doesn't let a trifle like this bother him and proceeds to write 4 or 5 pages of miscellaneous rambling on the topic. After the reader wades through all this, he feels that the student knows something about the topic and gives him a certain amount of credit. A more honest student, also knowing nothing about the question, omits it and, of course, gets a zero for that question. Such a premium on words lowers validity.

Thirdly, validity is affected adversely by the fact that frequently papers are graded for several things simultaneously. A reader of a biology paper begins taking off credit for poor spelling or grammar and the biology score gets lower and lower because of these deductions. Thus the grade does not show what the student knows about biology but is a hybrid that reveals achievement neither in biology nor in English. In such cases the paper should have two grades— one based upon achievement in biology, the other upon mastery of spelling and grammar.

THE ESSAY TEST IN THE CLASSROOM

Despite low validity and reliability, this type of test item is very popular with teachers.

Uses of Essay Tests

Essay tests are very popular as measures of classroom achievement. Over the past years much has been written about the relative merits of the essay test and the objective test. Basically the claims may be reduced to two major ones as Scannell (15) has shown: (1) the essay tests foster skill in writing and (2) the essay tests are more realistic in terms of adult needs. Let us take up the first claim that the use of the essay test promotes skill in writing. An essay test more or less typical for a class period of about one hour contains from 4 to 6 questions. In answering those questions the student usually begins with item 1, briefly thinks about it, takes the first idea that comes into his head, develops this idea for 8-10 minutes, stops, then goes on to the next question and repeats this procedure. No one will argue that students do not need practice and training in writing. But it is unfortunate if this time spent on examinations is the chief or only amount of time in the school program that can be devoted to the development of writing skill. To write a genuine essay requires time. The writer must do some thinking and organizing, probably constructing an outline. He most likely would want to spend as much time as the entire testing period on these preliminary activities. For certain types of examinations, where essay tests are used, there is considerable merit in allowing the student a "take-home" examination, giving him a week or so to complete it.

Notice that the essay test being discussed so far is actually concerned with the organization and expression of ideas. In many courses, items included in essay tests are in reality not essay tests at all. Consider such an item as to name the main parts of the eye and to give the function of each part. Actually this is a short-answer question requiring nothing but the recall of factual information. As has been shown, such material can be more efficiently and economically measured by the use of objective test items.

The second alleged merit of the essay test item is that it is much more realistic in terms of adult needs. This implies that, in taking an objective test, such as a multiple-choice test, one merely checks a space on the answer sheet, but that various life activities require one to organize his ideas and offer them in writing. Actually when multiple-choice items are well made, one does much more than merely make a mark on an answer sheet. One has to evaluate, to make decisions, to apply facts and principles, and to carry on other types of thinking when confronted with the 4 or 5 given solutions to a well-written question. Isn't this a common occurence in daily living? Isn't the bridge or chess player always confronted with several possibilities, one of which will lead to more desirable results than the others? Isn't the individual about to purchase a new automobile or hi-fi set confronted with a similar group of possibilities? Isn't it so that in daily living we are constantly facing situations where we have to make a choice among the various possibilities offered? In these situations we apply what we know, what we have learned from experience, and then we hope that we have made the best choice in our decision. One might further ask just when or how often one has to organize and write out his ideas in situations similar to those that he encountered as a student. Also it might be added that these essays are written for a person who knows much more about the subject than does the writer.

If we cannot truly assert that essay tests foster skill in writing and answer adult needs better than objective tests, why use the essay tests? Probably for most classroom situations they are unnecessary except to evaluate how well a student can write a theme or essay. If we want to assess style, quality, and other aspects of writing, it is obvious that the essay test item has to be used. Even here though studies have shown that objective tests of writing ability can predict achievement in writing, the latter measured by both teachers' estimates and grades received, better than do the essay tests. Typical of these studies is that reported by Huddleston (10) in which she used an objective verbal test, the English examination of the College Boards, a paragraph revision test, an English essay examination, and a total English test score based upon the last 3 of these. Scores on these tests were correlated with teachers' ratings taken over two years of English and with course grades in English averaged over a similar two-year period. Results showed the essay test to be more valid than the paragraph revision test, but less valid than the verbal test, the College Board English test, and the total English test. The verbal test predicted the most accurately of any of the tests.

In the Educational Testing Service study (6) described in the section on reliability it was noted that reliable essay scores were obtained for a group of students who wrote 5 essays. These total essay scores became the criterion in a study designed to investigate how well these scores agreed with scores on an objective test of English composition measuring usage, sentence correction, paragraph organization, prose groups, error recognition, and construction shifts. An interlinear, a badly written passage that examinees are asked to edit, was also used. It may be recalled that the total essay scores were quite reliable, the coefficient being .84. The obtained correlations in this study ranged between .46 and .71 with a median value of .64. When scores on various combinations of three of these subtests were summed to make a one-hour examination, the highest correlation of such a sum with the criterion was .78. When this coefficient is corrected to remove the effects of unreliability in the measures, the correlation between the best combination of objective tests and the criterion is about .89. Thus the objective items on the English composition test are as effective in ranking students' writing ability as a trained group of readers would be using a sizable sample of their writing. The use of the interlinear for one of the objective items increased the predictive effectiveness slightly. A full hour of such interlinears correlated about .68 with the criterion. Also an hour-long essay test was administered and results from this correlated with the same criterion with a resulting coefficient of .69. Thus the one-hour objective test measured writing ability more effectively than either the interlinear or the hour-long essay test.

In another study reported in the same Educational Testing Service publication one answer is given to the question as to whether prediction would be increased if a sample of students' writing was used along with scores on the *Scholastic Aptitude Tests*, both *Verbal* and *Mathematical*, and with high school rank. The following results were obtained in an Eastern liberal arts college:

Predictors	Criteria	
	Semester English	Semester Average
V + M + rc	.42	.66
V + M + rc + ECT	.46	.68
V + M + rc + WS	.46	.67

where:

V = Scholastic Aptitude Test—Verbal
M = Scholastic Aptitude Test—Mathematical
rc = high school rank
ECT = english composition test
WS = writing sample

From the above it is seen that there is only a slight increment in prediction when scores on the english composition test or the writing sample are used. Neither adds anything of practical importance to the original 3 basic predictors.

Essay tests have also been used to measure a student's interests and attitudes. School counselors use them in this manner to obtain information for educational and vocational counseling. Sims (16) has recently written on the use of the essay test as a projective device. This sort of technique implies that, when the individual is responding to it, he unwittingly reveals information about his own adjustment problems. People let things slip out. Proper interpretation of these statements aids in an evaluation of one's adjustment problems.

Construction of Essay Tests

The main problem in making essay-test items is finding or stating questions that are neither too general nor too specific. Consider the following items:

1. Discuss electricity.
2. Discuss intelligence.
3. Write an essay on the Civil War.

Each is so general that on any one of them 30 students could each spend 30 minutes and the 30 papers would have nothing in common. If behavior is to be evaluated and graded, then there has to be something in common on which to do the grading. Each of the above questions is appropriate for the topic of a book, but hardly for a test item. These items are unclear in purpose and difficult to grade.

Let us rewrite the second of the above questions. First we let it read:

2. Discuss the history of our concepts of intelligence.

The item is still broad, but it should force the respondent to answer it developmentally.

Next the item is written:

    2. Discuss the various theories of intelligence held by psychologists from about 1880 to the present.

This question specifies the limits within which the discussion must take place. Such an item allows the instructor to assess the relative importance that students place on the various theories and on the relationship among the theories. However, it is questionable if it is good measurement practice in an achievement test to have situations where the relative importance of the components enters into the appraisal.

Then the item is expanded further:

    2. Discuss the leading psychological theories of intelligence from 1880 to the present. Give the basic concepts of each theory, name several important individuals associated with each, and critically evaluate each theory.

This item as it now stands is very specific as to what is to be discussed. It gives the student an opportunity to recall basic information and to show that he understands the various theories of intelligence.

Finally the item is written:

    2. Discuss intelligence from the unifactor, two-factor, and multifactor points of view. Give ideas of the proponents and opponents of each theory.

The wording here limits the discussion to the 3 stated theories and to the notions of the advocates of each. It may be almost entirely a recall item prompting the student to do little more than list ideas remembered from class lectures or texts. The problem is entirely organized by the statement of the question. Thus, it provides little opportunity to test students' ability to organize. The third and fourth statements of this question about intelligence are the best items. The issue is between being too general and too specific. There are no rules to help here. Common sense and experience are important in the writing of essay-type test items.

In making an essay examination, we should note alongside each item its numerical value or the time to be allotted to it. The examinee then knows how his time is to be distributed, and we avoid the situation where the student spends time on a question all out of proportion to its value.

If students are to be compared on their relative achievement, it is advisable to have all students respond to all items. In other words, on a typical achievement test, there should be no choice, for, if sampling is allowed, it is impossible to compare performances. It is not unfair to expect all students to answer all items that are valid measures of achievement in the course of study being pursued. It is very probable that choice on an essay test helps the poor student more than it does the better one. Sometimes on examinations that are very broad in scope, such as the preliminary examinations written by students taking their doctorate, a wide choice is allowed among questions to be answered. Even in this situation, this practice is debatable. It might be better to narrow the field and have students write complete tests in more limited areas that specifically pertain to their course of study.

A different problem comes up in the writing of themes or in the writing of a theme on a test. It is generally accepted that an individual can write better on a topic in which he has an interest or on a subject in which he has been involved. It follows then that to ask all students to write on the same theme will result in variability in grades on these themes that is basically related to a student's interest in the topic. Given another topic any student might do better or worse. It has often been the practice to offer a limited choice when it comes to the writing of a theme on an achievement test.

Grading Essay Tests

The grading of essay tests is probably more important than writing the items. The following procedures should be followed:

1. Make all papers anonymous. This can be done by turning back the covers if the answers are written in an answer book, or by

assigning a number, unknown to the reader, to each paper. This numbering can be done by the students. The first student in each row can assign numbers to all papers in his row. When the papers are graded, then names and numbers can be associated. Bias, prejudice, or the "halo effect" affect grades when this procedure is not followed. By "halo effect" is meant the influence of one or two of an individual's characteristics or traits on our over-all rating or opinion of him. Suppose that an attractive, well-mannered girl leaves out several important parts of the answer to a question. The teacher is certain that this girl knows the correct answers and that she merely forgot to write them down. No credit is deducted. On the other hand, a boy who never gets his work done or does not hand it in on time and who is also an all-around general nuisance omits the same answers as the girl. Since he never does anything correctly or on time, he loses 10 points for his omissions. All human beings are affected in one way or another by other individuals. The nature of these interactions strongly influences our conscious and unconscious behavior toward others.

2. Take the first item of the test and make an outline of all the points which are to be covered. Give each of these a value. Do this for all the items on the test.

3. Take the first paper and read the first answer. Compare the student's response with the outline already made. Next read the response to the first question on all the papers. Then continue with the second question and so on until all questions have been read. This procedure leads to consistency as the reader or grader is attending to one question at a time. Also the effects of fatigue described earlier are controlled.

Some prefer, rather than make a check list as described above, to use a sorting method. This procedure is as follows: (1) Read rapidly through all the answers to the first item on the test and on the basis of your opinion of the answers sort the papers into five piles: (a) very superior, (b) superior, (c) average, (d) inferior, (e) very inferior. (2) Reread the items in each group and pull out and reassign any which are felt to be in the incorrect pile. (3) Assign values to the item depending on the pile into which the paper has fallen. For example, a 20-point question could, on the basis of the

5-point breakdown above, be assigned 20 points for "very superior," 16 points for "superior," 12 for "average," 8 for "inferior," and 4 for "very inferior." (4) Continue this process as described above until all items on the test have been graded.

Unless a method similar to the two described is used, the teacher might just as well take his papers and throw them up the stairs, assigning the highest grade to the paper that reaches the highest step. Reliability here by chance would be zero. Haphazard reading of essay-test items does not produce reliability coefficients much higher than this.

Engelhardt (8) summarized the use of the essay test, covering some points that we have already commented upon:

1. Use an essay test to assess achievement that cannot be more efficiently measured by the use of objective tests.
2. Structure questions that are used in grading so that all will attack the question in the same manner and their work may then be evaluated in a comparative fashion. Unstructured questions are useful in assessing attitudes and the like, the responses to which are not graded.
3. Only questions that can be answered in the allotted time should be used. A few good, well-thought-out questions may make a better test than a series of short items or one or two general and long ones.
4. Use the words "contrast," "compare," "evaluate," "explain," and the like in the questions as items containing these words are thought provoking.
5. Allow no choice in the students' responses to the items.
6. Use a point system of scoring based upon those elements that are expected to appear in the answers.
7. Score questions on the basis of points. Forget all about the system with a top score of 100 per cent and with such a value as 70 per cent being the passing point.
8. Score papers anonymously.
9. When two or more teachers use the same test, let the teachers agree upon the scoring procedure to be followed, try out this procedure on a few papers, and then have all the teachers read all questions, or have one teacher read one particular question

on all of the papers, another teacher another question, etc. Such a process improves reader reliability as we have shown.

10. Compute a cumulative score from the reading of several essays since such scores are more reliable than the score of any one essay taken separately. This was pointed out in the 1963 report of the Educational Testing Service (6).

Comparison of Essay and Objective Examinations

When these two types of examinations are compared, the following differences or similarities show up:

1. The essay test is usually less reliable than the objective test.

2. The objective test is usually more valid than the essay test because of its greater sampling of content material.

3. Essay tests are economical in time and effort when it comes to making them; expensive in both of these aspects when it comes to reading and scoring them. The reverse is true for objective tests.

4. Essay tests are cheap from an institutional point of view in that questions may be and often are written on the board and students supply their own paper for their answers. In the making of objective tests especially for large classes, reams of paper are needed.

5. Essay tests save time when the group tested is small. A class of 10 is much more suited to an essay test than a class of 100.

6. Guessing may be a problem on objective tests just as bluffing may be a problem on an essay test.

7. Both may be used to measure the various outcomes of learning such as the application of knowledge to new situations, the solution of problems, the evaluation of material and of ideas, etc. The assessment of such processes is not confined to the peculiar domain of the essay test provided that the essay test builder is skilled in the art of test item writing.

8. In the past it was claimed that a student studied one way for an objective test, in another fashion for the essay test. This was probably true when the objective test did nothing but measure the recognition and recall of factual matter. But with the newer and better type of objective items in use today built to measure

the diverse objectives of education, we have no evidence that study habits used in preparation for these objective tests are different from those used in getting ready for an essay test. Students study to pass tests. If the tests stress the assessment of varrious educational objectives, these the students will prepare for regardless of the type of test to be taken.

9. The essay test item is more life-like and realistic than the objective test item. This we have shown to be not true. If anything, the situations set up for objective test items are more similar to those encountered in daily living.

10. Students prefer essay tests to objective tests. Inconclusive research has been carried on related to this question. Perhaps, the real issue here is whose essay tests, whose objective tests. It is the writer's opinion that students are more concerned with the quality and validity of the various test items that they have to answer than they are with the basic forms in which the items appear.

Evaluation of Products

There are other situations in academic work where the techniques described above for grading essay examinations can also be used. The home economics, shop, and agriculture teachers frequently have to evaluate student products or projects and assign grades or scores to each. The procedure is basically the same. First, make a list of exactly what is going to be rated or graded. Then assign points to each listing on the basis of what your experience shows to be correct and rate the product or project. The sorting method described above can be used in still other areas. Students in special areas who want detailed information on how to evaluate products and projects should consult Adkins (1) or Micheels and Karnes (13).

EXERCISES

1. Using the principles described in this chapter, make an essay question in your subject-matter area for each of the following activities:

a. Comprehension
b. Explanation
c. Criticism and evaluation

d. Discussion
e. Interpretation
f. Summarization

2. Take each of the items above and outline the points that are to be used in evaluating the students' responses.
3. Duplicate the responses to an essay-test item and pass them out for grading by each member of the class. Summarize, compare, and discuss the results.
4. As a special project, students whose major teaching area is agriculture, home economics, industrial education, or physical education should make up a check list for the evaluation of a product, project, or activity in their area. Science students can do the same for a laboratory experiment or demonstration. English and social studies teachers can work on the evaluation of themes and essays.

REFERENCES

1. Adkins, D., *et al. Construction and analysis of achievement tests.* Washington, D. C.: Government Printing Office, 1947. Chapter 5.
2. Anderson, C. C. The new STEP Essay Test as a measure of composition ability. *Educ. Psychol. Measmt.,* 1960, 20, 95-102.
3. Ashburn, R. R. An experiment in the essay-type question. *J Exper. Educ.,* 1938, 7, 1-13.
4. Cureton, E. E. Definition and estimation of test reliability. *Educ. Psychol. Measmt.,* 1958, 18, 715-38.
5. Diederich, P. B. The use of essays to measure improvement. *College English,* 1949, 10, 395-9.
6. Educational Testing Service. Composition test shows high validity as reliable criterion of writing ability. *ETS Developments,* 11:1, Jan. 1963.
7. Educational Testing Service. Judges disagree on qualities that characterize good writing. *ETS Developments,* 9: 2, Feb. 1961.
8. Engelhardt, M. D. Improving classroom testing. *What research has to say to the teacher,* No. 31. Washington, D. C.: National Education Association, 1964.
9. Falls, J. D. Research in secondary education. *Kentucky School Journal,* 1928, 6, 42-6.
10. Huddleston, Edith. Measurement of writing ability at the college entrance level: Objective vs. subjective testing techniques. *J. exper. Psychol.,* 1954, 22, 165-213.
11. James, H. W. The effect of handwriting upon grading. *The English Journal,* 1927, 16, 180-85.
12. Meyer, Max. Grading of students. *Science.* 1908, 28, 243-50.
13. Micheels, W. J., and Karnes, M. R. *Measuring educational achievement.* New York: McGraw-Hill, 1950.

14. Sale, W. M. College Entrance Examination Board Examinations in English. *Report of Freshman English Conference,* Syracuse University. Syracuse, N. Y.: Syracuse University Press, 1946. Pp. 41-4.
15. Scannell, D. P. To write or not to write: That's the question. *Bull. of Education,* University of Kansas, Vol. 14, No. 2, 1960.
16. Sims, V. M. The essay examination as a projective technique. *Educ. Psychol. Measmt.,* 1948, 18, 15-31.
17. Starch, D., and Elliott, E. C. Reliability of grading work in mathematics. *School Review,* 1913, 21, 254-9.
18. Starch, D., and Elliott, E. C. Reliability of the grading of high school work in English. *School Review,* 1912, 20, 442-5.
19. Vernon, P. E., and Millican, G. D. A further study of the reliability of English essays. *British j. stat. Psychol.,* 1954, 7, 65-74.

CHAPTER 1

ITEM ANALYSIS

$\mathbb{A}$fter the objective test has been scored, the next step should be to make an item analysis. We make an item analysis usually to determine two characteristics of an item. The first of these is the difficulty of the item. In item analysis, difficulty is defined as the percentage of the examinees who marked the item correctly. The second characteristic is the measure of discrimination between two groups. When we use achievement tests, the two groups are the good and the poor students. With a personality inventory, the two groups are the well-adjusted and the poorly adjusted students, and with tests of special abilities, they might be the good workers and the poor. A third result can also be obtained by an item analysis: how well each distractor is working. Each of these three characteristics will be included in the discussion that follows.

ITEM ANALYSIS OF A SMALL CLASSROOM TEST

Diederich (4) has described an easy way of making an item analysis for a test given to an ordinary class. His method, which has proved popular with some teachers, is described below. This method is a desirable one, for the teacher's work is kept to a minimum. First the papers are arranged from high to low on the basis of total scores and then the median is obtained, dividing the class into two equal halves. Suppose that there are 37 students in a class, that the median of the test under consideration is 62, and that 3 students have scores of 62. First, all of the papers higher than the median are passed to the right and those with scores lower than the median to the left. The classroom will than be divided with the high papers on one side and the low ones on the other. Next the 3 papers at the median are taken. One is given to the high group and the other to the low group. The individual with the extra paper is asked to be score-keeper and his paper does not enter the item analysis. A tally sheet similar to that shown in Item-Analysis Worksheet No. 1 is placed on the board.

The teacher starts by calling out item 1 and asking all those holding papers on which item 1 is answered correctly to hold up their hands. A student to serve as a counter has previously been appointed for both groups. Each of these individuals now counts the number of hands in his section and calls them out for recording by the score-keeper. This process is continued until all items have been counted and tallied. If the test was a difficult one and there were a large number of omissions, these omissions should also be counted. This is particularly true of items appearing on the last quarter or so of the test. All of this can be done in a very few minutes, the actual time depending upon the length of the test.

The teacher may then copy, or have copied, this material from the board and complete it later. The values in column 3 (H + L) are first converted to percentages. In this case each value in column 3 is divided by 36, the number of papers, and this quotient is then multiplied by 100. These values represent the difficulty of the items, the percentage of students who responded correctly to the item. When the number of omits is high for any item, the number of correct responses should be divided by the number who actually respond to the item (the number of students minus the number of omits). Column 4 (H −L) is a measure of how well the item discriminates. Diederich points out that for items in the middle range of difficulty, that are responded to correctly by 25-75 per cent of the students, a difference (H − L) to be significant should be equal to at least 10 per cent of the number of students in the class. In this case 10 per cent of 36 equals 3.6 which is rounded to 4. When items are beyond this range of difficulty, that is when items are easy or difficult, a high-low difference of 5 per cent of the class may be taken as acceptable. In the example used here this would be a difference of 2.

Fig. 10:1. ITEM-ANALYSIS WORKSHEET NO. 1

Item	(1) H	(2) L	(3) H + L	(4) H − L	(5) Difficulty (Per cents)	(6) Discri- mination
1	18	2	20	16	56	+
2	18	18	36	0	100	0
3	12	6	18	6	50	+
4	6	12	18	−6	50	−
5	14	2	16	12	44	+
6	3	1	4	2	11	+
7	10	4	14	6	39	+
8	18	17	35	1	97	0
9	etc.	etc.				

H = number of "highs" who answered item correctly.
L = number of "lows" who answered item correctly.

These values of 10 and 5 per cent were arrived at from a study of the research done over the years on test construction. As we shall see below, the discriminatory value of an item is expressed as an index of discrimination. These are often presented as correlation coefficients. One such coefficient that is widely used in test work is the biserial correlation coefficient, called the biserial r. This statistic is a correlation between total test scores and responses to each of the individual items. Or in other words, it is an indicator of how well success on any particular item is related to success on the test as a whole. Since these are correlation coefficients, they can be evaluated as to "goodness" or significance. In practice, test makers like such coefficients to be .35 or higher. Items with biserial r's below this, at least for samples of the size being discussed here, are not significant, and items with such coefficients contribute nothing to the discriminatory power of the test. Diederich notes that when the class is split at the median, for items whose difficulty values fall within the band 25-75 per cent the biserial correlation coefficient is equal to approximately three times the high-low difference expressed as a per cent of the class. Thus if H − L is 4 and if this is 10 per cent of the class, the biserial r will be 3 times this 10 per cent or .30. If it is 6, or 15 per cent of the class, the coefficient will be about .45. These approximations are quite acceptable until the difficulty values of the items are outside the band 20-80 per cent. Then a H — L difference of 2 may be taken as significant.

Instead of dividing the papers at the median and having two equal halves, it is also possible to take the top 27 per cent and bottom 27 per cent of papers. (The reasons for choosing 27 per cent are discussed below.) Results are tallied in the same way as above. Now the per cent correct in the upper 27 per cent is placed in the first column, the per cent correct in the lowest 27 per cent in the second column, the difficulty value of the item (an average of the values in the first two columns) in the third column, and the discrimination index in the fourth column. This last value is obtained by entering a table such as the ones constructed by Flanagan (8) or Fan (7) with the computed high and low percentages and obtaining actual correlation coefficients from this table. It should be noted that the difficulty values obtained are estimates of the difficulty values that would be obtained if every paper had been used. Actually the differences between such difficulty values obtained from just the high and low groups of papers and those obtained by using all the papers are slight or trivial.

A method that is simpler, but probably more time-consuming because the teacher would have to do it himself, is to take the top 10 and the bottom 10 papers. Responses to each item are then tallied for the high and low groups, difficulty values computed by taking the total number of correct responses and dividing it by 20, and finally an indication of each item's discrimination is made. This last part of the analysis is done arbitrarily. One might set a standard such that, in order for an item to discriminate, the difference between the number of correct responses in the top 10 and the bottom 10 papers must be at least 2.

Now let us return to Item Analysis Worksheet No. 1 to study the results. An item is considered acceptable or not on the basis of both its difficulty value and its index of discrimination. Over the years research has shown that items of 50 per cent difficulty not only make the most discriminations but discriminate throughout the range of test scores. So test makers try to have the average item difficulty at 50 per cent with not much variability on either side of this. However, it is often difficult to achieve this, and most teachers and test builders usually end up with both easier and harder items. Then one criterion to use in selecting items is the closeness of the difficulty value of the item to 50 per cent, the closer, the better. Secondly we look to see if the item discriminates significantly.

Of the items in the table, numbers 2 and 8 are immediately discarded since they do not discriminate. Both are also very easy items and are undesirable on this point also. Such items actually add nothing to the effectiveness of the test. Item 4 discriminates negatively. Such an item should be studied more closely to see what is wrong. Perhaps the scoring key is in error or perhaps the better students are reading into the item something that the item writer did not intend to have there. Ambiguities in items may lead to such negative results. Items 1, 3, 5, and 7 are all acceptable items because their difficulty values are near the middle of the range and they all discriminate. Item 6 is a very difficult item and using a H — L difference of 2 instead of 4 it can be said to discriminate between the two groups. However, with items like this it is difficult to determine whether the results are brought about merely by chance or these obtained differences are real ones.

With multiple-choice items a teacher or test maker also wants to know how well each of the distractors is working. A new tally is now made, this time regarding the responses to each part of the item. Summaries like the following result:

Item 12	Responses					
	A	B*	C	D	E	Omit
High Group	1	16	0	1	0	0
Low Group	2	7	7	2	0	0

*Correct response.

This analysis gives the teacher an idea of the types of errors his students are making. Also it reveals which distractors are not working and which are working in reverse—that is, those distractors that are the choice of more of the high-scoring students than of the low-scoring ones. Such information is useful in making revisions of items. Diederich suggests that after the initial analysis has been made, the teacher look over the data on the board and select those items that do not discriminate or are too easy or too difficult. Then for these items in question, the high and low parts of the class should state how many students responded to each part of the item and how many omitted each item. This is all done using the score-keeper as before. Diederich feels that it is too much work to do this to all of the items.

ITEM ANALYSIS OF A LARGE CLASSROOM TEST OR ACCUMULATED TESTS

A Conventional Approach

Sometimes a teacher has a large number of papers on the same test or has accumulated papers from several classes over a period of time. When he has 100 or more papers much more reliable item analyses can be made. We shall now look at this procedure. Usually the teacher selects his upper and lower groups by taking the highest and lowest 27 per cent of the papers. This goes back to the work of Kelley (10) who showed that maximum discrimination indices were obtained when these percentages were used. Some later studies (6) have shown this not to be so, but that, whether 10, 20, or other percentages were used in setting up the upper and lower groups, these differences in size had little or no effect upon the reliability of the test. However, many of our calculation aids are based on the 27-per-cent method, and consequently many people still use it.

After the two groups have been set up, a tally is made of the number in each group responding correctly to each item. This now becomes a laborious operation when performed by hand. Scoring machines have item-counters that produce a graphic summary of the correct responses to each item as the papers of the upper group are passed singly through the machine. Then a similar summary is obtained for the lower group. These frequencies are changed into per cents and entered on a worksheet as shown below. An estimate of the difficulty of the item can be obtained by averaging the per cents found in columns 1 and 2. Davis (3) (in 13) has shown that maximum discrimination of an achievement test which would discriminate throughout the range is obtained when the distribution of item difficulties or average item difficulty tends to be around 50 per cent. Items selected for an achievement test should range from very easy to very difficult, with a majority clustering around the 50-per-cent level.

Fig. 10:2. Item-Analysis Worksheet No. 2

Item	(1) Per cent Correct Upper 27%	(2) Per cent Correct Lower 27%	(3) Difficulty	(4) Discrimination
1	90	40	65	.56
2	80	30	55	.51
3	42	50	46	—.08
4	50	50	50	.00
—	—	—	—	—
—	—	—	—	—
—	—	—	—	—
80	20	4	12	.36

To complete column 4, we can use any number of nomographs or computing devices. Actually the index of discrimination used by many people is a correlation coefficient that shows the relationship between total score on the test and the response to every single item. On an 80-item test, 80 separate correlation coefficients would have to be computed (1). This would discourage many from making item analyses. Davis (3), Fan (7), Davidoff and Goheen (2), Guilford (9), Flanagan (8), and others have developed nomographs or short, labor-saving charts that enable one to obtain these correlation coefficients, or transformations thereof, directly from the charts by entering them with the percentages correct in both the upper and lower groups. Such nomographs by Guilford, Flanagan, and Davidoff and Goheen may be found in Downie and Heath (5), Chapter 16. That similar results are obtained by the use of different item analysis statistics has been repeatedly demonstrated by research. Such studies as those by Kuang (11) or Ely (6) present evidence of this. The discrimination indices found in column 4 of the table were obtained by the use of Flanagan's table.

Another way to see whether or not an item discriminates is to see if there is a significant difference between the percentage in the high group answering the item correctly and the percentage in the low group. Here we are actually testing whether or not the observed difference between the two percentages is a real one or one that may best be accounted for by chance. A short-cut procedure for doing this was developed by Lawshe and Baker (12), who developed a very practical nomograph. This nomograph for testing the difference between two percentages may also be found in Downie and Heath (5), p. 150.

When correlation coefficients are used, a test of significance can be applied to determine whether or not the coefficient is different from zero and, thus, if the item is really discriminating. Tables for testing the significance of correlation coefficients can be found in the appendixes of statistics books. If a teacher had 100 or more papers, he might say that any item which had an index of .20 or above was actually working.

It should be noted that, if we had a test made up of two or more subtests, the item analysis should be made by subtests—that is, each item is studied against a subtest score. The upper and lower groups should be set up each time for each of the subtests.

With a large number of papers it is possible to make a rather detailed study of the workings of each of the distractors. Suppose that we take item 2 in the worksheet on page 219 and examine all the responses of the individuals of both upper and lower groups. The results are shown in Table 10:1. An inspection of this table shows that distractor A is a good one, working as it should. Distractor B is being missed by more good students than poor ones. Such an item part lowers the discrimination index. This distractor should be examined carefully to see if the cause of the trouble can be ascertained. It may be that there are certain ambiguities present which are affecting only the better students. At any rate the distractor should best be rewritten before being used again. Distractor C again is a good one. Distractor E, which was selected by a total of 3 in the two groups combined, is of little value as a part of the item. Since it failed to attract examinees, it also should be carefully inspected and rewritten.

After these changes have been made the item is ready to be re-administered. A second item analysis will reveal whether or not the item has been improved. Sometimes there is no improvement. Item statistics can even deteriorate. After several unsuccessful attempts at improving an item, the item should be rewritten from a new approach or thrown out.

The Use of Computers in Item Analysis—A New Approach

In recent years a good share of the drudgery associated with mak-

Table 10:1. ANALYSIS OF RESPONSES TO A SINGLE ITEM

	Upper 27%	Lower 27%	
Distractor A	4	33	370 papers
Distractor B	15	5	Upper 27% = 100
Distractor C	0	20	Lower 27% = 100
Answer D	80	30	Item Difficulty = 55%
Distractor E	1	2	Flanagan $r = .51$
Omits		10	
	$N = 100$	$N = 100$	

ing an item analysis has been eliminated by programming item analyses for computers. The report of Weisbrodt *et al.* (14) describes the adaptation of the test scoring services of a large university to analysis by computers. A major responsibility of a university testing service is to assist faculty members in the building and scoring of their classroom tests. The use of computers makes it possible to furnish the teaching staff with a large amount of basic test data and provide a very efficient scoring service for their tests. It was felt that if item analysis data were available to the teaching staff they would become more interested in improving their tests.

In the program described by Weisbrodt, students use an electographic pencil to place their answers to test items on a 100-item mark-sense card. These mark-sense cards are read and punched and then run through an IBM 1401 computer for scoring. The machine scores the cards and makes a print out of the number of rights, wrongs, and omits for each student. Along with this the mean and standard deviation of the test are obtained and each student's score is changed to a standard score with a mean of 50 and a standard deviation of 10. Also a frequency distribution of the scores is printed. This can be used for posting grades for the students are identified on it only by number. By this process 100-item tests are processed at the rate of 110 papers per minute.

Next the data on the 100-item mark-sense cards are converted to a format necessary for use with the IBM 7094 computer. This machine can analyze as many as 999 items at once. The size of the group is of no importance. The print out from this computer contains all of the following: the item difficulty, the test mean, the test standard deviation, the correlation of each item with the total score (the discrimination index), the correlation of the responses to each of the distractors with the total score, the reliability of the test (as a Kuder-Richardson No. 20 measure of internal consistency), and the standard error of measurement of the test. The discrimination index obtained here is a point biserial correlation coefficient which for all practical purposes may be interpreted in the same way as the biserial r previously mentioned. This computer is capable of making a complete analysis in about 30 seconds of a 100-item test responded to by 1000 examinees.

Obviously, when the number of test papers is large, the computer is the most efficient means of scoring and analyzing the papers. But this is expensive in time and money. Cards have to be punched and made available to the computer, and computer time is in itself expensive. Setting up the original program may also require considerable effort. For teachers who do not have a large number of papers or who do not have access to computers, the previously discussed item analysis techniques are still important.

Advantages Resulting from an Item Analysis

First of all, if a test is worth giving, it is worth going over and discussing in class. Usually there is not time to consider every item, nor is there any need to. From the item analysis, the teacher can see immediately the strong and weak points of his class and remedial work can be applied before any new work is taken up. Discussing a test in class is a good learning experience, sometimes even for the teacher. Results of these discussions will make any teacher a better item-writer because ambiguities and errors will soon turn up.

Secondly, the teacher can set up for himself a pool of items. A copy of the test can be cut up and each item attached to a 5 by 8 card by a cellulose adhesive (Fig. 10:3). This is quicker than typing the items onto cards. Then, below the item, can be recorded the date on which the item was used, the number and per cents in high and low groups answering it correctly, the test on which it was used, the difficulty of the item, and whether or not the item discriminated. The correct or keyed response can be starred (or circled) on the item itself. Items can be filed by subject matter, unit, section, or text, even the page of the text from which the idea for the item was obtained. Many times an item analysis reveals that an item needs

Text	2	2	50	NMD	7/7/1967
SOURCE	CHAPTER	SECTION	PAGE	PREPARED BY	DATE

The I.Q.'s of unrelated individuals correlate about
```
      A  .90
      B  .65
      C  .50
     *D  .00
```

FORM	M	N										
DATE	7/67	10/67										
HIGH GROUP	82%	78%										
LOW GROUP	26%	22%										
DIFFICULTY	54%	50%										
DISCRIMIN-ATION	.56	.56										

Fig. 10: 3. CARD SHOWING ITEM ANALYSIS DATA

repair. Take, for example, an item which measures an important aspect of a course and which has negative discrimination or is too easy or too difficult. Such do occur. The item can be revised before being filed, and then it will be ready to be tried again in its new form on the next appropriate test. An item pool makes test construction a much simpler operation once the item pool has been set up. Each time a test is made some new items should be constructed and tried out.

Thirdly, after making an item analysis, a teacher knows something about the difficulty of each item. These difficulty values can be used in locating the items on future tests. It is good psychology to start a test with some easy items. Here the teacher needs a couple of items that everyone can answer. Nothing upsets the morale and performance of an examinee more than being unable to do the first task on a test. Also a test is more efficient when items are arranged in order of difficulty so that each student can accomplish more by working through the easier ones and those of moderate difficulty before coming to the most difficult ones.

Finally, when a teacher resorts to making item analyses of his tests, he will in the end produce tests of higher reliability. As the ambiguous items, those which have negative discrimination, and those with no discrimination are removed from tests, test reliability is bound to rise. And, as was pointed out in Chapter 4, if tests increase in reliability, they also increase in validity. A more reliable test becomes one in which we can have more confidence.

Use of Outside Criteria

The methods discussed so far in this chapter are referred to in the literature as METHODS OF INTERNAL CONSISTENCY. Each item is studied by comparing the responses to it with the total test scores. A good item is answered correctly by the good students, etc. With some types of tests it is possible to use an outside criterion—that is, scores on some other test or measure in addition to the total test scores. The same techniques as above are applied, but our upper and lower groups are selected on the basis of scores on this outside criterion. Such indices, when computed, are called MEASURES OF ITEM VALIDITY. In dealing with predictor tests it is the usual procedure to calculate for each item an index both of internal consistency and of validity. Items selected for the final form of the test are those that correlate highest with the outside criterion and lowest with the total test score.

EXERCISE

It is suggested that the teacher make available some completed objective tests so that the items may be analyzed, using 3 or 4 of the different techniques described in this chapter. When finished, compare results obtained by the different methods.

REFERENCES

1. Conrad, H. S. Characteristics and uses of item analysis data. *Psychol. Monographs: General and Applied.* Vol. 62, No. 8, 1948.
2. Davidoff, M. D., and Goheen, H. W. A table for the rapid calculation of the tetrachoric correlation coefficient. *Psychometrika*, 1953, 18, 115-21.
3. Davis, F. B. *Item analysis data.* Harvard Education Papers, No. 2. Cambridge: Graduate School of Education, Harvard University, 1946.

4. Diederich, P. B. *Short-cut statistics for teacher-made tests.* Evaluation and Advisory Service Series, No. 5. Princeton, N. J.: Educational Testing Service, 1960.
5. Downie, N. M., and Heath, R. W. *Basic statistical methods.* 2nd ed. New York: Harper and Row, 1965.
6. Ely, J. H. Studies in item analysis. 2: Effects of various methods on test reliability. *J. appl. Psychol.*, 1951, 35, 194-203.
7. Fan, Chung-Teh. *Item analysis table.* Princeton, N. J.: Educational Testing Service, 1952.
8. Flanagan, J. C. General considerations in the selection of test items and a short method of estimating the product-moment coefficient from the data in the tails of a distribution. *J. educ. Psychol.*, 1939, 30, 674-80.
9. Guilford, J. P. *Psychometric methods.* 2nd ed. New York: McGraw-Hill, 1954.
10. Kelley, T. L. The selection of upper and lower groups for the validation of test items. *J. educ. Psychol.*, 1939, 30, 17-24.
11. Kuang, H. P. A critical evaluation of the relative efficiency of three techniques in item analysis. *Educ. Psychol. Measmt.*, 1952, 12, 248-66.
12. Lawshe, C. H., and Baker, P. C. Three aids in the evaluation of the significance of the difference between percentages. *Educ. Psychol. Measmt.*, 1950, 10, 263-70.
13. Lindquist, E. F. *Educational measurement.* Washington, D. C.: American Council on Education, 1951. Chapter 9.
14. Weisbrodt, J., et al. Use of IBM 1401 nad 7090 computers in a university testing service. *Educ. Psychol. Measmt.*, 1964, 24, 659-62.

CHAPTER 11

STANDARDIZED ACHIEVEMENT TESTS

In this chapter we shall take up first a discussion of the test batteries used in the elementary and junior-high school. Then attention will be given to subject-matter tests and tests of general education applicable to high school and college. Since reading tests are so numerous, these will be discussed separately. The chapter will close with a discussion of some achievement batteries used as selection devices by professional schools and of a few tests that are in categories by themselves.

ELEMENTARY-SCHOOL TESTS AND BATTERIES

These tests first appeared toward the close of the first decade of this century as a result of the work of E. L. Thorndike and his students. Stone published the first standardized arithmetic test in 1908. At the same time various achievement scales appeared. Thorndike and L. P. Ayres each published a scale for the evaluation of handwriting. These consisted of a piece of prose in samples of handwriting ranging from very superior to almost illegible, each of which had a value or score attached to it. A student's writing of the same piece of prose was taken and run along the scale until the examiner determined which scale specimen it most closely resembled. It received the value of that specimen as its score. Similar scales were developed for evaluating compositions and themes. It should be apparent that such devices as these were rather highly subjective in spite of their scientific appearance.

As time went on many achievement tests appeared, measuring the major subjects taught in the public-school curriculums. An examination of some of these older tests reveals that their major value was in determining how well students had learned the facts of a given area of instruction. An analysis of some of them showed a better than 90-per-cent devotion to the appraisal of this single, lone objective. Today, with our newer tests and batteries, the emphasis is on some of the other important objectives of education, as will be seen below.

The Uses of Achievement Tests

There are two problems involved in the use of standardized achievement tests. The first is to determine how well they meet the objectives of the local school or teacher. Frequently, when students do not do too well on such tests, it is found that many items are related to subjects and processes not yet covered or not included in the local curriculum. A careful analysis of test and curriculum is in order then before any test is purchased. The second problem is to gauge the effect that the use—or perhaps it would be better to say misuse—of these tests frequently has upon the type of learning which goes on in any classroom. In schools where a teacher is considered "good" or "bad" on the basis of the number of students who do well or "pass" on these tests, much time may be spent getting ready for these examinations at the expense of everything else. As a former high-school teacher in New York State, the writer has seen how the *Regents' Examinations* (state-wide achievement tests) influenced classroom activities in some schools. He has known of high-school teachers who, in the fall of the year, had each student purchase a copy of a review book which contained a collection of old Regents' Examinations. The year's work consisted of going over these questions until almost everyone knew the answers. After all, if enough years are covered, there are not too many new questions that can appear in the future which have not been discussed at least from some angle. Also, since these examinations are made up in advance, some teachers feel that there is little use in paying attention to what is going on in the world. The writer recalls that which occurred on D-Day, June 1944. A senior in a history class suggested to his teacher that they set up a radio in the classroom and listen to the invasion news. The teacher's reply was in the negative since, she stated, there would be nothing concerning the invasion of France on the *Regents'*

Examinations for that year. These tests were to be taken in a few days. The misuse of tests in this way can act as a strait jacket on the curriculum. As we shall see later, there are far better ways of evaluating a teacher and the effectiveness of his instruction than by using the scores obtained by his students on achievement tests.

The Widely Used Test Batteries

In discussing elementary-school batteries, a brief look will be given to several of the more widely used ones.

THE METROPOLITAN ACHIEVEMENT TESTS.* For many years this battery has been one of the most widely used elementary school batteries. The earlier forms were traditional in their approach to measurement in that they were chiefly aimed at testing the attainment of factual material. Over the years, this approach has changed and the 1964 edition is pointed at other important outcomes of education. Currently 6 levels of the battery are available, from grade 1 through grade 12. The first 3 of these, Primary I, grade 1.5, Primary II, grade 2, and Elementary, grades 3–4, measure the basic skills associated with reading and arithmetic. The other 3 batteries, Intermediate, grades 5–6, Advanced, grades 7–9, and High School, grades 9–12, in addition to measuring these skills and others such as language and work-study skills, also have a high percentage of very factual materials that require little reasoning or problem solving for the response.

The time needed to administer these batteries varies from about one hour and a half for the lowest level to over 6 hours for the high school battery. Several forms are available at each level and for the Intermediate and Advanced levels there are both partial and complete batteries. The latter differ basically by including tests that measure social science and natural science information.

STANFORD ACHIEVEMENT TESTS.* This is another battery that has been through various editions since its first appearance in 1923. The description that follows refers to the 1964 revision that was built for use in grades 1–9. Five levels are provided: Primary I, grades 1.5–2.5; Primary II, grades 2.5–3.9; Intermediate I, grades 4–5.5; Intermediate II, grades 5.5–6.9; and Advanced, grades 7–9. All of the

*Published by Harcourt, Brace & World.

Word Meaning
A very large ravine is called—
  1 a channel   2 an elevation   3 a basin   4 a canyon ....
The dead body of a wild animal is a—
  5 vestige   6 carcass   7 corpuscle   8 corruption ....
Something written about or talked about is—
  1 a token   2 a topic   3 a title   4 an article ....

Arithmetic Reasoning
Pine City is 120 miles from Milton. To go from Pine City to Milton by bus takes
4 hours and by train only 2¾ hours. How many hours less does it take to go
by train?
  f 1¼   *g* 1¾   *h* 2¼   *i* 6¾   *j* not given ....
How many 1-inch by 2-inch pieces of candy can be cut in a pan which is 8
inches by 10 inches?
  a 20   *b* 36   *c* 50   *d* 80   *e* not given ....
Dan says there are 2 quart and 2 pint packages of ice cream for the party. How
many people will all of it serve if a pint serves 4 people?
  f 4   *g* 12   *h* 16   *i* 24   *j* not given ....

Social Studies
A country with many great dikes is—
  5 France   6 Holland   7 England   8 Italy
The highest officer of a city usually is the—
  1 alderman   2 mayor   3 chief of police   4 councilman ....
Who built one of the first successful steamboats?
  5 Hayes   6 Ford   7 Fulton   8 Wright ....
The Nile River flows through—
  1 India   2 Egypt   3 Arabia   4 Syria ....

Science
Dew on the grass comes from—
  1 water rising from the ground   2 rain during the night
  3 moisture in the air   4 the grass itself ....
A "closed season" protects—
  5 wild life   6 swimmers   7 hunters   8 travelers ....
Insect larvae are the chief food of some—
  1 bees   2 flies   3 birds   4 worms ....

Study Skills
On which syllable is ĭt-ēr-ā'shŭn accented?
  1 first   2 second   3 third   4 fourth ....
In an index the topic under *lumbering* discussing the process would be—
  5 North America   6 exports   7 distribution   8 methods of ....
The most direct reference to the Inca Indians of Peru, South America, would
be found in an index under—
  1 Inca Indians   2 South America   3 Peru   4 Indians ....
Where would you look for an account of the Westward Movement in the
United States?
  5 dictionary   6 history book   7 weekly magazine   8 atlas .....

Fig. 11:1. REPRESENTATIVE ITEMS FROM DIFFERENT SECTIONS OF THE *Stanford
Achievement Test*, INTERMEDIATE BATTERY, GRADES 5-6.*

* Used by permission of World Book Co., Copyright 1952.

batteries test the usual language, reading, and arithmetic skills (Fig. 11:1). The measurement of both social studies and science appears in the Primary II battery, grades 2.5–3.9. Tests of study skills appear at all levels. The several upper-level batteries have many content items along with those measuring skills especially in the social and natural sciences. Of the various batteries offered for use in the elementary school, the *Stanford* stands out as the one that measures both achievement of basic skills and content. Its sections on testing study skills compare well with material found on the *Iowa Tests of Basic Skills*.

Scores on both the *Metropolitan* and *Stanford* batteries are reported in stanines (standard scores ranging from 1 to 9 with a mean of 5 and a standard deviation of 2), as well as in grade-placement and centile scores. Various types of answer sheets and scoring services are offered to users of both batteries. Eventually 4 forms of each *Stanford* battery will be available. In summary it is felt that the 1964 revision of the *Stanford Achievement Tests* provides for adequate assessment in continuous programs in grades 1–9. This battery has had many ardent supporters in the past, and it will probably continue to be used because of this familiarity with it and because of the attempts made by its authors to keep abreast with elementary school education.

THE IOWA TESTS OF BASIC SKILLS.* These tests are used from grades 3 to 9 to measure various skills used in reading, work-study, language and arithmetic (Fig. 11:2). The emphasis is entirely upon the fundamentals of elementary school learning. In this way the battery differs from most of its competitors. These tests do not offer specific measures of achievement in geography, literature, history, science, and the other subjects studied during these elementary school years. There are two basic reasons for tests like these. In the first place the acquisition of these basic skills represents a more permanent type of learning than that associated with the acquisition of factual information. A good share of the content of the elementary school curriculum consists of specific facts which, once learned, are easily and soon forgotten. Once studied and tested, these particular facts may never again appear either in the classroom or in any aspects of the

*Published by Houghton Mifflin Co.

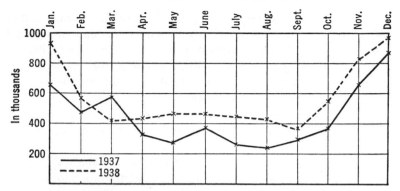

Questions are based on the line graph above.

During what month of 1937 were more hogs sold than in the corresponding month of 1938?
1 **January**   3 **June**
2 **March**   4 **December**

During what month in the latter part of 1937 did the sales again reach the January level?
1 **February**   3 **May**
2 **March**   4 **November**

Which seems the safest conclusion to draw from this graph?
1 **The price of hogs is highest in December**
2 **The number of hogs being marketed is steadily increasing**
3 **Late fall and early winter are the chief hog marketing months**
4 **August is the poorest month to market hogs**

During what one-month period was there the sharpest decline in number of hogs marketed?
1 **From April to May, 1937**
2 **From July to August, 1937**
3 **From December to January, 1938**
4 **From January to February, 1938**

Fig. 11:2. ITEMS FROM TEST B, "WORK STUDY SKILLS," *Iowa Every Pupil Test,* FORM L., A forerunner of the *Iowa Tests of Basic Skills* *.

student's daily life. On the other hand students read, talk, use numbers, and study every day. Effective achievement in these skill areas should be the basic objective of the early school years.

* Used by permission of Houghton Mifflin Co., Copyright 1940.

Another reason for emphasizing the acquisition of skills rather than content is the great variability in school curricula and school organization. Such diversification makes it almost impossible to construct content-oriented tests that are suited to different local conditions. Such different literature is read, such different texts used, such different points of view stressed in teaching, as in the various parochial schools, that rare is any test of content that may be used as a valid measure of achievement under all these variable conditions.

The Iowa Tests of Basic Skills cover 5 areas: vocabulary, reading comprehension, language skills (spelling, capitalization, punctuation, usage), work-study skills (map reading, reading graphs and tables, knowledge and use of reference materials), and arithmetic skills (concepts and problem solving). The tests are assembled in a multi-level booklet, containing six separate but overlapping tests for the six grade levels to be tested. In this way students in grade 5, for example, respond only to items appropriate for this grade. They do not have to waste time on items too easy for them or those that are inappropriate for their level of achievement. Also there are certain students in most classes who are less advanced than the rest of the class. Such students as these could be given the level lower than the one that their class is taking. This would result in a feeling of achievement on their part, rather than the usual one of frustration to which they are no stranger.

There are 4 equivalent forms of this battery available. Approximately 280 minutes of testing time are needed for the administration of the entire battery. This time may be conveniently spread over 4 days of testing with 75 to 80 minutes each day, including time for passing out papers, reading directions, and collecting materials. The publisher provides various types of answer sheets and scoring services. Scores are presented in grade equivalents or in grade centiles. Also, along with national norms, regional, large-city, and Catholic school norms are presented.

These tests then evaluate the basic learnings of elementary school education. They do not turn the clasroom into a cramming session to learn facts, facts, and more unrelated facts so that the student will do well on factual tests and the teacher will appear to be effective. These *Iowa* tests cause the aims of both teacher and students to be focused on these permanent outcomes of education. Time spent on these skills is well spent. From such skill-centered classes should come students who can handle academic work at higher levels better than some of today's students do.

THE CALIFORNIA TESTS. Another battery that should be mentioned here is the *California Achievement Tests*.* This covers five levels: a "Lower Primary" battery for grade 1 and the first half of grade 2, an "Upper Primary" for the second half of grade 2 and grade 3 and lower 4, an "Elementary" battery for grades 4-6, an "Intermediate" battery, 7-9, and an "Advanced" battery for grades 9-14. This series differs from those described previously in that it has batteries for senior high school and junior college. Each level is made up of five tests: reading vocabulary, reading comprehension (following directions, use of references, the interpretation of maps and graphs, etc.), arithmetic fundamentals, arithmetic reasoning, and mechanics of English, grammar, and spelling. The 2 reading tests are published separately as the *California Reading Test;* also published separately are the two arithmetic tests and the one related to language. Again it might be noted that these are tests the emphasis of which is placed entirely upon basic skills. Time required with this battery runs from 90 minutes for the primary battery to 150 minutes for the advanced one. A unique feature of these batteries is the section on the cover devoted to a diagnosis analysis of learning difficulties in which the student can summarize his weaknesses by encircling the items missed.

THE SEQUENTIAL TESTS OF EDUCATIONAL PROGRESS (STEP).† These tests were developed, according to the authors, on the following four assumptions: (1) the primary goal of education is the growth of the individual; (2) education is a broadly concerned, continuous, and cumulative process; (3) the basic aim of education is the development of critical skills and understandings; and (4) evaluation should be based on the student's application of these skills and understandings in new situations. The last of these is a measure of the success of the educative process. Tests have been developed for 4 levels: college freshmen and sophomores, grades 10–12,

* Published by the California Test Bureau.
† Published by the Educational Testing Service.

grades 7–9 and grades 4–6. The purpose of the batteries is to pro-vide a measure of those basic skills that it is hoped all students would possess by the time they left school. To do this, separate tests were constructed in 4 areas of comunications skills: reading a vari-ety of materials with understanding; writing, in which the student selects the best revision from suggested changes in materials written by students; essay, in which themes are written on selected topics; and listening, in which the student has an opportunity to compre-hend, interpret, and evaluate what he hears. Three additional tests measure achievement in mathematics, science, and social studies. The mathematics tests assess a broad understanding of general math-ematical concepts, the science test, the student's capacity to apply his scientific background to both familiar and new situations, and the social studies tests, those concepts deemed basic for the effective de-velopment of the student's relationship to the world in which he lives. Two forms of the battery are available at each level.

In general, this is a well-made group of tests. They are capable of giving an excellent evaluation of the general aspects of education noted above. If the examiner is interested in testing specific course content, other types of tests such as those described below must be used. Probably a well-balanced measurement program has room in it for both types of instruments.

The Ideal Use of Test Batteries

All these test batteries that we have been describing are expen-sive, both from the point of view of cost and the amount of school time devoted to administering them. It would seem logical then that they should be used in ways that make it possible to get as much from them as possible. This should mean a fall testing program, because when these tests are administered at the beginning of the school year and the results given to the teachers at once, they be-come most useful. First, they reveal the over-all achievement picture of the class. A teacher has to know where to start. It is not a good idea to assume that everything taught in the previous grades has been learned. These tests give a good picture of the strong and weak points of the total class. The effects of the summer vacation may be noted, especially if similar tests had been administered at the close of the spring semester. Secondly, they can be used for individual diagnosis. This can be done by the students themselves. Each can determine his high points and those areas or skills that need special attention and effort during the coming year. Thirdly, these autumn tests can be used in setting up reading groups and other study groups on the basis of students' present status. Finally, to evaluate growth in the best possible fashion, we have to know where individuals are at the beginning of the learning period. The administration of a second form of the same test at the end of the year will show us just where progress has been made and how much.

When these tests are administered only in the spring, they tend to be used for grading, promotion, and, sometimes, teacher evaluation. It seems highly advantageous to allow teachers to have these tests for fall use if they so desire. Perhaps, this should be the required time for administering them, with the spring use being made optional.

It is felt that achievement batteries administered in grades 1 and 2 are hardly necessary. Practically everything that goes on in these two grades is related to success in reading. If a child has not learned to read, then there is little use in giving him these batteries. If everything in these grades is so dependent on success in reading, it would follow that the logical way to measure achievement is by the use of a reading test alone.

HIGH-SCHOOL AND COLLEGE TESTS

While some of the tests described above may be used in high school and beyond, they are basically elementary school tests, some of which in a general form have been adapted to a large part of the educative program. High school and college achievement tests fall into two basic types. One consists of regular achievement tests that can be used at the end of a regular course, such as high-school physics, plane geometry, etc. The usual pattern is for a publisher to issue tests that cover the courses most frequently found in the academic programs of most high schools. Very few tests are published for such areas as home economics, agriculture, or industrial arts. The second type of test is of a general survey nature. These are usually constructed to measure over-all achievement at the completion of grade 12. Colleges and universities use the identical test to appraise the over-all attainment of entering freshmen. Some of these tests measure in the area of general education. By this is meant the common core of learning to which all high-school students are exposed.

Achievement Test Series

The Cooperative Achievement Tests* have long been accepted leaders in the measurement of achievement in both high school and collge courses. In the past, some of these tests, which are still available, took the form of general proficiency tests in the areas of mathematics, natural sciences, and social studies (Fig. 11:3). Today the emphasis is upon achievement tests in specific subject-matter areas or for a particular course of instruction. These *Cooperative* tests have traditionally been built in an attempt to measure various outcomes of education along with the testing of a student's knowledge of the factual material of a particular course. Usually there was emphasis on the application to new situations of principles learned in the course. One of the newer *Cooperative Tests* is the *Cooperative Modern Language Test* developed with the cooperation of the Modern Language Association of America and the U.S. Office of Education. These tests cover five modern foreign languages, measuring skill in reading, writing, listening, and speaking. These new language tests measure all possible uses to which a foreign language might be put.

Another series of achievement tests is the *Evaluation and Adjustment Series.*† At the present time, some 20 tests are available in this series measuring the major courses covered in high-school instruction. These tests, like those just discussed, are well made from the viewpoint both of good test construction and of emphasis on the various objectives of the high-school courses.

The Essential High-School Content Battery † is a rather long battery, taking almost 4 hours of testing time and covering high-school mathematics, science, social science, and English. The authors of this test discuss the varied aims and objectives of secondary education, such as vocational training, preparation for further schooling, participation in democratic living, and others. They feel that, in spite of where the emphasis is placed, students should show competence in the 4 areas measured by this test. This test was designed to appraise

---

* Published by the Educational Testing Service.
† Published by Harcourt, Brace & World.

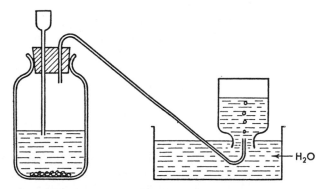

This apparatus is used to prepare and collect certain substances in gaseous form.

Which of the following substances could best be prepared and collected with this apparatus?
56–1   Carbon dioxide
56–2   Bromine
56–3   Chlorine
56–4   Hydrogen sulfide
56–5   Helium . . . .

Suppose the apparatus were used to prepare and collect hydrogen. Which of the following might appear in the balanced equation for the reaction?
57–1 SO_2
57–2 $2H_2SO_4$
57–3 HCl
57–4 $2ZnCl_2$
57–5 $ZnCl_2$ . . . .

This apparatus should not be used to prepare gases which are
58–1   very poisonous.
58–2   highly soluble in water.
58–3   explosive when mixed with oxygen.
58–4   lighter than air.
58–5   heavier than air. . . . .

Fig. 11:3. AN APPLICATION TYPE OF TEST ITEM FROM THE *Cooperative Chemistry Test, Form X.**

this common body of knowledge and skills, which it is expected all high-school students would possess. In other words, this is an attempt to measure that part of the school curriculum which is common to all students in spite of the special curriculum in which he or she might be registered. Each of the four subtests is broken down into shorter tests. For example, the science test consists of three parts: (A) "Science Information," (B) "Using the Concepts of Science," and (C) "Using the Scientific Method."

The Iowa Tests of Educational Development

The last of the high-school batteries to be discussed is the *Iowa Tests of Educational Development.** This battery, which takes a little less than 8 hours to administer, consists of 9 subtests that may be purchased separately or all in one booklet. The first four of these subtests—(1) "Understanding of Basic Social Concepts," (2) "General Background in the Natural Sciences," (3) "Correctness and Appropriateness of Expression," and (4) "Ability to Do Quantitative Thinking"—are a series of general background tests, one for each of the major areas of high-school instruction. The next three subtests—(5) "Interpretation of Reading Materials in the Social Sciences," (6) "Interpretation of Reading Materials in the Natural Sciences," and (7) "Interpretation of Literary Materials"—offer a check on reading comprehension in 3 of the major areas of the curriculum. Test (8), "General Vocabulary Test," according to the authors, is a measure of not only the student's ability to comprehend the meaning of words commonly encountered in his reading but also his general ability for school learning. Test (9), "Uses of Sources of Information," is a measure of the student's ability to use standard reference material and current literature for answers to specific problems.

The authors state that the major purpose of this battery is to help the classroom teacher become more quickly and reliably acquainted with the educational needs of individual pupils in order to effect better teaching. A teacher would want to know how much the students already know about any subject and how adequate a background they have for its study or how much skill is already acquired.

* Published by Science Research Associates.

Also a teacher must know what each student's capacity to learn is and how well he can use the instructional material at his disposal. In other words, this is a diagnostic test battery and as such should be administered at the beginning of a school year or term. The tests do not cover any specific high-school course but are broad enough to cover the objectives and responsibilities of several or all members of the school faculty. They cannot be used in the spring of the year to evaluate the teaching of any one instructor in a special subject-matter area.

This Iowa battery can be used with students in the second half of the eighth grade up to the entering college freshman. The writer feels that, because of the nature of the content, it would be best used in the senior high school. Bright eighth-graders might do well on it, but the average and poorer students might turn in very unreliable performances. This battery, like the others previously discussed and prepared for this level, is an excellent piece of test construction. Any of these merit use as models by every classroom teacher in the construction of his own tests.

READING TESTS

Reading tests may be classified into three types: reading survey, reading diagnostic, and reading-readiness tests. The first two are achievement tests, both measuring attainment in reading. The third, reading-readiness tests, are basically tests of mental ability. They are included in this chapter simply as a matter of convenience.

Reading Survey Tests

Reading survey tests usually measure two basic factors: reading comprehension and reading rate. Frequently, these tests also give an estimate of the size of the examinee's vocabulary. Reading comprehension is usually measured by presenting paragraphs of material from different subject-matter sources. These paragraphs are read and then a series of multiple-choice items, based on the reading material, is answered. The subject matter of the paragraphs is varied considerably. Some cover current social problems, history, physical and natural science, literature, and other areas. These are frequently

13. halo
13–**1** monument
13–**2** angel
13–**3** shrine
13–**4** crucifix
13–**5** ring of light . . . . 13( )

20. dawdle
20–**1** diminish
20–**2** make jokes
20–**3** pamper
20–**4** waste time
20–**5** shove . . . . 20( )

I do not mean by beauty of form such beauty as that of animals or pictures, which the many would suppose to be my meaning; but understand me to mean straight lines and circles, and the plain or solid figures that are formed out of them by turning-lathes and rulers and measurers of angles; for these I affirm to be not only relatively beautiful, like other things, but they are eternally and absolutely beautiful.

70. The writer thinks that his idea of beauty is
70–**1** easy to understand.
70–**2** the only one that is correct.
70–**3** not held by many people.
70–**4** only relative.
70–**5** simpler than others. . . . . . . 70( )

71. The writer sees beauty mainly in
71–**1** nature.
71–**2** painting.
71–**3** sculpture.
71–**4** poetry.
71–**5** geometric figures. . . . . 71( )

Fig. 11:4. ITEMS FROM THE *Cooperative English Test,* READING COMPREHENSION, C1. FORM T. (The paragraph is used to measure both speed and comprehension.) *

* Used by permission of the Educational Testing Service, Copyright 1943.

arranged in order of difficulty with the easier ones coming first. Measuring comprehension presents no particular problems.

Speed of reading, though, is another matter. We might justifiably raise the question whether it is actually possible to measure this aspect of reading, because it is doubtful if an individual has such a thing as a reading rate. When an individual reads, he adjusts his reading rate to the level of difficulty of the material that he is reading. When he reads humor and light novels, he reads rapidly; when he attacks a philosophical treatise, he may creep along. The best that these rate scores can give is an *average* rate of reading. The meaning and value of such a score has been questioned by many.

Survey tests are very numerous. Every test publisher has at least several that were developed by reading specialists. Some of the reading subtests of the batteries discussed earlier in this chapter are published separately, as was noted above. These are basically survey tests. Survey tests are used at the beginning of the school year, being given to all students and used as a screening device. The practice today is to pick out the poor readers and to see what help can be offered them. Most universities devote a large amount of time, money, and space to developmental and remedial reading clinics. The first type of clinic is concerned with trying to make better readers of individuals by guidance and practice. The second concentrates on the severely handicapped reader, first diagnosing, then treating. In the elementary school, results of reading survey tests can be used by a teacher in setting up reading groups within a class. Since reading is a special area of instruction at this level, these survey tests can be used as end-of-year examinations to evaluate attainment.

Reading Diagnostic Tests

Reading diagnostic tests are basically concerned with everything that the reading experts believe goes into the reading process. A look into any one of these shows that they generally measure comprehension and speed first. Then there are tests of word discrimination; various aptitude data tests, such as visual tests, memory tests, motor tests, vocabulary, the use of indexes and dictionaries, the reading of maps and charts; and other types of tests. Some of these tests are group tests and are very similar to survey tests. Examples of group tests are the *Iowa Silent Reading Test* * and the *SRA Reading Record*.† Other diagnostic tests are much more of a clinical nature and are frequently administered as individual tests. Sometimes various mechanical devices are used to assist in making the diagnosis. *Durrell's Analysis of Reading Difficulty* * is an example of this type. Special training in reading, especially remedial reading, is a prerequisite to correct and effective use of tests of this type.

A different approach to the measurement of reading is found in the *Gilmore Oral Reading Test*.* The purpose of this test is to analyze the oral reading performance of children in the first eight grades of school. The test measures accuracy of oral reading, comprehension of material read, and rate of reading. This is an individual test. The student is given a booklet containing the paragraphs to be read and is seated across from the examiner who records errors, time, and answers to questions in a record blank. This test is very useful to those attempting to appraise objectively this important objective of elementary education.

Reading-readiness Tests

Reading-readiness tests are usually administered during the last month of kindergarten or during the first few days of first grade. While most of these appear to be group tests, they are usually administered to from 6 to 8 pupils so that the examiner can see that everyone is doing what he is supposed to be doing. For many boys and girls, this is their first experience with paper-and-pencil tests, or with any type of test. Usually these tests are of such a nature that the child makes marks or draws lines in the test booklet using a large primary pencil.

Most of these tests cover such areas as word meaning, understanding of sentences, simple information, copying exercises, and matching exercises made up of figures, letters, numbers, and words. In

---

* Published by Harcourt, Brace & World.
† Published by Science Research Associates.

"Mark the pigeon."

"Mark the one you use to cut grass."

"Draw a frame around the one the same as the one shown in the frame."

647

674 467   647 746

"After the spoon, mark the nine."

   5   7   9 |

"Draw a picture just like this in the space beside it."

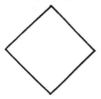

Fig. 11:5. Representative Items from the *Metropolitan Readiness Test* *

* Used by permission of the World Book Co., Copyright 1949.

general terms, these subtests are used to measure a child's ability to understand language, to test his experiential background (After all, reading consists of bringing meaning to the printed page. Breadth of meaning is related to amount of experience.), to determine his perceptual ability (recognizing similarities), and to evaluate his motor control. An inspection of the intelligence tests used at this level will reveal that they tap the same abilities. However, reading-readiness tests can be administered to small groups at once and are, from this point of view, more efficient than such intelligence tests as the *Stanford-Binet*. Scores on these readiness tests correlate highly with scores on intelligence tests. It might be mentioned that one of these tests, *Metropolitan Readiness Test* (Fig. 11:6),* contains an item which asks the child to draw a man. As will be shown in the chapter on intelligence, Goodenough used this as the only item on her test to measure the intelligence of children.

The manuals for these reading-readiness tests contain a set of norms, each of which has associated with it a rating or score that gives an indication of a child's probable success in reading. For example, the *Metropolitan Readiness Test* has 5 letter ratings A (Superior), excellent risk for first-grade work; B (High Normal), a good risk for first-grade work, provided that health and emotional factors are all right; C (Average), likely to succeed in first-grade work, but will need individual diagnosis and help; D (Low Normal), likely to have difficulty in first-grade work; and E (Poor Risk), chances for failure are high. Further kindergarten work or individual work is essential.

An example of the usefulness of the *Metropolitan Readiness Test* was shown by Mitchell (3) who analyzed results obtained using the test with almost 1200 first graders in a county in Virginia. Scores on this test were correlated with various scores on the Primary Battery I of the *Metropolitan Achievement Tests*. He found that the total scores on the *Metropolitan Readiness Test* were good predictors of achievement in grade 1 when scores on the *Metropolitan Achievement Tests* were used to measure this achievement. He reported that

* Published by Harcourt, Brace & World.

the correlation of the *Metropolitan Readiness Test* with word knowledge was .56, with word discrimination, .56, with reading, .51, and with arithmetic concepts and skills, .63. Other evidence of validity presented was that less than 10 per cent of those labelled "poor risks" in the fall of the year reached the grade norm in May, and that less than 10 per cent of those rated as "superior" in October failed to meet the grade norm in May.

It should be apparent that these tests measure only one aspect of the traits or capacities needed for success in reading. Of course, for a child to learn to read, intellectual development has to have progressed to a certain point. The usual mental age mentioned as being the minimum required is 6 years and 6 months. But, in addition to this, a child has to have developed and matured physically. He must be able to speak, hear, and see distinctly and well. And, thirdly, he has to have progressed to a certain point in respect to social development. Fourthly, he has to have reached a desirable emotional adjustment. These readiness tests measure only part of the picture. For better prediction, scores from these should be interpreted in the light of the other background data that may be available in greater or lesser amounts to the kindergarten or first-grade teacher.

These reading-readiness tests can be used in two general ways. First, if an elementary school is having a large entering group of first graders, different sections can be set up on the basis of these scores. It is a much simpler task to teach groups that are similar in basic abilities. However, some educators reject such practices as being inconsistent with a democratic philosophy. If such groups are set up, they should be flexible enough for a child to be moved from one to another easily when later evidence shows that he has been misplaced. It might even be desirable to hold back the children in the bottom group and have them spend another year in kindergarten. They might just as well be kept there because, if promoted to first grade, their activities there will have to be similar to the type that they had in kindergarten. The evidence from these tests shows that low scorers on them have not matured enough to profit from first-grade instruction. Secondly, the results can be used by the individual teacher in setting up reading groups in his own room. The same ends are attained as by setting up classes on the same basis. The first group would be taught to read right at the start of the school year; the second group might experience a delay of several months during which it carries on more readiness activities; and the third group might spend most of first grade doing no reading. At least with these tests the first-grade teacher can adapt instruction to the level of every child in her group.

ARITHMETIC AND MATHEMATICS TESTS

As in the area of reading, we find survey tests that are basically concerned with a student's level of attainment. As opposed to this there are tests that are of a diagnostic nature, the emphasis being upon the type of mistakes made by the student. Such tests as these are widely used with elementary-school children.

At the present time, there is one type of test used in this area that is rather unique. It is referred to as a *prognosis test*, and its purpose is to give an indication of how well a student will do in a new area of instruction, such as elementary algebra or plane geometry. The *Orleans Algebra Prognosis Test* * consists of a series of so-called "lessons" and "tests" made up to measure learning on these lessons. On page 2, for example, is found a lesson on the use of letters in algebra to represent numbers. For example:

$$ab \text{ means } a \text{ times } b$$
$$\text{If } a = 2 \text{ and } b = 6, \text{ then}$$
$$ab = 2 \times 6 \text{ or } 12$$

At the top of page 3 is a 12-item test on the use of these algebraic symbols. The bottom of page 3 contains the second lesson, which is tested on the top half of page 4. There are 11 of these lessons and tests and a twelfth test, which serves as a sort of a final examination covering all things taken up in all the previous lessons.

The best way to use prognosis tests is to base them upon methods and results in different schools or, if there are two or more teachers

---

* Published by Harcourt, Brace & World.

in the same school teaching the same subject, to consider each teacher separately. Suppose that we have a school in which the same teacher has 2 sections of beginning algebra or plane geometry. At the beginning of the year, each student is given a prognosis test in his respective area, and all these scores are compared with grades obtained at the end of the first semester. The records of those who dropped the course during the semester because of lack of ability must be included. Sometimes other students, for reasons not related to ability (such as absences caused by illnesses or accidents), do not do so well. These results should be disregarded. After data have been collected on several classes, and, if well-made tests are used for evaluating the semester's work, the teacher should be able to set up a table that will show the probability of a student's passing or failing the teacher's course on the basis of his score on the prognosis test. Since the percentages of failures in beginning algebra and in plane geometry are high, some schools have found these tests to be most helpful in counseling students. These tests will solve the problem that frequently arises in ninth grade as to who should take the regular courses in beginning algebra and who might better enter the course covering general arithmetic.

Other prognosis or aptitude tests for algebra and geometry use a different approach in that they are essentially measures of attainment in arithmetic or algebra studied up to the time of taking the test. The *Iowa Algebra Aptitude Test* * and the *Lee Test of Algebra Ability* † are of this type. The first of these consists of four tests: (1) "Arithmetic," a review of the fundamental processes; (2) "Abstract Computation," the use of letters as computational symbols; (3) "Numerical Series," the usual type of number series in which the rule is to be discovered and the number that comes next determined; and (4) "Dependence and Variation," determining changes that take place in a second number when various changes are made in a first number. These tests, though different in their make-up, can be used in the same fashion as was described for the *Orleans Test* discussed above.

* Published by Bureau of Educational Research and Service, State University of Iowa.
† Published by California Test Bureau.

SPECIAL ACHIEVEMENT-TEST BATTERIES

Frequently, achievement tests are assembled into special batteries for very specific purposes. For example, medical colleges, law schools, dental schools, many privately controlled universities and colleges, industries, and employment services have special tests or batteries that are administered to applicants. While an intelligence test is usually included, these batteries are, for the most part, made up of achievement tests in subjects related to the study or employment to which the individual is seeking admission.

An example of one of these batteries is the *National Teacher's Examination*, which is discussed in detail (pp. 433) in Chapter 18 in this book, "Teacher Evaluation." An example of a battery developed at the high-school graduate level is the *Engineering and Physical Aptitude Test.* * This battery covers a review of high-school mathematics, the ability to handle algebraic formulas, a review of physical science, a set of arithmetic problems, vocabulary, and mechanical comprehension. The purpose is to select individuals for training in work related to physical sciences and engineering.

For many years the Association of American Medical Schools has been interested in the use of tests in the selection of students. At the present time, the *Medical College Admission Test* * is administered nationally twice annually, spring and fall, at centers scattered over the United States. The battery is made up of the usual elements found in predictors of academic achievement. There are 4 parts to the battery: Verbal, Science, Quantitative, and General Information (humanities and social sciences), altogether making up about 300 items. Over the years this battery has been found to be effective in selecting students who will do well in medical school. That it is, as might be expected, a good predictor of academic success in medical school is beyond doubt. But it probably has little or nothing to do with an individual's ultimate success as a physician, especially as a general

* Published by the Psychological Corporation.

practitioner. The main use of such batteries is to keep academically undesirable candidates out of professional schools.

Tests used by dental schools are similar to this medical-school battery in that they usually measure verbal and numerical ability in addition to achievement in such predental areas as biology, chemistry, and physics. Dental-school batteries are unique in that they also have included tests of spatial ability and of manipulation. The latter calls for such things as shaping and carving objects in chalk or plaster and measurements of manual and finger dexterity.

The *Law School Admission Tests* * differ from both medical and dental batteries in that they are basically concerned with a lawyer's major activity, the manipulation of words. Subtests on this battery bear such labels as "Reading Comprehension," "Paragraph Reading," "Interpretation of Data," "Best Arguments," "Debates," etc.

When these batteries are used alone they are, in many cases, no better predictors of success in academic work than are the grades that an individual has earned in previous schooling. That is to say, an individual high-school grade average is about the best predictor of academic success in college. A student's grades as an undergraduate are good predictors in both the graduate and professional school. Over the years, an individual tends to repeat his performance in similar learning situations. When prediction is based upon a combination of these high-school grade averages, scores on these selection tests or batteries, and, perhaps, such scores as those obtained from an interest inventory, it usually increases in accuracy. Such multiple prediction is beyond the scope of this book. Scores on these achievement batteries, like the scores obtained from those special aptitude batteries that will be discussed in Chapter 13, "Evaluation of Special Abilities," are all dependent to a great extent upon intelligence. Since intelligence-test scores correlate significantly with future academic success, scores on these tests do also. The moot question is whether or not an individual's previously earned grades plus an intelligence-test score are not better predictors of success than are the results of these special batteries just discussed. Certainly these batteries are much more expensive in terms of time and money.

* Developed and administered by the Educational Testing Service.

Another very different type of achievement test is the *Watson-Glaser Critical Thinking Appraisal.** This test may be used both with high-school and college students and with adults. The appraisal made with this instrument is that of a very common objective held by all teachers, namely, teaching students to think. This test, which takes a little less than an hour to administer, consists of 5 parts. The first of these, called "Inference," contains data presented in short paragraphs below which appear half a dozen inferences. These are to be evaluated on a 5-point continuum from "definitely true" to "definitely false." The second part, "Recognition of Assumption," consists of determining whether the truth of given statements depends upon the truth of various assumptions listed below. The third part, labeled "Deduction," is made up of items in which 2 statements or premises are given, followed by several proposed conclusions. The student is to accept the premises as true and to evaluate whether or not each conclusion follows from the statement. In the fourth part, called "Interpretation," short paragraphs are followed by a series of concluding statements. These are to be appraised as to whether or not each follows from the given data. The fifth part, "Evaluation of Arguments," consists of the statement of a question, followed by a series of 3 or 4 arguments. Each is to be evaluated for strength or weakness. Teachers who are interested in evaluating the ability to think should welcome this effort in a very difficult area.

*Published by Harcourt, Brace & World.

REFERENCES

1. Buros, O. K. *The fifth mental measurements yearbook.* Highland Park, N. J.: The Gryphon Press, 1959.
2. Buros, O. K. *The sixth mental measurement yearbook.* Highland Park, N. J.: The Gryphon Press, 1965.
3. Mitchell, B. C. The Metropolitan Readiness Tests as predictors of first grade achievement. *Educ. Psychol. Measmt.*, 1962, 22, 765-72.

Older editions of *Buros'* yearbooks and the catalogs of the various test publishers are also useful references.

PART III

MEASUREMENT OF INTELLIGENCE,
SPECIAL ABILITIES, ADJUSTMENT, AND
INTERESTS AND ATTITUDES

CHAPTER 12

MEASURING MENTAL ABILITY

In this chapter we shall consider tests of intelligence or, as they are frequently called, tests of academic ability. Attempts to define what these tests measure have concerned psychologists for the last 50 years. The definitions of intelligence have been many and varied. Some representative ones are as follows:

> Wechsler (52)—Intelligence is the aggregate or global capacity of the individual to act purposefully, to think rationally, and to deal effectively with his environment.
> Goddard (16)—The degree of availability of one's experiences for the solution of immediate problems and the anticipation of future ones.
> Terman (45)—The ability to think in terms of abstract ideas.
> Stoddard (43)—Intelligence is the ability to undertake activities that are characterized by difficulty, complexity, abstractness, economy, adaptiveness to a goal, social value, emergence of originals, and to maintain such activities under conditions that demand a concentration of energy and a resistance to emotional forces.
> Binet (in 18)—The capacity to judge well, to reason well, and to comprehend well.

These definitions are of two general types. The first might be called a "cognitive" type and is typified by such definitions as the ability to carry on abstract thinking, the ability to learn, the ability to manipulate symbols, etc. The second is concerned with the "adaptive" processes of an individual to his total environment, as exemplified by Stoddard's definition given above.

255

Hunt (27) made a comprehensive study of the ways in which intelligence has been regarded since man first began to write on the subject. He showed that our current concepts of intelligence go back to the middle of the nineteenth century to the work of Charles Darwin and his theory of the survival of the fittest. Darwin's cousin, Sir Francis Galton, in 1869 published a book on the inheritance of genius in which he showed that famous Englishmen tended to come from a small group of families and concluded that high mental ability was inherited. Galton later established a laboratory in which he measured many men mostly with sensory and psychomotor tests. He and his associates mostly believed that intelligence was fixed and entirely determined by heredity. This had a tremendous effect on the concepts of mental organization held by American psychologists over the first half of the twentieth century. Prominent American psychologists such J. M. Cattell, G. S. Hall, H. Goddard, E. L. Thorndike, L. M. Terman, and Florence Goodenough were all strong advocates of this position.

As the years went by much evidence was accumulated to show that, while heredity had something to do with intelligence, it was not the only determiner. Studies of the intelligence of identical twins reared apart showed much lower correlations than those obtained from identical twins reared together, about .74 for the former, .90 for the latter. Studies by Jones (28) and Bayley (3) showed changes in individual IQ's over a period of time. Research performed at the University of Iowa and summarized by Stoddard (43) revealed the effects of environment on intelligence test scores. This lead psychologists to try to determine what proportion of intelligence was determined by heredity and what by environment. This rather pointless activity led to dissonant results.

The work of Hebb (25) and Harlow (24) based upon experiments of animal learning, evidence from neuropsychology, suggestions from the programming of electronic computers for problem solving, and data from the developmental studies of children (Piaget, in 5) lead Hunt (27) to conclude that "intelligence should be conceived as intellectual capacities based on central processes hierarchically arranged within the intrinsic portions of the cerebrum. These central processes are approximately analogous to strategies for information processing and action with which electronic computors are programmed." A concept of genetically predetermined fixed intelligence is incompatible with these concepts. Hunt's concepts are, of course, based upon the belief that each child inherits a basic capacity. Most important are the effects of learning in childhood and the implications for desirable and effective learning situations during the early years of development in the modification of this inherited basic capacity.

HISTORY OF INTELLIGENCE TESTING

The earliest systematic attempts to measure man's intelligence took place in the psychological laboratory of Wilhelm Max Wundt in Germany. The emphasis here was basically on reaction time. One of Wundt's students, H. Ebbinghaus, devised test items, many of which we still use today, in attempting to solve this problem as the Germans saw it. In the last decades of the nineteenth century, Germany was the Mecca of American scientists. One such scientist who went to Wundt's laboratory and obtained his Ph.D. there was J. McKeen Cattell. Cattell returned to this country, and he and Clark Wissler began measuring the reaction time, sensitivity to pain, color discrimination, and other psychological aspects of American students. These results were correlated with university grades and the resulting coefficient was approximately .00. This about ended the reaction-time approach to measuring mental ability.

About the end of the nineteenth century, officials connected with public education in Paris became concerned about the number of students in French schools who seemed incapable of profiting from schoolroom learning. Two Frenchmen, Alfred Binet and Théodore Simon, were commissioned to devise some sort of instrument to separate the feebleminded from the other children. After several years' work, Binet and Simon published, in 1905, the first intelligence test as we know it today. By 1908, Binet, having worked further with it, published another scale. This differed from the first in that it was an age scale. Each item was worth so many months' mental age. Here we have the first appearance of the mental-age concept. Binet's first test was a point scale, as are most of the tests in use today. In 1911, the year of Binet's death, appeared another revision of his test.

Binet's test was soon brought to this country and translated into English. (H. H. Goddard was an early user of this in the Vineland Training School.) The results of these translations were none too reliable, so two other American psychologists, Lewis Terman and F. Kuhlmann, both worked on adaptations or revisions, not translations, of the Binet scales. The more noted of these, Terman's *The Stanford Revision of the Binet-Simon Intelligence Scales*, appeared in 1916.

After the United States entered World War I in 1917, a number of psychologists were commissioned to construct a group intelligence test that could be used with all draftees for screening and assignment. Since Terman's test (and the others of that day) were individual tests, none was applicable to mass testing. So under the direction of A. S. Otis, R. M. Yerkes, and others the *Army Alpha* and the *Army Beta* tests were constructed. The first of these was used with literate individuals and the latter with illiterates and those who could not read or write English. Thus, for the first time in history, large groups of individuals were tested.

So successful did these tests appear that in the 1920's they were readily adopted by schools and industry. Everyone became IQ-conscious. There was great acceptance and enthusiasm and very little critical appraisal. As the years went by, research led to refinements. In the 1930's, L. L. Thurstone (49) published the results of his factorial studies (discussed below), and the beginnings of the appraisal of intelligence as consisting of more than a single, general trait were at hand. In 1939, another individual test, this one for adults, was constructed by David Wechsler. The Selective Service Acts before and during World War II led to some 10 to 12 million men's taking the *Army General Classification Test*. Since World War II, emphasis has been on the factorial approach to the measurement of intelligence and attempts have been made to control some of the environmental factors that apparently greatly affected test scores.

Theories of Intelligence

We shall now take a brief look at some of the major theories that psychologists use in describing the organization of mental life. The first and oldest theory is the UNIFACTOR THEORY, which describes mental ability as a single general capacity. This theory was taken into psychology directly from biology. Apparently this general trait is what was measured by our earlier tests of intelligence.

In 1904, Charles Spearman proposed his 2-factor theory. Here intelligence was conceived as a general factor (g), which was similar to the unifactor mentioned above, plus other factors that he called specific (s). Diagrammatically, his theory can be shown as

The correlation between 2 or more tests depends on the amount of g factor they have in common. In the above diagram, the ovals labeled S_1 and S_2 can be considered as separate mental tests, each with a varying amount of g and each with its specific s. This g factor of Spearman is described as a special sort of energy that can be applied in making comparisons or drawing inferences.

As Spearman's work continued, he found that he had to revise his theory to take care of group factors as shown below (42).

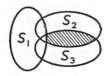

A group factor is shown as the darkened space above. Specific factors three (S_3) and two (S_2) have something in common. This is what Spearman called a group factor. Spearman's group factors included mechanical, arithmetical, musical, logical, and psychological abilities and 3 others that he called "perseveration," "oscillation," and "will." British psychologists today tend to follow Spearman's theories or modifications of it.

A modern rendering of Spearman's work is illustrated in the concepts proposed by Vernon (51, 52). At the top of his schema he has the general intellectual factor, g. Below this are his major group factors, one verbal-educational and the other spatial-practical-mechanical. Each of these can be further analyzed into minor group factors. When this is done, the verbal-educational group usually yields number, scholastic, fluency, and divergent thinking factors. The other major group includes perceptual, physical, psychomotor, spatial, and mechanical factors. Vernon notes that there are cross links between the two major groups such as in a test of clerical ability. Here one finds a combination of verbal ability and perceptual speed. Similarly mathematics and science bring together verbal, numerical, and spatial abilities. Finally Vernon notes that at the bottom of his system come specific factors related to single, simple tests. These may be turned into additional minor group factors by devising additional tests.

Americans, on the other hand, have adopted primarily the theories of the Thurstones (49). This man and wife combination administered 57 tests requiring approximately 15 hours of work to a large group of high-school students. These tests consisted of practically all known types of verbal and nonverbal mental activity as exemplified by the existing intelligence tests. As a result of treating this mass of data statistically by a complex process called "factor analysis," the Thurstones were able to isolate a small group of factors which they called *"primary mental abilities."* Briefly these are:

N   (number) the ability to carry out the 4 basic arithmetic processes rapidly and accurately

V   (verbal) the understanding of ideas expressed in word forms

WF   (word fluency) the ability to write and speak with considerable ease

M   (memory)

R   (reasoning) problem solving, profiting from experience, etc.

S   (spatial) the ability to visualize spatial relationship

P   (perception) perceptual speed.

The first 6 of these factors are published as an intelligence test, called the *Chicago Test of Primary Mental Abilities.** The first 6, less the test for memory, are also published as the *SRA Primary Mental Abilities Test.*†

This concept of the Thurstones is referred to as the MULTIPLE

* Published by Science Research Associates.
† Published by Science Research Associates.

FACTOR THEORY (48). Tests built in the light of this theory can be so constructed that they measure one or more of the factors. One test could be devised to measure only the spatial factor. Another such as the *Army General Classification Test* contains items covering the verbal, numerical, and spatial factors. We shall see in the discussion of tests, both in this chapter and in those that follow, how this factorial approach is applied to all facets of human abilities and personality.

Research of the Army Air Forces Testing Program of World War II as summarized by Guilford (21) verified some of the above factors, verified 7 others fairly well, and suggested 15 others as worth-while hypotheses for further investigation. A diagram of mental organization as visualized by this theory would look like this:

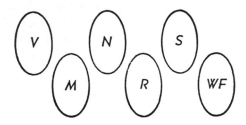

In his later work, Guilford (20, 23) proposed a 3-way organization of mental ability. He visualizes this model as a block with one side labeled "Operations," another, "Content," and the third, "Products." One face of the block consists of 5 operations, these in turn intersecting the 4 content categories, which in turn intersect the 6 products categories. The divisions in each of these 3 categories are as follows:

Operations
1. Memory—retaining information
2. Cognition—recognizing patterns, facts, etc.
3. Convergent thinking—proceeding from information to a specific correct answer
4. Divergent thinking—proceeding from information to a variety of adequate solutions as in finding titles to fit a plot

5. Evaluation—decisions concerning goodness or appropriateness of ideas

Content

1. Figural—directly perceived objects, events, drawings
2. Symbolic—letters, numbers, etc.
3. Semantic—verbal
4. Behavioral—interpretation of human behavior

Products

1. Information—units
2. Classes of units
3. Relations between units
4. Systems of information
5. Transformations
6. Implications.

The block made from the above then contains 120 cells (5 x 4 x 6) each of which represents an ability, a factor, or a type of task that may appear on an intelligence test. A common factual item on an intelligence test would be classified by this system as Memory, Semantic, and Unit of Information.

In the 1966 article Guilford noted that to date he and his students had actually identified 75 of these factors or abilities, or to state it in another way, 75 of his cells were occupied. Actually he has isolated 80 abilities, but he has found that several of the cells contain more than one factor. Guilford believes that the single-score approach to intelligence has worked well, but now the time has come to use a multiple-score approach. However, there is strong opposition to this. McNemar (30) has accused theorists like Guilford of fragmenting mental ability into more and more factors of less and less value. There will be a further discussion of this conflict later when special aptitude batteries are discussed.

The student may feel that these two major theories of mental organization are very dissimilar; actually they are not. When Thurstone built his factors into tests and administered these tests, it was found that there were positive intercorrelation among all of the factors (48). This seems to make the concept of a general intellectual factor unavoidable as this is the only way that these intercorrelations can be interpreted. In actual practice, the users of tests in America today usually accept the idea of a general factor. We continue to use the well-established individual and group tests which measure general intelligence. On a few of these tests, such as those used to predict academic success, verbal and quantitative scores are obtained, or on other tests verbal and performance scores. This is the major concession made to Thurstone's ideas, although his methods are widely used in research. As will be seen in Chapter 13, attempts to predict behavior using the multifactor tests have been disappointing.

It should be noted that there is a tendency for some individuals to regard Thurstone's or Guilford's factors as basic components when speaking of the organization of mental life, just as the chemist or physicist uses elements or atoms when discussing the nature of physical objects. On the other hand, members of the British school have maintained that factors were mainly classifications of similar tests and no more than that. Vernon believes that g is not the same whenever cognitive tests are used. This he regards psychologically as the general level of one's thinking skill, varying in saturation from one particular measure to another. Earlier, Spearman maintained that one and the same g was found in any intellectual test. It seems that the British point of view is in accord with Hunt's ideas which were previously described.

Another problem that has created controversy over the years is the organization of mental abilities from birth to adulthood. Garrett (15) postulated that mental ability is of a general nature in early life and that during the teens and somewhat later there is an increasing differentiation of this general ability into a number of more highly specialized aptitudes, perhaps as a result of maturation. However, this has not been substantiated by research, which has shown that the amount of general ability has stayed the same or increased with age. Typical of this research is that of Weiner (55) who analyzed the scores of 1400 subjects on the *General Aptitude Test Battery* (Chapter 13) drawn from over 10,000 cases. He took 200 individuals in the 14-15 age group and 200 other individuals in 6 other age groups, the last one being made up of people 45-54 years old. He applied factor analytic procedures to his data and found that in this battery a general ability factor accounted for about 20 per cent of the variability at ages 14-15, stayed at about this level during the twenties, and increased slightly in the 30- and 40-year-old groups. He clearly demonstrated that general ability does not decrease in prominence in successive age groups. As others have also shown, he demonstrated that, if it changed at all, it increased.

What Intelligence Tests Measure

We might begin discussion in a negative fashion by stating what intelligence tests do not measure. We have no intelligence test today that measures innate ability. The probability is high that we shall never have such a test. Intelligence tests measure the extent to which this innate potential has been modified by environment. In other words, they measure what an individual has learned and, hence, these tests are really achievement tests. If one doubts this, let him examine the items making up most of our verbal tests. Without schooling or book-learning an examinee is lost. When we administer tests of this type, we have to make an assumption that everyone being tested has had an equal opportunity to learn. This doesn't mean just equal schooling. It includes also the effects of the home on learning. All homes are not equally conducive to learning.

To be realistic about this, we must admit that this assumption of equal opportunity to learn is never met. Many scores obtained with intelligence tests reflect a child's background as much as anything else, and every single test score, therefore, should be interpreted in the light of what is known about each individual's background. The literature of psychology and education is filled with so-called "barren environment" studies, such as the study of the test scores of hill folk, canalboat children, and slum children. Alongside these are found the studies that show the increases of intelligence test scores of southern-born Negro children that are brought about by increased length of residence in northern urban centers. Inequalities of educational and cultural opportunities affect test scores. Terman (46) showed the effects of socio-economic status of parents on test scores. For example, with children in the 2- to 5½-year age group the mean IQ of children of professional people was 116.2, of semiprofessional and managerial workers, 112, of clerical and skilled trade workers, 104, of rural owners (as opposed to renters or hired hands), 99.1, and of day laborers, both urban and rural, 94. Similar differences were shown in 4 other age groups that he studied. It can be argued, and perhaps with a certain amount of validity, that differences in these scores are brought about by inheritance and selection. The nature–nurture controversy as to which of these factors affects mental ability most may be pursued by those interested in reading Stoddard (43) or the *Yearbook* of the National Society for the Study of Education (32). Our tests, then, measure the present status of an individual, the results of the modification of certain amounts of potential brought about by contact with environment.

TYPES OF ITEMS ON INTELLIGENCE TESTS

An inspection of a group of tests of academic ability will show that they tend to be made up of similar types of items. All tests do not contain the same kinds of items. Some, for example, consist of a predominance of verbal items—vocabulary, general information, reading, analogies, "same-opposites," and the like. Other tests are made up of items of the so-called "nonverbal" type. Examples of these are number series, picture series, and items dealing with spatial relationships. Still other tests tend to be made up of many of these different kinds of items, either grouped according to type or all mixed up. On the pages that follow are some examples of the more commonly encountered intelligence test items.

1. *General Information*
   An eight-sided figure is called a(an) (A) hexagon, (B) octagon, (C) polynomial, (D) pentagon, (E) cube.
   How far is it from New York City to San Francisco?
   How tall is the average adult American male?
   Galileo was famous as a (A) chemist, (B) philosopher, (C) physicist, (D) geologist, (E) theologian.
2. *Vocabulary*
   Eulogize means the same as (A) celebrate, (B) elate, (C) lament, (D) apologize, (E) laud.
   What is the second letter of an eight-letter word meaning the same as "to near"?
   Obtuse means the same as (A) pointed, (B) dense, (C) fat, (D) perpendicular, (E) blunt.
3. *Logical Choices and Judgment*
   Metal always has (A) weight, (B) shine, (C) great value, (D) grayish color.

A restaurant is never without (A) customers, (B) chairs, (C) waitresses, (D) dishes, (E) counters.

A steamship always has (A) passengers, (B) cargo, (C) guns, (D) funnel.

Leather is used for shoes because it is (A) cheap, (B) obtained from cows, (C) durable, (D) absorbent.

4. *Same–Opposites*

(*Directions:* One of the words at the right means the *same* or the *opposite* as the word at the left. Underline this word which is the *same* or *opposite*.)

hot   humid   cold   balmy   baked

graceful   honest   awkward   fast   strong

eulogize   celebrate   elate   lament   apologize   laud

5. *Verbal Analogies*

Abundant is to scarce as cheap is to (A) costly, (B) bargain, (C) economical, (D) inexpensive.

Water is to pipe as electricity is to (A) filament, (B) cord, (C) wire, (D) power.

Alloy is to element as brass is to (A) bronze, (B) steel, (C) copper, (D) statue.

6. *Disarranged Sentences*

(*Directions:* Rearrange the following to make meaningful sentences.)

soup at served is dinner sometimes.

the over sun plains up parched hot came the.

7. *Memory*

(*Directions:* Listen and repeat these numbers exactly as I say them to you.)

8   6   1   3   9   2

7   4   8   1   6   9   3

(*Directions:* Listen and when I am through you are to repeat these numbers backward.)

2   7   4   9   5   3

6   1   4   8   2   7

8. *Reasoning*

If the first two of the following sentences are true, the third is (A) true, (B) uncertain, (C) false.

Some of my friends are Democrats. Some of my friends are teachers. Some of my teacher friends are Democrats.

X is either W, Y, or Z. X is not Z. Therefore (A) X is W, (B) X is either W or Y, (C) one cannot tell whether X is W or Y.

9. *Classification*
   (*Directions:* Underline the word which does not belong in the group.)

oak	maple	hemlock	elm	ash
perch	bass	pike	frog	catfish
brass	silver	iron	zinc	gold

10. *Differences*
    (*Directions:* Which of the following differs from the others?)

BBCA	DABB	CBAD	DBBC
elbow	knee	ankle	thigh
pond	stream	river	brook

11. *Arithmetic*
    $31 + 43 + 46 + 35 = ?$
    $87 \times 9 = ?$
    $12 \div \frac{3}{4} = ?$

12. *Problems*
    If two apples cost 15 cents, how many apples can be bought for 45 cents?
    A car travels 18 miles in 20 minutes. How many miles per hour is the car going?
    Two men caught 48 fish. X caught three times as many as Y. How many did Y catch?

13. *Number Series*
    (*Directions:* Look at this series of numbers. What number comes next?)
    90, 30, 10, 3⅓, 1⅑   ?
    12, 18, 15, 21, 18, 24   ?
    (*Directions:* Which number does not belong in this series?)
    2, 5, 4, 6, 8, 10   ?

14. *Following Directions*
    Cross out the letter which is the same as the last letter of the fifth word of this sentence.
    r   h   i   w
    Cross out the odd number that is not in a triangle and that has a letter with it.

    Write the second largest of these numbers backward.
    64   78   56   98   79   _____

15. *Figure Analogies*

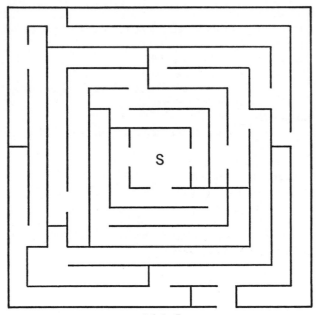

A is to B as C is to ? *

16. *Mazes*

Adult I
Porteus Test. Vineland Revision.†

* From the 1941 edition of the *American Council on Education Psychological Examination.* Used by permission of the Educational Testing Service, Copyright 1941.

† Reproduced by permission of C. H. Stoelting Co.

17. *Missing Parts*
   What is missing in each picture?

18. *Absurdities*
   What is silly about this picture?

19. *Spatial Relationships*

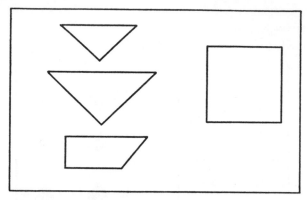

Mark the square to show how the pieces at the left will fit
into it.*

THE MEASUREMENT OF INTELLIGENCE

To measure intelligence we use either an individual or a group test.

Individual Tests

Individual tests are so called because of the fact that they are
administered to only one person at a time. Basically they are of 3
general types: highly verbal, like the *Stanford-Binet;* about half
verbal and half of a performance nature, like the Wechsler Scales;
and mainly of a performance nature, like the various preschool
batteries.

THE STANFORD-BINET TESTS. In 1916 Terman published his first
edition of the *Stanford Revision of the Binet-Simon Intelligence
Scale.* From 1916 until 1937, when it was superseded by a new edition of 2 forms, *L* and *M*, this was by far the most widely used individual intelligence test. These 1937 tests, *L* and *M*, were very similar in form and content. Actually in their development they were
two parts of a longer test. The correlation between the two forms
was .91. It was hoped that these two forms would be used interchangeably or that one could be used in certain cases as a check

* From the *Revised Beta Examination.* Used by permission of the Psychological Corporation, Copyright 1935.

upon the other. Actually this did not work out as most of the forms sold and used were form *L*'s.

The current edition of the *Stanford-Binet,* issued in 1960, incorporates in a single scale, called *Form L-M,* the best subtests from forms *L* and *M* of the 1937 revision. Only those items that were most discriminative were selected for the new scales. Thus the less satisfactory items and all duplicate items were eliminated. Also some items that were otherwise satisfactory were relocated on the test.

Form L-M may be administered to any person from 2-year-olds to adults. The test consists of a series of items or subtests that are arranged by half years. Between the ages 2 to 5 there is a test for each half year. From ages 5 to 14 there is one test per year. These are followed by one "average adult" test and 3 "superior adult" tests. Each item or subtest is worth so many months of mental age (MA). For example, at Year II there are six items each worth one month.

In administering the test one usually starts out with a test close to the subject's chronological age. For example, a typical 9-year-old boy would be given the items on Year IX first; next he would be given the items on Year X. Then the examiner would continue upwards until an age level is reached in which the boy misses every item. Suppose that he also missed an item or more on Year IX. He then would be given Year VIII and this procedure is followed downward until an age level is reached on which all items are answered correctly. This bottom age is called his *basal age.* It is assumed that he can answer correctly all items below his basal age. After the test is scored, the mental age values for all items responded to correctly, are summed and added to the basal age. This sum is the boy's mental age. Normally the scattering of successes and failures spreads over several age levels.

To a great extent the items on the *Stanford-Binet* are of a verbal nature. For example, on Year VI item 1 is a vocabulary item; item 2 is about differences ("What is the difference between . . ."); item 3 contains mutilated pictures ("what part is gone?"); item 4 is labeled number concepts ("Give me 6 blocks. Put them here"); item 5 is made up of opposite analogies; and item 6 is tracing a maze. On other tests simple arithmetic problems are found. Memory is measured by the repetition of digits or of sentences. Reasoning is sampled through the use of simple and complex problems. Spatial ability is measured by having the examinee draw geometric figures or by having him observe designs that are completed or are being made, and their attempt to reproduce them. All these different types of items measuring different aspects of mental ability are added together to give a single score.

The most significant difference between the 1960 edition and the previous one is in the type of IQ used in reporting scores. The authors have abandoned the old ratio IQ, that is $IQ = \dfrac{MA \ (100)}{CA}$ and have substituted in its place a deviation IQ with a mean of 100 and a standard deviation of 16. Binet IQ's are currently a type of standard score.

These deviation IQ's are easily read from an extensive table in the manual which has MA across the top and CA on the sides. The highest CA listed is 18-00, for the authors believe that mental growth stops typically at age 18 instead at age 16 as they previously maintained (4). When adults are given this test, a chronological age of 18 is used in entering the tables. (See 35).

The IQ is considered to be a measure of the rate at which an individual is developing mentally. Since a child's mental age is always rising, the IQ gives an indication of how relatively fast or slow this development is. IQ's tend to be relatively stable over the years. As Bradway, Thompson, and Cravens (7) have pointed out, there is considerable stability to test scores. These workers tested about 100 subjects ranging in age from 2 to 5½ years with the 1937 *Stanford-Binet* and followed this up with retesting 10 years later (adolescence period) and 15 years later (young adult period). The correlation between original scores and those obtained 10 years later was .65, and with scores obtained 25 years later, .59. The correlation between scores obtained in adolescence and those obtained 15 years later was about .85. Later Bradway and Thompson (1962) reported a study based upon 111 subjects who were given the *Stanford-Binet* both as preschoolers and as adolescents and later as adults were administered both the *Stanford-Binet* and the *Wechsler Adult Intelligence Scale*. The correlation between preschool IQ and adult *Stanford-Binet* and total WAIS score was .59 and .64. Those between adolescent IQ's and adult IQ's were .85 and .80 respectively. In this latter study the average increase in IQ on the *Stanford-Binet* from adolescence to adulthood was 11 points, indicating that normal mental growth continues beyond age 16.

Other studies confirm these results. When the period between testings is shorter, it follows that the correlation between the two sets of scores are higher. Test-retest correlations when the intervening period is six months or a year result in coefficients in the .80's and .90's. Lowered correlations are the result of various factors such as changes within the individual himself, differences in testing conditions, and the effects of reactions to different test administrators. However, in spite of all this, the *Stanford-Binet*, when correctly administered and scored, gives a reliable measure of a child's mental ability.

Ever since the *Stanford-Binet* has been used, individuals have been classified by the use of descriptive terms for each IQ level. The earlier test had these levels ranging from "idiot" to "genius." In the 1937 revision, these terms are less specific and less vivid, as they should be. The following distribution is from Merrill (31).

140+	= Very superior
120-139	= Superior
110-119	= High average
90-109	= Normal
80-89	= Low average
70-79	= Borderline
69 and below	= Feeble-minded

Such a system is useful in reporting the results of intelligence tests to parents, students, or others concerned. The writer believes that there is nothing sacred or mystical about intelligence-test scores that necessitates their being kept in locked files to be used only by those who have been duly initiated, the professional psychologists. If one of the major purposes of testing is to obtain information useful in counseling, these intelligence-test scores would seem to be the most basic part of the picture. If the purpose of educational and vocational counseling is to enable individuals to make realistic decisions in respect to their future lives on the basis of what they know about themselves, it then follows that a very poor job will be done unless the individuals have a reasonably accurate picture of their own mental abilities. Most individuals, as a result of school experience, have a pretty good idea as to where they stand on the continuum of intelligence (9). Teachers and others have no qualms about giving students grades and scores on achievement or classroom tests. What correlates higher with intelligence-test scores than these scores? This is not an argument for revealing specific scores or IQ's to students or parents, but merely a suggestion that this band or level approach be used when teacher or counselor sits down with student or parent to discuss a child's ability.

Something must also be said about the lower end of this intelligence continuum. In the past, anyone with an IQ of less than 70 on the *Stanford-Binet Test* was automatically labeled as feeble-minded. Today, the criterion of feeble-mindedness has been altered to include the social usefulness of the individual. The problem narrows down to whether or not a person is able to function in our society. Such basic questions as employability, physical self-care, delinquent behavior, and the like must be considered before an individual is institutionalized. There are many individuals with measured IQ's below 70 who today lead useful lives outside of institutional walls.

The *Stanford-Binet,* though widely accepted and used, is subject to criticism, some of it quite valid. First, the test is highly verbal. With such an emphasis on words, some children are penalized because all individuals do not possess the same amounts of all abilities. Secondly, many of the situations are academic, reflecting schoolroom activities. This is a liability when we have to test adults with a test so made. To adults, the test has no face validity. Thirdly, many psychologists feel that a single score is a poor way to represent an individual's mental ability. The trend today is toward concern for multiple abilities rather than one general ability. Fourthly, this test is time-consuming, both to administer and score. Also, any person desiring to administer it must have considerable special training. Usually a one-semester university course concerned with the administration and scoring of between 25 and 50 tests is considered a minimum. Fifthly, as pointed out earlier in this chapter, this test seems to have a bias in favor of white, urban, middle-class Americans. The use of the test with hill folk, Negroes, Indians, or lower-lower class urban children produces results of questionable validity. Finally, this test is held responsible by some for promoting the

continued use of the IQ as a measure of mental ability. Many feel that the age scale should be replaced by a point scale and the IQ scores by standard scores. In the test's favor it can be stated, first, that it is well developed and well constructed. The techniques used and the time spent in making this test should serve as criterions to be followed by all test-makers. Secondly, the test is fairly accurate. When correctly used, it produces reliable and valid results. Thirdly, more research has been carried on with this test than, perhaps, with any other test. Such research makes the test invaluable.
test invaluable.

THE WECHSLER-BELLEVUE INTELLIGENCE SCALE. In 1939, Wechsler published the first edition of the Wechsler-Bellevue intelligence scale, referred to as the WB. It was rather widely used by the U.S. Armed Forces in World War II. Two forms were available for the first edition. A revision, the *Wechsler Adult Intelligence Scale* (*WAIS*), was published in 1955 (53). These two editions were described as for use with adolescents and adults, but mostly they were used with adults. In 1949, Wechsler published the *Wechsler Intelligence Scale for Children* (*WISC*) (54). This test, similar in content and make-up to the adult test, is for use with children ages 5 through 15.

Wechsler was severely critical of other existing tests for several reasons. He felt that (1) they put too much emphasis on verbal tasks; (2) they placed too much emphasis upon speed; (3) they contained childish situations, ridiculous to adults; (4) they were not standardized on adults, usually only children and adolescents were used or only individuals in school; and (5) that the IQ as conceived by Terman and others was of questionable use and validity.

According to Wechsler, mental growth ceases in the early 20's. For a while an individual is on a plateau, and then the growth curve goes down at different rates for different individuals. Since this does happen, Wechsler argues that adults at different age levels should be compared with adults of the same age levels. Hence he has set up norms for 30-, 40-, and 50-year-olds. Whether mental capacity declines as Wechsler sees it is a moot question. It is possible that an individual who has lived 20 or 30 years as an adult in a not-too-stimulating environment and who has not performed some of the manipulations on this test since he left school would score lower,

Picture Arrangement Item

Object Assembly Item   Block Design Pattern

Fig. 12:1. SAMPLE ITEMS FROM THE WECHSLER TESTS *

the older he becomes. Another individual whose life consists of manipulating words and numbers would show no or slight decline.

The Wechsler-Bellevue (WB) consists of 11 subtests. Six of these make up the verbal score and the remaining 5, the performance score. The various tests are listed below:

1. *Information.* A test of the subject's knowledge about the world and its culture. Twenty-five items.
2. *Comprehension.* A test of practical judgment and common sense. Ten questions such as: Why are shoes made of leather? Why can't deaf people learn to talk?
3. *Digits Forward. Digits Backward.* For repeating digits forward, the series include from 3 to 9 digits; digits backward, from 3 to 8.
4. *Arithmetic.* Solution of 10 problems of an increasing degree of difficulty.
5. *Similarities.* Twelve items such as: In which way are an egg and a seed alike?

* Reproduced by permission of The Psychological Corporation, Copyright 1955.

5A. *Vocabulary*. Forty-two words ranging in difficulty from *apple* to *traduce*.

6. *Picture Arrangement*. Six sets of cards, such as a cut-up comic strip, to be arranged in order of the time in which the scene pictured on each fits into the entire story.

7. *Picture Completion*. Fifteen cards containing drawings with an important part missing. Subject is to tell what this part is.

8. *Block Design*. Seven colored designs on cards to be duplicated using a set of from 4 to 16 cubes painted differently on each side.

9. *Object Assembly*. Three puzzles, a man, a profile, and a hand, made of plywood, to be put together.

10. *Digit Symbol*. Code substitution. The numbers 1 to 9 are each represented by a given symbol. Subject then translates a series of numbers into these symbols.

This test is a point scale in contrast to the *Stanford-Binet*, which is an age scale. The raw scores are transformed to weighted scores. These are summed and the manual entered for the three IQ's, a verbal, performance, and total or full-scale IQ. As was mentioned in Chapter 3, these IQ's are standard scores with a mean of 100 and a standard deviation of about 15. Each subtest is also transformed to standard scores with a mean of 10 and standard deviation of 3. It might be mentioned in passing that, while the entire scale, or the two subscales, are unquestionably reliable, the same cannot be said of some of the subtests based upon 3 to 10 items. The published research of psychology abounds with studies made using these subtest scores as measures for separating groups. It is no wonder that one psychologist has difficulty producing the same findings in a situation similar to one of which he has read (37, 38).

Scores on this test correlate highly with *Stanford-Binet* scores. Coefficients of from .80 to .93 are the usual thing (38). This does not mean that scores on the 2 tests would be very similar for individuals but only that an individual's rank in the 2 distributions would tend to be about the same. Brighter subjects score higher on the *Binet*, and duller ones higher on the *Wechsler*.

The WB test has been more widely used in clinical psychology than in counseling situations, although lately its use in high schools and colleges has been increasing. A study by Silvania (39) revealed this test to rank first as the measure of intelligence used in university counseling bureaus. There is no question that its widespread use was brought about because it is an individual scale for adults, based on adults. The first edition was based upon adults in New York City, many of whom were patients in Bellevue Hospital. These norms were found to be inadequate for university students. The test is an easy test for these students. Super (44) went so far as to question the use of this test in educational and vocational counseling.

The 1955 revision, retitled the *Wechsler Adult Intelligence Scale* (*WAIS*), differs little from the original *Wechsler-Bellevue* (*WB*). It contains no new types of subtests and about two thirds of the items are from the earlier edition. Forty items have been added, but 23 of these are on the Digit Symbol subtest. Better norms have been produced using a stratified sample with controls on sex, urban-rural residence, white race *vs.* nonwhite, geographic region, occupation level, and occupation. Otherwise the test is very similar to the original.

PERFORMANCE TESTS. A third type of individual test used to measure intelligence comes under the heading of "performance" tests or batteries. Some of these, such as the *Cattel test* (1947) are especially constructed for infants. Others, such as the *Minnesota Pre-School Scale* (19) or *Merrill-Palmer Scales,* are for use with the pre-school child, ages 2 and up. Still others, such as the *Grace Arthur* (2) and *Porteus Maze* (36), are used with children and adolescents. Usually these are administered to those who have no or very poor verbal ability. Hence, these are useful in measuring the intellectual ability of the feeble-minded and dull as well as the deaf and the dumb.

These scales consist of completing formboards or pictures, solving puzzles or mazes, making block designs, assembling objects, and performing other similar tasks. This type of test measures a kind of ability quite different from that measured by the *Binet*. We should not be surprised to find that the correlation between these tests and the *Binet* or other verbal tests is lower than that found between the *Stanford-Binet* and the *Wechsler*. Most coefficients tend to fall within a band between .50 and .80. These performance tests are tools of the teacher in special classes or schools. Most of them require special study and skill. Because of this specificity, no more attention will be given to them here.

Group Tests

As opposed to individual tests, we have group tests. This type is much more common because of the practicality of administering a test to a group of individuals simultaneously. As with individual tests, these group tests can be classified into different types, verbal, nonverbal, or a combination of both. The nonverbal tests are used chiefly with kindergarten and primary-grade children who have not learned to read and, hence, would do nothing or poorly on verbal tests. Some group tests administered to older individuals contain both verbal and nonverbal parts.

VERBAL GROUP TESTS. The kind of test classified as verbal is by far the most commonly used type of intelligence test. Most of these strongly emphasize verbal ability. Some are made up completely of items testing this ability. Almost all these tests are timed tests, with an emphasis on speed. However, most of the tests are arranged in an increasing order of difficulty and, by the time work on the test is stopped, most of the individuals have gone about as far as they can go. The writer has demonstrated this to a class that complained about not having enough time. Another form of the same test was given and the students were told to work on it until all items were answered. Seven out of 25 students lowered their scores on the second administration. There was a general increase, but not a significant one.

Some of these tests, like their lineal antecedent, the *Army Alpha,* yield only a single score, an IQ or a centile score. In this category are found such tests as the various *Otis Tests,** *Henmon-Nelson,†* *Kuhlmann-Anderson,‡* and the various *Pintner Tests.** As opposed to this there are longer tests, such as the *California Test of Mental Maturity,§* which has a language and a nonlanguage score each broken down into a series of subscores. Other tests are based upon the results of factor analysis. Among these are the *Holzinger-Crowder Uni-Factor Tests,** and the *SRA Primary Mental Abilities.¶*

* Published by Harcourt, Brace & World, Inc.
† Published by Houghton Mifflin Company.
‡ Published by Personnel Press, Inc.
§ Published by California Test Bureau.
¶ Published by Science Research Associates.

These tests are similar in that each is made up of the same general kinds of test items. These include such types as those measuring word meaning, arithmetic computation and problems, "same-opposites," analogies, number series, block-counting, and reasoning. Sometimes the items are arranged in an increasing order of difficulty with the item types mixed up. That is, the test might start with an easy vocabulary item, followed by a simple problem, and then an easy item of another type; then another round is started using more difficult items. Tests arranged in this order are called SPIRAL OMNIBUS TESTS. The *Otis Self-administering Tests of Mental Ability* and the *Henmon-Nelson Test of Mental Ability* are examples. Most of the other tests are arranged into subtests on the basis of item type or of factors using one type of item to measure each.

At the end of this chapter will be found a brief description of some of the newer and more widely used intelligence tests. This list is by no means exhaustive, merely giving a sample or two of the different types. Buros' *Mental Measurements Yearbook* (8) and the catalogues of the various test publishers should be consulted for a more complete listing.

USES OF GROUP INTELLIGENCE TESTS. The results of group intelligence tests can be put to various uses, but here we will mention only 5 main applications.

1. To group students of various levels into different sections of the same grade. Suppose that in a certain school there are enough students for 4 sixth grades. Some schools might set up a "fast" section, made up of the top quarter of the students, two regular sections, and a "slow" group made up of the bottom quarter of the group. Some educators frown upon such a procedure as being undemocratic or not lifelike. Others argue that, from the viewpoint of teaching, learning, and achievement, such a sectioning method is by far more efficient than mixed classes.

2. To set up groups within grades. A teacher in a school that does not set up classes on the basis of ability can still use these test results to set up little groups within his own grade and adapt instructional materials, processes, and rate of achievement to the capacities of the students in each of the various groups.

3. To study motivation. A teacher may get some insight into an individual student's motivation when his achievement is compared

with his measured capacity to learn. There have been a few schools in the United States that have attempted to appraise and grade students by evaluating what has been accomplished from the viewpoint of each individual's ability to achieve. Such efforts have run into endless difficulties, mostly because they have to coexist with the conventional approach. These schools were forced to keep two types of records, one for their own uses with parents and students and another in case a student transferred to another system. A student of very limited ability with a record of "A's" and "B's" would cause unforeseen problems if he transferred to another school using the conventional methods.

4. To aid in counseling. Here we are concerned with the use of tests in helping each student to understand his own strengths and weaknesses so that he can make the most appropriate educational and vocational choices in line with his abilities.

5. To secure admission to another school or college. Some private secondary schools, colleges, and universities use these tests in selecting their students. For any given test, a school can set up local norms and usually can set up a critical cutting score. A student who scores below this is usually not admitted because research in this school has shown that students who fall below this point have academic difficulties.

EVALUATION OF GROUP TESTS. So far group tests have been criticized for putting too much emphasis on the verbal aspects of intelligence and for the pressure created by the time limits, which some people consider undesirable. Many of these tests are criticized for "low ceilings." By that is meant that they cannot measure the mental ability of the brighter students whose scores all tend to pile up near the maximum score.

These tests have been criticized because of the cultural biases that are reflected by their use. Porteus (36) was one of the early workers who first tried to rule out cultural effects when he developed his series of mazes and used them to measure the mental ability of aborigines in the South Seas and others. R. B. Cattell has a series of tests called *Culture Fair Tests** that are made up completely of nonverbal items that are supposedly only slightly related to any culture. Forty years

* Published by the Institute for Personality and Ability Testing.

ago Goodenough began using a test of one item—draw a man*. Each of these authors sought to develop a test that would cut across all cultures and have universal use. Goodenough's test requires the use of pencil and paper drawing. Just as soon as something like this is introduced into a test, we have cultural differences before we even start.

A group of American sociologists at the University of Chicago has made another and different approach to the problem (14). As sociologists they are interested in class structure and the effect of an individual's position in this class structure on his scores on any test of mental ability. In the course of their research, they examined every item on our most widely used intelligence tests and found that, statistically, the majority of items contained a class bias. This means that if a child is a member of a middle-class group he has a better chance of getting the item right than a child from a lower-class home. Activities and objects used and tested on these intelligence examinations tend to be drawn from our middle-class culture.

As a result of this study, Davis and Eells developed two tests entitled the *Davis-Eells Games* (12), a "Primary Form" for grades 1 and 2 and an "Elementary Form" for grades 3 to 6. In this test the child has to do no reading. All instructions are read slowly and clearly to the pupils. An attempt is made to develop a spirit of fun and play, both in the directions and in some of the items. Each item consists of a picture with a 1, 2, and 3 alongside it, as illustrated on page 283:

> Look at the first picture. It shows a woman; it shows a man with a bump on his head; and it shows a broken window. A boy is outside the window. I'm going to say three things about this picture. Look at it and find out the thing that is true.
> No. 1: The man fell down and hit his head.
> No. 2: A ball came through the window and hit the man's head.
> No. 3: The picture does not show how the man got the bump on his head. Nobody can tell because the picture doesn't show how the man got the bump.
> Which number was true? †

* Now available as the *Goodenough-Harris Drawing Test* and published by Harcourt, Brace & World.

† Adapted from *Directions for Administering and Scoring Davis-Eells Games*, World Book Company, 1952.

These items are basically concerned with the understanding of verbal problems. Other parts of the *Games* cover money problems, best way of doing things, and analogies.

Scores are given as indices of problem-solving ability, which the authors say may be regarded as an IQ, but they recommend that the

Fig. 12:2. Two Items from the *Davis-Eells Games*, Elementary Form *

* Used by permission of the World Book Co., Copyright 1952.

Index of Problem-Solving Ability (IPSA) term be used because it is a more accurate description of the measure obtained from using the test.

The test was designed to be free from the cultural bias that was known to influence results on other group tests. To date, the research on this test, though not intensive, points out that the *Davis-Eells Games* do not do this. In one study, Smith (40) pointed out that both the *Davis-Eells Games* and the *California Test of Mental Maturity* showed cultural bias when upper and lower socio-economic groups were used. Altus (1), in another study again comparing performance on this test with the *California Test of Mental Maturity* and two achievement tests, found that scores on the *Games* correlated much lower with scores on the reading and arithmetic tests than did scores on the *California Test:* reading .48 *vs.* .79; arithmetic .43 *vs.* .67. She also showed that children from a bilingual background and/or lower-class homes did better on the *Games* than on the *California Test.* The trends, however, were so slight that she recommended more research.

Later research, as exemplified by that of Knief and Stroud (29), was consistent in showing that these tests discriminated according to social class almost to the same extent as do the commonly used intelligence tests. Noll (33), the one voice to the contrary, using a large number of students in grades 2-6 showed that scores on the *Davis-Eells Tests* and socio-economic measures correlated close to zero. The same socio-economic measures produced substantially higher correlations when compared with Otis IQ's.

Further evidence of the group differences brought to light on our tests of intellectual ability are revealed in a study of percentages of freshmen passing the *Selective Service College Qualification Test* (see Table 12:1). These data are based upon the first and second administration of this test and were compiled by the Educational Testing Service (13). It must not be forgotten that the purpose of *SSCQT* was to defer qualified students in engineering and the physical sciences from induction into the U.S. Armed Services, at least until after training was completed. Manpower shortages in these areas was the reason. This explains the differences in the percentages passing in the major fields of studies, but it does not explain the

Table 12:1. PERCENTAGES OF FRESHMEN PASSING SSCQT BROKEN DOWN
BY GEOGRAPHIC REGION AND MAJOR FIELD OF STUDY

	Series	1	2		Series	1	2
New England		54	61	General Arts		48	49
Middle Atlantic		60	60	Humanities		52	54
E. North Central		55	56	Social Sciences		57	55
W. North Central		57	56	Education		27	30
South Atlantic		40	44	Business & Commerce		42	35
E. South Central		32	35	Physical Science & Math.		64	69
W. South Central		39	35	Engineering		68	68
Mountain		52	50	Biological Science		59	62
Pacific		55	56	Agriculture		37	44
All Divisions		53	54	All Fields		53	54

differences based upon geography. These seem related to socio-economic conditions.

RELIABILITY AND VALIDITY. The reliability of practically all the full scales of the commonly used group tests of mental ability is high. The usual internal-consistency, parallel form, or test-retest (with a rather short interval between test and retest) coefficient is typically above .90. Test-retest reliability over the years, as has been shown for the *Stanford-Binet*, is also moderately high. This was demonstrated by a study of Owens (34) using the *Army Alpha*.

In this study, Owens in 1950 readministered identical copies of the *Army Alpha* to a group of 127 individuals who had previously taken the test as college freshmen in 1919 when their mean age was 19 years. Owens found a correlation of .77 between the total scores on this test over the 31-year period. Since the range of ability of a group of college students is much restricted, this represents a rather remarkable consistency in test scores and offers us some confidence in the use we make of such intelligence test scores.

These group tests have been and are still being validated in 3 ways. First, scores on a new test are correlated with those obtained from another test. The *Stanford-Binet* in the past was very commonly used for this. When we follow this practice, we have to assume that the test against which we are working is valid. Secondly, tests of mental ability have been correlated with grades received in various school subjects, over-all academic averages, or level reached in school (amount of schooling) as criteria. Thirdly, ratings of teachers, supervisors, and commanding officers of enlisted personnel in the Armed Forces have been used as criteria. As might be expected, this third approach to validation produces the lowest correlation coefficients because of the unreliability of these criterion measures.

Typically, validity coefficients using schoolwork as criteria fall within the band .40-.60. A review of the years of research on this topic shows a median value of about .50. Frequently we encounter coefficients in the .70's, but these are the exception. The homogeneity of the group being studied also is an important aspect of validity. In the elementary school where variability is greatest, correlations should be highest. Then they should decrease in size in high school and college as the student population becomes more and more similar. In graduate school some research has produced validity coefficients between .10 and .25. This is to be expected, because the range of ability among graduate students, though large, is quite curtailed when compared with the population in general.

Group vs. Individual Tests

Some psychologists in the past and present have written and acted as if a really valid measure of an individual's mental ability could be obtained only by using an individual test. If schools operated on this assumption, only a very few children would be tested because of the time and expense needed to administer individual tests. Fortunately for a large part of the population, the current crop of group tests give a reliable and valid measure of an individual's ability. Perhaps the bottom 10 per cent should be given individual tests because of the group tests' great emphasis on verbal ability and reading and the deficiencies of these abilities in this low group. With the upper 10 per cent we sometimes run into the problem of "low ceilings." An individual test, such as the *Stanford-Binet,* allows a child a chance to go to his limit. However, this is not true for late adolescents and adults. The writer feels that, for the great majority of our boys and girls, all the information that is necessary for effective learning and counseling can be obtained with group tests. Too much valuable time is wasted giving all counselees *Wechslers,* a not uncommon practice on some university campuses. The individual test is a clinical instrument. Many insights into an individual's adjustment can be obtained by a keen observer during the testing period. Some feel that this information is more important than the MA score obtained. This may be true. But school personnel do not have the time nor is there really a need to treat all students in such a fashion.

General Precautions

In summarizing the use of these tests of mental ability, we must emphasize several points. First, too much confidence should not be placed in a single test score. We noted above that individuals tend to reproduce their performance from test to test. However, there may be variation, and we never know when we may have one of these discrepant scores. Secondly, every time a test is administered and entered in the record the information inserted should contain the name of the test, form, level, and date of administration. When a specific type of norm was used in obtaining the score, we should enter this also. It is important to know whether an individual was compared with entering college freshmen on a national basis, a local group of entering freshmen, eighth-graders, adults employed in a certain vocation, or some other group upon whom norms have been made. Thirdly, we should be concerned with the motivation of the individual. We should be alert for the person who seems indifferent to the test. A test administrator, when the testing groups are of classroom size, can frequently spot these cases. Everyone does not have equal motivation. Some boys and girls have very little, especially if they come from homes of low socio-economic status. Fourthly, and this ties right in with the above, each test score must be interpreted in the light of what is known about an individual's home background, because the type of culture he has been exposed to does have an effect upon intelligence-test scores. These tests measure achievement and, as was stated earlier, are used on the never-met assumption of an equal opportunity to learn for all.

Representative Group Intelligence Tests

ARMY GENERAL CLASSIFICATION TEST. The first civilian edition of the *Army General Classification Test* was issued by Science Research Associates in 1947. This test was designed as a measure of general learning ability and may be used with high-school and college students as well as with adults. Forty minutes is the time allotted for taking. The test consists of 3 types of items, which measure the verbal, numerical, and spatial factors of intelligence. See Figure 12:3. These items are arranged in spiral form, with groups of verbal, numerical, and spatial items following one another at increasing levels of difficulty throughout the test. Both self-scoring and machine-scoring answer sheets are available. Conversion scores are given to change the raw scores to percentile scores or to the *AGCT* type of standard scores with a mean of 100 and a standard deviation of 20. Also *AGCT* scores for a large number of civilian occupations are presented.

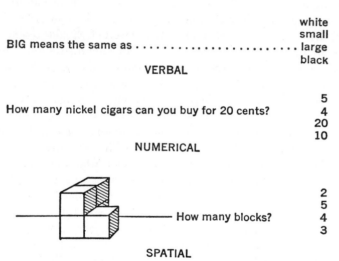

Fig. 12:3. REPRESENTATIVE ITEMS FROM THE CIVILIAN EDITION OF THE *Army General Classification Test* *

THE ACADEMIC PROMISE TESTS (APT). This battery was published in 1959 by the Psychological Corporation for students in grades 6-9. Actually it was an outgrowth of the *Differential Aptitude Tests* which this company had previously published for high school youths. The battery is composed of 4 tests: Verbal (V), 15 minutes; Language Usage (LU), 15 minutes; Abstract Reasoning (AR), 20 minutes; and Numerical (N), 40 minutes. Seven scores are obtained,

* Reproduced by permission of Science Research Associates, Copyright 1947.

one for each of the above four tests, a verbal score (VTLU), a non-verbal score (NTAR), and a total score. The test may be administered in one or two sessions. Time limits are adequate enough so that the emphasis is on ability rather than speed; hence they are chiefly power tests.

Answer sheets are used with these tests and raw scores are transformed to centiles each of which is the midpoint of a band of percentile ranks. Separate norms for boys and girls in grades 6, 7, 8, and 9 have been developed on a very large national sample. Correlations between scores on this battery and grades in English, mathematics, social science, and natural science are given. Median r's are typically between .40 and .60.

CALIFORNIA TEST OF MENTAL MATURITY. In 1963, the California Test Bureau published a new edition of the *Mental Maturity Series* of batteries consisting of 8 levels: (0) for kindergarten and grade 1; (1) for grades 1-3; (1H) a transitional form for between grades 3 and 4; (2) for grades 4-6; (2H) a transitional for grades 6 and 7; (3) for grades 7-9; (4) for grades 9-12; and (5) for grades 12 to college and adults. Thus the eight levels have been designed to provide for the sequential measurement of mental abilities from kindergarten to adult life. Two editions are available for each of these levels, a two-period test, the *Long Form*, and a one-period test, the *Short Form*. The *Long Form* consists of a Language Section that contains subtests of verbal comprehension, inferences, delayed recall, and number problems, and a Nonlanguage Section consisting of tests of opposites, similarities, number series, numerical value, analogies, manipulation of areas, and the like. On the *Short Form*, 7 subtests are present, these being mostly similar to those of the *Long Form*. However, two contain fewer items and one test is entirely different (Delayed Recall).

In addition the tests are also organized by factor analysis into the following factorial composition: Factor I, Logical Reasoning; Factor II, Spatial Relationships; Factor III, Numerical Reasoning; Factor IV, Verbal Concepts; and Factor V, Memory. The Spatial factor is not obtained with the shorter form.

Both forms yield deviation I.Q.'s for the language and nonlanguage sections as well as for the total score. These were obtained by first obtaining the scaling relationship between scores on the *Short*

Form with *Form L-M* of the *Stanford-Binet*. This approach to scaling allowed for meaningful comparisons of I.Q. scores on both tests in terms of I.Q. distribution, means, medians, and standard deviations. Finally the *Long Form* was equated and scaled to the *Short Form* and all comparable derived scores made equivalent. Answer sheets are available for those forms used in the primary grades. These tests, though timed, are basically power tests.

HOLZINGER-CROWDER UNI-FACTOR TEST. The Holzinger-Crowder battery of tests, based upon factor analysis, was published by Harcourt, Brace & World, Inc., in 1952. These tests, intended for grades 7-12, measure in one booklet 4 separate factors: verbal, spatial, numerical, and reasoning. The purpose of the test is to provide information for educational and vocational counseling of junior and senior high-school youth. A 32-page manual is provided to assist the teacher or counselor in interpreting and using the scores both singly and in combination.

Two classroom periods are needed for the complete administration of the battery. Scoring can be accomplished by means of a stencil, which may be used by hand or inserted into a scoring machine. Centile norms are available by grade for each of the 4 factors and for a general over-all measure of scholastic aptitude. This score may be translated into an IQ.

HENMON-NELSON TESTS OF MENTAL ABILITY, REVISED EDITIONS. These tests of mental ability, published by the Houghton Mifflin Co., first appeared in the 1930's. After many years of use they were revised in the 1950's. There are two forms, A and B, four different levels: Grades 3-6, 6-9, 9-12, and college through first year of graduate school. These are spiral-omnibus type tests made up of 90 items on the first 3 forms and 100 items on the college level edition. Items, arranged in order of difficulty, are of various types: vocabulary, sentence completion, opposites, general information, analogies, number series, figure analogies, and the like. Since there is an overlap in the grades covered by the forms, it is recommended that the form used for the overlapping grade be the one that best fits the school organization, or that the school use the lowest level with groups suspected of being below average in mental ability.

Four types of norms are provided: deviation IQ's, mental age equivalents, grade equivalents, and grade centiles. For college freshmen, separate centile norms are provided for verbal (V), quantitative (Q), and total (T) scores. For the three lowest levels both consumable and reusable test booklets are available. Various types of answer sheets and an answer card may be obtained for the latter form. The college form can be obtained for use with a variety of answer sheets. The consumable forms contain the self-scoring device of carbons used on the earlier editions.

In terms of time needed for administration, these are rather short tests, 30 minutes being required for the first three forms and 40 for the college level one. They give a good, rapid estimate of the mental ability of a student and doubtless are as good a prediction of school success as many longer tests.

LORGE-THORNDIKE INTELLIGENCE TESTS. The Lorge-Thorndike batteries were issued by Houghton Mifflin Co. in 1954. Five levels are covered in the series. Level I, for kindergarten and grade 1 and Level II for grades 2 and 3 are basically nonverbal tests as they do not require reading, although a comprehension of oral language is required. Level III, for grades 4-6, Level IV, for grades 7-9, and Level V, for grades 10-13, each include a verbal and a nonverbal battery. It is recommended that Level IV be used for the general run of the population and that Level V be reserved for high-school graduates. The verbal series is made up of subtests labeled: "Word Knowledge," "Sentence Completion," "Verbal Analogies," and "Arithmetic Reasoning." The nonverbal series (entirely pictorial, diagrammatic, or numerical) on the two lowest levels consists of pictures of common objects and of simple geometric figures that are used to measure "Oral Vocabulary," "Cross-out" (the one that doesn't belong), and "Pairing" (the two that go together). The 3 higher levels are made up of "Figure Analogies," "Figure Classification," and "Number Series."

These batteries are essentially made up of time-limit power tests. Any single test of the top 3 levels easily fits into a class period. The bottom 2 levels have no time limits. A consumable edition, in which answers are marked in the test booklet, is available for all 5 levels. A reuseable edition can be obtained for both the verbal and nonverbal forms of Levels III-V. Norms are present for changing raw scores to IQ equivalents (standard scores with a mean of 100 and a standard deviation of 16), age and grade equivalents for Levels I-III, and grade percentile ranks for Levels IV and V.

In 1964 a multilevel edition of these tests was produced for grades 3-13. This has in one test booklet both a verbal and a nonverbal battery, the former being made up of five subtests: vocabulary, verbal classification, sentence completion, arithmetic reasoning, and verbal analogy. The nonverbal battery uses items that are either pictorial or numerical. These are arranged in three subtests: pictorial classification, pictorial analogy, and numerical relationships. Along with providing greater flexibility in the testing program, this multilevel edition reduces both costs per pupil and the problems associated with storage and inventories.

The most recent test in this series is a level H designed for the group testing of college freshmen. Two forms are available both containing verbal and nonverbal batteries.

THE OHIO STATE UNIVERSITY PSYCHOLOGICAL EXAMINATION. The Ohio State test, which may be obtained from either the Ohio State University Research Foundation or Science Research Associates, has been available in newer and more improved forms ever since 1919. This test is used mostly with high-school seniors and entering college freshmen. However, it can be used with other brighter high-school students. Some universities even use it at the graduate level. This test is a real power test. In 2 hours most students finish it. Also this test is exclusively verbal, being made up of items measuring word meaning and verbal comprehension. Answer sheets are available for machine scoring, or self-scoring pin-punch answer pads may be purchased. Raw scores are converted into percentile scores.

OTIS SELF-ADMINISTERING TESTS OF MENTAL ABILITY. The *Otis Self-administering Tests* are among the older tests, having first appeared in 1922. However, they are still widely used in both industry and education, and are published in an "Intermediate" Form, grades 4-9, and a "Higher" Form, grades 9-12 and college, by Harcourt, Brace and World, Inc. These are of the spiral omnibus type of test which requires either a 20- or 30-minute working period. Age norms are available for the computation of deviation intelligence quotients.

The *Otis* tests give a good rapid measure of the mental ability of the general run of the population. The ceiling is too low to be of much value in dealing with university students.

Another widely used series is the *Otis Quick-scoring Mental Ability Tests*. Three levels are available: "Alpha," grades 1-4, "Beta," grades 4-9, and "Gamma," high school and college. The first of these requires 25 minutes of working time and the other two 30 minutes each. Mental-age equivalents and deviation IQ's are available for both the Alpha and Beta forms and only the latter type for the Gamma form.

THE SCHOLASTIC APTITUDE TEST (SAT) OF THE COLLEGE ENTRANCE EXAMINATION BOARD. This three-hour battery is given to hundreds of thousands of high school seniors annually. Two very basic skills are measured, verbal and mathematical. The verbal part (V) evaluates the student's knowledge of the meaning and relationships of words and his ability to interpret prose passages. The mathematical section (M) covers basic mathematics through elementary algebra and geometry.

Since the battery has been in use in one form or another since 1926 to predict success in the freshman year of college, a tremendous amount of research has been done with it and from this we have learned much about some rather important questions related to such tests used in the selection of freshmen. With this battery it has been shown that an average gain of 10 points on each section, V and M, can be expected on a second testing. Another gain, only slightly less than 10 points for each section can be expected between the second and third testing. Thereafter the effect of practice on scores is negligible. Other studies were conducted on the effects of cramming and coaching, which were found to cause an average increase of less than 10 points, a small difference on a scale of 200 to 800 and one that can hardly be expected to affect decisions relevant to college admission. Studies of the results of fatigue and anxiety were also made. Basically these showed that this three-hour battery did not bring about any noticeable fatigue or poor scores related to this. Also the effects of anxiety were much less than students and parents are apt to believe.

As noted, this battery is mostly used as a predictor of academic success. This it does well with correlations between scores and freshman grades ranging between .40 and .60 and higher, depending upon the school. However, there are times when a freshman class is so homogeneous in respect to mental ability, especially when the cutting score used in selection is high, that the resulting correlation coefficients are low and the battery is accused of having no predictive value. When a freshman class is so selected, one might expect practically all students to be successful and hence the test has actually done a lot of predicting. Since the results of this test vary so from college to college, each school should make a study of the effectiveness of the battery for its particular situation.

SCHOOL AND COLLEGE ABILITY TESTS (SCAT). This series of tests first appeared in 1955, produced by the Educational Testing Service to supersede the American Council on Education Psychological Examination (ACE) which had been used for many years with high school seniors and entering college freshmen. At present the SCAT covers 6 levels: college juniors and seniors, college freshmen and sophomores, grades 10, 11, 12, grades 8, 9, 10, grades 6, 7, 8, and grades 4, 5, 6.

The test consists of 4 parts: I, 30 sentence-completion items, II, 25 numerical-computative items, III, 30 vocabulary items, and IV, 25 numerical-problem-solving items. All of this adds up to 70 minutes of actual testing time; so the test can be administered in two sessions of about 45 minutes each or in one 80-minute session, including time for handing out material and giving instructions. Parts I and III are combined into a verbal score (V) and II and IV into a quantitative score (Q). Raw scores on these two parts and also the total raw scores are converted into centile ranks. These 3 scores are entered upon a profile sheet, not just as points, but as centers of a band, each such band being a built-in safeguard against over-interpretation of single test scores. The size of the band is equal to a standard error of measurement taken on each scale of the student's obtained score.

Tests are sold to be used with IBM or other answer sheets. Various types of norms are provided such as national (fall), national (spring), grades 4-14, urban, and the separate college classes. This test, like its predecessor, is an adequate predictor of academic success.

SRA PRIMARY MENTAL ABILITIES TEST. The *SRA* test for ages 11-17 is a shortened version of the *Chicago Tests of Primary Mental Abilities*, also available from Science Research Associates. The *SRA Primary Mental Abilities* is a 40–45-minute test measuring the following factors of Thurstone's: (V) verbal, (N) numerical, (S) spatial, (R) reasoning, and (WF) word fluency. The *Chicago Test of Primary Mental Abilities*, requiring about 2 hours for administering, measures the above 5 factors plus an additional one, memory (M). Centile scores are available for each of the factors as well as the total score. Profile sheets can be filled out showing the strengths and weaknesses of each student. These are proposed for use in counseling. Research has not borne out conclusively that these should be so used.

A lower-level test for ages 5-7 includes measures of verbal, spatial, motor, quantitative, and perceptual speed factors. Another level is available for ages 7-11. This measures verbal, numerical, spatial, reasoning, and perceptual factors.

REFERENCES

1. Altus, G. T. Some correlates of the *Davis-Eells Test. J. of Consulting Psychology*, 1956, 20, 227-32.
2. Arthur, Grace. *A point scale of performance tests, revised form II. Manual for administering and scoring the tests.* New York: Psychological Corporation, 1947.
3. Bayley, Nancy. Consistency and variability in growth from birth to 18 years. *J. Genetic Psychol.*, 1949, 75, 165-96.
4. Bayley, Nancy. On the growth of intelligence. *Amer. Psychologist*, 1955, 10, 805-18.
5. Berlyne, D. E. Recent developments in Piaget's work. *Brit. J. educ. Psychol.*, 1957, 27, 1-2.
6. Bradway, K. P., and Thompson, C. W. Intelligence at adulthood: A 25-year follow-up. *J. educ. Psychol.*, 1962, 53, 1-14.
7. Bradway, K. P., Thompson, C. W., and Cravens, R. Preschool IQ's after 25 years. *J. educ. Psychol.*, 1958, 49, 278-81.
8. Buros, O. K. *The sixth mental measurements yearbook.* Highland Park, N. J.: The Gryphon Press, 1965.

9. Carter, H. D. Should college students be told their intelligence test scores? *California J. educ. Res.*, 1952, 3, 66-72.
10. Cattell, Psyche. *The measurement of intelligence of infants and young children.* New York: Psychological Corporation, 1947.
11. Cattell, R. B. *Culture Fair Test.* Champaign, Ill.: Institute for Personality Testing, 1959.
12. Davis, A., and Eells, K. *Davis-Eells Games.* New York: Harcourt, Brace & World, 1953.
13. Educational Testing Service. Group differences affirmed by SSCQT figures. *ETS Developments*, Vol. II, No. 1, p. 1, Sept. 1953.
14. Eells, K., *et al. Intelligence and cultural differences.* Chicago: University of Chicago Press, 1951.
15. Garret, H. A developmental theory of intelligence. *Amer. Psychologist*, 1946, 1, 372-8.
16. Goddard, H. H. What is intelligence? *J. Soc. Psychol.*, 1946, 24, 51-69.
17. Goodenough, Florence. *Measurement of intelligence by drawings.* Yonkers-on-Hudson, N. Y.: World Book Co., 1926.
18. Goodenough, Florence. *Mental testing.* New York: Rinehart, 1949.
19. Goodenough, F., *et al. The Minnesota pre-school scales: revised manual.* Minneapolis: Educational Test Bureau, 1940.
20. Guilford, J. P. Intelligence: 1965 model. *Amer. Psychologist*, 1966, 21, 20-26.
21. Guilford, J. P. The discovery of aptitude and achievement variables. *Science*, 1947, 106, 279-82.
22. Guilford, J. P. The structure of intellect. *Psychol. Bull.*, 1956, 53, 267-93.
23. Guilford, J. P. Three faces of intellect. *Amer. Psychologist*, 1959, 14, 369-79.
24. Harlow, H. F. The formation of learning sets. *Psychol. Revue*, 1949, 56, 51-65.
25. Hebb, D. O. *The organization of behavior.* New York: Wiley, 1949.
26. Humphries, L. G. The organization of human abilities. *Amer. Psychologist*, 1962, 17, 475-83.
27. Hunt, J. McV. *Intelligence and experience.* New York: Ronald Press, 1961.
28. Jones, H. E. The environment and mental development. In L. Carmichael (ed.), *Handbook of Child psychology*, Chapter 10. New York: Wiley, 1954.
29. Knief, L. M., and Stroud, J. B. Intercorrelations among various intelligence, achievement, and social class scales. *J. educ. Psychol.*, 1959, 50, 117-20.

30. McNemar, Q. Lost: Our intelligence? Why? *Amer. Psychologist.* 1964, 19, 871-82.
31. Merrill, M. A. The significance of IQ's on the Revised Stanford-Binet Scales. *J. educ. Psychol.*, 1938, 29, 641-51.
32. National Society for the Study of Education. *Intelligence: Its nature and nurture.* 39th Yearbook, Parts I and II. Chicago: Univ. Chicago Press, 1940.
33. Noll, V. H. Relations of scores on the *David-Eells Games* to socio-economic status, intelligence test results, and school achievement. *Educ. psychol. Measmt.*, 1960, 20, 119-29.
34. Owens, W. A. The retest consistency of the *Army Alpha* after thirty years. *J. appl. Psychol.*, 1954, 38, 154.
35. Pinneau, S. R. *Changes in intelligence quotient, infancy to maturity.* Boston; Houghton Mifflin, 1961.
36. Porteus, S. D. *The Porteus Maze Test and intelligence.* Palo Alto, Cal.: Pacific Books, 1950.
37. Rabin, A. I. The use of the Wechsler-Bellevue with normal and abnormal persons. *Psychol. Bull.*, 1945, 42, 410-22.
38. Rabin, A. I., and Guertin, U. H. Research with the Wechsler-Bellevue Test: 1945-1950. *Psychol. Bull.*, 1951, 48, 211-48.
39. Silvania, K. C. Test usage in counseling centers. *Personnel and Guid. J.*, 1956, 34, 559-64.
40. Smith, T. W. Comparison of test bias in the Davis-Eells Games and the California Test of Mental Maturity. *California J. educ. Res.*, 1956, 7, 159-63.
41. Spearman, C. General intelligence objectively determined and measured. *Amer. J. Psychol.*, 1904, 15, 201-93.
42. Spearman, C. *The abilities of man.* New York: Macmillan, 1927.
43. Stoddard, G. D. *The meaning of intelligence.* New York: Macmillan, 1943.
44. Super, D., and Crites, J. O. *Appraising vocational fitness*, 2nd ed. New York: Harper and Row, 1962.
45. Terman, L. M. *The measurement of intelligence.* Boston: Houghton Mifflin, 1916.
46. Terman, L. M., and Merrill, M. A. *Measuring intelligence.* Boston: Houghton Mifflin, 1937.
47. Terman, L. M., and Merrill, M. A. *Stanford-Binet Intelligence Scale.* Boston: Houghton Mifflin, 1960.
48. Thurstone, L. L. *Multiple factor analysis.* Chicago: University of Chicago Press, 1947.
49. Thurstone, L. L. *Primary mental abilities.* Psychometric Monograph No. 1, 1938.

50. Vernon, P. E. Ability factors and environment influences. *Amer. Psychol.*, 1965, 20, 723-33.
51. Vernon, P. E. *The structure of mental ability.* New York: Wiley, 1950.
52. Wechsler, D. *The Measurement of adult intelligence.* Baltimore: Williams and Wilkins, 1944.
53. Wechsler, D. *Wechsler Adult Intelligence Scale (WAIS).* New York: Psychological Corporation, 1955.
54. Wechsler, D. *Wechsler Intelligence Scale for Children.* New York: Psychological Corporation, 1949.
55. Weiner, M. Organization of mental abilities from ages 14 to 54. *Educ. psychol. Measmt.*, 1964, 24, 573-87.

CHAPTER 13

EVALUATION OF SPECIAL ABILITIES

In the previous chapter considerable space was given to a discussion of a very general kind of ability possessed by individuals, namely, mental ability or intelligence. We saw how, as a result of factor-analysis studies, this general ability was broken into a group of so-called "factors." In this chapter we shall consider what are usually referred to as the special abilities. Factor analyses of these abilities show them to be made up of some of the same factors as is intelligence plus some very specific factors.

In the past, tests that measured special abilities were usually referred to as "aptitude tests." A better term for them is TESTS OF ABILITY. A test of ability is a measure of an individual's current status. The term *aptitude* should be reserved for those tests that are used to predict an individual's future performance or status on the basis of what at present he can do or possesses. *Aptitude* does not necessarily have to be applied to the tests of special abilities discussed in this chapter, but any test that is used to predict future performance may be so classified. Hence, both achievement and intelligence tests and interest and adjustment inventories may all be thought of as aptitude tests when used to predict.

Usually, in discussing special abilities, we cover 4 major areas: mechanical, clerical, musical, and artistic. Consequently we will discuss them in that order. The chapter will conclude with a discussion of test batteries that have become very common during the past few years, being used to measure a group of abilities simultaneously. Tests of this type are usually not administered to large groups be-

299

cause their use is reserved for students who require individual assessment of various abilities before effective educational and vocational counseling can be provided. A few tests are administered to groups, however. These will be mentioned in the discussion.

EVALUATION OF MECHANICAL ABILITY

Before any discussion of tests of mechanical ability, we should attempt to define mechanical ability. A review of the literature shows us that this is almost impossible. Frequently, we find definitions that describe jobs and performances carried out. Thus, mechanical ability is defined as "the ability to succeed in the school shop, or that capacity to do work with one's hands, hand tools, or machine tools" The following statement by Bennett (2) demonstrates the extensiveness of this ability. "A mechanical job as the term is ordinarily used covers a wide variety of occupations ranging in level from day laborer to graduate engineer and in another direction from locomotive repairman to watchmaker." Bennett and Cruikshank (2) believe that research points up the following 3 major components in mechanical ability: (1) the capacity to understand mechanical relationships, involving complex abilities of spatial perception and imagination; (2) manual and finger dexterity and manipulative ability, the muscular coordination required by most mechanical jobs; and (3) motor abilities of strength, speed of movement, and endurance.

A factor analysis based upon 31 tests and such information as youth, schooling, and ratings by foremen was carried out by Harrell (15) with data collected on 90 cotton-mill machine fixers. He isolated 5 group factors: (1) perception, (2) verbal, (3) youth (inexperience), (4) agility (manual dexterity), and (5) spatial. In addition to these, there were 2 other factors that overlapped the above, linking them together. These are known as general mental alertness and motor speed.

Another group of 59 tests was administered to 2156 male subjects, divided into 9 geographic groups, by the Division of Occupational Analysis of the War Manpower Commission (34). Some of these tests were constructed by the Division, others were commonly used tests of mechanical ability. The tests made by the Division were short speed tests of perceptual and spatial ability and dexterity rather than verbal tests. As a result of subjecting these data to factor analysis, the following factors were obtained or suggested:

1. A verbal (V), numerical (N), and spatial (S) factor was readily established.
2. A factor difficult to interpret was found on about 24 tests. This was designated (O). It seems to be a g or general intelligence factor.
3. Two perceptual factors, (P), involving geometrical figures, and (Q), words and numbers, were noted.
4. An aiming factor (A) was found, apparently related to accuracy and precision of movement.
5. A speed factor (T) appeared.
6. Two dexterity factors, (F) finger and (M) manual, were noted.
7. A logical reasoning factor (L) was suggested.

All the above are summarized by the authors in stating that only a few hours of testing are necessary to sample the significant aspects of behavior. Since many occupations require the same basic abilities, occupations so related could be grouped together in fields. On the basis of a relatively small number of test scores, prediction could be made for a number of occupations. Such techniques as this will be discussed later under the heading of aptitude batteries.

Mechanical ability, then, instead of being a single trait, is really a complex made up of a large number of factors. In evaluating this ability, we shall separate the usual instruments used into 3 groups: (1) tests of mechanical information and experience, (2) tests of spatial ability, and (3) tests of manual and finger dexterity.

Tests of Mechanical Information

Among the earlier tests of mechanical information were the *Stenquist Mechanical Assembly Test* and the *Minnesota Mechanical Assembly Test*, both of which are now obsolete. Both made use of a box containing a series of compartments each of which contained a disassembled object such as a bicycle bell, a clamp for holding test tubes to a stand, an old-fashioned door lock, etc. The purpose was to reassemble these objects as rapidly as possible. One of the first paper-and-pencil mechanical tests was the *Stenquist Mechanical*

Aptitude Test, published in 1921. The first part of this test was concerned with various tools and their uses and the second part with an understanding of the movements and relationships of rather complex machinery.

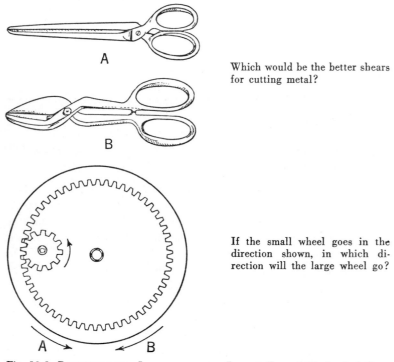

Which would be the better shears for cutting metal?

If the small wheel goes in the direction shown, in which direction will the large wheel go?

Fig. 13:1. REPRESENTATIVE ITEMS FROM THE *Bennett Test of Mechanical Comprehension* *

Today this aspect of mechanical ability is measured by such tests as the *Bennett Test of Mechanical Comprehension* and the *Differential Aptitude Test of Mechanical Reasoning.*† The emphasis here is upon the general principles of mechanics and other aspects of elementary general science or physics. The authors feel that these tests minimize the effect of formal training, but this seems doubtful.

* Used by permission of The Psychological Corporation, Copyright 1940.
† Both published by The Psychological Corporation.

The *SRA Test of Mechanical Aptitude* * has one part which covers the knowledge and use of common tools.

Tests of Spatial Ability

In the past, spatial ability was measured by individual perform-ance tests, such as the *Minnesota Spatial Relations Tests*,† which con-sist of 4 large boards each with 58 cutouts of various shapes, which are to be replaced in their correct holes. One set of pieces completes both boards A and B, and a second set, boards C and D. The test is administered and norms are available for average performance times on 2 boards or on 4 boards. Other tests, such as the *O'Connor Wiggly Blocks*,‡ consisting of a large block of wood (9 x 9 x 12 inches) cut into 9 wavy longitudinal sections, are concerned with working in 3 dimensions instead of 2. These 9 pieces are disarranged in front of the examinee. His score depends upon the time taken to reassemble them into the block.

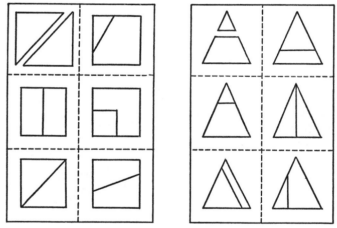

(The examinee selects the figure that results when the parts in the upper left block are assembled correctly.)

Fig. 13:2. SAMPLE ITEMS FROM THE *Revised Minnesota Paper Form Board Test* §

* Published by Science Research Associates.
† Issued by C. H. Stoelting Company and the Educational Test Bureau.
‡ Published by The Psychological Corporation.
§ Used by permission of The Psychological Corporation, Copyright 1941.

Such tests as these, being individual performance tests, are time-consuming and are not used extensively today. They have been replaced by paper-and-pencil tests, the most widely used of which is the revised *Minnesota Paper Form Board*.* This is a 20-minute test of 64 items, each consisting of a cut-up geometrical figure. The items are of the multiple-choice type, each with 5 responses. The task is to assemble the pieces mentally or perceptually and to mark that response which is the correct assembly. The studies carried on with this test have been many. It has been found to be related to academic work in engineering, art, and dentistry. Scores on it correlate sig-

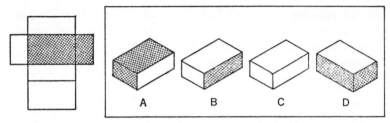

Notice—all the "boxes" made from this pattern are correct in **shape,** but the sides which you see are different. Some of these figures can be made from this pattern while others cannot. Let us look at them.
　—Figure A is correct. If the large gray surface is shown as the top, then the end surface of gray can be shown facing towards you.
　—Figure B is wrong. The **long, narrow** side is not gray in the pattern.
　—Figure C is correct. The two gray surfaces can both be hidden by placing the large gray surface at the bottom and the gray end to the back.
　—Figure D is wrong. The gray end is all right, but there is no long gray side in the pattern.

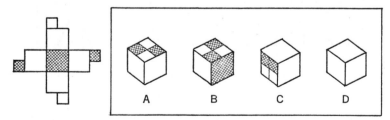

Study each pattern.
Decide which of the figures can be made from the pattern.

Fig. 13:3. SAMPLE MATERIALS FROM THE *Space Relations Test* OF THE DAT †

* Published by The Psychological Corporation.
† Used by permission of The Psychological Corporation, Copyright 1947.

nificantly with ratings of success on such jobs as toolmaking, aircraft engine inspector, certain machine operations, and various assembling tasks. Both the manual accompanying the test and Super (28) give many instances of its usefulness. The *Space Relations Test* of the *DAT* * is similar to this except that the initial item consists of a 2-dimensional pattern. The responses show this as folded into 3-dimensional objects. The task is to ascertain how many of those shown could be formed from the original pattern (Fig. 13:3).

Tests of Manual and Finger Dexterity

Manual-dexterity and finger-dexterity tests, by their nature, would have to be speed tests of performance. One of these, which measures mostly manual dexterity, is the *Minnesota Rate of Manipulation Test.*† This consists of a large board, with 60 circular holes in 4 rows. A circular disk or block fits loosely into each hole. The task consists of 2 parts: (1) "placing," putting the blocks from the table into the holes as rapidly as possible, and (2) "turning," turning the blocks in the board, as quickly as possible, bottom side up, using a standardized procedure.

Manual and finger dexterity is also measured by pegboards. These consist of a block of wood or metal with rows of drilled holes. *The Purdue Pegboard* ‡ consists of a board with a row of holes on each side. At the top of the board are 4 cups, holding pegs, collars, washers, and pegs. This test consists of 4 parts: (1) putting pegs into the right-hand row of holes, using the right hand using pegs from the right-hand cup; (2) a similar task for the left hand; (3) both hands putting in pegs simultaneously; and (4) an assembly task. This last consists of placing a peg with the right hand, a washer with the left, then a collar with the right, and topping it all by another washer with the left hand. Other pegboards, such as the *O'Connor Tweezer Dexterity Test*,§ as its name implies, require that each peg be picked up with a pair of tweezers.

There are a few tests that combine some of the above 3 types of measurement into one test. For example, on the *Macquarrie Test of*

* Published by The Psychological Corporation.
† Issued by Educational Test Bureau.
‡ Issued by Science Research Associates.
§ Issued by C. H. Stoelting Company.

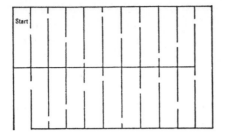

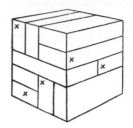

Tracing: Draw a curved line through the small openings in the vertical lines without touching them.

Blocks: How many blocks touch each block with an *X* on it?

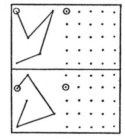

Pursuit: Follow each line with the eye from the space where it begins to where it ends at the right.

Copying: Copy each of the figures in the dotted spaces at the right.

Fig. 13:4. SAMPLE ITEMS FROM THE *Macquarrie Test of Mechanical Ability* *

Mechanical Ability,† the first 3 subtests are concerned with drawing and dotting tasks. These in part measure finger dexterity plus perceptual ability. The next 3 subtests are concerned basically with spatial ability. And the last test, a tracing test, taps perceptual ability. The *SRA Mechanical Aptitude Test* ‡ consists of 3 parts: mechanical information, spatial relations, and shop arithmetic.

It must be emphasized that the use of such tests as those described above is not the only way to obtain information about whether or not an individual possesses mechanical ability. First, a person may be asked to do a task that is a mock-up of the type of work he would

* Used by permission of the California Test Bureau, Copyright 1925.
† Published by California Test Bureau.
‡ Issued by Science Research Associates.

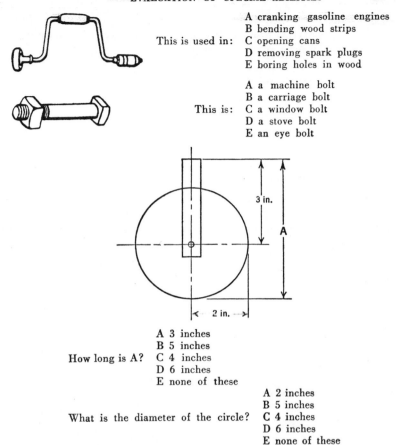

This is used in:
A cranking gasoline engines
B bending wood strips
C opening cans
D removing spark plugs
E boring holes in wood

This is:
A a machine bolt
B a carriage bolt
C a window bolt
D a stove bolt
E an eye bolt

How long is A?
A 3 inches
B 5 inches
C 4 inches
D 6 inches
E none of these

What is the diameter of the circle?
A 2 inches
B 5 inches
C 4 inches
D 6 inches
E none of these

Fig. 13:5. REPRESENTATIVE ITEMS FROM THE SRA *Mechanical Aptitudes* *

be doing later if hired. This is done many times by various industries. These work-sample tests or tasks have been shown to be highly effective in the selection of job applicants. Secondly, an investigation of an individual's hobbies may be in order here. Any boy who rebuilds old cars must have mechanical ability. An evaluation of products made in a shop course or on the job would also present evidence. And, finally, grades in courses where mechanical

* Used by permission of Science Research Associates, Copyright 1947.

ability is used should not be overlooked. Here we would include grades in mechanical drawing, shop courses, and even, perhaps, such courses as geometry and trigonometry.

Measures of Sensory and Psychomotor Skills

Usually, in evaluating mechanical ability, we try to obtain information on vision, color blindness, hand strength, auditory acuity, etc. These might be combined into a general grouping of sensory and psychomotor skills. Most teachers know that vision is usually tested by using a wall chart, usually the Snellen Chart, and hearing by some type of an audiometer. Color blindness, important in many jobs, is tested by such devices as the Ishihara Plates. Each plate consists of a background of dots of one color. A number is traced over this in dots of another color. Both colors are light in value, similar to pastels. An individual who is color blind will be unable to see the numbers. Since color blindness varies from total to just color blindness for red and green, responses to different plates will be different, depending upon the examinee's degree of color blindness. Two newer tests have been designed by Farnsworth.* In one of these 15 buttons have to be arranged in order according to color. On the other, the examinee sorts 85 caps of varying hues into 4 different series.

Measurement of the various psychomotor skills frequently requires special and sometimes rather expensive equipment. However, speed, as we have already seen, can be measured by the dotting and tapping tests of the *Macquarrie Test of Mechanical Ability* and by the various pegboards. Most physical education departments have dynamometers that are used to measure strength of grip. Tests used to measure reaction time, steadiness, coordination, and body sway are common tools of the experimental psychologist and are beyond the scope of this book.

Field and Level Concepts

Before considering the next type of special ability we shall digress and consider how these tests are used in modern educational and vocational counseling. This discussion will be limited to mechanical ability tests, although an analogous situation can be set up for the

* Published by The Psychological Corporation.

other abilities. Mechanical ability is conceived of as being a skill that is basic to successful performance in a wide range of occupations, from an engineer down to the operator of the simplest type of machine. This wide range of jobs has one thing in common: all require one or more of the aspects of mechanical ability previously discussed.

At the top level we find the professional people. Here are notably the engineers. They need high intellectual ability plus certain of the mechanical-ability factors. Dentists would also be found in this category. Below this we find the semiprofessional people and the skilled technicians. Intellectual requirements and training demands are not so great for this level, but they are still above that of the general run of the population. Laboratory assistants, dental technicians, and all types of so-called "technologists" are found at this level. Next comes the level of the skilled trades. Here one needs about normal intellectual ability, plus a large amount of mechanical ability. Included at this level are the artisans and skilled workers, such as toolmakers, plumbers, machinists, etc. Frequently an apprenticeship is necessary to enter these jobs. The next level consists of the semiskilled workers. Here are found the operators of the majority of the machines used in modern industry. A little training and some ability are needed but not much. Finally, there are the unskilled workers or laborers. No requirements on mental ability are demanded, but a certain basic mechanical ability is needed even for these tasks. A man can be a better pick-and-shovel operator or an ax handler and avoid harming himself and his fellow workers if he has some mechanical ability. So, in counseling, the counselor becomes acquainted with the requirements in terms of amounts of abilities needed for these different occupational levels. A good share of any field can be covered with the same tests.

EVALUATION OF CLERICAL ABILITY

If we consider all the different kinds of clerical jobs, we again notice that the range in ability needed is wide, just as with mechanical ability. When clerical ability is examined, it, like mechanical ability, is seen to be a composite of a group of abilities. A study of the tasks performed by clerical workers reveals that each requires the handling of arithmetic and language. These numbers and symbols are handled by a good clerical worker not only rapidly but accurately. Rapid observation then becomes an important factor in clerical ability. Tests that measure this are called PERCEPTUAL TESTS. This perceptual factor seems to underlie all clerical tasks. Some clerical workers need, in addition, skill in spelling, in rapid calculation, in taking dictation, typing, running business machines, and in many other specialties. None of our tests is made to measure all these things.

Probably the most widely used test of clerical ability is the *Minnesota Clerical Test.** This consists of 2 parts: number- and name-checking. The examinee goes through the test and, as rapidly as possible, puts a check on the line between the pairs of numbers and names that are identical. The items of the test are similar to the following:

59764		59674
8462046	X	8462046
William P. Benz		William P. Bentz
John William Co.	X	John William Co.

This test is an example of a true speed test. Time limits of 8 minutes for Part 1 and 7 minutes for Part 2 must be adhered to exactly.

This test has been shown to be very useful in such diversified activities as predicting grades in accounting ($r = .47, .49$), differentiating between rapid and slow typists, separating clerical workers presently employed from workers in general, and predicting different types of clerical success. Age, except for a slight slowing-up after age 40, seems to have no effect upon scores. Individuals with many years of clerical experience do not seem to have any advantage over younger clerks on this test. Correlations between scores on this test and intelligence-test scores for employed clerical workers, and university and high-school business students are between .20 and .25. Sex differences are significant on this test, as the manual reports that only about 16 per cent of men workers in the general population reach or exceed the median of women on both parts of the test. When employed clerical workers are studied, only 21 per cent of

* Published by The Psychological Corporation.

employed male clerical workers reach or exceed the median of employed female workers.

An example of a test of clerical ability that has broader coverage than the above is the *General Clerical Test*,* which is made up of 9 subtests. The first test, "Checking," is a perceptual task similar to that found on the *Minnesota Test*. The second test is concerned with alphabetizing. These two tests result in a clerical (perceptual) score. The next 3 tests, involving arithmetic reasoning, computation, and location of error, result in a numerical score. The remaining 4 tests measure spelling, reading comprehension, vocabulary, and grammar and result in a verbal score. This test usually produces the typical validity coefficients (.40-.50) when used to predict success in different clerical occupations.

In addition to these general tests there are quite a few specific tests, such as aptitude for shorthand, for typing, etc. References, for those interested, will be found in Buros (5). Also, again it is important to point out that there is important additional evidence which may be procured to evaluate a student's clerical ability. If he has had any business or commercial courses, grades received in these courses should not be overlooked. A person could also be given a work-sample test to see if he has any of the needed ability. While hobbies are not so important here as with mechanical ability, it is possible that some individuals might have hobbies which reflect this ability, such as keeping baseball and football statistics. Again this area can be graded into levels from the professional worker (the CPA) down to the unskilled one (the routine worker in the five-and-ten).

EVALUATION OF MUSICAL ABILITY

The name of the late Carl Seashore is synonymous with testing musical ability. In 1919, he issued the first edition of his *Measures of Musical Talent*. This was revised in 1938†. This current edition consists of 6 tests each placed on a separate side of a 12-inch record, 6 aspects of musical ability being measured: pitch, loudness, time, timbre, rhythm, and tonal memory. Pitch is evaluated

* Published by The Psychological Corporation.
† Issued by The Psychological Corporation.

by having the examinee determine whether the second of 2 musical sounds is higher or lower than the first. Loudness is measured by stating whether the second tone is stronger or weaker than the first. In the time test, the examinee is asked to determine whether the second tone is longer or shorter than the first. Timbre refers to tonal quality, and the examinee is asked to state whether two tones are alike or different in this respect. In the rhythm test, an evaluation has to be made of the similarity or difference of the rhythm of 2 pairs of notes. In the tonal memory test, series of 3, 4, or 5 tones are played twice in rapid succession. In the second playing one note is changed and the test-taker has to write the number of the one that is changed. In the past, the test was issued at several levels of difficulty, the different levels to be used with individuals of varying amounts of musical ability, but at present only the basic series is sold.

This test takes about one hour to administer. Two answer sheets are passed out, one for the record and the other for practice. Before each test starts each record is played for practice until all examinees understand what they are supposed to do. When there are no more questions, the trial for the record is then run. According to the manual, the test can be used with children in the fifth grade and on up. To take the test in the best manner, the student should sit at his desk in a state of attention in a forward position with his pencil poised above his paper ready to record his answer. Naturally, with a test like this, if the mind wanders for just a few seconds, all is lost. We might well wonder if 11- and 12-year-olds can concentrate as long as this test requires.

Scores are made into a profile showing results on each subtest separately. No total scores are used. Reliability coefficients for separate tests based on odd-even splits run between .62 and .88. The tonal memory subtest was found to be the most reliable one. Studies of validity show confusing results. Many of these studies have been conducted with students in musical schools—that is, they were used upon a rather homogeneous group, and correlation coefficients computed with measures obtained from such groups are apt to run low. Also ratings of music teachers have been used as criteria. Most ratings themselves can be criticized as possessing a certain amount of unreliability. One of the major studies was carried out by Stanton (22), who. over a period of years, administered the *Seashore Meas-*

ures and an intelligence test to all entering students at the Eastman·
School of Music, Rochester, New York. After administration, the
test scores were filed away, not seen by staff members. Stanton her-
self classified the students on the basis of the Seashore profiles and
intelligence-test scores into 5 groups: "safe," "probable," "possible,"
"doubtful," and "discouraged." Later the graduates were studied,
and it was shown that 60 per cent in the "safe" group were graduated, 42 per cent in the "probable," 33 per cent in the "possible,"
23 per cent in the "doubtful," and only 17 per cent in the "discouraged." Of course, it might be asked—and justly so—to what extent
are these results related to the intelligence-test scores? Stanton did
not consider this factor. Other studies have resulted in low to moderate correlations with grades in music courses and little or no relationship with intelligence. The test has been shown to have the
ability to separate professional musicians from amateurs and be-
ginners. Those who preferred classical music to other types scored
higher on the pitch, rhythm, and time subtests.

A new battery, the *Gordon Musical Aptitude Profile**, was de-
developed to evaluate the musical ability of groups of students to
aid in formulating educational plans in music and in adapting
music instruction to individual needs and abilities and to encourage
the musically gifted to participate in musical activities. The battery
measures three basic musical factors: tonal imagery, rhythm imagery, and musical sensitivity. Two subtests, melody and harmony, are
used to measure tonal memory, and two more, tempo and meter, to
measure rhythm imagery. Musical sensitivity is evaluated by three
separate subtests, phrasing, balance, and style.

All tests and directions are recorded on three tapes that may be
played on an ordinary tape recorder, each of the tapes taking less
than a regular class period. Students are asked to compare a selection with a musical answer and to decide if the musical answer and
the selection are alike or different, exactly the same or different,
or to decide which of the two renditions is indicative of a more
musical performance. Answers are placed on an answer sheet
where there is also a question-mark (?) column to be used when
the student is in doubt. Eleven scores are obtained, one for each

* Distributed by Houghton Mifflin and Company.

of the subtests, a total score for each of the three main divisions, and a composite score for the entire battery.

Norms are provided for grades 4-12 and additional norms for students participating in school musical organizations are also presented for elementary, junior high, and senior high schools. Reliability coefficients are in the .70's and .80's for the individual tests, in the .80's and .90's for the three component tests, and .94 for the entire battery. .Validity coefficients were first obtained by correlating test scores with judges' evaluations of students' tape-recorded musical performance. These studies yielded reasonably high coefficients. In a 3-year longitudinal study of all students enrolled in randomly selected 4th. and 5th. grade classrooms, musical aptitude scores were correlated with ratings of tape-recorded selections prepared in advance with teachers' help, with tape-recorded selections prepared without such help, and also with tape-recorded performances of sight-reading material. Teacher ratings and scores on a musical achievement test were also used with the following results:

	r
Selection prepared with teacher help	.49
Selection prepared without teacher help	.52
Sight reading	.51
All performance combined	.53
Teacher ratings	.37
Achievement test	.61

Also all students in this study were retested with the *Musical Aptitude Profile* after one year of intensive instrumental training to determine the effects of practice and training on test scores. The mean gain from test to retest on 250 exercises was less than 5 points and the coefficient of stability was .80.

Another battery is the *Drake Musical Aptitude Test** that was built to measure musical memory and rhythm for the purpose of estimating an individual's potential for a musical career. The complete battery is on the two sides of a 33 1/3 rpm record and may be administered in two 30- or 40-minute sessions. The battery may be used with students from grade 3 through college, and norms are provided for these various groups.

* Published by Science Research Associates.

Uses of Tests of Musical Ability

Many school systems find that such tests as these are very useful in selecting students to be given music lessons to prepare them for playing in school orchestras and bands or for singing in voice groups. Usually these tests are administered early in junior-high school. While these tests do not predict precisely which individuals will profit from musical training, they are useful in screening out those who have no musical talent. Much time, much money, and many heartaches could be saved if many ambitious American parents were aware of this. Frequently these tests will turn up hidden talent. In general they are useful in educational and vocational counseling, because students who score high on them tend to do well and succeed in musical curricula. And those who do poorly fail.

EVALUATION OF ARTISTIC ABILITY

Most of the techniques used in evaluating artistic ability are concerned with that type of ability involved in drawing and painting. Faulkner (9) grouped the evaluation methods into 5 types: (1) drawing scales, (2) art-judgment tests, (3) art-ability tests, (4) achievement tests, and (5) an evaluation of artistic products.

The first of these, drawing scales, consists of a series of scales that have been set up to measure the drawing ability of young children. The standards used are based upon realism rather than expression.

The second of these techniques, art-judgment tests, is widely used. One of the earliest of these, the *McAdory Art Test,* was first published in 1929. On this test, each item was made up of a series of 4 parts, to be ranked in order of preference. The items covered such areas as household furniture, clothing, textiles, and automobiles. Obviously, such a test would soon be out of date, if not continuously revised. Several attempts have been made to revise this test.

In 1930, Meier and Seashore issued *The Meier-Seashore Art Judgment Test.** The original test consisted of 125 pictures of works of art, in black and white, including old masters, Greek vases, Japanese

* Issued by Bureau of Educational Research and Service, State University of Iowa. Available through The Psychological Corporation.

prints, and other works of art. These differ considerably from the items on the *McAdory Test* in that, for the most part, they are time-less. Over the years, public appreciation of classical art remains about the same. There are no fads or cycles of appreciation in Greek vases. Each item consists of 2 parts, the original and another that has been altered in some way to change the symmetry, unity, or rhythm of the original. The student's attention is directed to that part of the work which has been changed. The examinee goes through the test marking the picture or drawing in each pair that he prefers. The original work is always, of course, the correct answer. A student's score depends then on the number of original pictures that he has selected, plus double credit for a selected few of these.

The revised edition issued by the same publishers and called the *Meier Art Tests, I: Art Judgment* consists of only 100 items. The original 125 items were subjected to an item analysis and the best 100 retained. Meier (19) in his manual describes the general make-up of artistic ability. This he conceives as consisting of 6 factors: manual skill, volitional perseveration, aesthetic intelligence, perceptual facility, creative imagination, and aesthetic judgment. He suggests that an attempt will be made to develop evaluation instruments to measure all of these.

This test can be used with students from junior-high school up and with adults. Reliability coefficients for the revised edition run between .70 to .84. Correlations of scores on this test with intelligence-test scores are very low or equal to zero. Correlations of art grades and scores on this test tend to fall in the .40's. Correlation between ratings of creative ability and scores on the *Meier Test* run between .40 and .69. The norms reported in the manual show that members of an art faculty scored higher than nonart faculty members, art students higher than nonart students, and older students higher than younger ones. Meier claims that these differences are due to selection processes rather than to training. This claim certainly is debatable. The writer feels that a good intensive course in the appreciation of art would raise scores on this test.

In 1963 appeared the *Meier Art Tests, II: Aesthetic Perception*, made up of 50 items based upon works of art ranging from the ancient to the modern. Included are pictures of paintings, abstract

Fig. 13:6. ITEM FROM THE ORIGINAL *Meier-Seashore Art Judgment Test.** (This item does not appear in the current edition of the *Meier Art Judgment Test.*)

designs, and sculptures. The subject is presented with four versions of each piece of art, one of which is the original, the other three varying in design, form, light or dark pattern, or in a combination of these characteristics. Some of the variations are slight, some rather considerable. The subject studies the 4 presentations of each item, observing how the pictures differ in regard to unity, proportion, form, and design, or how they vary as a whole. Finally the student ranks them from best aesthetically to poorest. Tentative norms are provided that were established upon high school students taking art courses and groups of college students.

A third test, *Meier Art Tests, III: Creative Imagination* is scheduled for future publication. This will complete the battery that with all parts used together will provide a measure of the basic components of aesthetic sensitivity.

Another test, similar to the Meier in basic structure but differing in its use of abstract geometric designs and lines in shades of gray, black, and white, is *Graves' Design Judgment Test.*† There are 90 of these, all except 8 being made up of pairs. The student goes through the booklet selecting the ones that he prefers or likes best.

* Used by permission of N. C. Meier, Copyright 1929.
† Published by The Psychological Corporation, 1946.

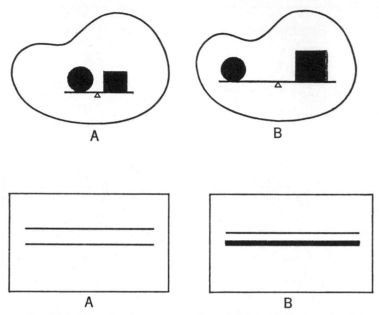

Fig. 13:7. Two Items from the *Graves' Design Judgment Test* *

Items for the final edition were selected on the basis of the agreement of art teachers as to which was the better design, more frequent selection of one design over another by art students than by nonart students, and as a result of an item analysis. Norms are presented for high-school and college students. To date, very little research has been published using this test.

Art Ability or Aptitude Tests

On all art ability tests, the student is given tasks to perform to see whether or not he can actually draw or paint. These tests are frequently long, preferably being used on an individual basis and being administered only to those who state a real interest in obtaining artistic training. They may all be called "work-sample tests." An older test of this type is the *Knauber Art Ability Test*,† which is made

* Used by permission of The Psychological Corporation, Copyright 1946.
† Distributed by The Psychological Corporation.

up of 17 subtests in which the student has to reproduce a drawing from memory, draw specified things, insert shadows into 2 compositions, create various abstract designs, borders, monograms, and carry out other diverse tasks measuring creative ability in art (17). The subtests are scored by comparing the students' drawings with a scale of standards presented in the manual. Subjectivity can enter the score here. This test seems very adequately to separate art students from nonart students, and art teachers from nonart teachers.

A more recent approach to the appraisal of artistic ability is found in the *Horn Art Aptitude Inventory* (16) designed for grades 12 and up. The test has been used to select applicants for art school; hence it may be looked upon as an achievement test. The test consists of 3 parts: (1) a "scribble" exercise, in which the student makes an outline drawing of 20 simple objects, such as a book; (2) a "doodle" exercise, in which the student has to draw simple abstract compositions with geometric figures; and (3) an "imagery" test, in which the student is given 12 cards each of which possesses a series of lines. These lines are to act as starting points about which he is to sketch a picture. Horn reports a correlation of .53 between scores on this test and mean instructors' ratings for a group of 52 art-school graduates. Also he presents data showing a correlation coefficient of .66 between freshman grades in art and scores on this test. Again, scoring with such a test is subjective.

A fourth approach to art appraisal is through the use of achievement tests. Some of the tests already discussed fall within this category. In addition to these, there are parts of our achievement batteries, such as the "Fine Arts" subtest of the *Cooperative General Culture Test*. Such tests measure a student's knowledge of the art of the past plus current developments.

And, finally, as an evaluation of artistic ability we can have the products of the individual who expresses an interest in art evaluated by one or more judges who are themselves competent in the specific area being appraised. Perhaps, in the long run, this method is as good as any.

Uses of Tests of Artistic Ability

The uses of these tests are very similar to those recommended for

Sample pictures B and C drawn on bases of key lines shown in A.

Fig. 13:8. ITEM FROM THE "IMAGERY" PART OF THE *Horn Art Aptitude Inventory* *

music tests. First, they can be effectively used to screen out those individuals who have little or no artistic talent. They will also show up those who will probably succeed in art training—that is, those who score high on the test. And they may uncover artistic talent in

* Used by permission of The American Psychological Association, Copyright 1945.

individuals who did not realize that they possessed any. These tests at present are no more than screening devices. Their development still has a long way to go before exact individual prediction can be carried out with them.

MULTIFACTOR TEST BATTERIES

Since World War II there has been an increasing emphasis on the use of multifactor batteries in the measurement of abilities. Such batteries are outgrowths of various selection programs set up during World War II both in the U.S. Armed Services and in civilian life. Practically all these are based upon factor-analysis research.

One of the oldest of these batteries is the *Differential Aptitude Tests (DAT)** (3, 4). This was designed for the educational and vocational counseling of high-school youth. At the present time it is used with university students in some counseling bureaus. The battery consists of 8 tests: (1) verbal reasoning (understanding of word concepts), (2) numerical ability (understanding of numerical relationships and facility in handling numerical concepts), (3) abstract reasoning (nonverbal measure of intellectual ability using diagram series), (4) space relations (a measure of spatial visualization and space perception), (5) clerical speed and accuracy (a simple perceptual task), (6) mechanical reasoning (items similar to *Bennett Test of Mechanical Comprehension* discussed previously), and (7 and 8) language usage (spelling and sentences). The first 6 of these are printed in separate booklets; the last two are combined in one. With these diagnostic batteries it is not necessary to administer the complete series to all students. Those believed appropriate for a specific examinee are selected and administered.

These *DAT* tests were first standardized in 1947. Since then, much research has been carried out, leading to the collection of both normative and validity data. Reliability coefficients for all tests except one are in the high .80's and .90's; mechanical reasoning, when based upon scores obtained from girls, resulted in coefficients in the high .60's and .70's. In the 1959 manual, about 4000 validity coefficients are summarized. These are based upon prediction of course

* Published by The Psychological Corporation.

grades for one or more semesters following the giving of the tests, prediction of course grades year by year for 4 years in one school system, prediction of achievement test results, and prediction of educational and vocational success. Super (27) summarizes this by pointing out that they show that the *DAT* scores well predict grades in English, social studies, mathematics, and science. He states that the tests look good for academic subjects, but only in a general sort of way. They seem to measure that which is involved in all these subjects, namely, intelligence. In the business and shop courses, the number and language-usage tests predict grades in bookkeeping and typing. To a certain extent, the spatial test predicts grades in vocational courses.

A long-range follow-up, using 1463 students who had previously taken the *DAT*, was made in 1954-55, 7-8 years after the students had graduated from high school (4). In general, those students who had graduated from colleges were markedly superior on all tests to the average of the high-school group of which they had been a part. This was most pronounced on the (1) verbal reasoning, (2) numerical ability, and (7 and 8) language usage tests (intelligence again). Those students who attended college but did not graduate were higher than the average of their high-school group but not so superior as those who finished college; those who attended special schools tended to fall around the average or slightly below; and those who had no more educational work beyond high school tended to be slightly below their class average. When occupations were analyzed, engineers were far above average on all tests. Others, such as draftsmen, technicians, businessmen, and salesmen, tended to fall around the average on all tests. Supervisors, foremen, factory workers, building tradesmen, and laborers tended to fall from slightly below to far below normal on all tests. With women, teachers in general scored highest on all tests. These were followed, in order, by nurses, stenographers, and clerks.

A second multifactor battery is the *Guilford-Zimmerman Aptitude Survey (GZAS)* * (14), which is composed of 7 tests. These are verbal comprehension, general reasoning, numerical operations, perceptual speed, spatial orientation ["the ability to form an awareness

* Issued by Sheridan Supply Company.

of the spatial order of things perceived visually" (13)], spatial visualization, and mechanical knowledge. By now the reader should be familiar with the nature of the trait measured by each of these. This test is for use with high-school and university students and with adults.

Reliability of this battery of tests is again high, all being very close to .90. Guilford (13·) shows that the first 6 have factorial validity, and, since the last (mechanical knowledge) was an achievement test, he states that it has content validity. He has also shown that his tests have "practical" validity, as he calls it, by correlating each test with an average grade based upon all subjects taken during the first year of college. The resulting correlations were .46, .34, .28, .16, .10, .17, and −.07, for tests 1 through 7, respectively. Verbal comprehension, general reasoning, and numerical facility (again intelligence!) do the best predicting of freshman academic success.

A third one of these batteries is the *General Aptitude Test Battery* (*GATB*), published in 1947 by the United States Employment Service (7, 8). This battery was standardized on adults gainfully employed in certain occupations and on those about to enter these occupations. In the current edition, 9 "aptitude" scores are produced using 12 tests either singly or in various combinations as shown:

G—Intelligence
    Part 3—Three-dimensional Space
    Part 4—Vocabulary
    Part 6—Arithmetic Reasoning
V—Verbal Aptitude
    Part 4—Vocabulary
N—Numerical Aptitude
    Part 2—Computation
    Part 6—Arithmetic Reasoning
S—Spatial Aptitude
    Part 3—Three-dimensional Space
P—Form Perception
    Part 5—Tool Making
    Part 7—Form Matching
Q—Clerical Perception
    Part 1—Name Perception

K—Motor Coordination
    Part 8—Mark Making
F—Finger Dexterity
    Part 11—Assemble
    Part 12—Disassemble
M—Manual Dexterity
    Part 9—Place
    Part 10—Turn

Tests 9, 10, 11, and 12 are performance tests, using apparatus, whereas the other 8 are paper-and-pencil tests.

Norms for this battery are expressed in occupational aptitude patterns, each of which consists of the cutting scores of the 3 most important aptitudes required by the family of similar occupations. Thus, a family of occupations might require G—intelligence, N—numerical, and V—verbal, and the minimum scores required on each are stated. An individual's profile is compared with these profiles to see which fields of work are most suited to his measured abilities. Part II of the *Dictionary of Occupational Titles* (U. S. Dept. of Labor, 1965) has the thousands of job titles found in Part I of this work organized into 22 broad areas of work such as art, clerical jobs, education and training, and the like. Included in each area are more specific worker trait groups each of which contains a qualification profile that specifies the general educational development, special vocational preparation needed, aptitudes, interests, temperaments, and the physical demands required by each job of those who would work at them. Certain parts of this qualification profile are expressed in terms of desired positions or placements on parts of the *GATB*.

Reliability coefficients are high and the validity coefficients present the usual picture. Super (25) feels that this test battery does do a fair job in differentiating among certain occupations.

Another multifactor aptitude test battery is the *Flanagan Aptitude Classification Tests (FACT)* * (10). This is made up of 14 tests, and the counselor's manual accompanying the tests contains a list of recommended tests for 30 occupations. Still another battery is Segal's

---

* Published by Science Research Associates.

*Multiple Aptitude Test,** covering essentially the same areas of human mental organization as the others.

Evaluation of Multifactor Batteries

In 1949, Super (23) wrote: "The day of the publication of isolated tests of single aptitudes will no doubt soon be past." Anastasi (1) noted that ". . . chief distinguishing features of contemporary psychology is its differential approach to the measurement of ability." However, Cronbach in the 1956 *Annual Review of Psychology* (6) concludes ". . . that while factorial scores may be useful for a theory of abilities, as soon as testors make inferences to behavior in significant situations, they encounter the same trouble as personality assessors." In other words, prediction of success in school subjects may or may not be done. We should now look into this and see why we have such a reversal of opinion.

In each issue of Volume 35 (1956-1957) of the *Personnel and Guidance Journal* appears an article devoted to a specific multifactor battery. Each article was written by at least one of the authors of the battery, and each is followed by a "comments" section by Super. The first of these, which appeared in the September 1956 issue, is Super's general discussion of these batteries (27). He starts off listing the things to be desired in tests used in counseling. First, he states what tests should describe. A test should tell us about a student's intelligence, his interests, attitudes, his special abilities, and his over-all adjustment. Secondly, a test should predict. It should be of some use in telling us what an individual's status, behavior, and attainment will be like in the future. It must tell not only what an individual will be like but what he will do. Thirdly, a test should be timeless. A test, such as the *Meier Art Judgment Test,* is of this nature. Likewise, the general run of our intelligence tests do not become useless as they get older. And, finally, he states that a test should be multipotential because people are of multipotential nature. A test should be so made that it can be applied to a large number of individuals in a large variety of jobs.

Super goes on to show that multifactor batteries are descriptive,

* Published by California Test Bureau.

timeless, and multipotential but not so good as predictors as other types of tests. The multifactor batteries are usually based upon attempts to achieve factorial purity for each test. This has focused attention upon simple, abstract items. Thus, these items tend to be abstract and general in content and, as such, are the exact opposite of a work-sample test. The specificity of this type of test gives it a validity which is much greater than the more general, abstract test. Custom-built tests, then, are better than these tests for the selection of employees for specific jobs, but they are not so good as these tests for counseling.

McNemar (18) also studied the results obtained with the *DAT* and pointed out that the *Verbal Reasoning* test was the best single predictor with *Language Usage* a close second and that the *Numerical Ability* test was the best predictor of achievement in school mathematics. Also he added that the remaining tests of the battery failed to demonstrate differential power in prediction, providing at most clues that are of little use to the school counselor. Vernon (33), again using data from the *DAT*, came to similar conclusions and observed that these multiple factor batteries failed to live up to their promise.

Summing up, it appears that these multiple factor batteries do predict, but not in a differential manner. Those parts of the batteries that contain the factors or measure the abilities found on our commonly used intelligence tests do predict grades in the basic academic subjects, but actually do no better than the intelligence tests. The verbal and numerical parts of the batteries carry most of the load in predicting. It follows that in terms of economics and efficiency the short 30- or 40-minute intelligence test is superior. The multiple factor batteries are initially expensive to purchase, they take several to many class periods for their administration, and they are usually sent to a center for scoring. At the present time, the evidence points to shorter, cheaper intelligence tests as the better for classroom and guidance purposes.

There is one study in which an attempt was made to determine the relationship between scores on aptitude tests and vocational success. This was carried out by Thorndike and Hagen (30), who sent a short questionnaire covering educational and vocational activities to 17,000 former Air Corps personnel approximately 12 years after they had been separated from the service. Each man had taken the battery given to Air Corps Cadets in World War II and had also completed a Biographical Data Blank. This battery measured general intellectual, numerical, perceptual-spatial, mechanical, and psychomotor abilities. On the follow-up questionnaire were such items as monthly salary, number of men supervised, self-ratings of job satisfaction and success, length of time in the occupation, etc. The authors found that, while there were real differences among various occupational groups, success in an occupation could not be predicted by these tests nor by items on the biographical questionnaire.

When this study was released, there was quite a stir about this latter finding. However, there are various factors that tend to make one wonder if this is really the last word on the subject. First, in this study the research workers were dealing with a very homogeneous group. Air Corps Cadets were a select group both mentally and physically, and with such groups correlations between traits and criterion measures tend to be low. Also the authors noted that only the more successful individuals tended to return their questionnaire. This is often the case in this type of research. Secondly the battery was set up originally to predict success in a military setting, but validation was accomplished in a civilian one. Thirdly, although the occupational groups used by the authors bore specific titles, they included in each many different types as may be observed when one considers the different assortment included in such generic titles as college professor or lawyer. Finally, many other factors such as interests, attitudes, and the like that are associated with ability in occupational success were completely disregarded. This problem is by no means solved.

Creativity

In recent years there has been considerable discussion in educational and psychological groups concerning the slighting of the creative individual when academic decisions are made upon the basis of intelligence tests alone. Much has been written on this topic and many tests devised which are supposed to measure creativity.

The basic difficulty here is the lack of agreement as to exactly what creativity is. From the types of tests devised, it is apparent that it means many different things to various individuals. An associated problem is creativity for what. Many think of creativity in association with the arts. Practically none of the work on this problem has been carried out in the area of the arts. A revue such as that made by Taylor and Holland (29) or an article by McNemar (18) give the reader an idea of the general state and lack of agreement in this area of measurement.

Some of the earliest efforts to measure creativity go back to the work of Guilford and his associates (12). These early workers created tests similar to the conventional IQ tests but purportedly measured other factors, for example, originality, various types of fluency such as ideational and expressional, flexibility, and sensitivity to problems. Later other characteristics not appearing on IQ tests were added, these including biographical, personality, motivational, and sociometric data. The majority of the results were analyzed by factor analysis. Often factors were obtained that were specific to the tests used. Sometimes factors were produced that were apparent in other studies. But in general, it appeared that creativity is a many factored thing. A very basic and important aspect of all of these studies is the omission of an investigation of the relevance of the factors to outside criteria of creativity. To date, because of this, little can be said about these tests as predictors of creativity.

The majority of studies have been carried out with individuals at the upper end of the distribution of mental ability. In other words we have a very restricted range in respect to intelligence. As has been pointed out, such a restriction of the range of talent in a sample leads to low correlations among traits. If one is concerned with scientific, engineering, literary, or architectural creativity and has criteria for such, it follows that there must be a relationship between intelligence and creativity. As one goes down the IQ scale, one finds that the chances for creativity become less and less. Actually it is impossible for a dull person to become creative in such areas as those noted above. It is granted that at high IQ levels there will be variability in creativity among individuals. To date we have no well-validated means of separating these individuals, but to claim that there is no relationship between intelligence and creativity, as some do, makes little sense.

REFERENCES

1. Anastasi, A. *Psychological testing.* 2nd ed. New York: Macmillan, 1961.
2. Bennett, G. K., and Cruikshank, R. M. *A Summary of Manual and Mechanical Tests.* New York: Psychological Corporation, 1942.
3. Bennett, G. K., et al. *Differential Aptitude Tests: Manual.* 3rd ed. New York: Psychological Corporation, 1959.
4. Bennett, G. K., et al. The Differential Aptitude Tests: An overview. *Pers. & Guid. J.,* 1956, 35, 81-91.
5. Buros, O. K. *The sixth mental measurements yearbook.* Highland Park, N. J.: The Gryphon Press, 1965.
6. Cronbach, L. J., in *Annual review of psychology.* Stanford, Cal.: Annual Reviews, 1956.
7. Dvorak, B. J. The General Aptitude Test Battery. *Pers. & Guid. J.,* 1956, 35, 145-52.
8. Dvorak, B. J. The new USES General Aptitude Battery, *Occupations,* 1947, 26, 42-4.
9. Faulkner, R. Evaluation in art. *J. ed. Res.,* 1942, 35, 544-52.
10. Flanagan, J. W. *Flanagan Aptitude Classification Tests: Counselor's booklet.* Chicago: Science Research Associates, 1953.
11. Gordon, E. *The Musical Aptitude Profile.* Boston: Houghton Mifflin, 1965.
12. Green, R. F., Guilford, J. P., et al. A factor analytic study of reasoning abilities. *Psychometrika,* 1953, 18, 135-60.
13. Guilford, J. P. The Guilford-Zimmerman Aptitude Survey. *Pers. & Guid. J.,* 1956, 35, 219-23.
14. Guilford, J. P., and Zimmerman, W. S. *The Guilford-Zimmerman Aptitude Survey, Manual.* 2d ed. Beverly Hills, Cal.: Sheridan Supply Co., 1956.
15. Harrell, T .W. A factor analysis of mechanical tests. *Psychometrika,* 1940, 5, 17-33.
16. Horn, C. A., and Smith, L. F. The Horn Art Aptitude Inventory. *J. appl. Psychol.,* 1945, 29, 350-59.
17. Knauber, A. J. Construction and standardization of the Knauber Art Tests. *Education,* 1936, 56, 165-70.

18. McNemar, Q. Lost: Our intelligence? Why? *Amer. Psychologist,* 1964, 19, 871-82.
19. Meier, N. C. *The Meier Art Tests, I: Art Judgment.* Iowa City, Iowa: Bureau of Educational Research Services, 1942.
20. Seashore, C. H. *The psychology of music.* New York: McGraw-Hill, 1939.
21. Seashore, C. H. *The psychology of musical talent.* New York: Silver Burdett, 1919.
22. Stanton, H. M. *Prognosis of musical achievement.* Eastman School of Music Studies in Psychology, No. 1, 1929.
23. Super, D. E. *Appraising vocational fitness.* New York: Harper, 1949.
24. Super, D. E. Comments (on the *DAT*). *Pers. & Guid. J.,* 1956 35, 91-3.
25. Super, D. E. Comments (on the *GATB*). *Pers. & Guid. J.,* 1956, 35, 152-4.
26. Super, D. E. Comments (on the *GZAS*). *Pers. & Guid. J.,* 1956, 35, 223-4.
27. Super, D. E. The use of multifactor test batteries in guidance. *Pers. & Guid. J.,* 1956, 35, 9-15.
28. Super, D. E., and Crites, J. O., *Appraising vocational fitness,* 2d ed. New York: Harper and Row, 1962.
29. Taylor, C. W., and Holland, J. L. Development and application of tests of creativity. *Rev. ed. Res.,* 1962, 32, 91-102.
30. Thorndike, R. L., and Hagen, E. *10,000 careers.* New York: Wiley, 1959.
31. U. S. Dept. of Labor, Bur. of Employment Security (USES). *Dictionary of occupational titles.* Vol. I: *Definitions of traits.* 3rd ed. Washington, D. C.: Government Printing Office, 1965.
32. U. S. Dept. of Labor, Bur. of Employment Security (USES). *Dictionary of occupational titles.* Vol. II: *Occupational Classification.* Washington, D. C.: Government Printing Office, 1965.
33. Vernon, P. E. Ability factors and environmental influences. *Amer. Psychologist,* 1965, 20, 723-33.
34. War Manpower Commission, Division of Occupational Analysis. Factor analysis of occupational aptitude tests. *Educ. psychol. Measmt.,* 1945, 5, 147-55.

CHAPTER 14

APPRAISAL OF PERSONALITY

One objective of American education commonly agreed upon is the achievement of satisfactory mental health by every student. In order to ascertain whether such a goal has been attained the student's personality has to be assessed. Over the past 60 years much has been written on this subject and many varied and interesting techniques and instruments developed in an attempt to evaluate personality. These assessment devices are on the whole much more complex and much less objective than those we have previously encountered. Perusal of the literature of both recent and past periods is apt to leave one with a sense of frustration because of the conflicting results reported. Gaier and White (8), in summarizing the research of the previous three-year period, stated that in general the whole was a picture of chaos with slight glimpses of promise. Both newspapers and popular magazines have in recent years run numerous articles about the failure of psychological tests to do what they claim to do. An examination of many of these articles and similar books shows that the largest part of the charges and criticism is directed at the various instruments used in the assessment of personality. Other psychological tests suffer from guilt by association.

Typical of such writings is a book entitled *The Brain Watchers* (9). Gross has built his case in part by quoting psychologists and the psychological literature. One has to admit that there are particles of truth in many of his charges. A major point of attack is upon the use of personality inventories in the selection, hiring, and promotion procedures of industry and government. Such inventories were not made to be used this way; the manuals of those inventories constructed by reputable psychologists recommend that these scales be used with caution, sometimes only for research. Another charge made by these critics is that the use of such inventories constitutes an invasion of one's privacy. Again there may be some truth to this in the use of some of the depth-probing psychological forms. But it seems that to apply this charge to all testing procedures is at best irresponsible. That there is a lot that we do not know about the techniques used in the assessment of personality will be obvious as we progress through this chapter. As each technique is presented attention will be drawn to both its limitations and its deficiencies. However, since desirable mental growth and development of an individual are important objectives of education, it follows that, if we wish to find out if these goals are being attained, evaluation becomes necessary despite some apparent limitations of the instruments used.

One of the major problems associated with the assessment of personality is that of finding suitable criteria against which to validate the inventories. Often there is a lack of usable criteria or a lack of agreement concerning the acceptability of a criterion among those using it, even among those of similiar background and training. The well-adjusted individual has over and over again been described as he who matures with age, stays relatively consistent in his behavior, conforms to the demands of society, and controls his emotional behavior. Such statements make good reading and have some meaning, but they are too general to be of much use in an assessment program. As one thinks about this problem, one has to conclude that "good" adjustment is a relative condition. What is good adjustment for one person may be exceedingly bad for another. The crux of the whole matter is the fact that it is exactly how the individual himself feels about his adjustment that makes it good or bad. Adjustment is also related to the culture in which one lives or to the various classes or subgroups within one culture. Exactly what is "good" or "normal" within one culture may not be in another. Consider the culture of the Eskimos or the Maoris and yours. Certain behaviors that are part of the daily way of life in one of these primitive societies might lead to social disapproval or even to arrest in your own. In our own culture different values are placed upon aspects of behavior within the different classes. The behavior of those in the middle classes is apt to vary considerably from that of persons in the lower or upper classes. Another point about behavior is that what is considered undesirable or acceptable this year may be desirable or unacceptable ten years from now. Thus, while it is difficult to decide exactly what is desirable behavior, it becomes even more difficult to build appraisal instruments with any valid accompanying normative data.

If adjustment is relative, individual, and related to one's culture, perhaps the most logical way to approach personality assessment is through an individual approach. If an individual's behavior is interpreted in the light of how he feels about it, then a large part of such appraisal has to be self-evaluation. A further problem is that all psychologists and psychiatrists are not in agreement about the importance of everyone's "being adjusted," that is, coming up to some arbitrarily established norms. Typical of this other approach is the thesis advanced by Lindner (17) that the only real progress in man's development was brought about by individuals who were unadjusted and nonconforming in their behavior. A glimpse into the lives lead by scientists, writers, and artists, both recent and past, reinforces this point.

Even if it is difficult or almost impossible to set up acceptable criteria of adjustment, this does not mean that no one has attempted to do this. For years teachers have had ideas as to what constituted good adjustment and what did not. A classical study by Wickman (31) investigated the teachers' attitude toward desirable adjustment. He had teachers select from a group of methods of adjustment the 10 they thought to be of most importance and the 10 of least importance. Another group of school psychologists was asked to do likewise. An analysis of his data revealed that the 10 activities the teachers felt to be of greatest importance tended to be ranked as of least importance by the psychologists. Ranked high by the teachers as evidence of poor adjustment were those activities that were conceived as threats to their authority in their classroom such as impertinence, cheating, untruthfulness, and destroying school property. On the other hand the school psychologists ranked high such traits as unsocialness, unhappiness, suspiciousness, and sensitiveness. The shy, quiet, retiring child was the model of good adjustment for some teachers. By selecting such traits as desirable and rewarding the possessor of them by better grades, teachers are actually contributing to poor mental health. Typically a young child is not like this; he is an active, growing, social organism. Sitting still in classrooms for hours on end is most unnatural behavior for most children. Understanding teachers are aware of this and act accordingly. That teachers have changed since Wickman's study and have become more understanding of boys and girls has been demonstrated by more recent studies (21). The basic psychological point here is that the quiet, retiring child is withdrawing from situations and repressing his feelings. Such behavior over time may lead to emotional problems of a type that never get solved. Avoidance behavior, day-dreaming, sulking, and the like are frequent results. On the other hand, the outgoing child works out his problems with no pile up of tension from day to day. He has little about which to worry.

Today we have better agreement about the nature of desirable behavior. However, the appraisal instruments that we use are not very good for assessing individual behavior. Many are best used with groups as a screening device useful in pointing out individuals who may be in need of psychological help. Many of the recent inventories have been built by avoiding the criterion problem. To do this the author demonstrates that his scale has construct validity, such as being capable of measuring certain factors. This in itself does not make any instrument any more useful in working with an individual.

In this chapter we shall consider in the following order the following assessment techniques: (1) observation, including the use of anecdotal records, rating scales, and check lists; (2) use of autobiographies and other personal documents; (3) sociometric techniques; (4) situational tests; (5) projective techniques, taking only a brief look at those that might possibly be used by a teacher or counselor; and (6) personality or adjustment inventories, probably the most widely used of all these methods.

APPRAISAL BY OBSERVATION

Before many of the instruments discussed in this chapter can be used, teachers must learn how to observe accurately. This can be done by any teacher's controlling his techniques as described below or by 2 or more teachers working together and comparing their results. It might be noted here that this technique is most useful with the nursery school or kindergarten child. A procedure, such as the following will aid in the improvement of the results obtained by observation.

1. Determine ahead of time exactly what is to be looked for. What is the purpose of the observation? What traits or what aspects of behavior are to be investigated? Such questions as these put meaning into the observation process.

2. Observe only one child at a time. A human being has all that he can do to watch one child, let alone a group of 20 or 30. When group behavior is to be studied, moving pictures and recordings must be used to do the observing in order to get a record of the many things going on at once.

3. In observing, be on the lookout for significant behavior. Many things a person does are trivial and reveal nothing about an individual.

4. Do your observing of a child at different times during the day. Daily observations of 7-year-old Johnnie at 11:30 a.m. would give us a lot of information about Johnnie as a hungry child, but very little about his behavior when not hungry. Spreading observations throughout an entire school day is called TIME SAMPLING. Usually a schedule is set up wherein each child is observed for a short period of time over the day. Research has shown that the evidence offered by an accumulation of these spread-out and short periods of observation furnishes a more valid picture of a child's behavior than does that obtained from fewer, longer periods.

5. Immediately after the observation period has ended, record and summarize the observed behavior. Techniques for doing this will be discussed below. Some observers take notes during the observation period. This is not always desirable or practical. The presence of a pad and pencil in a play scene of young children might result in behavior different from what might be obtained when these were absent.

Anecdotal Records

Observation is frequently implemented by the use of anecdotes or anecdotal records (Fig. 14:1). Hamalainen (11) has listed the purposes of anecdotes as:

Student: _____   Date: _____

Prepared by: _____

Exactly What Was Said and Done?

Any interpretations may be placed on the other side.

Fig. 14:1. AN ANECDOTAL RECORD FORM

1. to furnish the multiplicity of evidence needed for good cumulative records;
2. to substitute for vague generalizations about students specific exact descriptions of behavior;
3. to stimulate teachers to look for information that is pertinent in helping each student realize good self-adjustment;
4. to contribute toward an understanding of an individual's basic personality pattern.

Before an anecdotal record program can work efficiently, it must be completely accepted by the entire staff of the school. To achieve such acceptance, the entire faculty should work together in deciding exactly what it wants to do and the best ways of doing it. Such questions as "What is the best way of using the anecdotes?" "How shall they be collected and recorded?" "Exactly what aspects of behavior is the group going to be concerned with?" must be discussed and answered before a program can get started. In addition, most staff members need training in the use of anecdotes. Several training sessions should be set up, in which each staff member brings in at least one anecdote to be evaluated by the group. Staff members should also consider the desirable length of these anecdotes and the number to be written on each student per week.

The following suggestions should be noted in writing anecdotes:

1. The anecdote must be an objective, accurate, and reasonably brief description of significant behavior.

2. The behavior must be related to a certain amount of background information. The writer must remember that he may not be the only one who will read these. Unless these background data are present, little or no meaning may be conveyed to other readers.

3. Opinion has no place in the basic part of the record. For example, the following is not a good anecdote:

> Johnnie showed his usual streak of cussedness today when he deliberately grabbed a new pencil from Willie and broke it into two pieces.

It is better written like this:

> In the class this morning, Johnnie reached over to Willie's desk, took a new pencil which Willie had just bought, and broke it into pieces.

Frequently, at the bottom of the anecdotal record form or on the back, a space is reserved for opinions and interpretations. Sometimes another section is reserved for suggestions and recommendations.

How to keep opinions out of anecdotes is one of the most difficult problems related to this evaluative tool. Here is one thing upon which the suggested staff-training sessions could spend considerable time. Many experienced teachers find it difficult to write with complete objectivity. Under guidance they can be trained to do so.

4. The behavior recorded must be significant behavior. By this is meant that what is recorded in the anecdote must give insight into the developing personality of the student. The anecdote should lead to an understanding of the extent to which an individual's basic socio-emotional needs are being fulfilled or satisfied. Anything that leads to a better understanding of a boy or girl is significant.

5. Teachers have a tendency to write only anecdotes that reveal misbehavior. Some schools which started using anecdotes soon found

that they had large quantities of instances of negative behavior. Pick up any student's folder and one found much that was bad and little that was good. To avoid this, it was suggested to the teachers that every negative anecdote written be counteracted, so to speak, by a positive one. Some schools have gone so far as to use colored papers, such as green for positive anecdotes and pink for negative ones. In the long run, then, a teacher should attempt to turn out an equal number of both types.

6. Many anecdotal records should be regarded as confidential. There is no reason why the lurid details of misbehavior that might appear in a student's folder one year should be passed on to the next year's teacher immediately to prejudice him against the type of scamp he has on his hands. Anecdotes have to be summarized. In this summary we have an over-all picture of the general nature of a student's development. This summary becomes a part of the student's permanent record. Perhaps, it would be judicious annually to destroy most of the anecdotes.

7. How many anecdotes should a teacher write? Teachers feel that they have enough to do without having more piled upon them. This writing of anecdotes may become a tedious chore. However, this writer feels that, once a system is set up and is functioning, most teachers will see its merits. Hamalainen (11) suggests that, in large classes, a teacher should try to write at least one anecdote per week on every student. In small classes he should write as many as possible. A good rule might be that a teacher record any significant behavior whenever he sees it. For some students the absence of anecdotes would in itself be significant.

8. Before anecdotal records are used, someone must determine how and by whom they are going to be summarized. It is conceivable that, with the entire staff of a school busy writing anecdotes, the building would be crammed with papers, useful only when sold for waste paper. In the elementary-school grades the teacher himself might want to summarize his own anecdotal record. He might list the aspects of personality development that the school has set up as its objectives. The social-development section of most grade-school report cards will give an idea of what most of these are. These could be dittoed, and a separate sheet set up for each student in the class. After each objective would appear three spaces, labeled "weak,"

"average," and "strong." After it is written, each anecdote for each child should receive a number. Suppose the first objective on the dittoed sheet is *Courtesy*. An anecdote is written about Mary that shows her quite deficient in this objective. This is the first anecdote for Mary written this year. It is numbered "1" and, after this objective on Mary's sheet, the number 1 appears in the box labeled "weak." Thus each anecdote, after it is written, is classified and entered in the appropriate cell following the objective to which it is related. It is possible that some anecdotes will measure 2 or more objectives and be entered in more than one cell. A further advantage of such a numbering system is that the low numbers reveal the behavior at the beginning of the school year. Changes in behavior, for the better or the worse, are revealed by the higher numbers. A summary for a child's permanent record could easily be made from each child's sheet of classified and evaluated anecdotes.

In some schools, elementary teachers have to write letters to parents in lieu of report cards. It is inconceivable that a teacher can write meaningful reports of this type unless he keeps an almost running account of what is going on. In the absence of objective data, his letters, except in the cases of a few "problem" children and one or two "well behaved" ones, become platitudinous. Data must also be collected by the teacher who uses report cards where check lists are completed and social development evaluated. There is neither reliability nor validity to these either unless the teacher keeps some sort of record of significant behavior. When it is time to fill out the report cards every 6 or 9 weeks, many teachers have nothing upon which to complete the social-development part of the card as they do for the subject-matter section. One boy may have every mark he obtains influenced by a recent, single misdeed. Others, in the absence of any evidence, may obtain average marks or marks similar to those received last time.

In high schools and beyond, anecdotes are frequently sent to the counselor or counseling department where they are sorted, classified, and evaluated as described above. Jarvie and Ellingston (14) describe a system in which a dictaphone was placed conveniently for staff members to record rapidly their anecdotes. These were transcribed and handled in the usual fashion.

9. Another question that arises is who should write anecdotes. It would seem that the logical answer to this would be "all teachers." Whether a student is in his class or not should have no effect on a teacher as a writer. The validity of the system is enhanced when anecdotes come from the playground, cafeteria, shop, etc. A teacher should welcome these, rather than resent the concern of others with his students. Of course, in high school the system could function only in this fashion.

EVALUATIONS OF ANECDOTES. When anecdotes are used as they should be—that is, when they are written by objective observers—we have very useful, economical, and valid evidence of a student's adjustment. Anecdotes take time to write and more time to record, analyze, and summarize. These are the technique's greatest liabilities. Frequently, opinions get intermixed with the anecdote and we end up with more of the teacher's outlook and philosophy of life than of a child's behavior. Hamalainen (11) noted that the better anecdotes were written by the teacher who had taken work in child development, mental hygiene, and other areas of psychology.

Rating Scales

Another technique to implement observation is the use of rating scales. These were first used early in the nineteenth century by the British Navy to describe weather conditions. Later in the century Francis Galton employed them extensively in evaluating the vividness of images. In the early twentieth century Karl Pearson was using them in rating intelligence. During World War I psychologists employed them extensively in rating the efficiency of officers. A notable attempt here was W. D. Scott's *Man-to-Man Scale*. Since then they have been widely used in all types of personnel work, both in schools and industry.

There are many different types of rating scales (10). Some of the more widely used are described briefly below.

1. *Numerical Rating Scales*. At the top of the page on which ratings are to be made, different levels of the trait being rated are numbered. Below are listed the names of those being rated on this trait. The rater merely enters the appropriate number after each name to indicate judgment of the individual. A listing like this could be set up:

Abbott	1	2	3	4	5	6	7
Brown	1	2	3	4	5	6	7
Gray	1	2	3	4	5	6	7
White	1	2	3	4	5	6	7

Here he encircles the number that corresponds to his rating of that trait for each individual rated.

2. *Forced-Choice Technique.* For many years psychologists have used a research technique known as the method of paired comparisons. When this method is used, the rater compares each individual being rated with every other individual being rated in the general terms of "equal," "better," or "worse." Starting in the 1930's and increasingly during and after World War II, psychologists used a forced-choice inventory, involving a modification of the paired comparison method. Typical of these is the *Edwards Personal Preference Inventory* (see below) on which the subject is confronted with pairs of items and he is to select the one that best describes him. Theoretically each item could be compared with every other item on the inventory. However, with scales like the *Edwards PPI* this would lead to a very long and tiring inventory. Instead of doing this, an item may be compared with any other 10 or so items depending upon the length of scale desired. There is evidence that doing this within reason has small effect on the reliability of the inventory. Sometimes the items are arranged in triads, as on the *Kuder* inventories, or in sets of 4 or 5.

To build a forced-choice scale, items are tested to see if they differentiate between high and low criterion groups on the trait being rated. The statistic obtained is the index of discrimination of the item. Secondly, a measure of its attractiveness or social desirability is obtained, called the preference index. Items are then assembled into groups of 2, or of whatever number has been decided upon, on the basis of equal social desirability and different discrimination indices. Edwards (6) discussed in detail the method used in establishing social desirability values for his above-named inventory. It was hoped that having items of equal social desirability would force the rater to pick the really descriptive term in each group rather than the most socially desirable response.

Originally forced-choice scales were constructed in an attempt to control the effects of various response sets such as leniency, acquiescence, making socially desirable responses, and the like. Recent research on these topics has shown that forced-choice scales have not lived up to their expectations. These scales, like the conventional personality scale, may be distorted at will, but, perhaps, not so easily. In some situations they apparently work better than the others (24).

3. *Score Cards.* Whatever is being rated is analyzed into its component parts and a maximum score is assigned each part by an informed person. The rater assigns a value to each item as he passes judgment, and these values are totaled for the final score. (This method has been widely used in appraising school buildings and textbooks rather than in evaluating adjustment.)

4. *Simple Rankings.* The individuals being rated are assigned numbers, the one most superior for the trait in question being assigned number 1, etc. It is easy to pick out and rank the several high and low individuals for any given trait. The position given all others have little meaning.

5. *Graphic Rating Scales.* These are the commonest type in current use. A specific trait is put on a continuum with descriptive terms along the line to aid the rater in making a decision upon the case at hand. Here are examples:

How does he behave in a group of his peers?

1	2	3	4	5
Completely dominated, Submissive, Lost in group		Cooperates willingly, Both leads and follows		Aggressive, Takes control whenever possible

How would you rate his enthusiasm?

1	2	3	4	5
Apathetic	Rarely enthusiastic	Sometimes enthusiastic	Usually enthusiastic	Intensely enthusiastic

In reference to perseverence, he

1	2	3	4	5
Always finishes his tasks		Usually completes his tasks		Never finishes his work

These would be classified as DOUBLE RATING SCALES, because they have the opposite extremes at the ends of the continuum and an average at the center. Frequently the center is a zero point in a distribution of a trait. A SINGLE SCALE has zero at one end and a maximum at the other end. Other phrases could be written in on the above scales. For example, midway between the first and second judgments of the first scale could appear "Usually dominated by the group."

These scales have a twofold advantage: they are fairly simple and they are easily understood. If well constructed, with words of as precise a meaning as possible, they have many uses. In general, in constructing them, we should avoid such words as *very, some, average,* and *large,* which may have different meanings to different individuals. When setting them up on a page we should scatter the good and poor ends of the continuum in random fashion to prevent a rater's going down the page and checking an individual the same on each trait. The phrases at the ends of the continuum should not be so extreme as to be avoided by the raters. As shown above, each scale should be introduced by a question to which the rating gives the answer. In general, these scales, like test items, require thought, care, and revision. They can be improved with use.

Certain factors, however, enter into the use of rating scales, affecting their usefulness. The first of these is the so-called "halo" effect, which we described before as the influence of one or two outstanding traits (good or bad) on the rater's entire opinion of an individual. A person high on one very desirable trait tends to be rated high on all traits and vice versa. Secondly, raters tend to be lenient in that they seem to rate all their acquaintances "above average" on acceptable traits. Thirdly, raters tend to avoid making extreme judgments. The easiest solution is to give everyone a "break" by marking all near the center of the continuum.

RELIABILITY AND VALIDITY OF RATING SCALES. In the past much of the research done using rating scales has shown that their reliability coefficients were at best of moderate size, around .50. (See 30). Today, however, with the improved skills in the construction of rating scales, better analyses of what is being rated, and proper training of those who do the ratings reliability coefficients of a much larger size are frequent. In some cases these coefficients approach those obtained with some of our standardized tests. The reliability of a rating scale is directly related to the number of raters, in general the higher the number of raters the higher the reliability. The nature of the trait being rated also affects the reliability of ratings. Traits that are exemplified by overt behavior are much easier to rate than those that are not. An individual's need of constant prodding to get his work done can be rated much more reliably than the effect his manners and appearance have on others. So it follows that to increase reliability the builder of a rating scale should use those traits to which the rater can respond objectively and not those that require the rater's interpretation or subjective evaluation.

The size of validity coefficients obtained with the use of rating scales in prediction vary considerably, as with all such psychological instruments. An analysis of the structure of most scales will show that they possess content validity. The size of the predictive validity coefficients, like those associated with standardized tests, is closely related to the nature and goodness of the criterion being used.

Uses of Rating Scales. The use of rating scales varies from time to time. Graphic rating scales are less frequently encountered today than they were 30 years ago. Their use in assessing personality has been, at least in education, superseded to a great extent by the use of sociometrics, projective instruments, and personality inventories. Actually these latter scales are nothing but self-rating scales, which in one form or another enjoy very extensive usage. Nonetheless, graphic rating scales are still widely used in schools in the ratings of teachings and teachers by teachers, by administrators, and by students. In industry, rating scales are the most commonly used evaluative device. In some plants, every individual employed is rated at least once annually and the results used mostly for promotion or pay raises.

Check Lists

Very similar to rating scales are check lists. In general, they are easier to construct and easier to use than rating scales. Check lists can be constructed to cover all aspects of an individual's adjustment. They can be made to cover an appraisal of an individual's attainment of all of the school objectives. Personal difficulties and reasons for these difficulties could make up another type of check list. Finally, an individual's attitudes and interests can be ascertained by these lists.

An example of a check list used to evaluate a child's over-all behavior could be constructed in part as follows:

1. *Work Habits*
   _____ Finishes each task
   _____ Needs constant urging to finish most tasks
   _____ Gives up when the least difficulty arises
   _____ Almost never finishes anything
2. *Impression Made upon Others*
   _____ Happy, pleasant
   _____ Quiet
   _____ Self-controlled
   _____ Understanding
   _____ Obstinate, stubborn
   _____ Dreamy
3. *Getting Along with His Colleagues in Play*
   _____ Usually a leader
   _____ Gives and takes in his play
   _____ Popular in group. Always among those first chosen for games
   _____ A good loser
   _____ Possesses a bad temper when thwarted or losing
   _____ Prefers to be by himself
   _____ Always a follower
   _____ Unpopular, never chosen for games
4. *Etc.*

In the directions for such a check list, the rater should be told to consider each child and each trait very carefully and then to place a check in as many of the spaces as he thinks describe each individual. Users of check lists have found that they are most meaningful when the rater is asked to note on the sheet any evidence he has or reason he feels is the basis for his check marks. Any group of teachers can very easily set up such check lists to gather a large quantity of useful evidence of student growth.

APPRAISAL BY AUTOBIOGRAPHIES AND OTHER PERSONAL DOCUMENTS

In many schools, much important information about older elementary children and adolescents is acquired by having them write autobiographies. Obtaining various types of information may become the aim of these writings. Some teachers might be concerned only with attitudes and interests. Others might concentrate on an individual's philosophy of life and the values he holds. Again, the purpose of such an autobiography might be to get sufficient background material in the light of which to interpret other data at hand, especially to throw light upon the adjustment problems of many children and youth. Since so many different types of material can be obtained from an autobiography, it becomes necessary for the teacher or school counselor to determine ahead of time exactly what he wants to find out. After this he builds a short outline and gives this to the students to follow while writing. This is necessary if the desired information is to be obtained. Such an outline results in a so-called "partially structured" biography.

Counselors have been and still are the chief users of students' autobiographies. These autobiographies have been useful in providing information about a student's social, economic, and emotional problems. They frequently reveal that to which an individual aspires or what he expects to obtain in life. Usually a meaningful statement of an individual's level of aspiration is obtained. Finally, they provide intimate personal data. In some cases, students reveal in their writings things that they would not tell an individual in a face-to-face situation.

Frequently, writing an autobiography for the counselor is made into a regular English assignment. After corrections have been made, the theme is rewritten and made a part of each student's folder in the counselor's office. To the writer, this seems a dubious way of doing things. The attitudes of students toward various English teachers might seriously influence the nature of material included in the autobiographies. Counseling tends to be a personal and confidential relationship between the counselor and the student, and the English teacher becomes a not-always-welcome intruder. It is better to have these documents written for the counselor, even if a few grammatical errors get included in a student's record. This most important and useful appraisal instrument involves no special costs and, certainly, no training is needed for interpretation.

Other personal documents, such as diaries, have also been used in studying personality (1). However, the very intimate nature of most of these rules them out as useful devices except in a psychological clinic. In high schools, special types of diaries or logs can be used to keep account of a student's activities and his reaction to them. In some Schools of Education, practice teachers, when they go out to spend a semester or part of a semester in a new community, are required to keep daily logs of their activities and problems. These are gone over later with the supervising teacher.

APPRAISAL BY SOCIOMETRIC TECHNIQUES

Sociometry is concerned with the determination of relationships that exist in any group. The first major work in this country in this area was done by J. L. Moreno (19) and H. H. Jennings (15). In general, students are exposed to situations in which they have to make a choice involving their classmates. For example, a class may be starting a new series of projects in which the students are going to work in small groups. Each student is asked to write down the names of the 3 people in his class with whom he would like to work. Situations can be set up to cover such activities as field trips, class social events, and games. The teacher should, as far as possible, utilize these choices made by the students in setting up the work or play groups. If this is not done, the students are apt to have a "what's the use attitude" the next time that sociometric data are gathered since nothing tangible seems to result from these selection activities.

After a teacher has decided upon a project or event that merits a sociometric approach, he asks each student to take a small piece of paper and to write upon it the names of the 2 or 3 individuals with whom he would prefer to carry on the coming activity. In order for this technique to be effective, the members of any group have to have been together long enough for all to be known to each other.

The Sociogram

The collecting of the data is one of the easiest parts of sociometric technique. Analysis of the data is much more time-consuming. In analyzing, if the class is small, a diagram called a SOCIOGRAM as shown in Figure 14:2 can be constructed.

In Figure 14:2 a circle has been drawn for each girl. Annie's paper is taken up first, and Annie's first choice is seen to be Helen.

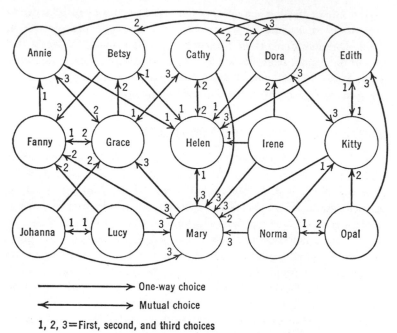

One-way choice →
Mutual choice ←→
1, 2, 3=First, second, and third choices

Fig. 14:2. Choices of 15 Sixth-grade Girls

An arrow is drawn from Annie to Helen. Since this is a first choice, a number 1 has been placed on the arrow near the head. (Instead of using numbers, first choices could be indicated by a colored arrow, say red, second choices by green, and third by black. Some workers feel that whether a choice is first, second, or third is of little importance and so they enter each in the same fashion.)

To continue, Annie's second choice is Grace, and her third choice is Dora. Arrows are now drawn to each of these girls and are labeled 2 and 3. Next Betsy's choices are taken up and each one entered. This process is continued until each choice of all 15 students has been drawn onto the sociogram. It will soon be apparent that if the group is of any size this picture becomes rather complex.

This sociogram gives the teacher a picture comparable to a photograph of a group of girls. This picture is specific to a certain day and these choices pertain to the specific proposed activity. These points should be remembered, because social situations change fairly rapidly. A teacher who uses sociometrics can easily keep up to date by the frequent collection of such data. Suppose that the data in Figure 14:2 are based upon a proposed social activity. With the same group a proposed educational or athletic activity might be used as a basis for additional choices. Both of these might produce an entirely different leader or leaders. It is true that every group has social leaders, educational leaders (bright students), and those who excel in athletics. Of course, there are some fortunate individuals who possess enough talents in all three areas to be chosen as a leader in each.

An analysis of Figure 14:2 shows that Helen and Mary have the largest number of choices. These two girls would be referred to as "stars of attraction." No one chose Irene. She is called an *isolate*. Notice that Johanna and Lucy each chose each other first. Such a choice is referred to as a *mutual choice*. Kitty, Norma, and Opal are almost a small group existing within the framework of the larger group. This situation is described as a *clique*. All these situations will usually be found in any classroom.

A sociogram tells us nothing about what is wrong with any boy or girl. Nor, as a matter of fact, does it reveal an individual's strong points. The user of the sociogram begins with the data at hand and starts to investigate. Why did no one choose Irene? What is there about her appearance, dress, personality, or background that is apparently related to this? What can I as a teacher do for Irene to aid her in becoming a part of this group? These are the types of questions that arise. The usefulness of the sociogram is realized when something is done about as many apparent problems as possible. Of course, not only the isolates should be examined. It would be a good idea to consider the desirability of a clique in any classroom. And is being the center of one or of several activities the best type of adjustment? A teacher might examine just how this "big frog" in the "small puddle" is fitted to get along in the future in a larger group where several "big frogs" will come together, as in high school.

Some teachers, on using sociograms for the first time, are disturbed by what appears when compared with what they expected to appear. Children frequently use different criteria in selecting their leaders. For example, with a group of sixth- or seventh-grade boys, the well-developed, manly boy, good in athletics, and dressed in messy jeans may be the almost unanimous choice of the others. At this level he might be selected by the girls too. For girls are ahead of boys in physical development, and in the sixth and seventh grades most of the boys in the girls' own classes would be considered too immature to be bothered with. Sociograms should be interpreted and investigated in the light of what we know about child development. Boy-girl choices would be expected in the primary grades, be absent in the intermediate grades, and recur at the time of adolescence. Finally, in looking at isolates and cleavages, the teacher should consider all such factors as religious and cultural backgrounds, socio-economic status, intelligence, personal development and appearance, race, length of time in a community, and other characteristics useful in analyzing individual adjustments.

The Tabular Method

There is another method of treating sociometric data as shown in Figure 14:3. On a large piece of paper the names of all the individuals in the group are set up across the top. Down the left-hand margin appears again the name of each child in the group. Under each student's name at the top are three columns to take care of first, second, and third choices. First, Annie's choices are taken. She chose Helen first, Grace second, and Dora third. So in the row in which Annie's name appears the space under "1" is encircled under Helen, the "2" under Grace, and the "3" under Dora's name. Betsy's paper is taken next and treated in the same fashion as Annie's. This is done until the choices of all students have been tabulated. At the bottom of the page a summary is made of the number of first, second, and third choices each child received. If we wished to quantify the results, we could multiply the number of first choices by 3, second choices by 2, and third choices by 1. If we felt that the order of choice was of little importance, we could merely give a score on the number of choices received.

This tabular method is not so revealing as the sociogram approach. But if we are carrying on a study using sociometry some such approach is necessary when the results are to be compared with some-

	Annie	Betsy	Cathy	Dora	Edith	Fanny	Grace	Helen
Chooser	1 2 3	1 2 3	1 2 3	1 2 3	1 2 3	1 2 3	1 2 3	1 2 3
Annie	1 2 3	1 2 3	1 2 3	1 2③	1 2 3	1 2 3	1②3	①2 3
Betsy	1 2 3	1 2 3	1 2 3	1②3	1 2 3	1 2③	1 2 3	①2 3
Cathy	1 2③	1 2 3	1 2 3	1 2 3	1 2 3	1 2 3	①2 3	1②3
Dora	①2 3	1 2③	1 2 3	1 2 3	1 2 3	1 2 3	1 2 3	1②3
Edith	1②3	1 2③	1 2 3	①2 3	1 2 3	1 2 3	1 2 3	1 2 3
Fanny	①2 3	1 2 3	1 2 3	1 2 3	1 2 3	1 2 3	1②3	1 2③
Grace	1 2 3	1②3	1 2 3	①2 3	1 2 3	1 2 3	1 2 3	1 2③
Helen	1 2 3	1 2③	1 2 3	1②3	1 2 3	1 2 3	①2 3	1 2 3
Total of 1, 2, 3	2 1 1	0 1 3	0 0 0	2 2 1	0 0 0	0 0 1	2 2 0	2 2 2
Score	9	5	0	11	0	1	10	12

Fig. 14:3. TABULAR ANALYSIS OF THE CHOICES OF 8 GIRLS

thing else. In the method described above, a high score would be indicative of a large amount of social acceptance and vice versa, but the real, precise picture has been lost. Remmers (24) offers other methods of analyzing sociometric data.

Guess Who Techniques

Another sociometric application is found in the use of *Guess Who?* or *Who's Who in My Group?* techniques. A series of situations like the following are set up, and the students are asked to write the names of all individuals in the group who meet the descriptions.

Are there any children in our class who are friendly with everyone? They like to talk or chat with any one in the class at any time. They are not "stuck-up." Who are they? ———————

Some boys and girls are very even-tempered. They never get mad or angry when anything goes wrong. Do we have any in our class? Who are they? ———————

A summary sheet can be made for each boy and girl in the class. On it we can note the number of times he or she has been mentioned by others for each of the questions. In making up such "Guess Who?" scales, we should include traits that are desirable and others that are undesirable.

A standardized sociometric test is the *Syracuse Scale of Social Relations**. Three forms are available, one each for elementary school, junior high school, and senior high school. Each form measures one specific psychological need, succorance, ratings of classmates as possible sources of aid when in trouble, this being common to all 3 forms. The other need assessed at the elementary level is called "achievement-recognition," on the junior high school form, "deference," some one to look up to as an ideal, and lastly on the senior high school form, "playmirth," some one whose company you would enjoy at a social affair.

All forms are administered and scored in the same manner. To begin with, on page 2 of the test booklet the student first builds a scale for his use. On the *Succorance* scale he is told that sometimes, when he gets into trouble, he is unhappy and he is asked to think over the time when he was very unhappy and would have liked to have talked over his troubles with some kind, sympathetic person. Then he is told to think of all the people that he has ever known and to write the name of the one that he would most liked to have gone to in the box at the right on the bottom of the page. Then he does the same thing for that person whom he would least liked to have helped him. This name he places in the box at the extreme left. Three other boxes are so filled, one at the center (medium) and one each between the center and each end. Then these five names are copied at the top of the next page of the test booklet in a series of 5 boxes and are used as a scale in assessing the members of the class in relation to this need.

The teacher then reads off the names of each member of the class in alphabetical order. Suppose that the first name on the roster is Ann Adams. The teacher tells the class to copy Ann's name on line 1 of this booklet. Then the teacher asks which of the five people at the top of the page is Ann nearest to when it comes to helping you when you are in trouble. The student places a mark in one of the

* Published by Harcourt, Brace & World.

five boxes that he feels Ann is most like. After doing this, he is asked to circle a term in the box into which he has placed his mark. For example if Uncle Bill's name appears in the center box, the student has to decide if Ann is "better" or "less good" than Uncle Bill on this trait and to encircle the appropriate term. Then the teacher reads the name of the second pupil on the class list and the above process is continued until each member of the class is rated. The same procedure is followed for the second need. At the bottom of the page, numbers appear at the base of the columns. These are used in quantifying results.

Five different pieces of information may be obtained from the scores. By looking at a student's answer sheet, the teacher may see how each student regards his fellow students. This can be made more precise by obtaining the mid-score of a student' ratings and using this as a rating of his feelings about the class as a group. Thirdly an average of these mid-score ratings can be taken to give an over-all class average that shows how the group regard their classmates. The last two results are obtained by placing each student's name on a double entry chart provided by the publisher and entering into it the evaluation made of him by all of his classmates. When this is completed, the horizontal scores will show how each pupil rated each of his fellow students and the vertical scores will show how he was rated by each of his classmates. Midscores of both ratings received and ratings made are next determined for each student. These ratings may then be converted to centiles. The authors also show how to use the results in identifying the members of cliques in the group.

As noted in the manual, a major purpose of the scales is to provide data relating to personal and social adjustment to be used with other information in promoting optimal growth and adjustment of the individual pupil. Secondly they may be used in identifying cliques and in the setting up of subgroups within the class for various educational and social purposes. Thirdly decisions related to classroom morale and parent-teacher relationships using these sociometric data may be made. A low class average of ratings would be indicative of low class morale and a teacher could then take steps to better such. These data could also be used to show parents how any child fits into the class group.

These scales are probably as well made and as useful as any instrument on the market for measuring social relationships. But like all sociometric devices, their use is time-consuming. Probably in the long run, the time and effort put forth pay off many times in the usefulness of the results received.

Evaluation of Sociometrics

Actually students have been using these sociometric techniques for many years. Choosing sides for a spelling bee or for a game are examples that have long been a part of the typical classroom scene. High-school and college seniors have been running contests to select the most beautiful senior, the one most apt to become rich, etc., all of which were published in the class yearbook.

In sociometrics, we have techniques that are economical; there is no cost, since odds and ends of papers can be used in collecting the data. They require rather considerable time in setting up the data into such a form that it can be analyzed. This is probably their chief limitation. The data collected are as timely—and certainly more valid—as those that could be obtained by any other method. Since we expect the picture to be a constantly changing one, our usual concepts of reliability do not apply (23). The types of information obtained are almost endless in number, and the clues as to who in any given group needs help are invaluable.

APPRAISAL BY SITUATIONAL TESTS

During the years 1924-1929, Hartshorne and May (12) carried on an intensive investigation of such so-called "ethical" traits as honesty. This study, summarized and reported in three volumes, is referred to as the *Character Education Inquiry*. A large number of the tests used in this study were of a situational nature. Situations were set up as part of the classroom work, homework, or recreation period. In all of these an individual was given a chance to be dishonest. Such problems as these were presented: Children were given a finely graded series of weights to arrange in order from lightest to the heaviest. The only possible way to arrange them correctly was to look at the bottom of each where the weight was recorded. Students were allowed to grade their own papers after copies had been made of their original papers. Games were played using coins. The chief purpose of this was to see how many coins were returned.

The chief finding of all of this was that there was no general trait that individuals possessed and that could be labeled honesty. For by far the majority of the individuals, honesty might best be described as relative or situational. A child might be scrupulously honest in his financial dealings, yet think nothing of cheating on a classroom test. Adults seem to follow the same pattern as far as this trait is concerned.

During World War II, the Office of Strategic Services (OSS) began to set up situational tests for the selection of personnel for military intelligence (22). Candidates for this service stayed at a house for a 3-day period during which they were subjected to a series of tests to evaluate: (1) how well each held up under pressure and frustration; (2) what qualities each had as leaders; (3) how resourceful each was and how good his judgment was; (4) his social intelligence; and (5) how well each could keep secrets and mislead others. These situational tests were all rather hastily thought out and put into effect. As far as their over-all validity is concerned, those investigations that were made produced low coefficients. The war ended before much of the work was completed.

After the war situational tests were set up in a university and used there in the selection of graduates for training in clinical psychology (16). To be brief, the experiment did not work. Several paper-and-pencil tests of intelligence and interests proved to be better predictors than the situational tests.

APPRAISAL BY PROJECTIVE TECHNIQUES

Today, the major tools of the clinical psychologists in assessing personal adjustment are the so-called "projective techniques." As previously noted, a projective device usually places the examinee in a situation where he has to describe something, relate a story, or respond to given words. In responding, the individual, it is hoped, will unwittingly reveal things about himself. The subject "projects" his own feelings and problems into the situation at hand, and his responses are evaluated by the clinical psychologist, the result being an assessment of the person being tested.

Since projectives are generally used by a trained clinical psychologist and since most schools do not have such an individual on their staff, very little time will be given to a description of these instruments. The interested reader will find them described in detail in Anderson (2) or Bell (3). Of all of these, the one most widely used is the familiar *Rorschach* or *Inkblot Test* (21). Here the subject responds by relating what he sees in a series of both black and white and colored inkblots. A second instrument is the *Thematic Apperception Test,* usually called the *TAT* (20). In this test, an examinee responds to a series of 20 suggestive or rather vague pictures. He is

Fig. 14:4. INKBLOT SIMILAR TO THOSE USED ON THE RORSCHACH TEST

asked to tell a story about each one, in which he relates what he thinks has happened and also what he thinks is going to happen. The series of descriptions are then evaluated and an assessment made. A third technique is known as sentence completion. Rotter's *Incomplete Sentence Blank* is an example of this type (29). On this test appear 40 words or phrases called "stems," such as *Boys,* or *In school.* The person taking the test considers each of these stems separately and turns it into a complete sentence such as "Boys are fun," a rather typical feminine response. Responses are evaluated on a 7-point scale and a quantitative score obtained. Of the many projective techniques, this is one that can be mastered in a short time with a little practice. Finally, with children, play materials (such as dolls and toys), drawing, and painting are widely used as projectives. An analysis of finger-painting, the shapes and colors of drawings and paintings, and the observation of children playing with certain toys frequently reveals much about a child's adjustment and his problems.

As has been noted, projective techniques require special training on the part of the user if they are to be applied correctly. But training in the administration and scoring of these devices does not in itself assure that the instruments have any validity. For some, such as the *Rorschach*, different scoring methods have been devised by various users. Such different scoring systems often lead to different interpretations of the same data. The scoring of the majority of projectives is very subjective. And then there are usually no norms against which to compare individual performance. As with the use of standardized tests, the administrator of a projective should attend to the frame of reference of the subject when he is responding. If a subject knows that a projective is being used with a certain purpose in mind, he will respond from that reference point. For example, if subjects are told that the *Rorschach* is a measure of creativity or of artistic ability, or that it is used in establishing whether or not a person is mentally ill, he will respond differently in each case. Also responses to the *Rorschach*, like the responses to group tests, are influenced by the environmental conditions in which the test is administered. Familiar or pleasant surroundings will evoke responses different from those obtained in unfamiliar or unpleasant situations.

The reliability problem encountered with projectives is similar to that associated with essay tests: attention is mostly focused on scorer reliability. A group of well-trained persons all using the same methods will produce reliable results. Of this there is little question. However, practically nothing is known about the reliability of projectives as psychological instruments.

An examination of the psychological journals will show a great number of articles reporting research based upon projective techniques. When such research is summarized, the results are at best confusing. Probably many of the results reported, though positive in nature, are caused merely by chance. With so much research done, it is inevitable that some results will be significant, and probably these are the ones printed in the journals. In the past there has been a tendency to disregard cross-validation, that is, repeating the research with another group to see whether the results obtained with the first group hold up.

The validity of projectives seems almost nonexistent. It follows then that such devices have little use in school work. Some psychologists question whether they have any use in any type of situation. Some clinical psychologists who do use them disregard the over-all results, merely using them to obtain insights into behavior as the subject responds in the testing situation.

APPRAISAL BY PERSONALITY OR ADJUSTMENT INVENTORIES

Personality inventories first appeared during World War I when Robert S. Woodworth constructed his *Personal Data Sheet*. He was attempting so to adapt a psychiatric interview that it could be administered to a large group of individuals at one time for screening purposes. After the war, these inventories were widely used, like the group intelligence tests that appeared at the same time, but it was soon noticed that they were not as reliable as they might be. The use of adjustment inventories, over the past 30 years, has been cyclical. Periods of doubt followed periods of acceptance. But, in spite of all this, they have remained extremely popular and are still widely used in education, industry, and the Armed Forces.

The typical adjustment inventory is made up of from 100 to almost 600 items. Such questions as the following are typical:

Do you have frequent dizzy spells?
Do you feel that most people are better than you?
Do you get easily discouraged?
Do you cross the street rather than speak to an acquaintance?

Usually the person being examined has the choice of 3 answers to each item: "yes," "no," and "?" (Don't know). A few items allow for only a "yes-no" response.

In using these inventories, we work under the assumptions that personalities have a certain amount of stability and that over a range of similar situations the same reactions will be elicited. Different individuals possess varying amounts of each trait. The more responses of a certain nature an individual marks, the more certain we can be that he possesses the trait being measured. The above assumptions seem logical within a trait-and-factor system of psychology. Meeting these assumptions is not the chief problem involved in the use of these inventories. Other problems will be discussed below.

Users of personality inventories are usually confronted with the following questions when they begin to think about the results obtained with these instruments:

1. *Are the responses of these individuals honest or true?* As an individual works his way through one of these questionnaires, he soon sees that there are many items which in good society he should mark in a certain direction. So instead of revealing that he departs from the social norm, he marks the items in the socially desirable direction. Many of the items are related to very personal religious, sexual, and emotional problems. He really never knows who will get hold of the results. Then the question comes up as to why should he, the examinee, respond to these items honestly. So goes the line of reasoning. One currently used inventory, *The Minnesota Multiphasic Personality Inventory* * has a lie (L) key, which consists of a group of items that most persons would mark in a certain direction, such as "I seldom get angry." When a person marks these items in the opposite direction, counter to the usual response, his score on the (L) key rises, and any user of such results would best conclude that the results at hand are an underestimation of the real situation. Most of these inventories have no lie key.

A large part of the current research is centered upon an examination of exactly what these personality inventories measure. While the results of the research are by no means in agreement, the findings of Jackson and Messick (13 and 18) are typical of many studies. In the second of these the authors analyzed eight studies made with the *Minnesota Multiphasic Personality Inventory* using factor-analytic techniques. They concluded that the very consistent findings in these studies indicated that the largest single factor associated with the *MMPI* may be interpreted in terms of acquiescence. In the second study, analyzing data that they themselves collected, they concluded that 75 per cent of the variance associated with the *MMPI* could be identified as acquiescence and social desirability. However, a few studies have produced diametrically opposite findings. Rorer (25), and Rorer and Goldberg (26, 27) have shown that as a result of their studies acquiescence is not an important determinant of responses on the *MMPI*. Their findings were based upon administering the *MMPI* and a reversed *MMPI* to the same group of subjects and studying the results.

* Published by The Psychological Corporation.

Whether or not one obtains valid results with these inventories is to a great extent determined by the attitude of the examinee. If he knows that the responses to the inventory are to be used to help him and if he accepts this, then his responses are apt to be much more honest and to the point.

2. *Does the individual understand the questions?* Associated with this question is another. *Does the individual understand enough about his psychological make-up and functioning to respond meaningfully to these items?* According to Forbes and Cottle (6), the reading-difficulty level of the more widely used personality inventories ranges between the fifth- and eighth-grade levels. Compared with other tests, these levels are low. But these are only averages, and there are probably many students in high school who would have some difficulty in understanding what some of the items are all about.

In reference to the second of these questions, no answer seems available. To the writer, it seems a highly dubious practice to expect children in the lower grades to respond to these items with any amount of understanding of what the questions are all about. The writer also feels that many adolescents and adults lack enough insight into their own behavior to complete these inventories meaningfully.

3. *How can such inventories be interpreted when actually there is no ideal type of behavior?* As was noted earlier in this chapter, what is good adjustment for one individual may be poor adjustment for another. There is no way of knowing how an individual feels about his response when he makes a mark on an answer sheet. These inventories are set up in such a way that, when individuals achieve the same score, it has to be interpreted in the same way for both. Actually this makes little sense.

4. *How has the inventory been validated and what is its reliability?* It is difficult to find adequate criteria against which to validate these inventories. Criteria used are mostly the ratings of psychologists, psychiatrists, and teachers. As ratings, their reliability tends to be low. When scores are correlated against unreliable criterion ratings, the ensuing validity ratings are low. The published reliability coefficients of these inventories generally fall in the .70's and .80's.

At the end of this chapter some of the currently used personality inventories are described. Only a few of the many published ones are discussed there in order to give a general idea of what these instruments are like. For further information, the interested reader should consult Buros (4) or the catalogues of the various test publishers. In general, these inventories can be grouped into categories. First, we have the older ones patterned after Woodworth's *Personal Data Sheet* of World War I. These are merely collections of items that are supposed to measure certain traits. In a temporal sequence, these were followed, secondly, by the inventories of R. B. Cattell, J. P. Guilford, and L. L. Thurstone, all of which are based upon factor-analysis studies. The techniques used in developing these are similar to those that were used earlier in the studies of intelligence. A third type, such as the *Mooney Problem Check Lists* * and the *SRA Youth Inventory*,† are based upon an analysis of the problems with which youth of different ages are faced. The *Mooney* consists of a list of problems covering such areas as health, finances, and vocational plans. The examinee is told to read through the list carefully and, when he comes to a statement that suggests one of his problems, to underline it. Next he is to go back over all those that he has checked and encircle the suggested problems that are bothering him most. Then, on the back of the inventory he is asked if he really thinks that the items checked give a good picture of his problems. After that he is asked to summarize his problems in his own words, and, lastly, on another page, he is questioned as to whether or not he would like to have more time in school to discuss these personal problems and, if he could, with whom in the school would he like to discuss them. There are advantages to a list like this. First, no labels are placed upon a student. Some of the classifications obtained from some inventories have no place upon the lips of teachers when describing children. No keys yet developed are valid enough. A second advantage of this list is that it is up to the student whether or not he wants to check any problems and talk about them with a teacher or counselor. No one is forced to fill out or complete this check list as with the conventional inventory. The writer feels that person-

---

* Published by The Psychological Corporation.
† Published by Science Research Associates.

ality instruments of this type have these advantages that should lead to their greater use in the public schools.

A fourth type of inventory is set up in forced-choice format. Typical of such is the *Edwards Personal Preference Inventory* which has already been discussed. Several others developed by Gordan are briefly described at the end of the chapter.

Uses of Personality Inventories

There were times in the past when large groups as a whole had personality inventories administered to them. For example an entire freshman class would be given an inventory for the sole purpose of screening out those individuals who might be in need of psychological help. In the light of what has already been said, this seems to be a highly dubious procedure and very expensive in both time and money. Rather than using these inventories like this, it seems that they might better be used by the counselor when dealing with individual cases. In these face-to-face situations, there is a good chance that desirable rapport has been established between the two and the counselor can explain the purpose of the inventory and discuss the value that may be derived from it if it is responded to correctly.

As has been noted, both industry and various governmental agencies have used these inventories in the selection, hiring, and promotion of employees. That these instruments have any validity for this is doubtful. Over and over again we have been presented with research that has shown how easy it is for a subject to make himself appear as he so desires. When one's future is at stake, it is obvious that he is going to make himself appear in the best of all possible lights.

What then about the use of these inventories in schools? Probably there would be no loss if 90 per cent of them disappeared today. An instrument like the *Mooney Problem Check List*, when properly used, may become an effective tool of the counselor. Use of techniques already discussed in this chapter will probably lead to more valid assessments of personality than can be obtained from these inventories.

SOME REPRESENTATIVE PERSONALITY INVENTORIES

Bell Adjustment Inventory

The *Bell Adjustment Inventory, Revised Edition, 1962**, represents one of the older type of inventories. One form is available for grades 9-16. This new edition yields 6 scores: Home Adjustment, Health Adjustment, Submissiveness, Emotionality, Hostility, and Masculinity-Femininity. The inventory is composed of 200 items that are responded to on a "Yes," "No," or "?" ("Can't Say") scale. This inventory is practically self-administering and scored easily in comparison to some of its competitors. Evidence is presented that the *Bell* differentiates among groups identified as falling high or low on a continuum representing each scale. As Vance, in Buros (4), pointed out, this revised edition is accompanied by sufficient evidence in the manual to justify its trial use a screening device. The earlier edition had been used in part for this since its publication in 1934.

California Personality Inventory

The *California Personality Inventory* (CPI)* was constructed to make a multidimensional evaluation of the personality of normal individuals. It is made up of 480 statements to which the subject responds "True" or "False." Eighteen scores result bearing such titles as "Dominance," "Sociability," and "Tolerance," all being more or less socially desirable aspects of behavior. Psychopathological characteristics are not assessed. This also is essentially self-administering and untimed, requiring about an hour for completion. Much research demonstrating its reliability and some validity has appeared in recent years. Some of these studies have shown that the CPI is measuring 4-5 traits rather than the 18 claimed by the author. However, such a condition is not unique with this inventory. The *CPI* is probably one of the best personality inventories, if not the best, for use with normal individuals of age 13 and above.

California Test of Personality

The revised edition of the *California Test of Personality* † (1953) is made up of two forms covering 5 different levels: "Primary,"

---

* Published by Consulting Psychologists Press.
† Published by California Test Bureau.

kindergarten-grade 3; "Elementary," grades 4-8; "Intermediate," grades 7-10; "Secondary," grades 9 through college; and "Adult." The "Adult" form is made up of 180 items. Lower forms are made up of progressively fewer items. A score for "Self-Adjustment" and one for "Social Adjustment" as well as a total score are available. Each of the 2 major sections is made up of 6 subsections. Scores are available for each of these, but because of the small number of items on each (ranging from 8 to 15 depending upon the level) scores based upon these are apt to be quite unreliable.

The items are answered on a "Yes-No" basis, and most individuals can complete the instrument in a 45-minute period. IBM answer sheets can be obtained and these may be hand-scored or machine-scored. Scoring is simple.

An examination of the items will reveal that many of them ask the examinee how he feels about certain things rather than whether or not he does them. Many of these inventories concentrate almost exclusively upon feeling. It is felt that this is apt to produce more valid results.

Edwards Personal Preference Schedule

Published for university students, the *Edwards Personal Preference Schedule* * (1954) is based upon a list of manifest psychological needs. These are: (1) achievement, (2) deference, (3) order, (4) exhibition, (5) autonomy, (6) affiliation, (7) intraception, (8) succorance, (9) dominance, (10) abasement, (11), nurturance, (12) change, (13) endurance, (14) heterosexuality, and (15) aggression. In addition to these, there is a measure of test consistency and profile stability. There are 225 pairs of experiences and activities. Each pair is supposedly made up of 2 items of equal social desirability. The pairs were produced by taking situations that represented these 15 needs and arranging them so that each need is paired with every other need twice. This is a modified paired-comparison approach. Students are to read each pair and select the one that they feel to be more characteristic of themselves. No items are to be omitted. Fifty minutes is adequate for university students to complete the inventory.

* Published by The Psychological Corporation.

Subsequent research, of which there has been a large quantity, has failed to demonstrate that the items on this inventory are of equal social desirability, that scores can not be influenced by attempts to distort them, and that it measures these 15 manifest needs as claimed. Also most of the studies concerning predictive and construct validity show the validity of the *EPPI* to be of a dubious nature. Many of these research results are conflicting or confusing because of the type of score obtained with the *EPPI*, called an ipsative score. This means that, because of the forced-choice nature of the scales, a subject's score on one scale is influenced by his score on the other. That is, it is impossible to be high on all scales or low on all. Most inventories use normative scores, each score reflecting an absolute level on each variable. The use of ipsative scores leads to questions concerning the use of our conventional statistical and factorial methods and clouds the interpretation of the results obtained with *EPPI* research.

Since the *EPPI* takes considerable time to administer, since it is most efficiently scored on a computer, and since research has shown it to be wanting in validity, a counselor should seriously consider the use of one of the competing normative scales for use in his guidance program. There seems to be little other than extra cost that this instrument can add to his program.

Gordon's Inventories

Gordon has three personality inventories, a *Personal Inventory*,* a *Personal Profile*,* and a *Survey of Interpersonal Values.*† The first two of these are brief, 18-20 item forms, requiring 10-15 minutes to administer. Both are made up of items of a forced-choice nature and both assess four different aspects of personality. For a more complete evaluation both forms should be administered at the same time. Evidence presented in the manuals shows these two inventories to be equal to some of the longer ones in respect to validity and all round utility. The third, the *Survey of Interpersonal Values*, like the first two suitable for junior high school through college, is composed of 30 triads of items that measure six aspects of personality. Research on this form is not as complete as on the other two, but it also seems to be a useful, short, easily scored inventory.

* Published by Harcourt, Brace & World.
† Published by Science Research Associates.

Guilford-Zimmerman Temperament Survey

The result of Guilford's factorial studies in personality is the *Guilford-Zimmerman Temperament Survey* * (1949). This inventory for high-school and college students consists of 300 items covering 10 traits or factors. These are: *G*, general activity; *R*, restraint; *A*, ascendance; *S*, sociability; *E*, emotional stability; *O*, objectivity; *F*, friendliness; *T*, thoughtfulness; *P*, personal relations; and *M*, masculinity. Answer sheets are used, and from these all 10 subscores can be obtained by the use of only 2 scoring stencils.

The items are expressed or stated in the affirmative, using second-person pronouns, and not as questions or using first-person singular. Three categories of responses, "Yes," "No," and "?", are used. This inventory is longer than most of the others. But if subtest scores are to prove reliable, longer tests or inventories have to be constructed. The items on this inventory are also of such an innocuous nature that its use in the public schools cannot cause trouble.

Minnesota Counseling Inventory

The Minnesota Counseling Inventory† is based upon two earlier scales, *The Minnesota Multiphasic Personality* and the *Minnesota Personality Scale.* Items from these two inventories were rewritten or reworded to make them more acceptable to high school students and their parents. It was for the former group that the inventory was made. Altogether there are 355 items on the instrument, and these are responded to on a true-false basis. Nine scores are obtained, 7 that may be referred to as clinical: Social Relationships, Family Relationships, Emotional Stability, Conformity, Adjustment to Reality, Mood, and Leadership. The other two, categorized as validity scales, are the Question Score based upon the number of items omitted, and the Validity Score, based upon the lie (L) scale of the *MMPI*.

Since this inventory is derived from the *MMPI* and since it has been shown that response sets such as acquiescence and the tendency to give socially desirable responses are important variables affecting *MMPI* scores, there is no reason for assuming that such factors do

* Published by the Sheridan Supply Co.
† Published by The Psychological Corporation.

not have a major effect here also. The high school counselor will probably find that this scale has little to add to his program.

Minnesota Multiphasic Personality Inventory

The *Minnesota Multiphasic Personality Inventory* * (1943) differs from all those described above in that it may best be called a "clinical instrument." As such, it has very limited use in the public schools. The intimate and personal nature of many of the items demands that the inventory be used with older adolescents and adults rather than with a high-school population. Two types of scales are present, the so-called "validity" scales and the clinical scales. The 4 validity scales are: (1) a "cannot say" or "?" key, which consists of the number of items that the examinee is unable to mark either "true" or "false"; (2) a lie (*L*) key, which is intended to identify those individuals who are trying to falsify their score by choosing responses that seem to them to be more socially acceptable than others; (3) a validity (*F*) key, which is a check on the correct taking and scoring of the scale; and (4) a correction (*K*) scale, which is meant to sharpen up the discriminating ability of the clinical scales. There are various clinical scales; however, usually only 9 of these are scored. These scales bear such clinical names as "hysteria," "paranoia," and "psychopathic deviate." It is felt that high-school counseling can get along without the use of such labels, which may be carelessly attached to various boys and girls.

Of all our personality inventories, this is probably the one that has had most use, and on which the most research has been based (See 4 and 5.) A large part of this recent research has been centered on the effects of various forms of response set, such as acquiescence, *upon* MMPI scores. Some of the results make one wonder if the *MMPI* measures much more than these response sets. Even if this were not so, it is doubtful that any clinically oriented instrument such as this has any place in the public schools.

Mooney Problem Check Lists

The *Mooney Problem Check Lists* * (1950) are available in 4 levels: junior and senior high school, college, and adult. The college

* Published by The Psychological Corporation.

and high-school forms consist of 330 items covering 11 areas: health and physical development; finances, living conditions, and employment; social and recreational activities; social-psychological relations; personal-psychological relations; courtship, sex, and marriage; home and family; morals and religion; adjustment to school or college work; the future: vocational and educational; and the curriculum and teaching procedures. The junior-high-school form has 210 items, which cover 7 different and appropriate areas. These inventories are self-administering, can be completed in less than 50 minutes by practically everyone, and provide *no* tables of norms. The checked problems are summarized within each area. The advantages gained by the use of such check lists have been discussed earlier in this chapter.

SRA Youth Inventory

The *SRA Youth Inventory* * (1949) is a check list of about 300 items. This inventory is a result of a series of surveys of the problems of high-school students. These were analyzed and grouped into areas called: (1) My School; (2) After High School; (3) About Myself; (4) Getting Along with Others; (5) My Home and Family; (6) Boy Meets Girl; (7) Health; and (8) Things in General. The inventory is self-administering and of such a length that any student can easily finish it in a class period. Machine answer sheets and also self-scoring carbon answer sheets are available. Percentile norms are presented for rural and urban high-school boys and girls.

In addition to the above keys there is a Basic Difficulty Score, which is based upon 109 items that experts believe to be indicative of basic personality disturbances. It is suggested that the counselor apply the key to all papers after the students have scored their papers for the 8 keys listed above in order to obtain the Basic Difficulty Score for each student. Papers should then be arranged in order, with those having the highest basic difficulty score on top. Those individuals should be the first ones scheduled to see the school counselor.

In the 1956 revision, Form S of the *SRA Youth Inventory* for grades 7-12, instead of marking whether or not each item is a prob-

* Published by Science Research Associates.

lem by placing a check in a box or upon an answer sheet, the student places his response in one of 3 boxes or the circle provided. If he feels that the item is one of his most serious problems, he places his mark in the first box, which is the largest box. If he feels that it is a moderate problem, then he marks the middle or medium-sized box. And the smallest box is to be used only when the student feels that the item is a small or occasional problem. Finally, there is a small circle to be marked when a statement does not express the way that the student feels. An intensity score is obtained by multiplying the number of marks in the largest boxes by 3, the number in the medium-sized boxes by 2, and the number in the smallest boxes by 1. Items that are marked by checking the circle have no value in computing the intensity score. Another edition, the *SRA Junior Inventory* is for use in grades 4-8.

The Sixteen Personality Factor Questionnaire

This inventory and others similar to it such as the *IPAT High School Personality Questionnaire* were developed by R. B. Cattell at the Institute for Personality and Ability Testing. They are supposed to measure all aspects of personality as revealed by factor analysis. The 16 *PFQ* is for use with individuals ages 15 and over. This inventory consists of 2 forms, A and B, each composed of 187 items, each of the various factors being assessed by 10 to 13 items. It is suggested that forms A and B be administered at the same time. Norms are presented for these combined scores. While Cattell has expertly developed these different inventories, they are by no means acceptable to many other test builders and to users of tests. One of the basic problems is whether or not these 16 factors are "the" basic factors of personality. There is evidence that these factors can by the method of factor analysis be reduced to a smaller number of factors. A second problem is associated with the low reliability inherent with scales made up of such a small number of items. Also little has been done validating the scales other than through the use of factor analysis. Little is known of their predictive validity. Finally Cattell uses esoteric terms in reporting his results, such as "premsia" and "harria." At present these inventories may be useful in research, but it seems that they have little to offer the high school or college counselor for his program.

REFERENCES

1. Allport, G. W. *The use of personal documents in psychological research.* Social Science Research Bulletin, No. 49, 1942.
2. Anderson, H. H., and Anderson, G. L. *An introduction to projective techniques.* New York: Prentice-Hall, 1951.
3. Bell, J. E. *Projective techniques.* New York: Longmans, Green, 1948.
4. Buros, O. K. *The sixth mental measurements yearbook.* Highland Park, N. J.: Gryphon Press, 1965.
5. Dahlstrom, W. G., and Welsh, G. S. *An MMPI handbook.* Minneapolis: Univ. of Minnesota Press, 1960.
6. Edwards, A. L. *The social desirability variable in personality assessment and research.* New York: Dryden Press, 1957.
7. Forbes, F. W., and Cottle, W. C. Determining readability of standardized tests. *J. Appl. Psychol.,* 1953, 37, 185-90.
8. Gaier, E. L., and White, W. F. Trends in the measurement of personality. *Rev. educ. Res.,* 1965, 35, 63-81.
9. Gross, M. L. *The brain watchers.* New York: Random House, 1962.
10. Guilford, J. P. *Psychometric methods.* New York: McGraw-Hill, 1954.
11. Hamalainen, A. E. *An appraisal of anecdotal records.* New York: Bureau of Publications, Teachers College, Columbia University, 1943.
12. Hartshorne, H., and May, M. A. *Studies in deceit.* New York: Macmillan, 1928.
13. Jackson, D. W., and Messick, S. Acquiescence and desirability as response determinants on the MMPI. *Educ. psychol. Measmt.,* 1961, 21, 771-90.
14. Jarvie, L. L., and Ellingston, M. *A handbook on the anecdotal behavior journal.* Chicago: University of Chicago Press, 1940.
15. Jennings, H. H. *Leadership and isolation.* New York: Longmans, Green, 1943.
16. Kelly, E. L., and Goldberg, L. R. Correlates of later performance and specialization in psychology. *Psychol. Monographs,* Vol. 73, No. 12, 1959.
17. Lindner, R. L. *Prescription for rebellion.* New York: Rinehart, 1952.
18. Messick, S., and Jackson, D. W. Acquiescence and the factorial interpretation of the MMPI. *Psychol. Bull.,* 1961, 58, 299-304.
19. Moreno, J. L. *Who shall survive?* Washington, D. C.: Nervous and Mental Diseases Publishing Co., 1934.

20. Murray, H. A. *Thematic Apperception Test: Manual.* Cambridge: Harvard University Press, 1943.
21. National Education Association. *Teacher opinion of pupil behavior, 1955-1956.* Research Bulletin, Vol. 34, No. 2. Washington, D. C.: National Education Association, 1956.
22. OSS Assessment Staff. *Assessment of men: Selection of personnel for the Office of Strategic Services.* New York: Rinehart, 1948.
23. Pepinsky, P. N. The meaning of "validity" and "reliability" as applied to sociometric tests. *Educ. psychol. Measmt.*, 1949, 9, 39-49.
24. Remmers, H. H. Rating methods in research on teaching. In N. L. Gage, ed. *Handbook of research on teaching.* Chicago: Rand McNally, 1963. Pp. 329-78.
25. Rorer, L. G. The great response-style myth. *Psychol. Bull.*, 1965, 63, 129-56.
26. Rorer, L. G., and Goldberg, L. R. Acquiescence and the vanishing variance component. *J. appl. Psychol.*, 1965, 49, 422-30.
27. Rorer, L. G., and Goldberg, L. R. Acquiescence on the *MMPI*. *Educ. psychol. Measmt.*, 1965, 25, 801-17.
28. Rorschach, H. *Psychodiagnostics. A test based upon perception.* Berne, Switzerland, 1942.
29. Rotter, J. B., and Rafferty, J. E. *The Rotter Incomplete Sentence Blank: Manual.* New York: Psychological Corporation, 1950.
30. Symonds, P. M. *Diagnosing personality and conduct.* New York: Appleton-Century, 1931.
31. Wickman, E. K. *Children's behavior and teachers' attitudes.* New York: Commonwealth Fund, 1928.

CHAPTER 15

EVALUATION OF INTERESTS

We shall begin this chapter by examining the importance of interests, both from the viewpoint of the educative process and from that of an individual's daily living. As noted in Chapter 7, all stated objectives of American education include the development of interests of one type or another as an important goal of school experiences.

Interests have been described as one of the main aspects of the learning situation. Interests are the *motivators* of learning. Without them, very little learning takes place in many individuals. Children are no different from adults in having strong likes and dislikes about many activities. A knowledge of these likes, dislikes, and indifferences on the part of the teacher, and, perhaps, an awareness of them also by the student, have a lot to do with whether or not any learning takes place in a classroom. A common example of the importance of interests is found in a high-school English class where a boy who is supposed to be writing a theme on his summer experiences is idly sitting in his seat looking off into space. When asked by the teacher why he is doing nothing, he replies that he can't think of anything about which to write. The teacher asks a few questions and finds that the boy spent two previous summers working as a general handy man on a "dude" ranch. Then he asked why did the student not write about some of his experiences there. The only reply was that the student didn't think that the teacher would be interested in something not connected with the school.

Almost every teacher has had in class the very bright student who does not work and either manages to just get by or fails. From the point of view of these students there is little going on in school to interest them. Frequently, the work is so simple that they already know it and are bored. On the other hand, some good students can go into any class and come out with top grades. Perhaps they are so conditioned that when they are put into any classroom learning situation there is nothing to do but produce. Students with no more interests in chemistry than an aboriginal Hottentot get "A's." Other students are selective in the subjects in which they receive good grades and, as pointed out above, some fail in everything.

Interests are of importance in themselves. It seems logical that an adult's possession of diversified and mature interests should lead to a better and more satisfactory adult life than he would have without such interests. Everyone is acquainted with the contented adult with his hobbies and activities for his spare time. He has never known boredom. Contrast this man with the individual who just can't stay home. There is nothing to do. There isn't much outside the home for this man either. But he is always pursuing something, never landing anything. The thought of doing something by himself or for himself scares him. His interests, psychologically, are those of a young adolescent. It follows that achievement in interests is an important outcome to be hoped for from our school experiences. Every teacher should have 2 concerns when it comes to interests: (1) the possession of socially desirable interests by all students, and (2) the maturation and development of these interests as the student grows older.

Interests are also of the utmost importance in educational and vocational counseling. When dealing with the adolescent student, we find that a knowledge of his abilities is only one part of the picture when it comes to making future educational and vocational plans. A high-school student may have high academic ability and the proper background courses to study engineering successfully in college. However, many students with such qualifications do not succeed. The student's interests must be considered. Does he really want to be an engineer or is this vocational plan merely the hope of a parent frustrated in his own desires? A study of the boy's interests soon reveals what the real picture is. Several standardized inventories exist that are most useful in vocational and educational planning. These will be discussed later.

NATURE OF INTERESTS

It should be stated first that all interests are learned. In this respect they are similar to attitudes. In fact, they are a special type of attitude. In the past (Smith and Tyler [20]) teachers were shown to have such an attitude about interests as that one interest was as good as another so long as it was not antisocial. Another feeling was that the absence of interests was, at the most, unfortunate. Since we know that interests are learned, such teacher attitudes as these are untenable.

Super (32) classified interests into 4 groups depending upon the way in which information about them is obtained. First, there are expressed interests. The individual states that he is interested in this or that activity. Such statements frequently are quite unreliable, merely reflecting passing fancies. It might be noted here that, in general, the younger the child the less reliable the stated interests. Secondly, there are manifest interests. When a person collects stamps, builds model railroads, or plays a violin, these activities are taken as manifestations of real interests in these activities. But again, for some individuals these interests may not be real. An adolescent boy may engage in an activity, such as amateur theatricals, merely because his best girl of the moment is active in these. Later he has a new girl, and, along with her, a new manifest interest may appear. Thirdly, there are tested interests. Our assumption here is that, if a person knows something about a subject and scores high on an achievement test in that area, he has an interest in that subject. Above we noticed that some students get good grades in subjects which they state they detest. There is one test, the *Michigan Vocabulary Profile Test* (11), which is used as a measure of this type of interests. On this test there are 8 areas, such as mathematics, physical sciences, fine arts, and sports. A high score in an area may or may not be an indication of an interest in that area. Fourthly, there are inventoried interests. Here an indication of a student's interests is obtained by having him choose among a large number of activities those that he likes and those that he dislikes.

Strong (27) listed five characteristics of interests that summarize in part what has already been said. First, he noted that interests are acquired in the sense that a feeling or feelings become associated with an activity as it is carried on. These feelings may be the results of a single or of many experiences. Playing football as a young boy may have associated with it feelings that exist as an interest in football throughout life. Secondly, interests are permanent or persistent. However, sometimes they do change, such as having a dislike become a like or the other way around. Thirdly, interests vary in intensity and one can state or rank his relative preferences for different interests or activities. Strong combines the fourth and fifth characteristics and calls them acceptance-rejection and readiness to act. For example, if one person asks another if he would care to read a certain book that the first has recently purchased, the second person might say "No, thanks" or "Yes, I would like to very much." With acceptance-rejection there is an implication of action, direction, and choice. The associated value, or feeling quality, decides whether any activity will be accepted or rejected, resumed or discontinued.

In evaluating interests, the teacher has to be aware that many times these so-called "interests" as obtained in any of the above ways are merely reflections of what a student feels is socially desirable. If a teacher asks a group of high-school students what their vocational plans are, he may obtain results that show that 80 or 90 per cent of the boys are going into professional work, a level in which about 10 per cent of the population of the United States is engaged. There is no realistic attempt on the part of students to investigate these so-called "interests" from the viewpoint of the special abilities required for each, the amount of training needed, or the cost of such training. Glamour enters into the selection of some of these so-called "stated interests." In the movies or on television, an adolescent girl sees the attractive life of nurses. This is mostly social and romantic. Nursing then becomes an interest and a life goal. After training starts, the less glamorous and even sordid aspects of the profession appear as a result of working with the diseased and injured. The potential nurse is disillusioned and often gives up her plans.

EVALUATION OF GENERAL INTERESTS

We shall first take up general interests that are related to learning situations or that are ends in themselves. Vocational interests will be discussed separately.

By Check Lists

The usual approach is to make check lists covering various types of activities. For example, these check lists could be labeled "magazines," "books," "radio or television programs," "hobbies," "athletics," and "organizations and clubs." The list is presented to the student and he checks the activity in which he engages. With the older students, we encounter the usual problem of misinterpretation when using these lists. It is socially desirable to read books or certain magazines; hence the student checks a few of each to show that he conforms. Some English teachers control this tendency toward social conforming by having the student write a short summary of the book he has checked as having read. With young children these check lists work better.

The writer once worked with a group of teachers in an entire consolidated school—that is, one having students ranging from grades 1 to 12—on a project evaluating interests. Check-list results on radio programs, hobbies, movies, and reading were obtained for students in all 12 grades. Since the results were summarized together, changes in interests over the 12 years could be noted. As might be expected, interests changed with maturation. What was popular in first grade was mostly gone by twelfth grade. But two rather disturbing situations did appear in the summary. The first was the persistence of some of the 6-year-old interests at the twelfth-grade level. When 20 per cent of the seniors listen regularly to the same radio or TV programs as do 6- or 7-year-olds ("The Lone Ranger" and similar blood-and-thunder serials), the writer feels that something has gone amiss. The same comment applies also to the way enlisted men (and some officers too) in World War II confined most of their reading activities to comics. The second point was the lack of stated interests on the part of the juniors and seniors in the so-called "better" programs and books. Symphonic and educational programs were mentioned by only a small minority. These ratings may be an underestimation of what actually exists, because, at this time of life, the individual is strongly influenced by his peer group and may not reveal publicly what actually he is interested in for fear of ridicule.

The construction of these interest check lists is very simple. As a starting point, when they are first used, we can get the information by asking each student to take 3 slips of paper and on the first to list his 3 or 4 favorite television programs, on another the 3 or 4 magazines he reads frequently, and on a third, his hobbies. In this way items for a check list for future use can be obtained. This list is valid because it contains the types of activities that are engaged in by students in a given geographical area.

By the Questionnaire

Another method of appraising interests is through the use of the questionnaire. Here a rather long list of some 30 or 40 items is set up, covering such things as "subjects liked best," "subjects liked least," "hobbies," "vocational plans," "part-time job activities," and any other items related to school or job activities. This type of approach, because of its nature, should be used only with older students. It becomes useful in the high-school counseling program. Here a lot of useful information for a counseling interview can be obtained ahead of time and valuable counselor time saved. Of course, unreliable information is just as apt to appear here as on any of the other appraisal instruments.

By Student Writings

Students reveal their interests in their writings. The subjects selected by students for their English themes and the thoroughness with which the subject is handled are indicators of interest. Sometimes students are asked to write their autobiographies. The student is given a partial outline to insure the discussion of certain points about himself. This semistructured essay should be assigned by the school counselor when the chief use is to provide information for counseling (as we saw in the previous chapter). In this we include a statement of a student's academic interests, his hobbies, and vocational plans. Students tend to elaborate on the latter quite fully, and usually

Fig. 15:1. INTEREST INDEX

First 23 Items from *PEA Interest Index* (8.2a) *

Directions: As you read each item below, underline one of the three letters after the number of that item on the answer sheet. Underline L (like) if you like or want to do what that item says. Underline I (indifferent) if you neither like nor dislike it. Underline D (dislike) if you dislike it or would not enjoy doing it. Try to mark every item, and to underline the letter which most nearly expresses your usual feeling toward it.

To underline L, I, or D, fill in the *whole space* between the dotted lines under these letters with a *heavy black mark,* using a *very soft pencil.* Otherwise the scoring machine may not count your answers accurately.

1. To write stories.
2. To learn how to go about getting a job.
3. To go on trips with a class to find out about conditions, such as housing, unemployment, etc., in various parts of your community.
4. To take part in class discussions of literature.
5. To visit stores, factories, offices, and other places of business to find out how their work is carried on.
6. To correspond in a foreign language with a student in another country.
7. To play baseball (either hard or soft ball).
8. To take part in a campaign against countries or business firms which treat people unjustly.
9. To speak a foreign language.
10. To play gymnasium games, such as dodge ball, relays, two-deep, etc.
11. To decorate a room.

12. To sing songs at parties, picnics, etc.
13. To attend public meetings to protest against something which you regard as unfair.
14. To learn how to cook well (in camp or at home).
15. To sing in a glee club, chorus, or choir.
16. To put eggs into an incubator and open one every day to see how the chick develops.
17. To sketch or paint.
18. To try to estimate the answer in problems involving size, weight, distance, etc.
19. To experiment with plants to find out how various conditions of soil, water, and light affect their growth.
20. To carve wood, soap, or stone.
21. To make chemical compounds.
22. To make things of wood, metal, etc.
23. To do the arithmetic necessary in planning trips or parties for the class.

an indication of the level to which a student is aspiring can be obtained. Not only in the English class and for the counselor but in all other areas, important information on interests can be obtained. Performance in the art class, in the music class, in gymnasium, or shop—all have valuable clues to the presence or absence of interests.

In evaluating academic interests, some schools have followed the practice described by Smith and Tyler (20) of constructing an academic interest inventory that covers all the areas of knowledge taught in that specific school (see the PEA Interest Index). For example, each teacher makes up a list of 15 or 20 activities related to his area. The biology teacher, for instance, might include such items as "going on bird hikes," "reading about man's development," and "making an insect collection." Each teacher would write his list of items, and these would be combined into a general check list of academic activities related to school courses.

EVALUATION OF VOCATIONAL INTERESTS

In appraising vocational interests, the usual procedure is to employ a standardized inventory. Here we shall discuss those most usually encountered.

Kuder Preference Record

The *Kuder Preference Record* * consists of a large group of items arranged in triads like this:

Direct an orchestra	( )	( )
Compose music	( )	( )
Repair musical instruments	( )	( )

The student has to select the one he would prefer to do most and the one he would prefer to do least. Each time he is forced to make a choice among the responses, and all items are to be answered. Two editions of Form C are available, one for hand-scoring and the other for use with IBM answer sheets. The hand-scoring edition involves the pin-punch method widely used with tests published by Science Research Associates. This edition is best suited to the public schools. The test can be administered in one period and scored during the same period the next day. Scoring is nothing more than counting pinholes. The scores are entered on profile sheets and centile scores for each area so obtained. The student completes his own profile sheet (Fig. 15:1).

Form C of the *Kuder* measures interest preferences in 10 broad interest areas: outdoor, mechanical, computational, scientific, persuasive, artistic, literary, musical, social service, and clerical (Fig. 15:2). Any score at or above the 75th centile is to be considered as

* Published by Science Research Associates.

43	38	50	54	35	10	15	4	38	52
Outdoor	Mechanical	Computational	Scientific	Persuasive	Artistic	Literary	Musical	Social Service	Clerical

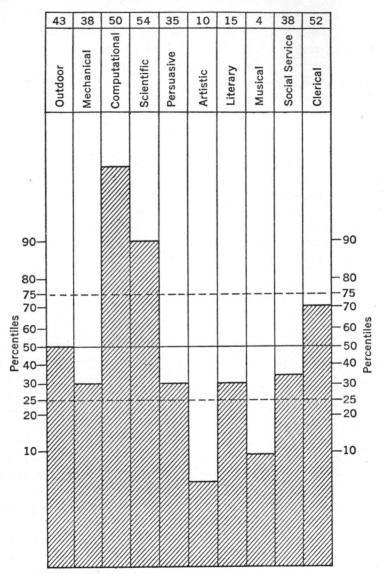

Fig. 15:2. KUDER PREFERENCE RECORD PROFILE OF A MALE *

* Adapted and used by permission of Science Research Associates, Copyright 195L

being significant as an indicator of interest in that area. Very low scores are also important in that they show that an individual is rejecting a specific area of interest. In addition there is a verification scale (V) and, for any subject whose V score in not within the range of 38-44, a serious doubt is cast on the value of the subject's responses.

Form D differs from Form C and earlier forms in that keys are available for specific occupations rather than for the broad preference areas listed above. This inventory consists of 100 triads similar to those described above and responded to in the same way. This form also has a V scale on which honest, cooperative subjects score between 49 and 60, the maximum score, and those really trying to fake results have scores of 44 or less. These leave a small band where results may be classified as doubtful. Most of the scales developed on Form D are of a professional nature, such as Counseling Psychologist, School Superintendent, and Accountant.

Kuder (13) pointed out that there were other ways of building an interest inventory instead of using Strong's general reference group (see below). He proposed to develop one in which the keys were established by differentiating among a number of specific occupations. Kuder's method consisted of setting up as response weights for differentiating between two occupations the actual difference between the proportions of the two groups (A and B) marking each particular response. The formula for the weight to be assigned to an item is simply $p_a - p_b$. The existence of electronic computers makes it possible to set up scoring keys in this manner and to use them.

Kuder administered the items of Form D of the *Kuder Preference Record* to a large group of subjects in different occupations (his criterion groups) and by the use of the technique just described set up item weights for the various items. As a result he had 79 occupational and 19 college-major scales for men and 37 and 13 of each respectively for women, and Form DD of the Kuder was born. On this inventory the subject responds to the inventory in the usual way, the items are scored electronically, and a profile sheet produced with the results printed on it. An entry on such a sheet for a male subject might look like this:

Printer
XXXXX   .42

The .42 represents a correlation between the individual's response and the response characteristic of each of the criterion groups. The line of X's depicts graphically the extent of the relationship with the group represented. The first X represents a score of .20 to .24 and each succeeding one an additional .05.

In addition to the occupational and college-major scales there are a verification scale (V) for checking the degree of confidence that can be placed in a subject's responses and eight experimental scales. The latter are to be used as the inventory is further developed in setting up masculinity-femininity, maturity, and other such scales.

When this inventory is used, Kuder recommends that each subject rank his occupational and college-major scores separately and look at the scores within each group in reference to each other. Obviously the larger the difference between two scores, the greater the real difference in interests. The author adds that occupations that fall within less than .07 of the top score are recommended for primary consideration as this .07 represents a true difference in rank. Similarly the college-major scales should be studied, and for the women, scores on the men's occupational scales as well.

The purpose of the scores, as pointed out by Kuder, is to show the subject various possibilities either for work or for study in reference to his own interest pattern. The scores along with other information should be used by him in making an intelligent decision about his interests. The inventory was developed with these four groups in mind: (1) eleventh and twelfth graders who are soon to be faced with a vocational or educational choice; (2) students who will drop out of school early as in grades 9 or 10; (3) college freshmen as an aid in selecting a major; and (4) adults in counseling, placement, rehabilitation, and job-training centers.

Another Kuder interest inventory, Form E, *New General Interest Survey*, was developed for use in grades 7-12, in college, and with adults as a measure of degree of preference in the same 10 areas that are found on Form C. Kuder suggests that this instrument be used as part of a comprehensive exploratory program with junior high school students. The use of a simplified vocabulary also makes it adaptable to adults with reading difficulties.

USES OF THE KUDER PREFERENCE RECORD. Probably the greatest use to which the *Kuder* inventory is put is as a tool in counseling.

Here it is used in 2 ways. First, a young student who has made no decision as to his vocational or educational plans fills out the Record as an exploratory move to see just what his interests are. Sometimes it is used to confirm a choice already made or to show that the area chosen is not one in which the student is interested. If a student scores high in the scientific area, for example, he is not told of any special vocation that he should enter or train for. In the manual are suggested occupations ranging from the professional level down to that of skilled workers where scientific interests are apt to be found (14). The student might like to get more information about these jobs from reading about them. If a student finds that he has 2 high scores, then jobs reflecting both these interest areas are suggested for the student's investigation. It is also possible that an occasional student will be found who has no significant score. Perhaps he is still immature as far as interests go—that is, his interests have not yet crystallized. Or it might be as suggested by Kuder (14) that, because of an equal balance of his interests in all 10 areas, nothing shows up. And it might be that he has no interests except in the areas of labor or personal services.

A second use of the *Kuder* is as a teaching device. Somewhere in eighth or ninth grade, the social-studies curriculum may contain a unit on the world of work. Since most students have to come to a decision about their future early or later, it seems that toward the end of junior high school is a good place to start deciding. Through use of the *Kuder*, the major areas in which men work can be investigated. Research has shown us that interests do change. The vocational interests of a ninth-grader are not to be accepted as final. There is still no harm in this short course in vocational orientation at that point of life. As a matter of fact, there is no reason why the *Kuder* cannot be taken every year throughout high school. The language of the *Kuder* is simple enough for it to be used in junior high. A page in the test booklet describes in very simple terms some of the more technical vocabulary with which the young student might be unfamiliar.

Form C of the *Kuder* is most useful in dealing with junior and senior high-school students because of the fact that it is not geared to the professional level. Occupations are lumped into these 10 broad general areas of interests, and vocations at all the ability levels in each area are considered. The *Kuder* then can be useful with the entire secondary-school population rather than with just the top 10 or 20 per cent of the students as would be the case if only professional occupations were considered.

Strong Vocational Interest Blank

The *Strong Vocational Interest Blank* * consists of 400 items, most of which are responded to on a "like," "indifferent to," or "dislike" basis. The items are broken down into groups made up of professional occupations, college academic subjects, amusements, activities, types of people and everyday activities, and a self-rating personality inventory. At the present time there are two forms: one for men and one for women. Sometimes women, especially at the university level, are given the men's form. In the manual, Strong recommends that the inventory not be used with individuals below age 17 except in the case of unusually mature 15- or 16-year-olds. The reason for this is that he feels that the change of interests is considerable between ages 15 and 20, and, hence, unless the individual tested is very mature, the results obtained will be subject to considerable change. Darley (8) states that this inventory can be used with ninth- and tenth-grade students with IQ's of 105 and above.

The inventory was developed by using as subjects mature men known to be successful in their occupations. Success was defined as earning at least a certain minimum annual income. According to Strong (30), the average age of these groups was 40 years. Items that distinguished men in a specific profession from other professions or professional men in general went to make up the various keys. Then, if a student marks this inventory in such a way that he receives a top score (A) on the physicians key, it means that his inventoried interests are similar to those of successful physicians. Items bear positive or negative weights for the various occupational keys.

When it is realized that there are about 50 keys currently in use on the blank for men, we see that hand-scoring of this inventory is out of the question. At the present time, the usual practice is to use special answer sheets and to send the papers out to various test bu-

* Published by Stanford University Press.

reaus where a complete scoring job and profile are furnished for about $1.25 per student.

The *Strong* is scored for some 40-odd professions, which may be grouped into the following areas (see Fig. 15:3):

> Scientific—psychologist, physician, etc. (Group I)
> Technical—mathematician, physicist, engineer, etc. (Group II)
> Social Welfare—minister, YMCA secretary, high-school social-science teacher, etc. (Group V)
> Business Detail—accountant, banker, purchasing agent, etc. (Group VIII)
> Business Contact—sales manager, real estate salesman, and life insurance salesman (Group IX)
> Verbal—advertising man, lawyer, author-journalist (Group X).

In addition, there are a few scattered professions, such as musician (Group VI), president of a manufacturing concern, production manager (Group III), CPA (Group VII) and a rather heterogeneous group (IV) made up of such diverse occupations as farmer, carpenter, aviator, printer, policeman, and mathematics-physical science teacher.

In addition to the above occupational keys, there are 3 nonoccupational scales. The first of these, the Occupational-Level, or O-L, Scale, was defined by Strong (30) as a scale that contrasts the interests of unskilled men with those of business and professional people earning certain annual salaries. Darley (7) indicated the scale to be an index of a man's level of aspiration, whether an individual was aiming at professional status and leadership or whether he was content to exist and operate at a more routine level. There has been considerable evidence that this scale does measure level of aspiration [Kendall's study (12), for example], but Barnett, Super, and others (2) in a summary of several studies using the scale put the actual validity of the scale in doubt. In spite of this, many counselors use scores that lie in either extremity on this scale as a measure of an individual's occupational motivation.

The second of these scales called the Masculinity-Femininity (M-F) Scale was defined by Strong (30) as an index that separated the interests of males and females. Darley (7) described it later as the

SEE OTHER SIDE
FOR EXPLANATION

LAST   NAME   FIRST

STD. SCORE

DATE

◀— LETTER GRADE

GROUP	OCCUPATION
I	DENTIST
	OSTEOPATH
	VETERINARIAN
	PHYSICIAN
	PSYCHIATRIST
	PSYCHOLOGIST
	BIOLOGIST
II	ARCHITECT
	MATHEMATICIAN
	PHYSICIST
	CHEMIST
	ENGINEER
III	PRODUCTION MANAGER
	ARMY OFFICER
	AIR FORCE OFFICER
IV	CARPENTER
	FOREST SERVICE MAN
	FARMER
	MATH-SCIENCE TEACHER
	PRINTER
	POLICEMAN
V	PERSONNEL DIRECTOR
	PUBLIC ADMINISTRATOR
	REHABILITATION COUNSELOR
	Y.M.C.A. SECRETARY
	SOCIAL WORKER
	SOCIAL SCIENCE TEACHER
	SCHOOL SUPERINTENDENT
	MINISTER

C   B-   B   B+   A
C+

0   10   20   30   40   50   60   70

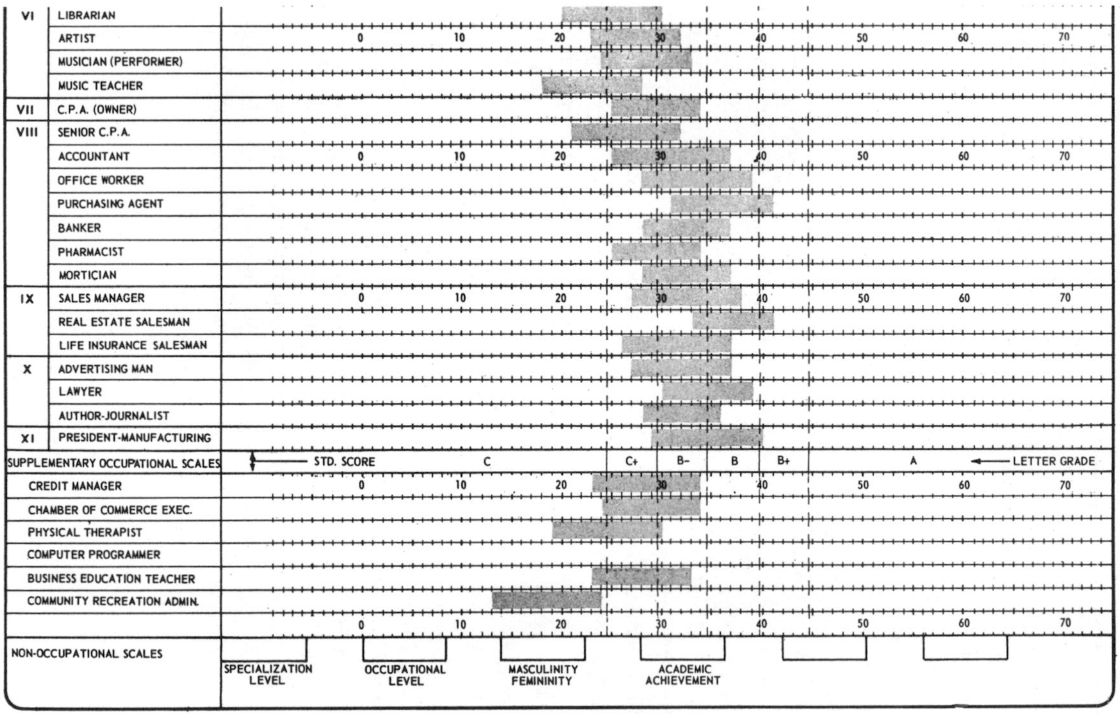

Fig. 15:3. Profile Sheet for the Strong Vocational Interest Blank *

* Used by permission of Testscor, Inc.

"continuum based upon the extent to which the individual's attention is held by technical, depersonalized, manipulative, concrete activities or objects in his environment (masculinity) or by cultural, aesthetic, personalized, symbolic, appreciative activities or objects in his environment (femininity)." Thus masculine interests are defined as interests in concrete objects and processes. An engineer and a physicist have such masculine interests. Feminine interests relate to people or to cultural, aesthetic, and appreciative activities. A clergyman, social-studies teacher, or poet may be said to have feminine interests.

The third of these nonoccupational keys, the Interest-Maturity (I-M) Scale, was noted by Strong (30) to contrast the interests of 15-year-old boys with those of men between the ages of 23 and 27. Darley (7) stated that interest-maturity reflected the "well-organized, socially sensitive, generally mature, tolerant, insightful individual." The idea behind this I-M Scale was that the more similar one's interests were to those of a 15-year-old, the more they were apt to change, since the typical 15-year-old supposedly has unstable interests. There is evidence that the I-M Scale does not clearly do this, but it may be used as an index of general maturity of outlook (8).

Obtained scores on this inventory are changed to a system of letter grades. According to Strong (30), a score of A, as noted above, for any occupation means that the individual has likes and dislikes similar to those men classified as successful in the given occupation. Individuals with scores of B are less like the norm group, and C grades signify no likeness between the examinee and the norm group. In using the scales, scores are actually reported as A, B+, B, B−, C+, and C. Many users of the *Strong* today have the papers scored by Hankes' Testscor, Minneapolis. One of their profile sheets is shown in Figure 15:3. Strong showed that the shaded areas on this chart covered the range of the average chance scores, plus and minus 1 standard deviation of these chance scores for each occupation. An inspection of Figure 15:3 shows that this chance area tends to occupy the C and B− grades. Scores to the right of this band are the ones usually considered when interpreting a *Strong* profile. It is equally important to consider scores to the left of these shaded areas, because they probably mean, in many cases, that the individual has rejected an interest in these occupations.

Darley (7) originated the pattern concepts used in analyzing *Strong* blanks. He has defined a "primary" pattern as the interest type in which an individual shows a preponderance of A and B+ scores. The "secondary" pattern has a preponderance of B+ and B scores, and the "tertiary" pattern contains a majority of B and B— scores on the specific occupational keys. These various preponderances have to be on the specific keys within an interest type. For example, an A on the mathematician scale, and B+ on the physicist and engineer keys would constitute a primary interest pattern. Hagenah (8) analyzed the interest patterns of 1000 University of Minnesota students and found that 193 of these students had no primary interest pattern, 410 evidenced single primaries, 303 double primaries, 88 triples, and 6 quadruple. In a similar fashion she analyzed the secondary and reject patterns.

Strong worked on this inventory for over 30 years. He and others have collected quite a lot of data that attest to its usefulness, stability, and validity. Strong's chief study (30) has been with a group of Stanford University engineers who first took the inventory as freshmen in 1931 and were retested in 1939 and 1949. For this group, Strong found a correlation of .69 between the freshman choice and the occupation engaged in nineteen years later. One half of the students continued in the occupation of their early choice or changed to a closely related occupation, whereas only one fifth of the group changed to an occupation quite unrelated to their early choice. Another point of interest is that 50 per cent of these men as freshmen had, at the age of 18.7 years, selected the occupation to which they were to devote their lives. Also, those who changed their occupations selected, as freshmen, jobs with lower prestige value than did those who stayed in the occupation of their first choice. Similar results were found by Trinkaus (33) working with Yale alumni.

Powers (19), using a more heterogeneous group than Strong, reported a mean Pearson r of .69 for 109 individuals tested in 1931 and again in 1941. Stordahl (24) followed a group of high-school seniors over a 2-year period and found Spearman rank-order correlation of .74 and .72 for metropolitan and nonmetropolitan males, respectively.

Reliability coefficients have been computed for the presently used scoring scales using the odd-even method. These r's range between

.73 and .93, with a mean value of .88. The lowest of these, .73, is for the CPA scale.

In reference to predictive validity, Strong (30) lists 4 propositions by which this type of validity can be demonstrated:

1. Men continuing in occupation A obtain higher interest scores in A than in any other occupation.

2. Men continuing in occupation A obtain higher interest scores in A than other men entering other occupations.

3. Men continuing in occupation A obtain higher interest scores in A than men who change from A to another occupation.

4. Men changing from occupation A to occupation B score higher in B prior to the change than in any other occupation, including A.

That these propositions are true can easily be demonstrated by consulting Strong's own work (28, 30) or that of others (8).

The 1966 Revision

Strong (25, 26) and others (31) discussed the need for revision of the widely used *Strong* blank and the methods used in updating the 1938 edition. As the years went by certain items became obsolete and invalid because what they referred to, such as certain magazines or occupations, either changed or disappeared. In 1966, the new edition of the Strong was finally published. About 100 of the old items were completely replaced because of obsolescence or of their inability satisfactorily to differentiate between occupations, and another 50 items were rephrased either to update them or to lower their level of reading difficulty. In the end the 1966 revision includes 399 items. While the system of scoring was not changed to that type using unit weights as many users of the inventory had urged, the scoring was simplified by reducing the range of item weights from $\pm$ 4 to $\pm$ 1. This still leaves the inventory with a complicated scoring system that will encourage users of the instrument to continue to use computer scoring facilities as they did with the earlier edition.

A number of new scales have been added to the profile sheet (Figure 15:2). In Group III Army Officer and Air Force Officer have been added making an area of interests reflecting the supervision of others in technical jobs. Librarian, Artist, and Music Teacher have been added to Group VI, developing a cluster of cultural-aesthetic activities. Several of the older occupational scales were also dropped and new ones inserted in the various groups or added as supplementary scales at the bottom of the profile sheet.

One of the nonoccupational scales, Interest-maturity, was dropped in the revision because over the years little evidence was produced that it had any validity. A new nonoccupational scale, Academic Achievement, has been developed. Scores on this scale correlate about .35 with college grades and are related to persistence in school. High school seniors who later earned no college degree had a mean score of 29 on this scale, those who later obtained a bachelor's degree a mean of 39, those who attained a master's degree had a mean of 45, and the average score of these high school students who eventually obtained a doctorate was 62.

On the earlier forms the shaded areas on the profile sheet were referred to as areas of chance scores, these being based originally on the throw of dice, the boundaries of each band being set as plus and minus one standard deviation about each mean chance score. Stephenson (22, 23) questioned this interpretation and showed that these chance scores were quite reliable in a test-retest situation. He demonstrated that, when university students were asked to fake chance scores, they could not. Campbell (4) suggested that a better way to demonstrate that a score was or was not of significant interest was to compare it with a distribution of scores obtained by the men-in-general group rather than a distribution obtained by throwing dice. He proposed to replace these so-called chance bands by men-in-general bands, each such band being taken as a standard deviation on each side of the men-in-general mean for each occupation.

At this point we might contrast the *Strong* with Form C of the *Kuder*. The *Strong* is based upon the interests of successful persons in various occupations. The *Kuder* was constructed statistically by studying the relationship of each item with various area or group scores. The *Strong* is best scored by an outside agency for a fee; the *Kuder* is actually self-scoring. The examinee merely counts pinpricks to obtain his score. The *Strong* is definitely constructed for a limited group, those who are contemplating the professions; the *Kuder* covers a wide range of human occupations from skilled jobs up to the top professions. The *Strong* is limited to individuals 17 years and over, except in early maturing or bright individuals. This more or less confines its use to high-school juniors and seniors and above. The *Kuder* can be used in junior-high school, as was noted previously.

Minnesota Vocational Interest Inventory (MVII)

Clark (1961) published a book in which he described the *Minnesota Vocational Interest Inventory (MVII)*,* an instrument that was developed using enlisted men in the Navy and that was later adapted to cover the activities of skilled tradesmen in civilian life. The *MVII* is made up of 570 items arranged in groups of three, that is, in 190 triads such as:

> Be a grocer
> Be a printer
> Be a shop foreman.

No attempt was made to arrange these in any order or in any particular groupings. The subject responds to each by selecting the one that he likes to do most and the one that he dislikes.

In his research Clark found that the interest patterns of men in different skilled occupations have the same sort of uniqueness as those of men in various professional groups. As on the *Strong,* Clark established keys that separated workers in a specific occupation from workers in general. A key for baker would be working effectively if it resulted in a distribution of scores for bakers that differed significantly from a distribution of scores for those in a workers- or tradesmen-in-general group or from a distribution of scores of workers in another occupation. Clark used large numbers, 225 or more, to establish occupational keys for workers in a group of skilled trades such as baker, carpenter, mechanic, printer, retail sales clerk, and the like. Instead of using the complicated weighted scoring method of the earlier *Strong* blanks, the author used a unit system, each choice being worth only one point. Clark's inventory is very similar to the *Strong* in many respects, except for the fact that instead of being built for professional and subprofessional workers, it is geared to the skilled tradesman or craftsman.

The profile sheet for the first edition has 21 specific occupational

* Published by The Psychological Corporation.

and 9 area scales, the latter being titled: Mechanical, Health Service, Office Work, Electronics, Food Service, Carpentry, Sales-Office, Clean Hands, and Outdoors. These area scales consist of clusters of items that correlated positively with each other. Also on the profile sheet there is a shaded band for each occupational scale, this area representing the range of scores for the middle third of a group of skilled tradesmen from various occupations, tradesmen-in-general. Such shaded areas may be used as reference points in determining the significance of a subject's scores.

In his book, Clark (6) reported research based upon use of the *MVII* with enlisted personnel in the Navy. He presented evidence that showed that scores on the *MVII* were positively related to course grades in a Navy Electronics Technician School and that certain naval personnel who were satisfied with their jobs scored significantly higher on specific *MVII* scales than those dissatisfied. Clark also reported that satisfied industrial education teachers scored significantly higher on the Industrial Education Teacher Scale than did dissatisfied teachers. Along with such evidence as this the *MVII* certainly seems to have content and construct validity. To date, with few exceptions, most of the research with this instrument has been done using enlisted naval personnel as subjects. One of the few nonmilitary studies follows.

Barnette and McCall (3) administered the *MVII* to over 1100 vocational high school boys in grades 9 and 12 in a large city, these boys being enrolled in various curricula such as food service, printer, electrician, mechanic, and the like. Scores on the *MVII* were compared with a boy's choice of training program. Results were more clear-cut for the twelfth graders than for the freshmen, but even for the seniors the findings were confused. Best results were obtained with the food handling, printing, and electrical scales. Students in the building trades, machinist, mechanics, and welders programs tended to have highest *MVII* scores on scales not related to the training program of their choice. Results were even poorer with the freshman group, but this is to be expected as research has shown that the vocational interests of students of this age level have not yet crystalized. The authors also noted that the test items were apparently too difficult in vocabulary level for these students.

The main purpose of the *MVII* is to show how much an individual's interests are like those engaged in a variety of occupations. Its major use is with students whose education will be terminated with high school graduation, students in vocational and technical schools, applicants for apprentice training, drop outs, and unemployed adults. To the extent that it is true that a person who is interested in a job is a more satisfactory worker than one without such interests, this becomes a useful counseling instrument. In the years to come, the *MVII* will be a basic and essential part of the counseling record.

The Occupational Interest Inventory

The *Lee-Thorpe Occupational Interest Inventory* * consists of 2 levels, *Intermediate Form,* for grades 7-12 and an *Advanced Form* for grades 9 up to adulthood. Structurally, the test is divided into: (1) fields of interests—personal-social, natural, mechanical, business, the arts, and the sciences; (2) types of interests—verbal, manipulative, and computational; and (3) levels of interest—in routine tasks, in tasks requiring considerable skill, and in tasks requiring expert knowledge, skill and judgment.

Research reports on studies using this instrument have been rather scanty. The *Inventory* has been rather widely used during the past 10 years, but validity evidence is still scarce. MacPhail (18) has reported on its use in separating various categories of degree groups in a university.

Another interest inventory also published by the California Test Bureau is the *Picture Interest Inventory* for grade 7 and higher. In this inventory the subject responds to pictures instead of words. In the first part of the instrument there are 53 triads of pictures, each picture depicting a person performing a particular type of work. As in other such item arrangements, the examinee responds by marking the one that he likes most and the one that he likes least. On the second part there are 30 pictures of an occupational activity and the subject responds to them on a "like-dislike" basis. The areas of interest measured are very similar to those encountered on the *Occupational Interest Inventory* and correlations are presented showing the relationships between these two inventories as well as the re-

* Published by California Test Bureau.

lationship between the scales on the *Picture Interest Inventory* with various scales on the *Kuder* and the *Strong*. This instrument has possibilities in evaluating the interests of slow readers and non-English-speaking subjects.

Gordon in his *Occupational Check List** has developed an inventory for use with students whose education stops with high school graduation or earlier. He has 240 items such as "drive a heavy truck" and "lubricate and service automobiles," all of which are occupational tasks generally referred to as skilled, semi-skilled, or unskilled. The items are distributed through five broad areas: business, outdoors, arts, technology, and service. The subject goes through the inventory and indicates the activity that he would like to do by underlining that item. When finished, he goes over the items that he has marked and circles the numbers in front of the ones that he would like to do the most. There follows a page on which he is asked to describe the job he would like for his life work and to give the reasons for his choice. On the next page he is asked to name and describe any other jobs that he would like to do that are not included in the check list. Finally there are two questions asking if the student plans to enroll in a regular college or university and the other requesting that he make a guess as to what kind of work he will be doing five years hence. This inventory is very similar in format and in the methods used in completing it to the *Mooney Problem Check Lists*. As on the *Mooney*, there are no norms. The major role for the check list is as a counseling instrument in which the student has a chance to consider occupational activities prior to the counseling interview.

The Study of Values

The Study of Values† was first marketed in 1931 by Allport and Vernon. It was revised in 1951 and again in 1960 and is now known as the Allport-Lindzey scale. Spranger (21) classified men into the following types:

1. theoretical—dominant interest is the discovery of truth.
2. economical—interested in what which is useful.

---

* Published by Harcourt, Brace & World.
† Published by Houghton Mifflin Company.

3. aesthetic—sees highest values in form and harmony.
4. social—highest value is love of people.
5. political—interested primarily in power.
6. religious—highest value called unity. A mystic.

The authors constructed the scale for the purpose of placing an individual's interest in one or more of the above groups.

For many years this inventory has been used in evaluating the interests of university students. One reason for this rather limited use is the difficulty of its reading index, which was shown by Forbes and Cottle (10) to be 12.7 years. The authors of the current revision state that it can be used successfully with high school seniors. The 1960 form differs from the previous ones in that it not only has extensive student norms based upon about 8000 students but also occupational norms for specialized vocational groups, the latter based upon about 10,000 individuals spread throughout professional and semiprofessional occupations. The inventory is so constructed that the mean score for each of the 6 values in the standardization groups is 40 and significant departures from this in one direction or another separate the two sexes, various university groups, and the various occupational groups.

Dukes (9) summarized the vast amount of research that has been carried out with this inventory. Students in different curricula and adults in different occupations do have distinctive profiles. Because of this, *The Study of Values*, when used with other information about subjects, is a useful counseling device.

Appraisal of Vocational Interest Inventories

It might be well, in concluding our discussion, to consider some of the liabilities of these interest inventories. In the first place, they can be faked (17). Over and over again examinees in studies have been asked to make themselves appear to have this or that interest. There is no question but that this can be done. The problem of faking, though, should not be so important with school groups where really nothing is at stake and the entire counseling procedure is set up to aid the students. Where such inventories are used as part of an employment battery, the problem of faking is much more important. Secondly, there is the problem of difficult vocabulary and of an understanding of what is involved in many of the occupations that appear on these scales. Forbes and Cottle (10) have shown the average grade level by five formulas for estimating readability of the *Kuder* to be 8.7, *Lee-Thorpe*, 9.5, and the *Strong*, 11.4. From this it can be seen that some high-school students will have difficulty with all three. Thirdly, the possibility of always receiving socially acceptable choices is always present. Perhaps many students select these without once thinking about it. But in spite of these 3 conditions or factors, we have in these instruments of vocational interests 3 of the most useful and valid of the many used in assessing human traits.

REFERENCES

1. Allport, G. W., and Lindzey, G. *A Study of values.* 3rd ed. Boston: Houghton Mifflin, 1960.
2. Barnett, G. J., Stewart, L. H., and Super, D. Level of occupational interest: deadweight or dynamism? *Educ. psychol. Measmt.*, 1953, 13, 193-208.
3. Barnette, W. L., and McCall, J. N. Validation of the *Minnesota Vocational Interest Inventory* for vocational high school boys. *J. appl. Psychol.*, 1964, 48, 378-82.
4. Campbell, D. Chance on the *SVIB*: Dice or men? *J. appl. Psychol.*, 1963, 47, 127-29.
5. Clark, K. E. *The Minnesota Vocational Interest Inventory.* New York: The Psychological Corporation, 1965.
6. Clark, K. E. *Vocational interests of nonprofessional men.* Minneapolis: University of Minnesota Press, 1961.
7. Darley, J. G. *Clinical aspects and interpretation of the Strong Vocational Interest Blank.* New York: Psychological Corporation, 1941.
8. Darley, J. G., and Hagenah, T. *Vocational interest measurement.* Minneapolis: University of Minnesota Press, 1955.
9. Dukes, W. F. Psychological studies of values. *Psychol. Bull.*, 1955, 52, 24-50.
10. Forbes, F. W., and Cottle, W. C. A new method for determining the readability of standardized tests. *J. appl. Psychol.*, 1953, 37, 185-90.
11. Greene, E. B. *Michigan Vocabulary Profile Test.* New York: Harcourt, Brace & World, 1939.
12. Kendall, W. E. The Occupational Level Scale of the Strong Vocational Interest Blank. *J. appl. Psychol.*, 1947, 31, 283-8.
13. Kuder, G. F. A rationale for evaluating interests. *Educ. psychol. Measmt.*, 1963, 23, 3-10.

14. Kuder, G. F. *Kuder Preference Record, Vocational.* Chicago: Science Research Associates, 1956.
15. Layton, W. L. *The Strong Vocational Interest Blank. Research and uses.* Studies in Personnel Work, No. 10. Minneapolis: University of Minnesota Press, 1960.
16. Lee, E. A., and Thorpe, L. P. *Occupational Interest Inventory.* Los Angeles: California Test Bureau, 1956.
17. Longstaff, H. P. Fakability on the Strong Interest Blank and the Kuder Preference Record. *J. appl. Psychol.*, 1948, 32, 360-69.
18. MacPhail, A. H. Interest patterns for certain degree groups on the Lee-Thorpe Occupational Interest Inventory. *J. appl. Psychol.*, 1954, 38, 164-6.
19. Powers, M. K. Permanence of measured vocational interests of adult males. *J. appl. Psychol.*, 1956, 40, 69-72.
20. Smith, E. R., and Tyler, R. W. *Appraising and recording student progress.* New York: Harper, 1942.
21. Spranger, E. *Types of men.* New York: Stechert, 1928.
22. Stephenson, R. R. Chance versus nonchance scores on the SVIB. *J. appl. Psychol.*, 1961, 45, 415-19.
23. Stephenson, R. R. Faking "chance" on the SVIB. *J. appl. Psychol.* 1962, 46, 252-6.
24. Stordahl, K. E. Permanence of Strong Vocational Interest Blank scores. *J. appl. Psychol.*, 1954, 38, 423-7.
25. Strong, E. K., Jr. Good and poor interest items. *J. appl. Psychol.*, 1962, 46, 269-75.
26. Strong, E. K., Jr. Reworded versus new interest items. *J. appl. Psychol.*, 1963, 47, 111-16.
27. Strong, E. K., Jr. Satisfaction and interests. *Amer. Psychol.*, 1958, 13, 449-56.
28. Strong, E. K., Jr. Validity of occupational choice. *Educ. psychol. Measmt.*, 1953, 13, 110-23.
29. Strong, E. K., Jr. *Vocational Interest Blank for Men.* Stanford, Cal.: Stanford University Press, 1966.
30. Strong, E. K., Jr. *Vocational interests of men and women.* Stanford, Cal.: Stanford University Press, 1943.
31. Strong, E. K., Jr., et al. Proposed scoring changes for the Strong Vocational Interest Blank. *J. appl. Psychol.*, 1964, 48, 75-80.
32. Super, D., and Crites, J. O. *Appraising vocational fitness.* 2nd ed. New York: Harper and Row, 1962.
33. Trinkhaus, W. K. The permanence of vocational interests of college freshmen. *Educ. psychol. Measmt.*, 1954, 14, 641-6.

CHAPTER 16

APPRAISAL OF ATTITUDES

Attitudes are usually defined as the readiness to react toward or against some object or value. They may be considered as a sort of charge or potential that an individual has. When we are stimulated by the appropriate stimulus, our responses usually follow a predetermined pattern. *Attitude* is in itself a generic word, which includes such other aspects of personality as interests, appreciations, mores, and morals. We have previously devoted Chapter 15 to interests. This chapter will be devoted to general attitudes, which concern an individual's feelings about religion, races, politics, war, economics, and the like.

NATURE OF ATTITUDES

All attitudes are learned. Allport (1) has summarized the methods by which he believes an individual may possibly acquire an attitude. He talks first about "integration." An accumulation of experiences over a long period of time will influence an individual in a given direction, culminating in a certain attitude about the object or value. For example, continued failure in reading or on written composition over a period of years will cause a student to have an unfavorable attitude toward these. A hacking-up of such classical literature as the plays of Shakespeare may lead to complete disregard of such literature for the rest of the student's life. Secondly, Allport points out that attitudes may be built up by a process of "differentiation." Here a specific attitude results from the development of a more general one. Over the years a student builds up an undesirable attitude toward school because of unpleasant experiences with certain teachers. He now has a certain attitude not only against school but against everything associated with school. He dislikes arithmetic; he dislikes reading, both in and out of school.

Thirdly, says Allport, some attitudes are brought about by "shock." Unusually painful experiences for which a child has not been prepared result in the formation of certain lasting attitudes. A child is taken to a physician; a needle appears; and the child receives a shot in his arm. Or a child is taken to a dentist and the first thing he knows a tooth is being extracted. Such situations as these contribute to the formation of attitudes that may persist a lifetime.

Finally, attitudes are acquired by "adoption." This is a sort of social inheritance in which an individual first assumes a certain attitude by following the example of his family. As he grows older, attitudes held by his friends, his church, and his school tend to become his. This is probably the chief source of our attitudes. It is interesting to watch how young preschool children are blind to such things as skin color. This has no effect on play activities. Such an absence of undesirable racial attitudes is usually found in the primary grades, too. But soon something begins to happen and the attitudes of many parents come to the fore, resulting in the usual racial cleavages.

Attitudes possess various dimensions, some of which are important when we are attempting to evaluate them. Remmers (15, 16) has a very good discussion of these dimensions, 4 of which we will summarize.

1. *Direction.* An individual is usually for or against some object or value. This is the aspect of attitudes that is usually measured. The work of such opinion pollsters as Gallup and Roper is basically concerned with the extent to which the population is favorable toward a certain politician, an international event, or a new soap or toothpaste.

2. *Intensity.* As we begin to study attitudes, we soon become aware of the differences in the strength of feeling people have about them. People who are strongly in favor of or strongly opposed to a certain practice or object naturally have more intense attitudes than those closer to the center of this continuum. But even individuals at

the extreme, who apparently have the same intensity, may still be quite different. For example, as Cronbach (5) has pointed out, 3 different individuals may present the same very intense attitude against organized religion. The first of these individuals may have arrived at his conclusion as a result of prolonged thought and deliberation. The second may have adopted this attitude because his friends are presently in the same position. The third may have this attitude because of an extreme emotional experience; perhaps he has lost his wife and young children as the result of an auto wreck or fire. One of the 3 men possesses an attitude that might easily be changed, but not the other 2.

3. *Public* vs. *Private*. Attitudes may be public; with some attitudes we suffer no qualms about revealing them to our aquaintances. Our attitudes about the major political candidates in a presidential election, about the new model automobiles, or the new styles in women's hats would be examples of this type. Other attitudes possessed by many may be of a type upon which society frowns. A person liberal in his political or economic beliefs refuses to reveal them when national witch hunts are in practice. It took a Kinsey to get people to reveal intimate details of their sex life. Keeping data confidential or anonymous is one way of trying to ascertain these private attitudes. Kinsey's data are so kept that, if a person were to steal a filing case of it, all he would possess would be a collection of meaningless cards. The more an individual feels society does not accept his beliefs, the less he will be willing to reveal them.

4. *Generality* vs. *Specificity*. The evidence today, especially with adults, seems to point to generality as being an aspect of attitudes. If an individual is labeled as a "liberal," he will tend to be liberal in his attitudes toward politics, economics, religion, international affairs, etc. There is a general liberal attitude that permeates all his beliefs and feelings. This is in conflict with the findings of Hartshorne and May (9), which were discussed in Chapter 14. It may be recalled that they reported that a child possessed no such ethical trait which could be labeled "honesty." Honesty was found to be situational—that is, a child might be completely honest in one type of situation and cheat in another.

EVALUATION OF ATTITUDES

There are 3 principal reasons why it is important that we study or evaluate attitudes. First, the acquisition of desirable attitudes is one of the major objectives found in all lists of school aims. Teachers hope that, as a result of the learning process, students will become tolerant of other races and religions, will acquire an appreciation of art, music, and literature, and will be considerate of their own health and of that of the community. As a result of science courses, we expect each individual to become familiar with the scientific method, which, of course, is a very important attitude. Hence, attitudes are in themselves very important concomitants of all learning that goes on in schools at all levels.

Secondly, and more specifically than above, if an individual is to live effectively in our democratic society, he must possess those attitudes that will lead to this effective living. A well-run school can do much in preparing boys and girls for such desirable adult life. Sensitivity to and understanding of social problems, tolerance, and appreciation of the worth of every individual are important objectives to be attained here.

Thirdly, success in various occupations has associated with it certain attitudes. The successful and competent elementary-school teacher possesses attitudes that are different from those held by a university physics professor. An individual going into social work must possess attitudes different from those held by an individual joining a police force. Hence, attitudes are important from the viewpoint of good counseling procedures. Attitudes must be considered along with abilities and interests in setting up educational and vocational aims.

Thurstone-type Scales

The first method for evaluating attitudes that we shall take up is that which uses scales as made by Thurstone (18). In discussing this technique, Thurstone's *Scale for Measuring Attitudes toward the Church* (Fig. 16:1) will be used as an example. To begin with, a large variety of attitudes about the church are written by the scale maker. These must be comprehensive enough to cover all possible

A SCALE FOR MEASURING ATTITUDES TOWARD THE CHURCH

L. L. Thurstone and E. J. Chave

Check (✓) every statement with which you fully agree:

.8ᵃ 1. I think the church is a divine institution, and it commands my highest loyalty and respect.

5.2 2. I am neither for nor against the church, but I do not believe that church-going will do anyone any harm.

8.1 3. I feel the good done by the church is not worth the money and energy spent on it.

10.2 4. I regard the church as a monument to human ignorance.

7.2 5. I believe that the church is losing ground as education advances.

2.4 6. I feel the church is trying to adjust itself to a scientific world and deserves support.

8.5 7. The teaching of the church is altogether too superficial to be of interest to me.

.5 8. I feel the church is the greatest agency for the uplift of the world.

1.4 9. I think the church has a most important influence in the development of moral habits and attitudes.

3.4 10. I believe that the church is necessary, but like all other human institutions it has its faults.

10.6 11. I regard the church as a harmful institution, breeding narrow-mindedness, fanaticism, and intolerance.

7.6 12. The church is too conservative for me, and so I stay away.

3.6 13. I believe in the ideals of my church, but I am tired of its denominationalism.

1.3 14. I believe that the church furnishes the stimulus for the best leadership of our country.

6.3 15. I'm not much against the church, but when I cannot agree with its leaders I stay away.

9.0 16. I regard the church as hopelessly allied with reactionary forces.

2.7 17.ᵇ I believe that the church practices the Golden Rule fairly well and has a consequent good influence.

ᵃ These scale values do not appear on the scale but are inserted here to aid in understanding how the scale works.

ᵇ There are 45 items on the complete scale.

Fig. 16:1. A THURSTONE ATTITUDE SCALE *

attitudes about this institution. Next, the builder of the scale has to obtain a group of individuals to act as judges. Thurstone believed that at least 50 were necessary. The judges were then asked to take all these attitudes about the church, each of which now appears on a separate sheet of paper, and to sort them into 11 piles. At one extreme is the most favorable attitude and at the other, the least favorable. The neutral position is at the center. These piles are supposed to be separated equally on the continuum. Because of this, Thurstone's method is called that of *equal appearing intervals*. The median value ascribed to each item by the judges is taken as the scale value for that item. Items upon which there is widespread disagreement on the part of the judges are disregarded. This scale which measures attitude toward the church is made up of 45 items selected from the large original group. The scale values range from .5 for "I feel that the church is the greatest agency for the uplift of the world" to 11.0 for "I have nothing but contempt for the church." An item at the center with a scale value of 6.0 is "My attitude toward the church is best described as indifference."

In taking such a scale as this, the examinee goes down through the items checking every statement with which he fully agrees. The items are not arranged in the final form according to scale value but are mixed up. The scale values of all the items checked or endorsed are added. This sum is divided by the number of items checked by the student to obtain his score. A median value could be taken instead of the mean. In the manual of each scale are found tables for the interpretation of the various scores, ranging from strongly favorable (low score in this case) to strongly antagonistic.

The chief problem with these Thurstone-type scales is the tremendous amount of time required to construct them. Even if judges are available, and frequently they are not, the scales are a lot of work to make. Thurstone used 300 judges in setting up this one scale about the church. Remmers (14) has constructed a series of generalized scales in an attempt to get around this difficulty. In his scales, such as the one entitled *A Scale for Measuring Attitude toward Any School Subject* (Fig. 16:2), the examinee writes in the specific school subject involved and then goes ahead and checks it just as is done with a Thurstone-type scale. Also several, up to 5, things, practices, or objects can be rated on the same scale where space is provided for such. Remmers has shown a high agreement between scores on these generalized scales and Thurstone's more specific scales, when a generalized scale was set up to measure the same attitude as the specific one. Such scales as these, however, should not be used indiscriminately. Results should be checked for validity each time.

A Scale for Measuring Attitude toward Any School Subject

Please fill in the blanks below. (You may leave the space for your name blank if you wish.)

Name_____

Boy   Girl   (encircle one)   Date_____

Age when school started this year____ Grade (encircle one)   7, 8, 9, 10, 11, 12

What occupation would you best like to follow?

Directions:

Following is a list of statements about school subjects. Place a plus sign (+) before each statement with which you agree with reference to the subject or subjects listed at the left of the statements. The person in charge will tell you the subject or subjects to write in at the head of the columns to the left of the statements. Your score will in no way affect your grade in any course.

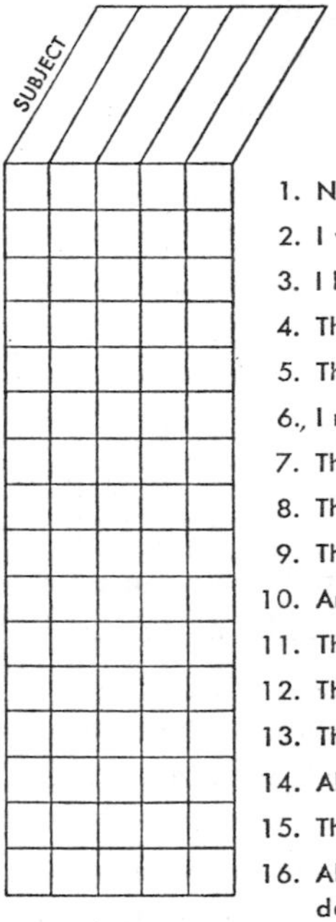

1. No matter what happens, this subject always comes first.
2. I would rather study this subject than eat.
3. I love to study this subject.
4. This subject is of great value.
5. This subject has an irresistible attraction for me.
6., I really enjoy this subject.
7. This subject is profitable to everybody who takes it.
8. This subject develops good reasoning ability.
9. This subject is very practical.
10. Any student who takes this subject is bound to be benefited.
11. This subject teaches me to be accurate.
12. This subject is a universal subject.
13. This subject is a good subject.
14. All of our great men studied this subject.
15. This subject is a cultural subject.
16. All lessons and all methods used in this subject are clear and definite.

Fig. 16:2. A GENERALIZED ATTITUDE SCALE * (Ella B. Silance—edited by H. H. Remmers)

* Reproduced by permission of the Purdue Research Foundation.

Thurstone validated his scale on attitudes toward the church by giving it to divinity students, active church members, nonactive church members, and nonattenders. The theological students and active church members scored higher than the other groups. Other scales were validated by associating scores on the scale with material obtained by the use of an autobiography. When answered carefully and straightforwardly, these scales appear to have validity. Reliability, computed on an alternate-form basis, tends to run in the .80's. There are 2 forms for most of the scales.

Likert-type Scales

The second type of scale to be discussed is called the Likert Scale (12). Compared to the Thurstone-type scale, this is very easy to construct. Again, a list of statements is drawn up that reflects both favorable and unfavorable attitudes about what is to be measured. The items are given to the examinees who, this time, respond to them on a 5-point scale: "strongly agree" (SA), "agree" (A), "no opinion or undecided" (U), "disagree" (D), and "strongly disagree" (SD). A large number of persons are given the scale and then an item analysis is made. Those items that correlate highest with the total score on the scale are selected for the final form. This is the method of INTERNAL CONSISTENCY.

When we score this type of scale, the favorable items have a value of 5, 4, 3, 2, and 1 ranging from "strongly agree" to "strongly disagree." For the unfavorable items the values go 1, 2, 3, 4, 5, from "strongly agree" to "strongly disagree." A high score then is obtained by marking the favorable items "strongly agree" and the unfavorable ones "strongly disagree."

Likert-type scales can be made in very much less time than Thurstone-type scales; no judges are required; and scoring is no more complicated. Studies have shown correlations between the results obtained by both types of scales, measuring the same attitude, to be high. As a result of this, Likert scales have to a large extent replaced those of the Thurstone variety. Both scales may not really tap attitudes if the examinees do not so wish. In an earlier chapter, under response set, it was noted that it was easier to be agreeable than disagreeable. This surely must be taken into account here.

Such self-report scales on which inferences are drawn from responses to statements of belief, behavior, feelings, and the like are all susceptible to two types of effects—that of the subjects' desires to present a certain picture of themselves and that of the results of response sets (2). Many times when confronted with an attitude scale, subjects can see the purpose of the scale, can see the implications of their responses, and thus can control the nature of their responses to create any impression that they so desire. Over the years much has been written describing methods of controlling such behavior. For example, responses to attitude scales are made anonymous, emphasis placed on the importance of right and wrong answers as a contribution to scientific knowledge, statements used stressing the fact that there is no right nor wrong answer to any item in the scale, attempts made to establish desirable rapport between the subject and the examiner, and many more such approaches used. Sometimes the items are so constructed that a continuous response of favorable replies is prevented. For example, using an item to which an unfavorable response is apt to be considered as desirable would bring this about. Such an item might be "Would you be willing to have an alcoholic serve as your U.S. Senator? Also the use of forced-choice items in which the subject has to make a decision between two equally sociably desirable statements (7) helps in part to bring about more valid responses.

Response sets are encountered in the tendency for individuals to agree (or disagree) with items regardless of the item content, to give extreme answers, or to select items in the center of the scale. The first of these response sets can be counteracted by writing items in such a way that for about half of the items agreement represents a favorable response and for the other half an unfavorable response. Various schemes have been tried out in attempting to control a subject's giving a certain type of response to all items. Westie (19) suggested presenting items in matched pairs, one referring to the attitudinal object and the other referring to some control object. He noticed that, when an item such as "Would you be willing to have a Negro bookkeeper live in the same apartment house as you?" is used and when subjects are given a 5-point scale upon which to respond, one can not know if subjects who answer "very willing" differ in their attitude from those who reply "willing." If a parallel item about a white bookkeeper is also presented, responses can be scored on the discrepancy between the subject's response to the Negro and to the white item and such a score removes the effects of response style from the score.

Error-choice Technique

A third method of attitude measurement is called the error-choice technique. This involves the construction of an achievement test. Hammond (8) has used items of a multiple-choice type with 2 responses. Usually half the items are straightforward and have a correct response. The remaining items have no correct given answer, and in responding to these an individual reflects a bias one way or another. What appears then to be an honest-to-goodness achievement test turns out to be a projective technique used in evaluating attitudes.

Kubany (10) in a study showed how this worked with medical students and social-work students in measuring their attitudes on national health insurance. He constructed a 50-item test on health, diseases, and medical care. Twenty-two of his items had no correct given answer. An example of one of his items follows:

Of the total recorded physical defects listed as causes of rejection during World War II, what percentage could have been prevented or corrected?
A. 25-30%
B. 15-20%
(The correct answer according to federal health specialists is 20-25%.)

The idea again then is that an individual's attitude will be revealed by the direction of his choice. Those who feel that medical care is not sufficiently available to all would be in favor of national health insurance and would tend to pick the higher of the 2 figures, the "A" response. Those who feel that medical care to all is sufficient and who, hence, would not be in favor of national health insurance would tend to take the lower figure, the "B" response. At the end of the test, each individual was asked a direct question as to whether he was in favor of or opposed to some form of national health insurance. On this test, a high score reflected an attitude in favor of national health insurance and a low one, an opposing attitude. The mean score for 42 social-work students was 14.6 and for 59 third-year medical students was 5.9. A test of the difference between the 2 means produced a *t* ratio of 20.9. There was only the slightest overlapping between the 2 groups.

Other research workers have used this type of test to examine labor-management relations and supervisory functions and the technique seems to be a valid one. It is felt that a lot more will be done with this method in the future.

Standardized Scales

A fourth method consists of the use of standardized scales. Typically, these present a series of items made up of situations in which each individual has to pick the one that he feels is correct. An item could read like this:

On a hot summer day a boy is given an ice-cream cone. He should reply to his benefactor:
A. One cone is hardly a taste on a day like this.
B. My father gets better ice cream at Smith's store.
C. It was nice of you to treat us today.
D. Ice cream is bad for the teeth.

Another type item, used in the New York Regents' Inquiry into the character and cost of Public Education in New York State, sets up a situation either in the school or in the community and the individual has to decide which course of action, if any, listed below the item he would follow.

In the past there were quite a few such instruments available for use. These have disappeared of late because it has been shown that the correlation between actual behavior and what a person says he would do is very low or nonexistent. In most of these instruments the acceptable answer is readily apparent. A group of Sunday School youths and another group of youths in a reformatory would achieve similar scores. Both groups know what society considers to be good behavior, but one group has disregarded these standards and has gotten into trouble.

Simpler Evaluation Techniques

Fifthly, many of the devices described in detail in Chapter 14 can be used in appraising attitudes. First, observational techniques implemented by the use of anecdotal records would be a rich source of information about a student's attitudes. Here we are using overt behavior and making inferences about the student's attitudes from this. Secondly, a student's writings, as exemplified by his themes, autobiographies, and diaries, contain a large amount of material about his attitudes, ideals, and appreciations. Thirdly, check lists of activities, free-time pursuits, and reading records or check lists would reveal, as was previously pointed out, a lot about interests and some information about attitudes as well. As far as reading goes, it has been stated, and probably correctly so, that we read not to change our attitudes but to further fortify or justify the attitudes we already hold. That is, a conservative Republican does not take to reading the Communist *Daily Worker*.

Free-response Technique

Sixthly, there is the free-response technique. Suppose the wives of potato-growers had been protesting the prices paid for potatoes. An item like this could be built:

> Statement. New York Wholesale Vegetable and Fruit Dealers today offered $1.00 per hundred pounds for potatoes.
> List all your ideas about the above statement which you feel are important.

Responses to questions such as this could be summarized into categories to the extent to which they reflect desirable social attitudes. Smith and Tyler (17) list 3 categories for such responses: (1) purely personal association (such as "I have enough potatoes" or "Never eat them"); (2) implications showing personal-social values (such as "If potatoes are so cheap, we should eat more of them"); and (3) responses showing wider social implications (such as "How can these growers live with such prices?"). In building items of this type, we may use any situation that might elicit different attitudinal responses. The local newspaper is a good source of ideas.

Another free-response technique is to present unfinished stories related to the attitude being measured and have the students complete the stories. From the endings which the students write, all sorts of information about individual problems and attitudes can be obtained. The following is an example of this technique:

You are a member of a group of 14- and 15-year-old white boys who have been in a summer camp for one week.
You are now fairly well acquainted with all the fellows in your outfit. At the beginning of the second week, another cot is placed in your tent and given to a Negro boy. Describe what happened.

Paired Comparisons

A seventh technique used in assessing attitudes is the method of paired comparisons. When we use this technique, the examinee is presented with a list of pairs of nationalities, practices, or whatever attitudinal object is being measured. Each nationality is presented in combination with every other nationality. For each pair the rater has to mark the one which he prefers. Scores could appear as a rank-order summary of his nationality or practices preference. This method, while free from response set and exacting—the rater has to compare each possibility with every other possibility—is time-consuming when the number of objects or practices to be rated is large. Forced choice techniques are modifications and simplifications of this method.

Opinion Polling

Eighthly, opinion polling or surveying is a method of attitude measurement. Frequently, the type of question used here is of the "yes–no" or "agree–disagree" type. In measuring opinions about current events, we might use such questions as: "The British are to be condemned for their invasion of Egypt" or "Russia is less effective in European politics than it was five years ago." Gallup, Roper, and other pollsters use a stratified, random sample in obtaining their responses. They do not go out on a street corner and ask the question of the first 100 individuals who come along and cooperate with answers. Findings from such an approach would be very restricted. The pollsters hope, on the basis of their sample, to be able to make an inferential statement about the percentages of the entire United States who agree or disagree with a certain question.

Great care must be taken in wording the questions, because it is possible to word statements in such a way as to obtain the response desired. Also questions have to be simple and unambiguous. Many individuals interviewed actually have no opinion on the question being asked. Some don't even have any idea about the situation or individuals involved in the question. The ignorance and apathy of a part of the population is sometimes startling. Hence, an informational question can be used first. If the person being interviewed knows nothing about this, the interview is terminated then and there. Frequently, after an individual has responded to an item, he is asked to answer an open-ended question, such as "Can you tell me why you feel this way?", "How strongly do you feel about this?", "Just what do you think about this situation?". The purpose of these open-ended questions is, in part, to obtain information that might be checked against the responses obtained on the attitude items. Also, it is an attempt to measure the depth or intensity of the attitude.

While opinion polling is widely used outside the schools, it is of less use to the classroom teacher than any of the other methods of attitude appraisal. Teachers of social studies might use it in the appraisal of the attitudes about and the knowledge of current events. Opinion polling could also be used by a school group to find out how the student body feels about various proposed courses of action. A project like this would be a good one for an eleventh- or twelfth-grade social studies class.

Suggestions for Attitude Scale Construction

Teachers frequently find it more useful to build their own attitude scales rather than use those made by specialists. These teacher-made scales have the advantage of fitting into the objectives of the local school. A group of teachers could get together and set up scales following the techniques discussed above. Corey (3) has suggested steps that are helpful. First, each teacher asks each student to write 3 or 4 statements that express various ideas about the attitude being appraised. As an example, about the attitude toward cheating he notes:

Cheating is as bad as stealing.
If a test isn't fair, cheating is all right.
I won't copy, but I often let someone else look at my paper.
A little cheating on daily tests doesn't hurt.

Next, the teachers edit the items, eliminating all duplicates and statements of facts rather than opinion. They list the following qualities that should be characteristic of the items which are selected to remain on the scale:

1. The statement must be debatable.
2. The statement should not be susceptible to more than one interpretation.
3. The statement should be short.
4. Technical terms should be avoided.

The third step is to administer to a group of students all the items that have survived the second step. The students are asked to put a plus sign in front of the ones they favor and a minus sign before the ones which they consider to be unfavorable. Statements that produce 80-per-cent agreement as favorable or unfavorable are accepted for the final form of the scale. Items below this value are discarded because of possible ambiguities.

After duplicating, the scale is ready to use. In the directions it is important to stress that this is not a test in that it is made up of a group of items with right and wrong answers. All are opinions and are to be answered to see how the students feel about the topic being covered. The items can be responded to as was described above for the Likert-type scale—that is, on a 5-point scale ranging from "strongly agree" to "strongly disagree." Quantitative scores can be obtained as on Likert-type scales.

It must be emphasized that the administration of these scales should be divorced from the giving of the usual achievement test that is to be graded. If this is not done, the concept of a grade stands to the fore, and what appears on the attitude scale are the responses that the student thinks the teacher wants him to put down or the responses he knows reflect the teacher's attitudes. Of course, we might get these in any case, but our chances are increased when these inventories become a part of an examination. It should not be necessary to state that these scales must not be graded on the basis of what the teacher feels to be the most desirable attitude being considered as the correct response.

When he was a high-school science teacher, the writer set up in the above fashion a collection of short attitude tests under such rubrics as "Concerning health and hygiene," "Concerning the earth, plants, and animals," "Concerning weather, water, etc.," "Concerning people, etc." He administered these short scales at the beginning of a unit of biology or general science for several reasons. First, the responses that appeared gave an indication of what might be stressed and what need not be. Secondly, he could see if the scientific attitude, the attainment of which was one of the major objectives of these courses, was really being adopted and applied, or whether he was merely getting the responses that represented the folklore, myths, and misinformation of the area (which, incidentally, was rural). Thirdly, the total administration of such a series of scales at the beginning of the year and again near the close indicated to him the extent to which desirable attitudes had been developed by the courses. Fourthly, there is no better way to get some students thinking or investigating a problem than to have their cherished beliefs shown to be not in line with scientific facts and principles.

Validation of Attitude Scales

We might summarize at this point the major techniques used in validating these scales. First, the method of Thurstone's of administering the scale to contrasting groups can be applied. Thus the responses of churchgoers could be compared with those of non-churchgoers, those of registered Republicans with registered Democrats. A scale resulting in significant differences between 2 such groups would be labeled as valid. Secondly, scores on scales can be interpreted in the light of what people write that they have done or believe. If the scale possesses validity, different size scores would go along with different descriptions of behavior. Thirdly, a group of judges can be used to validate the scales (6). In one study, a group of attitude scales was drawn up to measure the effect of a university's program of general education on certain attitudes. These scales covered such areas as politics, literature, civic relations, science, and music. Experts in different subject-matter areas were used to determine what the best response was to each item. For example, members of the Fine Arts College were asked to rate the items related to art. The students' papers were then scored, using the judgments of these experts as the best answers.

A fourth technique that can be used is the comparison of scale ratings with actual behavior. As will be shown below, this usually produces rather discouraging results, because people don't always seem to do what they claim they would or should do. Perhaps much of the behavior used as criterion measures is too complex and too changeable to be useful in validation studies. It is possible, through the use of observational techniques, to see how different students behave in specific situations. Many times this specific behavior is in line with a student's expressed attitude.

PROBLEMS OF ATTITUDE APPRAISAL

The major problem in attitude appraisal is how to get valid responses. As pointed out above, the correlation between responses on one of these paper-and-pencil questionnaires and observed behavior is apt to be very low. The classic example is the study by Corey (4), who administered a test to a group of educational psychology students near the end of the week. At the same time the class was given an attitude scale on cheating. This was anonymous but was secretly coded so that the student completing it could be identified later. Over the week end copies were made of the students' papers. During the first class period of the ensuing week, the students were allowed to correct their own test papers in class and thus were given a chance to cheat. The correlation between the attitudes expressed on this scale about cheating and actual cheating behavior was .02.

Another study that is widely quoted by social psychologists is one conducted by La Piere (11). He traveled around the United States with 2 well-dressed Chinese companions for a period of time during which they stopped at about 250 hotels and restaurants. Only once were they refused service. A few months later La Piere questioned by mail each of the housing and eating establishments visited as to its policy on catering to persons of different ethnic origin, such as Chinese. Over 90 per cent of the respondents categorically stated that they would not serve Chinese. He was forced to conclude that one's general appearance, neatness, cleanliness, plus good-looking clothes and baggage, had a lot more to do with the issue at hand than did skin color, straight black hair, and slanting eyes.

A second problem in attitude appraisal is that the approval of a general attitude does not always include the approval of specific attitudes which make up the general one. This arises when we measure attitudes such as our belonging to the United Nations or just plain internationalism in general. Many individuals are all in favor of these, as shown by opinion polls. Then more items are submitted about factors that are important if the United States is to be an effective member in an organization of nations. For example, trade barriers have to be eliminated or lessened, an international police force has to be established, radical financial arrangements have to be made, a free exchange of all types of ideas is all for the better. These new items cover conditions basic to a union of nations. Many of the individuals who wholeheartedly endorsed the general statement now are against those factors that are needed to make the general statement effective. Hence, it is probably not desirable to try to appraise complex objects. Better results might be obtained by examining the specifics and making inferences about the complex on the basis of an individual's response to these.

Another problem that enters into attitude appraisal is the change in attitudes over the years. Scales that are in use today may be worthless in a few years. When Thurstone first constructed his attitude scales about war, he found that many students were opposed to war. This was in the late 1920's. Ten years later the international picture had changed tremendously. In a few more years many of those who strongly opposed war under any conditions found themselves in the Armed Forces serving in World War II. Another example would be how what is considered radical or liberal by one generation becomes the accepted attitudes of the majority, even of the conservatives, in the next. Many of the liberal attitudes toward government introduced by President Franklin D. Roosevelt in the early 1930's are so considered today. Before any scale is used it should be examined in the light of how it fits into the world of today. The scale value on many of Thurstone's scales have changed considerably from what they were originally.

One other difficulty may be encountered. The administration of attitude scales usually turns up a number of individuals whose scores place them in the middle of the distribution—that is, they reflect a neutral attitude. It is difficult to know exactly what these neutral scores mean. Do they represent an individual who really is straddling the fence, who hasn't made up his mind in one direction or another? Or do they represent scores of an indifferent individual who is in no way concerned with us or with our scale? A third possibility is that they are brought about by the ignorance of the individual in reference to what is being measured.

A final word in respect to these scales and techniques. Throughout this chapter it has been stressed over and over again that the correlation between scores on these scales and observed behavior is low. Does this make the scales useless? The writer feels that the answer to this question is "No." If a person says that such and so is his attitude, then this is in itself important. In many cases where the attitudes involved are not too personal or private, the results at hand are probably pretty close to the truth. This would certainly be true in reference to many teacher-made scales that could be used in measuring the achievement of class objectives. But as the attitudes become more private, individuals will hold back, especially if they feel that they have something to hide. Making responses anonymous helps in part to get around this problem. However, if one of the chief purposes of evaluation is to help a student assess his strengths and weaknesses, anonymous papers are of little value. Perhaps the classroom teacher should become less concerned about some of these private attitudes and focus his attention on the so-called "public" ones. The latter still leave a big field in which to labor.

REFERENCES

1. Allport, G. W. "Attitudes." In C. Murchison, *Handbook of social psychology.* Worcester, Mass.: Clark University Press, 1935.
2. Cook, S. W., and Selltiz, C. Attitude measurement. *Psychol. Bull.,* 1965, 62, 36-55.
3. Corey, S. M. Measuring attitudes in the classroom. *Elem. School J.,* 1943, 43, 457-61.

4. Corey, S. M. Professed attitudes and actual behavior. *J. educ. Psychol.*, 1937, 28, 271-80.
5. Cronbach, L. J. *Essentials of psychological testing.* New York: Harper, 1949.
6. Downie, N. M., *et al.* The opinions of Syracuse University students on some widely discussed current issues. *Educ. psychol. Measmt.*, 1950, 10, 628-36.
7. Edwards, A. L. *The social desirability variable in personality assessment and research.* New York: Dryden Press, 1957.
8. Hammond, K. R. Measuring attitudes by error-choice: An indirect method. *J. abn. soc. Psychol.*, 1948, 43, 38-48.
9. Hartshorne, H., and May, M. A. *Studies in deceit.* New York: Macmillan, 1928.
10. Kubany, A. J. A validation study of the error-choice technique using attitudes on national health insurance. *Educ. psychol. Measmt.*, 1953, 13, 157-63.
11. La Piere, R. T. Attitudes vs. actions. *Social Forces*, 1934, 13, 230-37.
12. Likert, R. A technique for the measurement of attitudes. *Arch. of Psychol.*, No. 140, 1932.
13. McNemar, Q. Opinion-attitude methodology. *Psychol. Bull.*, 1946, 43, 289-374.
14. Remmers, H. H. Generalized attitude scales—Studies in social-psychological measurement. *Studies in Attitudes—A Contribution to Social Psychological Research Methods*, Studies in Higher Education 26, Bull. Purdue University, 1934.
15. Remmers, H. H. *Introduction to opinion and attitudes measurement.* New York: Harper, 1954.
16. Remmers, H. H., and Gage, N. L. *Educational measurement and evaluation*, 2nd ed. New York: Harper, 1955.
17. Smith, E. R., and Tyler, R. W. *Appraising and recording student progress.* New York: Harper, 1942.
18. Thurstone, L. L., and Chave, E. J. *The measurement of attitude.* Chicago: University of Chicago Press, 1929.
19. Westie, F. R. A technique for the measurement of race attitudes. *Amer. sociol. Rev.*, 1953, 18, 73-8.

CHAPTER 17

EVALUATION OF SOCIO-ECONOMIC STATUS

In earlier chapters where test scores were discussed, we emphasized that such scores must be interpreted in the light of what is known about an individual's background. We previously noted the relationship between scores on the *Stanford-Binet* and the occupations of parents. Terman (4) showed a difference of 20 points between the mean IQ scores of the sons and daughters of professional people and those of the children of rural owners. We also paid attention to the work of the University of Chicago sociologists in which they demonstrated that a class bias operated on all our group tests of mental ability (1). It may be recalled that the *Davis-Eells Games* were developed as a result of the work of these sociologists. Because the class or group to which an individual belongs or with which he identifies himself is important in our use of test results, in this chapter we shall discuss some of the attempts that have been made to evaluate this social-class belonging or membership.

TECHNIQUES FOR EVALUATING SOCIO-ECONOMIC STATUS

When we evaluate socio-economic status, the techniques that we usually employ are simple. The student often is asked to complete a questionnaire or check list that covers such items as location of home, contents of home, occupation of father, education of parents, and organizations belonged to. Sociologists and social psychologists, on the basis of their research, are able to ascribe an individual's score on one of these scales to a specific socio-economic class. In a large share of this work, the class structure proposed by Warner (5) is followed. Very briefly this is:

1. *Upper-Upper Class.* In this class in any community are found those members of a small group that is based on wealth and "oldness" of the family. "Oldness" usually refers to families who were early settlers in the community. Wealth is mostly inherited. This group includes 1.4 per cent of the population.

2. *Lower-Upper Class.* The newly rich, whose money comes from industry, make up this group. Of all the groups, the highest incomes are found here. Here we find 1.6 per cent of the population.

3. *Upper-Middle Class.* In this group (about 10 per cent of the population) are found the community leaders and "doers." Here are placed most of our business and professional families. Many of these may be wealthy, but they are more or less "upstarts" in the opinion of members of the first 2 groups.

These three levels are above the "Common Man."

4. *Lower-Middle Class.* In this group we find the top layer of the "Common Man." As a whole the group is neither rich nor poor. Clerks, a few skilled workmen, and small retailers are important members of this group. About 30 per cent of the population are in this category.

5. *Upper-Lower Class.* This class includes many of the semiskilled workers found in American industry (about 34 per cent of the population). It might well be labeled "working class." Warner describes them as "poor but honest" workers.

6. *Lower-Lower Class.* In this group are included the poor. Frequently, members of this group are on relief and are, in cities, the inhabitants of slums. Most of our unskilled workers, both urban and rural, belong to this group, which totals about 25 per cent of the population.

DEVICES FOR EVALUATING SOCIO-ECONOMIC STATUS

Sims Score Card for Socio-Economic Status

One of the earliest attempts for the evaluation of socio-economic status was the *Sims Score Card.** This scale of Sims' was made up

* Published by Public School Publishing Co.

of 23 items, covering education of parents, cultural activities engaged in, occupation of parents, and such things as the possession of a telephone, bathtub, and furnace in the home. The scale is for use with students in grades 4-12. According to the manual, it is to be administered as a group test, the examiner reading the items one at a time and the students then marking the appropriate response.

Scoring is accomplished by assigning weighted scores to the various responses. These are summed and divided by 23 (the number of items). The highest possible score is 36, which locates a student in the highest socio-economic group. Scores range downward to zero. The scoring system is laborious and slow and cannot be handled by machine.

The manual has nothing to say about validity and reliability. Certainly some students are going to respond to many of these items on the basis of the social desirability of the item. For example, consider the item on the possession of a bathtub. Some whose home does not contain a bathtub are going to mark this item "Yes." Because of the standards to which they are exposed in school, they feel that they should have a bathtub at home. This is true for many of the other items on the scale that refer to such things as books and magazines.

American Home Scale

The *American Home Scale* * contains 50 items set up in the following 4 sections:

1. *cultural*—which includes the contacts an individual has with books, magazines, people, and education;

2. *aesthetic*—which includes natural surroundings, such as birds and trees as well as the various forms of art;

3. *economic*—which includes all factors contributing to material welfare: food, shelter, clothing;

4. *miscellaneous*—which includes items independent of the above but contributing to socio-economic status.

Scoring, which may be done by hand or by machine, is much simpler than for the *Sims Score Card*. Raw scores for each of the 4 scales may be transformed to standard scores or centiles. High

* Published by Psychometric Affiliates, Chicago.

scores represent upper-class belonging, but no attempt is made in the manual to identify a specific score with a specific class. This scale may be used with students in junior-high school and above.

While the scale is newer, more comprehensive, and easier to score than that of Sims, it still suffers from the possibility that the responses obtained are not true ones but merely the socially acceptable answers. But this is inherent in the use of such scales as these.

Warner-Meeker-Eells Index of Status Characteristics

The *Index of Status Characteristics of Warner, Meeker, and Eells* uses 4 categories: (1) occupation, (2) source of income, (3) house type, and (4) neighborhood. The individual being rated selects the one item in each of these categories that best describes him and the score for each of these items is multiplied by a value as described below to obtain a total score.

Occupation *

1   Professional workers and owners of large businesses
2   Semiprofessional workers and lesser officials in large businesses
3   Clerical workers
4   Skilled workers, carpenters, plumbers, butchers, watchmakers
5   Owners of small businesses
6   Semiskilled workers, truckdrivers, waitresses, night watchmen
7   Unskilled workers, laborers, and servants

Source of Income
1   Inherited wealth
2   Earned wealth, living on savings or investments of the present generation
3   Profits, fees, royalties
4   Salary, based on a monthly or year's amount
5   Wages determined by an hourly rate
6   Private relief, friends, churches, associations
7   Public relief

* Detailed descriptions of each of the divisions of these categories may be found in (5).

Housing

1   Excellent houses, large, well-landscaped, and cared for
2   Very good houses, relatively smaller than above
3   Good houses, slightly larger than needed
4   Average houses, 1-2 story homes
5   Fair houses, not quite as good as "average" or smaller
6   Poor house, badly run down
7   Very poor houses, deteriorated beyond repair, unsafe, littered with junk

Dwelling Area

1   Very high, best houses in town located here
2   Well above average area, superior, but not having reputation of above
3   Area "nice and respectable" but not populated by society
4   Average area populated by workingmen
5   Below average, area close to industry or railroads
6   Low, run-down, semislum, houses set close together
7   Very low, slum district

Originally Warner used amount of income and education in addition to the above 4 categories. Later research showed that these two categories were unnecessary, and, since these data were of a type more difficult to obtain, they were eliminated. An ethnic factor, country or origin of family and race, is also important in social participation and must be considered with the above.

To arrive at a total score we perform the following operations:

$$4 \times \text{Occupation Score} = \underline{\hspace{2cm}}$$
$$3 \times \text{Source of Income Score} = \underline{\hspace{2cm}}$$
$$3 \times \text{House Type Score} = \underline{\hspace{2cm}}$$
$$2 \times \text{Dwelling Area Score} = \underline{\hspace{2cm}}$$
$$\text{Total} = \underline{\hspace{2cm}}$$

This total score is transformed to a social-class equivalent by the following table:

12-22	Upper Class
25-34	Upper-Middle Class
37-50	Lower-Middle Class
54-63	Upper-Lower Class
67-84	Lower-Lower Class

Sims SCI Occupational Rating Scale

The *Sims SCI Occupational Rating Scale** (SCI stands for Social Class Identification) differs from the earlier *Sims Score Card for Socio-Economic Status* and from the *American Home Scale* in that its real purpose is more or less disguised and the problem of obtaining valid responses is lessened. This instrument is for use with high-school and college students.

Sims SCI Scale consists of a list of 42 occupations, ranging from those of the unskilled worker up to professions. Examples are garbage collector, janitor, bricklayer, government clerk, Army colonel, high-school teacher, and United States ambassador. The examinee is to consider each of these occupations and to respond to it on the following scale:

S   If he feels that the people in this occupation belong to the same social class that he and his family do.

H   If he feels that those in this occupation generally belong to a higher social class than he and his family do.

L   If he feels that those in this occupation belong generally to a lower social class than he and his family do.

D   If he is not familiar enough with the occupation to be sure or if he does not care to answer for a particular occupation.

This scale can be completed in a very few minutes. Administration and scoring are very simple. A high score means that the individual identifies himself with the upper-upper class. The range of classes extends from the lower-working class, through the middle class, up to the upper-upper class, as shown on page 425.

In the manual, Sims published evidence supporting the validity of the scale. When the scale was administered to a large group of students from different occupational backgrounds, the mean score for students from homes where the father was a skilled worker was 16.9. The mean for students from professional homes was 25.6. The means for the other groups ranged in between these. He also showed differences in means for students in different types of schools, ranging from a mean of 25.1 for College of Arts and Science students down to 12.0 for trainees in a Veterans' Administration continuation school. Differences in scores between fraternity and sorority

---

* Published by Harcourt, Brace & World.

Fig. 17:1. INTERPRETATION OF SCI SCORES *

SCORE	SOCIAL CLASS LEVEL	EXAMPLES
1-6	lower-working	garbage collector, hired man, domestic cook
7-12	working	factory worker, automobile mechanic, telephone operator
13-18	middle-working	telegraph operator, railroad ticket agent, small grocery-store owner
19-24	middle	real estate salesman, high-school teacher, druggist, owner of large farm
25-30	upper-middle	newspaper editor, minister, civil engineer
31-36	upper	corporation lawyer, surgeon, mayor of a large city
37-42	upper-upper	university president, president of a large bank, United States ambassador

* Adapted from the manual for the *Sims SCI Occupational Rating Scale.*

pledges when compared with nonfraternity and nonsorority freshmen students were highly significant, producing in both cases *t* ratios of about 10. Both fraternities and sororities tend to draw their members from the upper socio-economic levels.

Sims also showed that this scale apparently conceals its purpose (3). He administered it to 69 college seniors and graduate students. When completed, the students were asked what they thought the scale measured. Only one student suspected the purpose to be something other than what it appeared to be but was not sure as to exactly what the scale measured. Since these sophisticated students did not know what the scale was measuring, there is less apparent need for seriously questioning the validity of the responses of less-informed persons.

Reiss (2) presented the results of many years of research at the National Opinion Research Center on the subject of the social status of occupations and the development of a socio-economic index for all occupations. The details of the development of the indices are spelled out in Reiss's book. In the appendix of that book he presents a socio-economic index for the various occupations following the detailed classification used in the Census of 1950. From this scale the following indices are taken as examples:

Dentist	93
Chemist	79
Real estate agent	74
Locomotive engineer	58
Bus driver	24
Bartender	19
Farm laborer	6
Porter	4

The author stated that this scale is not offered as a universally valid measure of socio-economic status. He recommends that other data such as the number of years of schooling completed and the amount of income be used to supplement these index values. A caution is also made that such scale values may change with time as do the bases for the scale values, that is the opinions held by individuals on the status of different occupations.

USES OF SCALES OF SOCIO-ECONOMIC STATUS

The most important use of socio-economic scales is to provide supplemental information for the interpretation of test scores, especially those obtained from intelligence tests. Educational and vocational counseling will be improved by their use, as has been pointed out previously. Scores obtained are also of use in curriculum planning. There is a definite relationship between the type of high-school curriculum followed by students and their home background. The use of these scales reveals the type of new student who will be enrolled, and, as a result, course offerings may be adjusted to them. However, we must remember that at present the chief ladder on which to climb up this socio-economic scale is education. This is apparent to some of the students and, to the extent to which this is so, students will depart from the predicted curriculum.

REFERENCES

1. Eells, K. E., *et al. Intelligence and cultural differences.* Chicago: University of Chicago Press, 1951.
2. Reiss, A. J., Jr. *Occupations and social status.* New York: Free Press of Glencoe, 1961.
3. Sims, V. M. *Sims SCI Occupational Rating Scale, Manual.* New York: Harcourt, Brace & World, 1952.
4. Terman, L. M., and Merrill, M. A. *Measuring intelligence.* Boston: Houghton Mifflin, 1937.
5. Warner, W. L., *et al. Social class in America.* Chicago: Science Research Associates, 1949.

CHAPTER 18

EVALUATION OF TEACHING

It is not unusual to pick up a newspaper or magazine and see such headlines as "Students at University X to Judge Faculty" or "A New Student Revolt." There has been an increasing amount of feeling on the part of college students that they are being neglected by their professors. It is true that many of the modern professors are oriented more toward research than toward teaching and thus do not teach undergraduates or grudgingly do so. This has caused many undergraduates to feel that they have been cheated in their college experience. The major result of this has been an increasing demand for students to be allowed to rate teachers. Some schools have even used student ratings as an official part in the granting of tenure to staff members. In this chapter, along with student ratings of instructors and of instruction, other techniques for evaluating the effectiveness of teaching will be considered.

THE PROBLEMS OF TEACHER EVALUATION

Teacher evaluation has been—and will continue to be—a major problem confronting educators. However, some beginnings toward a solution have been made. Barr (1) and his students have devoted years to the study of this problem from many angles.

A little thought soon reveals to us why teacher evaluation is such a problem. Good teaching first has to be defined, and this is an almost impossible task.

What Makes a "Good" Teacher?

If we read the writings on good and effective teachers, we soon see that a teacher may be "good" for any of a number of different reasons. One man may be a "good" teacher because of the way in which he conducts his class. He may be a drillmaster, but students learn a lot that they use in later life. A sort of halo appears about this teacher. Another may be a "good" teacher because of the effects he has on the personalities of developing boys and girls. Still another is a "good" teacher because his students do so well on tests, both local and state-wide. And another teacher is "good" because of the time and leadership he gives to the school's extracurricular program. Indeed, some teachers, especially in small communities, achieve this distinction because of their contributions to community activities during out-of-school hours. Leadership in professional organizations also helps a teacher to be considered "good," while another teacher is called "good," and steadily promoted, because of the large amount of research he produces and publishes. In many cases, it matters not how good or valuable this research is, just so long as it is published. No one teacher achieves the impossible and carries on all these activities. Very frequently a teacher possesses only one of the above abilities. So, it is difficult to define good teaching. The use of the ratings of such as criteria against which to validate our evaluation scales and tests leads to rather poor results.

Of course, for the purposes of a study, it is possible to define arbitrarily good teaching to be such and such and for us to go ahead with our study. However, what outcome emerges from such a study is of rather limited application.

What Qualities Should the Good Teacher Have?

Just as it is difficult to define good teaching, it is also difficult to decide which characteristics of the teacher are related to successful teaching. Studies over the last 50 years have shown low correlation between grades received while in training and teaching effectiveness. There is a cliché that states that the higher the grades, the poorer the teacher. This is, of course, a misstatement. Sheer academic success is only one part of what makes for good teaching, and a teacher's personality traits are probably much more important. Over the years, research work has shown that such traits as sympathy, good judgment, an interest in people, self-control, enthusiasm for the subject taught, and the like seem to be related to effective teaching. And even without doing research, we could arrive at the same findings. A good teacher should possess those qualities that enable him to get along well with others. Add to this a certain amount of enthusiasm for his work and his subject plus a bit of common sense and we have the good teacher. Intelligence and health are not too important because there is a high probability that most teachers possess enough of both to function adequately.

MEASUREMENT OF TEACHING ABILITY AND TEACHER EFFECTIVENESS

Despite the problems discussed above, the rating of teaching ability and teacher effectiveness is carried on in one form or another wherever there is a classroom. Usually one or more of the following methods is employed: (1) an evaluation of the changes brought about in students; (2) an appraisal of the teacher's achievement, attitudes, and knowledge of educational practices and principles; (3) ratings of the teacher by students; (4) teacher self-evaluation; and (5) ratings made by superiors.

Measurement by the Changes Brought About in Students

In its simplest form, this method consists of administering a series of tests at the end of one year or at the beginning of the second year and following this at the end of the second year with the re-administering of the same or similar tests. Scores of individual students are then examined and growth or the lack of it noted. However, as will be shown below, measurement of these changes is far more complicated than the administration and readministration of 2 sets of tests. But even if teacher evaluation were this simple, we would be left with many problems. For example, it is almost impossible to determine who or what is responsible for the growth measured. Some students learn in spite of the teacher. Some move ahead tremendously on the basis of their readings. Perhaps some progress because of their home environment. Other teachers may be responsible for the changes that come about in the students. Perhaps growth and maturation in themselves contribute to the increment. So it becomes almost impossible to say how much of any measured increment in a student's achievement is related to the work of any one teacher.

Chauncey and Dobbin (3) noted that, when tests are used in evaluating teaching, the following considerations must be made: Do the tests measure basically what the teacher is teaching and does the teacher accept the fact that they do? Exactly what are the chief characteristics of the group being taught? Is the teacher a member of the evaluation team or merely its victim? When such factors are disregarded, they found that: (1) the good teacher who happens to have children from a lower socio-economic background or from barren environments will not look good in comparison to other teachers; (2) a good teacher who has no part in the planning of the evaluation program and who consequently finds that the tests used have different emphases and subject matter will change his ways to teach what the tests measure even though the aims of the teacher were more desirable for the group being taught; (3) a good teacher who has to use a test that he feels does not fit well what he is trying to teach will by the use of quick reviews and cramming sessions get his students ready for the test; and (4) a poor teacher is protected by the testing for he can usually find out by one means or another the general nature of the material on the tests, concentrate on this, whether appropriate or not, and have his students do well. The net result of using tests in the assessment of teaching is to make the test to a great extent the master of the classroom learning situation. Those things that appear on the test are taught. Other things and objectives, perhaps more appropriate for a certain class, are disregarded because the teacher will not be assessed in reference to them.

If we are going to measure changes brought about in students, we must first decide what changes are important. The desired changes are, of course, the objectives of a given class or school and, in many cases, have been worked out in great detail. To measure growth in all these objectives over a given period of time is very difficult. Much time and planning is needed. We have no simple little battery of tests that will do this. Further consideration of objectives will reveal that most of them are related to future activities in which the student may or may not engage in long after he has graduated from school. One of our commonly stated school objectives is to prepare students to participate actively as informed citizens in our democratic society. An objective for a special course, such as health or hygiene, is to learn about and practice lifesaving and artificial respiration. We can give tests to see if a student knows anything about democratic living or artificial respiration, but the real criteria with which we should correlate teaching and learning actually exist way out in the future. Such criteria are said to be "remote." It might be possible for us to collect data on the community activities of alumni and rate them as desirable or undesirable. But the difficulties of the follow-up of former students and the study of them are so great that we usually do not use such as criteria. In some areas, such as lifesaving, a person may never have the opportunity to save a life. Perhaps he could, but the need to do so has never appeared. Thus we have no real criterion for this skill.

Tests to Measure Teaching Ability

Some 30 years ago, batteries of tests to measure teaching ability were quite common. Today none of these older batteries is used, but one of them is discussed below to show the general contents of these tests. Currently the *National Teachers Examination* and its related battery, the *Teacher Education Examination Program*, are the only ones in use. In addition to the test batteries, there are attitude scales toward teaching practices and child development, such as the *Minnesota Teacher Attitude Inventory*.

COXE-ORLEANS PROGNOSIS TEST OF TEACHING ABILITY. One of these is the *Coxe-Orleans Prognosis Test of Teaching Ability*.* Despite its title, the purpose of this test, clearly stated in the manual, was to set standards for admission to normal schools of the past. The test consists of 5 parts: I. "General Information"—78 items, both completion and multiple-choice, such as : "What is the name of the lofty tower in Paris?"; II. "Professional Information"—100 true-false items on child psychology and teaching; III. "Lessons in Education"—such activities as computing a median, scoring a paper, evaluating good test items; IV—a test of reading comprehension; V. "Problems in Education"—situational educational problems with a series of suggested solutions that are to be checked or ranked.

* Published by World Book Co.

This is a very long battery taking about 3 hours to administer. In the manual are presented the correlations between scores on this battery and a comprehensive achievement test in normal-school work given at the end of the school year in a group of normal schools. The average of these 10 correlation coefficients is .656. In the same table appear correlations between scores on the *Terman Group Test of Mental Ability** and the same achievement tests covering normal-school work for the same 10 schools. This time the average correlation is .664. Here again we have the same result that we have already noted several times before. The short, simple, intelligence test requiring about 30 minutes to administer predicts just as well or better than does a much longer battery. It must be recalled that concern here is limited to the prediction of grades only. This may have, as pointed out above, very little to do with teaching ability.

NATIONAL TEACHERS EXAMINATION. The purpose of this battery as stated in the accompanying bulletin is to provide objective examinations for those intellectual capacities felt to be essential for effective classroom teaching. No claim is made that this battery is a measure of teaching ability. However, the various tests do evaluate knowledge of subject matters, cultural background, mental ability, and certain understandings of teaching that are usually agreed upon as being related to succesful teaching. The battery is made up of two major parts: the *Common Examinations* given in the morning to all candidates and the *Teaching Area Examinations* of which the candidate takes one or two parts in the afternoon. The *Common Examinations* includes:

1. Professional Information (covering educational psychology, child development, educational measurement, etc.)
2. English expression
3. Social studies, literature, fine arts
4. Science and mathematics
5. Nonverbal reasoning.

The *Teaching Area Examinations* cover 13 areas:

1. Education in the elementary school
2. Early childhood education

* Published by World Book Co.

3. Biology and general science
4. English language and literature
5. Industrial arts education
6. Mathematics
7. Chemistry–physics–general science
8. Social studies
9. Physical education
10. Business education
11. Music education
12. Home economics education
13. Art education.

Each of the 13 area examinations is designed to measure an individual's competency in his major area of concentration. Candidates for elementary school positions take either "Education in the Elementary School" which covers the range from kindergarten through eighth grade or "Early Childhood Education" which is limited to material up to and through grade 3. Both tests cover knowledge of professional education and teaching methodology as well as elementary school literature, arithmetic, science, history, and the like. The tests for secondary teachers contain specific subject matter for each area and some material devoted to professional education.

This battery may be used in two ways. It makes an excellent device by which an institution may evaluate its individual seniors or graduate students in teacher education or to appraise the success of its own teaching program. Also it may be used by a school organization or system along with other information in the selection and hiring of teachers.

The *National Teachers Examination* is administered four times a year at established centers throughout the United States. Information concerning the location of these centers may be obtained by writing the Educational Testing Service. All arrangements to take the battery must be made in advance with the above agency.

MINNESOTA TEACHER ATTITUDE INVENTORY. An instrument that attempts to measure teacher-student relationships is the *Minnesota Teacher Attitude Inventory (MTAI)*.* This consists of 150 items to which the examinee responds on a 5-point scale, ranging from "strongly agree" to "strongly disagree." The items were constructed

* Published by The Psychological Corporation.

to cover the moral status of children in the opinion of adults; discipline and conduct problems, both in and out of the classroom; principles of child development and behavior; principles of education; and the personal reactions of a teacher, his likes, dislikes, and sources of irritation (4).

It is assumed that when a teacher scores high on this scale he understands students and should be able to work harmoniously with them. Such a teacher is the one found in the child-centered classroom. At the other extreme is the teacher who tries to dominate the classroom. In this he may or may not be successful; but, in either case, a situation is built up in which neither teacher nor students like school. High-school teachers concerned with academic subjects would be expected to score lower on this inventory than elementary teachers.

There has been quite a bit of research based on this instrument. Downie and Bell (6) showed that students scoring high on the *MTAI* tended to have backgrounds of experiences with young people, to express an interest in teaching, and to have been rated high by their instructors as good prospects for the teaching profession. Students who scored low tended to exemplify the extreme opposites. When the scale is used, we see that scores increase as a student progresses through teacher-training—that is, a senior tends to do better than a sophomore. Apparently, exposure to education and psychology courses brings about this change. But after he graduates and as he grows older as a teacher, the scores go down again. These trends are apparent in the norms provided in the manual which comes with the scale. Another factor that affects the scores is the type of curriculum in which the student-teacher is enrolled. A report (10) based upon 737 students taking education courses at Purdue University showed the raw score equivalents for the 50th centile to be for the Men's Physical Education majors, 5; Agriculture, 11; Industrial Education, 17; and males in the School of Science, Education, and the Humanities (Liberal Arts) to be 31. Females in this same school had a score of 38 and girls in Home Economics had an equivalent score of 32. The writer gave this inventory to 156 sophomores of both sexes in teacher-training at the State College of Washington and obtained a raw score equivalent of 55 for the 50th centile. A large part of these sophomores were girls who planned to enter the field of elementary education.

An individual's score on this scale reflects his learning of specific attitudes in education and psychology courses. Differences in attitudes among different schools and different philosophies of education permeating different campuses would lead to these differences. Straight academic teachers would tend to get lower scores. As we grow older, we become less enthusiastic, perhaps more realistic about students, and we score lower. Apparently there is a conflict between theory and practice operating here. This scale, when used with other evidence, offers possibilities in selecting certain types of teachers. Its real value will be demonstrated in the years to come when some of the long-term research now under way in teacher education is terminated.

There has accumulated to date a large amount of evidence that points to the fact that the *MTAI*, like other attitude scales, can be faked. Typical of such research is that of Polmontier and Ferguson (9) who administered the *MTAI* to three groups of teachers with at least two years of experience. All three groups were first administered the scale under standard instructions. Then Group I was re-administered the scale under standard instructions, while Group II was told to make themselves as permissive as possible in their responses and Group III was to reflect an authoritarian attitude. There were no differences among the three groups under normal instructions or between the test-retest scores for Group I (r = .95). However, for Group II the mean rose from 54 to 78 and for Group III fell from 55 to —14. Test-retest correlation coefficients for Groups II and III were .57 and .07 respectively.

In another study, Sorenson and Sheldon (15) summarized previous research, designed a more complicated study of their own, and concluded that students are apt not to fake the *MTAI* in a counseling situation, but would be much more likely to do so in a selection situation. Also they stated that groups of students are not likely to be able to fake the *MTAI* unless they receive a cue from the instructions, or elsewhere, as to what the scale is all about.

KELLEY-PERKINS HOW I TEACH SCALE. Another instrument that evaluates a teacher's knowledge of human growth and development is the *Kelley-Perkins How I Teach Scale.** Part I consists of 30 items to be evaluated on a 5-point scale extending from "decidedly harmful" to "decidedly beneficial." These items concern such classroom procedures and practices as keeping a record of all unusual behavior, telling a pupil he can succeed in any type of work if he really tries, and following the same exact schedule every day. The second part consists of 30 attitudinal items that are to be responded to using the response pattern of a *Likert Scale.* Two examples are "Dishonesty is a more serious personality characteristic than unsocialness" and "Children have no one to blame but themselves, if they are bad." The third part consists of 15 items related to child growth and development, which are to be responded to on a 5-point scale ranging from "undoubtedly false" through "uncertain" to "undoubtedly true." An example of this type of item: "The pupil who excels in one ability necessarily is poor in another."

STUDENT EVALUATION OF TEACHING

Much has been written in the past few years about student evaluation of teaching. The mention of student ratings is usually enough to start an argument any time a group of teachers gets together. One is led to wonder just why all the fuss.

The Arguments Against Student Evaluation

We will first look at some of the arguments frequently voiced against student evaluation. The most common of these is that students are in no position to know what is good teaching and that it takes experience and age to evaluate a complex process like teaching. The writer feels that nothing is further from the truth. It is rather platitudinous to say that no one is in the classroom more than the students. If they cannot tell good teaching from bad, then it follows that no one can. If there is agreement among a group of students that a certain instructor possesses this or that undesirable trait or follows this or that poor practice, then there must be some truth to it that merits looking into. What students feel about a teacher or a practice is in itself important. Another point here is that there is

* Published by Educational Test Bureau.

no other individual who is in a better position to rate a teacher than is the student. Some administrators rate teachers without ever observing them, using merely hearsay evidence or such things as the number of students that the teacher sends to the office for disciplinary reasons. Supervisors have a bit more evidence. But the students are in class every day and have a chance to see the teacher under all sorts of conditions. Frequently, when a second adult, such as a principal or supervisor, is in a classroom, the situation is quite different from what it is when they are not there. Thus any ratings these individuals might make are made under atypical conditions. Perhaps the students aren't experts on educational matters—nor should they be expected to be—but their opinions of the value of what they are exposed to daily should not be overlooked. Student evaluation of teaching does not let the students decide what should or should not be taught or how. As will be pointed out below, there is a little chance for this to happen when this technique is used correctly.

Another charge frequently made is that these ratings by students tend to set up popularity contests among the faculty. Again, the writer sees little justification for this charge. Ratings by students should be confidential between teacher and class. There is no reason for other teachers to become involved or be used for comparison in a given rating situation.

Others claim that such factors as ability of the student, achievement of the student, whether the course is a required or an elective one, sex of the instructor, and many other variables that might have something to do with grades, have an effect upon the type of rating received by the instructor. As will be seen below, there is very little to justify any of these claims.

It has been observed that these charges against student ratings tend to come from older subject-matter-oriented academicians at both the high-school and university level who have never tried such ratings—and, of course, never will. Perhaps because of some hunches, some of them wouldn't dare to have students rate them. (As one of these teachers told the writer, he would not have courage to pick the ratings up and face the results.) The autocratic classroom runs so smoothly from the teacher's point of view that any student interference, even suggestions, might lead to chaos. Many such claims are probably rationalizations of or other defenses against using these ratings by people who are afraid of the facts of life.

Student evaluation of teaching should be confidential between students and teacher, as we just said. Its sole purpose should be to improve teaching. The teacher gathers these data because he is interested in making himself a better teacher. Contrast this emphasis with the manner in which these student data have been used by some administrators who collected the information to use for promotion or even for discharging a teacher.

The writer uses such teacher-evaluation scales most of the time as follows: Toward the end of the semester he brings the rating sheets to class and, about 20 minutes before the end of the period, explains what is to be done and passes out the scales. A large manila envelope is put at the front of the room. Students put their completed rating sheets into this. The student who finishes last is asked to seal up the envelope and bring it to the instructor's office. The students are told that the ratings will not be opened until all the semester's grades are completed and turned in. This is meticulously done. The writer has also found it to be a good plan to be out of the room when the students are filling out the blanks and handing them in. Of course, no names are placed on the rating sheets. The writer feels that students like to fill out these sheets and that they usually do a careful and thoughtful job with them.

When a university pays little heed to the feelings of the students about the kind of teaching they receive, students have been known to take matters into their own hands and to run an evaluation of the faculty themselves. More than one faculty has found itself confronted with such an evaluation, and even more—with a little book sold to entering freshmen containing all that is to be known, good and bad, about each instructor and his practices. Many universities now have a service (usually operated by the testing or evaluation department), which will tabulate and summarize these rating sheets for instructors. The blanks are provided free. All that is needed is the interest and initiative of the instructor. These services are always confidential. Since students are ready for this practice and may do it any way, a wise teacher makes the most of the opportunity. All teachers are evaluated and rated by students whether a teacher wants it or not.

Again, an interested teacher capitalizes on this to his own improvement.

Two Studies of Student Evaluation

The writer (5) once had at his disposal about 16,000 evaluation forms on faculty members filled out by students. From these data an attempt was made to answer the question of the effect of certain variables upon these ratings. First, the grade point averages were considered. A dichotomy was made of students above "C" *versus* students below "C" and results studied. In this study, a questionnaire of 36 items was used. On only one item were the instructors marked less favorably by the higher group. This was the extent to which the course objectives were met. The lower group rated less favorably such items as fairness, objectivity, and promptness in returning and going over tests, and items related to student-instructor relations. When responses between students in required and elective courses were compared, no major differences were found. A comparison of responses of students in junior and senior courses with those in the freshman and sophomore courses showed the students in the upper division gave higher ratings to items related to intellectual stimulation and desire for more work in the area. When student ratings in large classes (over 30) were compared with those in small classes, it was found that 17 of the items covering instructional procedures, tests, and value of the course received less favorable ratings in the large classes. On the other hand, in the small classes 4 items covering instructor-student ratings received harsher ratings.

Data were also available as to age, rank, degree held, sex, and number of years on the staff of each instructor. Ratings of 257 staff members under 40 years of age were compared with those of 169 age 40 and over. No differences were found. The ratings of 59 full professors, 79 associate professors, 103 assistant professors, and 165 instructors were next studied. Here the full professors tended to be rated higher on such items as background of interests and experiences, humor, and effectiveness of presentation. All 3 ranks were rated higher than instructor on knowledge of subject matter. The ratings of 161 staff members with the doctorate, 191 with a master's degree, and 52 with only a baccalaureate degree were compared. Here there was a tendency for those with higher degrees to get higher ratings on knowledge of subject matter, organization of the course, and stimulating intellectual curiosity. The ratings of 300 male instructors when compared with those of 106 female instructors showed little difference. And, finally, being on the staff over 5 years had no effect on the rating when these ratings were compared with those on the staff less than 5 years. The intellectual ability of the students, except as measured through their grade-point averages, was not a variable considered separately in this study. Bryan (2), in an earlier study, showed no appreciable differences between the ratings of high and low IQ groups. Several other conclusions of Bryan's might be noted here. Since many more students than administrators were used in his study, he found the ratings of the former to be more reliable. (He had teachers rated by both students and administrators.) Also he noted that the amount of agreement between the ratings of high-school seniors and administrators were in direct proportion to the degree of contact that the administrator had with the teachers and pupils.

Riley and others (13) summarized a total of about 34,000 individual rating sheets on 384 faculty members of Brooklyn College. From a list of 10 qualities considered important to good teaching, each student was asked to note the top 3 for teachers in the arts, pure sciences, and social sciences, respectively. These 10 qualities were: (1) organization of subject matter, (2) speaking ability, (3) ability to explain, (4) encouragement to thinking, (5) attitude toward students, (6) knowledge of subject, (7) attitude toward subject, (8) fairness in examinations, (9) tolerance of disagreement, and (10) personality—the instructor as a human being. Then each student was asked to rate the teacher he met first, second, third, fourth, or fifth in the week's program, depending upon the first initial of his name. In addition he was free to rate 4 other teachers of his choice with whom he was currently enrolled.

It is interesting to note here that the qualities deemed essential for effective instruction varied considerably, depending upon the area of which the course rated was a part. The 3 teaching qualities considered most important to students in the arts were, in order: knowledge of subject matter, encouragement of thought, and enthusiasm for subject. In the pure sciences, ability to explain, organization of subject matter, and knowledge of subject were so listed.

And in the social sciences the 3 noted were encouragement of thought, organization of subject matter, and tolerance toward disagreement. It might be noted here that "sympathetic attitude," "fairness on tests," "pleasing personality," and "speaking ability" were given very low ratings. In general, students wanted their instructors to know their subjects well and on that score they rated their instructors satisfactorily. Students also wanted their instructors to stimulate thought, and it is here, according to the students, that their teachers failed most strikingly.

Some of the more specific findings were that the full professors tended to be rated highest in knowledge of subject matter. The lower ranks, however, were rated higher in enthusiasm for subject, attitude toward students, tolerance of disagreement, and in personal attractiveness.

An attempt was made to gain some insight into the factors influencing student judgment, and the following variables were studied in their relationship to the ratings given by students: students' grades, size of class, sex of student, year in college, and whether or not the class was required or elective. Of these, only grades produced any noticeable differences. On every attribute except one, "knowledge of subject matter," students with low scholastic standing were more critical than the better students. This criticalness of the poorer students was also noted in the previous study (5). In certain of the courses, differences in these variables produced differences in the ratings.

The research workers who carried out this study stated that "a collection of student ratings of instructors has no claim to validity as an over-all measure of teaching quality. Nor is the student conception of 'ideal' teaching presented as anything but a yardstick with which to measure student satisfaction with reality as he finds it." However, they pointed out that some faculty members had to be reassured that no duplicate of their ratings would be made for the president of the college, dean, or department head. Two hundred and eighty-four of the 384 Brooklyn College faculty who had been rated attended departmental meetings where the results of the survey were discussed. Of those present, about 200 expressed a favorable opinion, although only about 60 accepted the judgment of the students as valid. Some 150 considered the student ratings of themselves to be helpful, while 80 said that these were of no help at all. The president of Brooklyn College felt that the survey served its purpose because of the professional discussion it provoked on the campus and that some of the specific conclusions reached deserved further attention.

At this point, we might note that these two studies reported above and others have usually resulted in showing slight relation or none at all between IQ, achievement, and other variables, except that low grades seem to make students more critical. We can wonder if this is rationalization. Large classes frequently receive a greater percentage of poorer ratings than small classes. This fits in with a general feeling which Americans have that real learning takes place in the small class where there are intimate student-instructor relationships. These ratings have also been shown to be reliable. A sample of 300 papers were drawn from the 16,000 mentioned in the first study reported above, and a reliability coefficient of a trifle less than .95 was computed by the split-half method. In summarizing data, the writer has seen 4 almost identical profiles constructed on the basis of ratings turned in by 4 separate classes taught by one instructor. Reliability seems to be of no problem with these scales. It should be emphasized here also that this is a very economical evaluation device, costing little in terms of materials, and revealing a great deal of important information.

Remmers (11) summarized the research on student evaluation of teaching in part as follows:

1. The reliability of the ratings of teachers is a function of the number of students doing the rating. When 25 or more students perform the rating, reliability is as high as that of well-made psychological tests (12).
2. There is no relationship between grades received by students and their evaluation of teachers.
3. There is little or no relationship between students' ratings of a course and the difficulty of a course.
4. The sex of a student is not related to ratings given teachers by students.
5. The sex of the teacher is generally not related to the ratings received.

6. Alumni, 10 years after graduation, agree to a certain extent (r's from .40 to .68) with current campus evaluations in their average ratings of the same instructors and agree very highly ($r = .92$) on the relative importance of ten teacher characteristics (7).

7. Students can reliably discriminate among different aspects of an instructor's personality and of his course, and in any given institution there are wide differences among student evaluations of different departments and the teachers in each.

8. Students are more enthusiastic about such ratings than are instructors, but more instructors than students have noted improvement in their teaching as a result of student evaluation (12).

Methods of Obtaining Student Ratings

Once a teacher or a faculty has decided to conduct a student evaluation of teaching, he or they must decide on the method to employ.

Two Rating Scales. The most conventional approach to teacher evaluation is to build up some sort of a rating scale. The 36-item scale discussed above consisted of 4 parts: (1) "Instructional Procedures"—9 items on organization, assignments, student involvement in classroom activities and attainment of objectives; (2) "Tests, Examinations, and Quizzes"—6 items on validity of tests, grading, and the opportunity to discuss results; (3) "Value of the Course"—7 items on stimulation produced, cultural value, etc.; and (4) "Instructor-Student Relations"—14 items covering humor, appearance of instructor, understanding of students, and tolerance. Each of these items was to be evaluated on a 5-point scale from (A) "this course is one of the best (or most effective) that I've ever had in this respect" to (E) "one of the least effective." A wide space was left at the right-hand margin for student comments. The writer believes that sometimes the most revealing information appears in these comments and that the students should be encouraged to fill in these spaces.

Another widely used scale is the *Purdue Rating Scale for Instruction* (Fig. 18.1). This scale is printed on two sides of a sheet of paper. On the first page are 10 items for the rating of the instructor: interest in subject, sympathetic attitude toward students, fairness in grading, liberal and progressive attitude, presentation of subject

11. Suitability of the method or methods by which subject matter of the course is presented (recitation, lecture, laboratory, etc.).......................... $\overline{11A}$ $\overline{11B}$ $\overline{11C}$ $\overline{11D}$ $\overline{11E}$

12. Suitability of the size of the class (consider the subject matter and type of class—lecture, lab., etc.)............ $\overline{12A}$ $\overline{12B}$ $\overline{12C}$ $\overline{12D}$ $\overline{12E}$

13. The degree to which the objectives of the course were clarified and discussed .... $\overline{13A}$ $\overline{13B}$ $\overline{13C}$ $\overline{13D}$ $\overline{13E}$

14. The agreement between the announced objectives of the course and what was actually taught...................... $\overline{14A}$ $\overline{14B}$ $\overline{14C}$ $\overline{14D}$ $\overline{14E}$

15. Suitability of the reference materials available for the course............... $\overline{15A}$ $\overline{15B}$ $\overline{15C}$ $\overline{15D}$ $\overline{15E}$

16. Suitability of the laboratory facilities available for the course............... $\overline{16A}$ $\overline{16B}$ $\overline{16C}$ $\overline{16D}$ $\overline{16E}$

17. Suitability of the assigned textbook..... $\overline{17A}$ $\overline{17B}$ $\overline{17C}$ $\overline{17D}$ $\overline{17E}$

18. The use made of tests as aids to learning .... $\overline{18A}$ $\overline{18B}$ $\overline{18C}$ $\overline{18D}$ $\overline{18E}$

Fig. 18:1. SECTION OF THE *Purdue Rating Scale for Instruction*, PAGE 2 *

matter, sense of proportion and humor, self-reliance and confidence, personal peculiarities, personal appearance, and stimulating intellectual curiosity. Above each of these across the page is a continuum ranging from a wholly desirable or highly favorable condition on one end to its extreme opposite on the other. Each line is broken into 10 parts. The student selects the piece that best reflects his attitude and places a black mark in the appropriate space on the small answer card that is used with the scale. On page 2 there are 16 items on which the rater evaluates certain aspects of the course on a 5-point scale. Included here are such items as frequency of tests, uses made of tests, suitability of the texts and references, attainment of the course objectives, and the like. Again the student's responses are placed on the same answer card, no marks being made on the scale itself. These answer cards are then run through a computer and frequency counts made of the responses. Mean values are calculated

* Reproduced by permission of the Purdue Research Foundation. Copyright 1950.

for each item to be used in constructing a profile sheet for each class, thus revealing the instructor's strengths and weaknesses. The chief advantage of such a scale is that a large number of ratings can be summarized rapidly and the different classes of one instructor compared or the results among various instructors compared if they so desire. The structure of the scale and the small answer card used limit the students' responses to the items on the scale. Since it is impossible to write any additional comments on the scale, valuable information is often lost by this restriction.

THE INCOMPLETE SENTENCE TECHNIQUE. Lindgren (8) discussed the use of the incomplete sentence technique as a means of evaluating a course. He felt that the typical rating approach failed to reveal to an instructor how students really felt about a course, and he noted that filling out one of these questionnaires was like writing a letter of recommendation or rating a former employee. There is a feeling of relief now that the course is over and a desire not to hurt an individual's feelings. Since one will probably have no more to do with a given instructor, he can be charitable. A student might also evaluate himself and conclude that, after all, since he himself did not do his best, he should not blame the instructor too much for lack of success on the part of both. In this manner, Lindgren discussed the rating scales, and, as a result, he tried using a sentence-completion blank of some 33 items to evaluate a summer workshop. This was set up in the same fashion as was Rotter's (14), which was discussed in Chapter 14. As a result, Lindgren felt that he received information that was certainly more expressive and more interesting to him as a teacher. Also this nondirective approach resulted in keener insights into the feeling of the students about the course and its instructor.

For the past few years, the writer has been using an evaluation sheet, modified from Lindgren's, at the end of his course in elementary tests and measurement. A copy of it is shown on page 447.

One of the major objections usually made to such an approach is that the results are difficult to summarize or to quantify. However, if we want to, we can set up a 7-point scale for the evaluation of the responses to each item, as Rotter did with his sentence-completion blank. These can range from very undesirable or poor responses through neutral ones to most desirable or excellent responses. The

Fig. 18:2. EVALUATION SHEET *

Directions: Complete each of the following by making a complete sentence. Work rapidly and try to express your real feeling. Center all your remarks on this course and its instructor. Do not sign your name. When finished put your answer sheet in the manila folder on the front desk. *Answer every item.*

1. This course...
2. The best..
3. The worst...
4. What I liked most..
5. This class...
6. The main trouble..
7. Since I have taken this course..............................
8. I don't see...
9. This course has helped me..................................
10. What bores me..
11. Instructor X...
12. I shall be happy if..
13. The lectures in this course.................................
14. I feel that Instructor X....................................
15. Standardized tests...
16. I would like..
17. Statistics...
18. When this course is over...................................

writer, when he wishes to summarize his evaluation sheets, does no more than classify the responses to each item as positive, negative, or neutral. Many times the responses merely are read for the over-all ideas. To one who has many times used both approaches for gathering student opinion it seems that the amount of information obtained and the unusual insights discovered by the incomplete-sentence technique are never in any way approximated by the use of the rating scale.

Another free-response device that is frequently used is to set up a sheet as follows:

1. The (three) best features of this course are:
   a ....
   b ....
   c ....
2. The (three) worst features of this course are:
   a ....
   b ....
   c ....

* Adapted from Lindgren (1952), by permission of G. F. Kuder.

3. I would improve the course by:

    a ....
    b ....

Here again the student has a chance to put down those things about which he has strong feelings. Again the chief disadvantage is summarizing by hand.

With this we conclude our discussion of student rating of instruction. It is strongly recommended that teachers try these techniques and prove to themselves their merits and values.

Teacher Self-ratings

Another approach to teacher evaluation is to have the teacher himself complete such a scale as the *Minnesota Teacher Attitude Inventory* or the *Kelley-Perkins How I Teach Scale.* By comparing his responses with those given as most desirable, he will have a good idea as to how he compares with what is considered good teaching. It is a matter of common acceptance among educational psychologists that the best type of evaluation is self-evaluation.

Supervisor Ratings

In the past, there existed a vast number of rating scales and score cards to be filled out by administrators and supervisors on teachers over whom they had jurisdiction. Some of these still exist and are used in the same autocratic way as they were in the past, despite the fact that we now know that such ratings as these are of low reliability because of the rater's lack of information about the ratee. Granted that some supervisors know their teachers well because of real supervisory practices. Ratings of student-teachers by their supervisors are apt to be higher both in respect to reliability and validity. Contrast these, though, with those made by the principal who has to rate the entire faculty of a large school.

Summary

At this point the student or teacher might wonder which of the practices discussed in this chapter are best for him to use. The writer feels that, of all of those discussed, student ratings of the teacher and his methods are by far the most practical and fruitful when used by the teacher to gather information to make him a better teacher. Any teacher would profit also by obtaining one of the attitude scales discussed here, administering it to himself, and seeing how he compares with the various norm groups.

REFERENCES

1. Barr, A. S. Measurement and prediction of teacher effectiveness. *Rev. educ. Res.*, 1946, 16, 203-8.
2. Bryan, R. C. Pupil ratings of secondary school teachers. *School Review*, 1938, 44, 357-68.
3. Chauncey, H., and Dobbin, J. E. Should tests be used to assess teachers? In *Testing: Its place in education today.* New York: Harper and Row, 1964. Pp. 102-7.
4. Cook, W. W. *The Minnesota Teacher Attitude Inventory: Manual.* New York: Psychological Corporation, 1951.
5. Downie, N. M. Student evaluation of faculty. *J. higher Ed.*, 1952, 23, 495-7.
6. Downie, N. M., and Bell, C. R. The Minnesota Teacher Attitude Inventory as an aid in the selection of teachers. *J. educ. Res.*, 1953, 46, 699-704.
7. Drucker, A. J., and Remmers, H. H. Do alumni and students differ in their attitudes toward instructors? *Purdue University Studies in Higher Education*, 1950, No. 70, 5-61.
8. Lindgren, H. C. The incomplete sentence tests as a means of course evaluation. *Educ. psychol. Measmt.*, 1952, 12, 217-25.
9. Polmontier, P. C., and Ferguson, J. E. Faking the Minnesota Teacher Attitude Inventory. *Educ. Psychol. Measmt.*, 1960, 20, 79-84.
10. Purdue University, Division of Education, Committee on Selection and Guidance. *Purdue Norms for the Minnesota Teacher Attitude Inventory.* Report No. 2, Lafayette, Ind., April 1956, mimeo.
11. Remmers, H. H. Rating methods in research on teaching. In N. L. Gage, ed., *Handbook of Research on Teaching.* Chicago: Rand McNally, 1963. Pp. 329-78.
12. Remmers, H. H. *The Purdue Rating Scale for Instruction: Manual.* Lafayette, Ind.: University Book Store, 1960.
13. Riley, J. W., *et al. The student looks at his teacher.* New Brunswick, N. J.: Rutgers University Press, 1950.
14. Rotter, J. B. *Incomplete Sentence Completion Blank: Manual.* New York: Psychological Corporation, 1950.
15. Sorenson, R. G., and Sheldon, M. C. A further note on the fakability of the MTAI. *J. appl. Psychol.*, 1958, 42, 74-8.

APPENDIXES

APPENDIX

MAJOR PUBLISHERS AND DISTRIBUTORS
OF TESTS

American Guidance Service, Inc., 720 Washington Ave., S.E., Minneapolis, Minn. 55414.

Bobbs-Merrill Co., Inc., 4300 W. 62nd St., Indianapolis, Ind. 46206.

Bureau of Educational Research and Service, East Hall, State University of Iowa, Iowa City, Iowa 52240.

California Test Bureau, Del Monte Research Park, Monterey, Cal. 93940.

Consulting Psychologists Press, Inc., 577 College Ave., Palo Alto, Cal. 94306.

Educational Testing Service, Princeton, N. J. 08540.

Harcourt, Brace & World, Inc., 757 Third Ave., New York, N. Y. 10017.

Harper & Row, Publisher, 49 E. 33rd St., New York, N. Y. 10016.

Houghton Mifflin Co., 2 Park St., Boston, Mass. 02107.

Institute for Personality and Ability Testing, 1602 Coronado Dr., Champaign, Ill. 61822.

The Psychological Corporation, 304 E. 45th St., New York, N. Y. 10017.

Psychometric Affiliates, Box 1625, Chicago, Ill. 60690.

Science Research Associates, Inc., 259 E. Erie St., Chicago, Ill. 60611.

Sheridan Supply Co., Box 837, Beverly Hills, Cal. 90213.

C. H. Stoelting and Co., 424 N. Homan Ave., Chicago, Ill. 60624.

Western Psychological Services, 12045 Wilshire Blvd., Los Angeles, Cal. 90025.

APPENDIX

GLOSSARY

Ability Test. A test that measures an individual's current status. An example is a typing test administered to see how well a job applicant for a typing position can type. See GENERAL ABILITY and SPECIAL ABILITY

Achievement Test. A test usually administered at the end of a period of learning to measure growth and progress. The typical classroom test is of this type.

Age Equivalent. A system of scoring that is used on standardized tests in which the average score of various age groups is determined. Then an individual's score on a test may be translated into these equivalents. If a child is said to have a mental age of 8-8 (8 years, 8 months), this means that his score on the given test is the same as that of the typical child of 8 years and 8 months.

Age Norms. Values or norms that show the typical or average performance for individuals of different age groups on a test.

Age Scale. A test the results of which are expressed in years and months. The *Stanford-Binet* is an example of this. A typical score on this test might be 7 years, 7 months—that is, a mental age of 7-7.

Aptitude Test. As used in this book, such a test is employed to predict future behavior. It may be an intelligence test, achievement test, or personality or interest inventory. Many of our intelligence tests are called "scholastic aptitude tests" because they are used to predict an individual's future school performance.

Arithmetic Mean ($\bar{X}$ or M). The sum of the raw scores divided by the number of cases. More exactly, that point in a distribution about which the sum of the deviations equals zero. Also called simply *mean* or *average.*

$$\overline{X} = \frac{\Sigma X}{N}$$

Assumed Mean. The midpoint of an interval in a frequency distribution from which deviations are computed in calculating the arithmetic mean for group data. The assumed mean may be taken in any interval without affecting in any way the value of the mean.

Attitude. A learned tendency to respond in a certain way when aroused by a specific stimulus.

Average. See ARITHMETIC MEAN

Basal Age. A term used in *Stanford-Binet* testing to denote the highest age level at which an individual responds correctly to all of the items making up that level.

Battery. In general, a group of tests administered at one time for a specific purpose. More specifically, *battery* is reserved for the achievement tests used in the elementary schools, each of which is made up of 4 or more tests measuring different parts of the curriculum.

Biased Sample. A sample that gives a distorted picture of a group. For example, if we were to obtain a sample of homes in a given community by taking every twentieth name in a telephone directory, our sample would be biased because households without telephones are excluded. This would, however, give us an adequate sample of homes having telephones.

Ceiling. The upper limit of a skill or ability as measured by a test.

Centile (*C*). A point in a distribution below which fall that percentage of cases designated by the number of the centile. For example, C_7 is that point in the distribution with 7 per cent of the cases below it. PERCENTILE (P) is used synonymously with centile.

Central Tendency. A point in a distribution about which a majority of the cases tend to fall. The *mean, median,* and *mode* are measures of central tendency.

Chronological Age (*C.A.*). An individual's age as expressed in years and months, as 13-7.

Class Interval. See FREQUENCY DISTRIBUTION

Clerical Ability. In its simplest form, the ability to handle words and numbers (symbols) rapidly and accurately. Basically, perception.

Coefficient of Equivalence. The type of reliability coefficient obtained when parallel forms of the same test are administered to the same individuals.

Coefficient of Internal Consistency. The type of reliability coefficient obtained when either the split-half or *Kuder-Richardson* methods are used in computing it.

Coefficient of Stability. The type of reliability coefficient obtained when the same test is administered twice to the same individuals.

Continuum. A line along which a trait is conceived as being distributed. At one end of the line, we might find the absence of the trait and at the other end, the maximum amount. In dealing with personality traits, we frequently set up continuums with the maximum negative amount of the trait at one end, zero at the middle, and the maximum positive amount at the opposite end.

Correction for Guessing. Adjusting scores on objective tests to counteract the effects of students' guessing the correct answer. Considered to be of questionable usefulness and validity by some test workers.

Correction Formulas. The formulas used in correcting for guessing. Using such a formula, an individual's score on a test is the number correct minus the number wrong, this latter being divided by one less than the number of possible responses to the items. For 4-response multiple choice items, the score is

$$R - \frac{W}{N - 1}$$

Correlation Coefficient. A statistic used to measure the relationship between 2 sets of variables or data. The maximum value of this statistic is 1. Most often r (the *Pearson Product-Moment Correlation Coefficient*) is used to measure correlation. But note that this statistic is not necessarily a measure of a causal relationship.

Criterion. A set of scores, measures, ratings, products, etc. used in validating a test. Grades in school are used as criteria in validating intelligence tests. Ratings by foremen or units produced in a given period of time may be used as criteria in validating a test of mechanical ability. The criterion is that which the test is constructed to predict.

Critical Ratio (CR). A value obtained in testing the significance of differences by dividing the difference between 2 statistics by the standard error of the difference. For example, suppose the first mean ($\overline{X}_1$) is 84, the second mean ($\overline{X}_2$) is 78, and the standard error of the difference between the two means ($s_{\overline{X}_1 - \overline{X}_2}$) is 2. Then

$$CR = \frac{\overline{X}_1 - \overline{X}_2}{s_{\overline{X}_1 - \overline{X}_2}} = \frac{84 - 78}{2} = 3.00$$

This is interpreted as a standard deviation unit or a z-score, 2.58 being the 1-per-cent level, and 1.96 the 5-per-cent level. CR is used with large samples. With small samples, a t-test is used. These 2 are the same except for the matter of their use and evaluation. See t-TEST

Culture-free Test. Usually an intelligence test devised to rule out the effects of an individual's environment on his score. Mazes, "draw-a-man" tests, and some nonverbal tests are examples. Probably it is impossible to construct a really culture-free test.

Cumulative Frequency (cf). A column in a frequency distribution that shows for any given interval all the scores in the distribution that lie below the upper limit of that interval.

Curvilinear Relationship. A relationship that departs from linearity. For example, suppose that in the beginning of the range variable Y increases as variable X increases. But at a certain point, as variable X continues to increase, variable Y begins to decrease and continues to do so. The Pearson r or Spearman rho must not be used when data take this form. See LINEAR RELATIONSHIP

Decile. Each of 9 points in a distribution that divides the distribution of scores into 10 equal parts. For example, the tenth centile is equal to the first decile.

Decoy. See DISTRACTOR

Descriptive Statistics. A group of values used in describing a sample, such as mean, standard deviation, centiles, etc. See SAMPLING STATISTICS

Deviation IQ. A form of standard score which has a mean of 100 and a standard deviation of about 15, as compared to the conventional IQ, which is the ratio of mental age to chronological age. The results of Wechsler's intelligence tests are expressed in deviation IQ's.

Diagnostic Test. A test used to show an individual's weaknesses and strengths in a certain area of study. Such tests are frequently encountered in reading and arithmetic. Personality and interest inventories have "diagnostic profiles" that show an individual's high and low points in various areas measured by the instrument.

Discriminating Power. The extent to which an item separates contrasting groups, such as good students from poor students or well-adjusted individuals from poorly adjusted persons. Usually expressed as a correlation coefficient.

Distractors. Those parts of a multiple-choice item that are not the correct response. The incorrect responses to an item. Also called *decoys.*

Educational Age. Average-age norms covering the elementary school subjects. Suppose that on a test the educational age corresponding to a raw score of 68 is 8 years and 2 months (8-2). This means that children of a chronological age of 8 years and 2 months have an average score of 68 on this test.

Educational Quotient (EQ). The ratio of the educational age to the chronological age.

$$EQ = \frac{EA}{CA} (100)$$

End Test. A test given at the end of a period of learning.

Equivalent Form. See PARALLEL TEST

Error Score. An individual's obtained score is made up of 2 parts: the true component and the error component. The latter part, the error score, is that which is associated with the unreliability of the test. Daily fluctuations in an individual's traits, chance discrepancies in test administration and scoring, etc., contribute to this error score.

Extrapolation. Estimating values of a variable beyond the range of available data. If a line or pattern is established between 2 variables, and the assumption is made that the established pattern will continue, then it is possible to interpret scores higher or lower than those for which data are available.

Face Validity. A measuring instrument has face validity when it seems to be valid to the individual being measured. The taker feels that the test is fair and appropriate. But the instrument may have no real validity.

Factor. A theoretical component obtained by making a factor analysis. Also used in the interpretation of and as the name given to the results of a factor analysis, such as spatial factor, memory, etc.

Factor Analysis. Any method of analyzing intercorrelations among a set of tests or other variables in which an attempt is made to account for the complex group of intercorrelations in terms of several underlying factors.

First Quartile. See Q_1

5-per-cent Level. A level of confidence in which a probability statement is made that the chances are 95 in 100 of something's being so. There are 5 chances in 100 that it is not so.

Free-response Test. A test on which the items are of such a nature that the examinee responds in his own words. The essay examination and such projectives as the *Rorschach* are examples of this.

Frequency Distribution. A tabulation of scores, usually from low to high, showing the number of individuals who obtained each score.

Usually, to save space and to make the data easier to manipulate, the data are grouped into intervals of various sizes depending upon the data. The number of these intervals is usually between 10 and 20. For example, the lowest interval of a distribution might be 5-9. This interval includes all individuals whose raw score was 5, 6, 7, 8, or 9. The class interval (*c.i.*) for this interval is 5. Its lower limit is 4.5, its midpoint, 7, and its upper limit, 9.5.

General Ability. Another term used synonymously with *intelligence.* See SCHOLASTIC ABILITY

General Education. A term used to refer to that common core of learning which all high-school and college students study regardless of the curriculum or course of study in which they are enrolled.

Grade Norms. Norms used on standardized achievement tests indicating the average scores of students at different grade levels. With such norms a student beginning the sixth grade might have such scores as 6-3 in geography, 6-8 in history, etc. The first of these means that his score in geography is that of the average student three tenths of the way through grade 6.

Graphic Rating Scale. A scale on which a trait is spread out on a line (continuum) with descriptive phrases written along the line. The rater considers the individual in reference to the trait under consideration and places a mark on the line indicating his opinion of the amount of the trait possessed by the individual being rated.

Group Test. A test so constructed that it can be administered to more than one individual at a time.

Halo Effect. The tendency in rating an individual to let one of his traits, either desirable or undesirable, influence ratings on other traits.

Homogeneity. Tendency of a group to be alike. Little variation. Small standard deviation.

Individual Test. A test that can be administered to only one individual at a time. The *Stanford-Binet* and many performance tests are individual tests.

Inference. The act of making a logical statement, deduction, or conclusion on the basis of data at hand.

Intelligence Quotient (IQ). The ratio obtained by dividing mental age by chronological age.

$$IQ = \frac{MA}{CA}(100)$$

This is useful with children but of little value with adults because mental age does not continue to increase at a constant rate and it eventually ceases to sometime in late adolescence or early adulthood.

Interpolation. The act of estimating a value between 2 given values or points.

Interval. See FREQUENCY DISTRIBUTION

Inventory. As used in this book, the term applied to an evaluation instrument used to appraise personality, attitude, or interests. Differs from a test in that there are no right and wrong answers to the items.

Item Analysis. A statistical study of test results to determine: (1) the difficulty of each item, (2) the discrimination index of each item, (3) sometimes its correlation with an outside criterion, and (4) how well each of the distractors is working.

Item Difficulty. The percentage or proportion of individuals taking a test who respond correctly to an item. An item of 83-per-cent difficulty is one answered correctly by 83 per cent of the examinees.

Item Discrimination. Usually one of several kinds of correlation coefficient that shows the correlation between the responses to a single item and total test scores. A high index (large correlation coefficient) indicates high item discrimination as those who scored high on the test answered the item correctly and those who scored low answered it incorrectly.

Kuder-Richardson Formulas. Several formulas used in determining the reliability of a test. The most widely used of these is computed by using the difficulty of each item and the standard deviation of the test. The coefficients produced by this method are coefficients of internal consistency similar to those obtained by the split-half method. Like the latter, these should not be used with speed tests.

Level of Confidence. A term used to show the amount of confidence that can be placed in a statement about a true or population value. We say that the chances are 99 in 100 that the true or population mean falls between 2 values. Such a statement as this is made at the 1-per-cent level of confidence.

Linear Relationship. A relationship between 2 variables of such a nature that as one variable increases or decreases the other does likewise. The relation between the size of a community and the number of children in school is of this type: the larger the community, the larger the school enrollment.

Local Norms. Norms that are made by collecting data in a certain school or school system and using these to evaluate student performance in place of national or regional norms. See NORMS

Low Ceiling. Term applied to a test that is too easy for many examinees. Many tend to score at the top or near it and, instead of being spread out, all receive the same score. Many of our group intelligence tests have low ceilings.

Lower Limit of an Interval (or of a Number). In statistics, numbers are considered to be points on a continuous band. The number 17, for example, starts at 16.5, its lower limit, and ends at 17.499999+ (17.5), its upper limit. An interval, say of 9-11, has 8.5 as its lower limit and 11.5 as its upper limit. Its midpoint is 10.0.

Mastery Test. A test given with a single objective in mind—that of determining to what extent individuals in a group have learned or mastered a given piece of material or lesson which was assigned.

Mean. See ARITHMETIC MEAN

Mechanical Ability. A term applied to a group of factors or skills taken together. Usually we find that the ability to perceive spatial relationships, manual and finger dexterity, and mechanical knowledge or information are the basic components of this so-called "mechanical ability."

Median (Mdn.). That point in a distribution of scores with 50 per cent of the cases on each side of it. The midpoint of a distribution. Equal to C_{50} or P_{50}. The appropriate measure of central tendency when a distribution of scores departs from normal in its shape.

Mental Age (MA). A term used in which to express the results of some intelligence tests. A mental age of 12 years indicates mental ability the same as that of the average 12-year-old child. On the *Stanford-Binet,* each item is worth a certain number of months mental age. The sum of these for all of the items answered correctly results in an individual's mental age.

Midpoint of an Interval. The point halfway between the lower limit and the upper limit of a class interval of a frequency distribution. In the interval 10-13, the midpoint is 11.5, half the distance between 9.5 and 13.5.

Mode (Mo.). That score which appears most frequently in a set of scores. When scores are arranged in a frequency distribution, the mode is taken to be the midpoint of the interval containing the largest number of cases. The least frequently used measure of central tendency.

Multiple Correlation Coefficient (R). This statistic is used in prediction when more than 2 variables are involved. In simple prediction, we can predict grades (y) from intelligence test scores (x). Suppose now that we add high-school rank (w) and scores on a certain scale of an interest inventory (z). The correlation between y and the combination of w, x, and z which best predicts y is called the multiple correlation coefficient. Prediction efficiency is usually increased by using more than one predictor variable.

N. In statistics, the symbol designating the number of individuals or things.

National Norms. Norms based upon sampling supposedly representative and comprehensive enough to be considered truly national. Good national norms are difficult to obtain and set up and are often of limited use in the schools. See NORMS

Nonverbal Test. A paper-and-pencil test usually used with young children (those in the primary grades) in which the test items appear as symbols, figures, and pictures rather than words. A series of items made up of 4 objects, one of which is different and is to be marked, is typical of a nonverbal test.

Normal Distribution. A distribution of scores that is bell-shaped. The mean is at the center (point of greatest height) and 3 standard deviations measured off on each side of this mean will include practically all the cases. Much of our work in educational measurement is based upon an assumption of a normal distribution of psychological traits.

Norms. Statistics or values that describe the performance of various groups on a test or inventory. A student's score on the test can be referred to the norms accompanying the test and his performance evaluated as being good, average, poor, etc. Norms are *averages*, not *standards*. In any typical class, a teacher might expect half the class to be above the norm and the other half below the norm. See LOCAL NORMS; NATIONAL NORMS

Null Hypothesis. A statement of no difference that is set up when making a test of significance. Suppose that we have 2 means, *A* and *B*, and we wish to test to determine if there is a significant difference between the 2 means. We start out by stating a null hypothesis that we shall test, namely that mean *A* does not differ from mean *B* or, in other words, that mean *A* is equal to or is the same as mean *B*.

Objective Test. A test that is scored in such a way that no matter who scores it results are the same. Scoring keys or stencils are used.

Ogive Curve. A type of curve obtained by plotting cumulative proportions or percentages. Also called an *S*-shaped curve. Useful in setting up centile norms.

Omnibus Test. A test that contains all types of items mixed together rather than having them arranged by types. Usually a single score is obtained from the use of such a test.

1-per-cent Level. A level of confidence in which a probability statement is made that the chances are 99 in 100 of something's being so. There is 1 chance in 100 that it is not so.

Parallel Tests. Two tests are parallel when they have equal means and equal standard deviations and are composed of similar items measuring the same material, abilities, or objectives. In tests of special abilities or aptitude tests, each form should correlate similarly with the same external criterion. Also called *comparable, alternate,* or *equivalent* forms.

Parallel-Form Reliability Coefficient. A type of reliability coefficient obtained by first administering one form of a test to a group and following this with a parallel form of the same test and computing the correlation coefficient between the 2 sets of results. This is the technique usually used with speed tests.

Parameter. A population value. See STATISTIC

Percentile (P). See CENTILE

Performance Test. A type of test that requires motor responses, usually manual. Formboards, pegboards, mazes, work-sample tests, etc. are examples of this type. The opposite of paper-and-pencil test.

Point Scale. A type of test in which each item responded to correctly contributes a certain number of points to the individual's score. See AGE SCALE

Population. In statistical work, an arbitrarily defined group from which samples are drawn. For example, all fifth-grade children in a certain state might be a population. Or all freshmen engineering students in land-grant universities. *Universe* is used as a synonym.

Power Test. A test with no time limit. The examinee works until he answers all the items.

Pretest. A test given at the beginning of a period of learning or of a course to appraise initial status. Growth that has taken place is determined by the administration of an *end test* when the learning period is over.

Probability. The likelihood of an event's occurring. Chance. In measurement, predictions are made in terms of probability statements, such as that the chances are 99 in 100 that such-and-such will occur.

Product-Moment Correlation Coefficient (r). The most widely used method of correlating data when a linear relationship prevails. Developed by Pearson.

Profile. A graphic presentation of the results of an individual's performance on a group of tests.

Prognostic Test. Any test that is used to predict achievement. Used frequently in algebra and plane geometry.

Projective Technique. A disguised, frequently vague, situation to which a subject reacts. In doing so we hope that he will unwittingly reveal aspects of his own behavior which will aid the examiner in assessing the individual's adjustment. He "projects" himself into the inkblot or picture that makes up the instrument.

Psychograph. See PROFILE

Psychometrist. A person who administers psychological tests and other instruments.

Psychometry. The measurement of human traits, such as intelligence, special abilities, interests, etc.

Quartile Deviation (Q). A measure of variability. One half the distance between Q_1 and Q_3. Also known as the *semi-interquartile range.*

Q_1. The first quartile. That point in a distribution which has 25 per cent of the cases below it. Equal to C_{25}.

Q_3. The third quartile. That point in a distribution below which fall 75 per cent of the cases. Equal to C_{75}.

r. See PRODUCT-MOMENT CORRELATION COEFFICIENT

Random Sample. A sample so drawn that every individual in the population has an equal chance of being drawn into it. Random sampling is basic to the use of sampling statistics. See BIASED SAMPLE

Range. The distance between the high and low scores in a distribution of scores.

Rank-Order Correlation (rho). A method of obtaining a correlation coefficient by assigning ranks to each score of all individuals, getting the difference between these 2 ranks, squaring each of these, summing, and using Spearman's formula:

$$\text{rho} = 1 - \frac{6\Sigma D^2}{N(N^2 - 1)}$$

Rating Scale. A verbal or graphic device used in obtaining ratings of individuals. See GRAPHIC RATING SCALE

Raw Score. The original, untreated result that is obtained from a test or other measuring instrument.

Readiness Test. Any test that is used to ascertain whether an individual has attained the maturity necessary to profit from learning. Most commonly associated with reading.

Reading Age. Special type of age-equivalent score that indicates a child's reading ability in age terms.

Reliability. Consistency of measurement. A test is reliable to the extent that it consistently produces results which are similar. Reliability is expressed in terms of correlation coefficients or by use of the standard error of measurement.

Reliability Coefficient. The correlation coefficient obtained by correlating scores obtained from 2 administrations of the same test, between parallel forms of a test, or between halves of a test. See TEST-RETEST, PARALLEL-FORM, SPLIT-HALF, and KUDER-RICHARDSON COEFFICIENTS

Response Set. The tendency for an individual to respond differently to a test item in the form that it is in from the manner in which he would respond if the idea in the item were in some other form.

rho. See RANK-ORDER CORRELATION

Sample. A group drawn from a population. See RANDOM SAMPLE

Sampling Statistics. That branch of statistics which is concerned with the making of inferences about population values on the basis of sample values or in testing the significance of the difference between 2 or more statistics.

Scattergram (SCATTERPLOT). A double-entry chart used in the computation of the *Pearson Product-Moment Correlation Coefficient.* An inspection of the scatterplot gives an indication of the sign (positive or negative), size, and shape (linear or curvilinear) of the relationship.

Scholastic Ability. The ability to do successful school work. Book-learning ability is a synonym. Most of our verbal tests of intelligence measure this ability.

Semi-interquartile Range. See QUARTILE DEVIATION (Q)

Sigma. See STANDARD DEVIATION

Significant Difference. A difference between 2 statistics that is a true or real difference, not one attributable to chance.

Skewness. The tendency for some distributions of scores to pile up at either end of the distribution rather than at the center. A very easy test would produce such a distribution. Such a distribution is said to be *negatively skewed,* the tail going off to the left. A very difficult test would be *positively skewed,* the tail this time going to the right.

Sociometry. The determination of the social relationships among the members of a group.

Spearman-Brown Formula. In a special sense, the formula used when the reliability of a test is computed by the split-half method. Since reliability is related to length, longer tests being more reliable, and since the split-half method actually cuts a test down to half its size, the resulting coefficient indicates the reliability of a test only half the size of the original one. The use of the *Spearman-Brown Formula* raises this coefficient to what it should be for a test the same length as the original one. The same formula can be used generally to determine the reliability of a test any given number of times larger or smaller than a certain test.

Special Ability. Term used for such abilities as mechanical, clerical, musical, and artistic to separate them from general ability or intelligence.

Speed Test. A timed test made up entirely of very easy items. Given enough time on such a test, most examinees would have almost perfect or perfect scores.

Split-half Reliability Coefficient. A type of reliability coefficient obtained usually by correlating individuals' scores on the odd-numbered items of a test with their scores on the even-numbered items and correcting the results with the *Spearman-Brown Formula.* This technique should not be used with speed tests.

Spiral-Omnibus Test. A type of test in which the varieties of items are mixed up but arranged in order of difficulty. A test might start with a vocabulary item, then comes a problem item, followed by a reasoning type of item, etc. until one of each of all the different kinds used on the test is used. Another sequence of similar items then appears, but this time each is more difficult than the previous. This plan continues throughout the test with the items becoming increasingly more difficult.

S-shaped Curve. See OGIVE CURVE

Standard Deviation. The most widely used measure of variability, being used when the mean is used as the measure of central tendency and the data approximate a normal curve. A very useful statistic in measurement work because of this relationship to the normal curve, one standard deviation taken on each side of the mean together including approximately 68 per cent of the cases and 3 standard deviations (sigma units) including together practically all of the cases.

Standard Error. The standard deviation of a group of sample values about the population value.

Standard Error of a Score. See STANDARD ERROR OF MEASUREMENT

Standard Error of Estimate. A value that gives us an indication of the accuracy of our prediction. Suppose that a standard error of estimate of 3 is obtained by the formula:

$$s_{y/x} = s_y \sqrt{1 - r^2}$$

where s_y is the standard deviation of the test and r the validity coefficient being used in prediction. In this case, we are predicting Y from X. This standard error of estimate of 3 means then that for any given X value the chances are 2 out of 3 that the predicted Y value will fall in a band of 3 units on each side of the Y value as determined by the regression equation. The larger the validity coefficient (r), the smaller the standard error of estimate.

Standard Error of Measurement. An estimate of the size of the error of measurement in a score. All scores are unreliable to a certain extent. Suppose, using this formula, that we estimate the standard error of measurement to be 2:

$$s_e = s \sqrt{1 - r}$$

where s is the standard deviation of the test and r the reliability coefficient of the test. We can say then that the chances are 2 out of 3 that any individual's obtained score is within 2 units (the standard error of measurement) of his true score. The larger the reliability coefficient, the smaller the standard error of measurement.

Standard Score (z-score). A type of score in which each individual's raw score is expressed in the number of standard deviation units that it is from the mean.

$$z = \frac{X - \overline{X}}{s} = \frac{x}{s}$$

Standardized Test. A test that has been given to various samples or groups under standardized conditions and norms established.

Stanine (Standard nine). A type of standard score with a mean of 5, a standard deviation of 2, and a range between 1 and 9.

Statistic. A sample value. A value that describes a sample such as mean, median, standard deviation, etc.

Stem. The introductory part of a multiple-choice test item that is to be completed by one of the responses below or following.

Stratified Random Sample. A type of sample in which the population is first broken down into groups that make it up (such as freshman, sophomore, junior, and senior), and the proportion of the total that each group makes up then computed. Next, a random sample is drawn in each group. In this way, the proportions in the sample are the same as those in the population.

Subjective Test. Tests that are often scored on the basis of the attitudes, opinions, and idiosyncrasies of the scorer. The essay test is an example of this. Different scorers get different results.

Sum of the Squares. A value obtained by subtracting each raw score from the mean, squaring each, and adding these squares. Used in computing standard deviation.

$$\Sigma x^2 = \Sigma (X - \overline{X})^2$$

Survey Test. A general achievement test in a certain subject where the emphasis is on one or two aspects of that subject, such as rate of reading and level of comprehension. Used in screening groups and frequently in sectioning. See DIAGNOSTIC TEST

Test of Significance. A test made to see whether or not 2 or more observed differences are true differences and not the type brought about by chance fluctuations.

Test–Retest Reliability Coefficient. A type of reliability coefficient obtained by administering a test to a group, then readministering the same test and running a correlation coefficient between the 2 sets of scores.

Time-Limit Test. Test so constructed that the time allotted for working is usually ample enough to give individuals an opportunity to reach their limit or the top of their ability.

Third Quartile. See Q_3

True Score. A score that would be obtained if we had a perfectly reliable measuring instrument. If it were possible to test an individual over and over again with the same test, the mean of all of these test scores would be an estimation of an individual's true score. True scores are never obtained.

T-Score. Normalized standard score with a mean of 50 and a standard deviation of 10.

t-Test (See CRITICAL RATIO). A test of significance that, when used for testing differences, is the ratio of the difference between 2 statistics divided by the standard error of the difference. The resulting ratio, when N is small, is interpreted using a special table. When N is large, this is interpreted in the same manner as the critical ratio.

Universe. See POPULATION

Upper Limit of an Interval or Number. The theoretical upper limit of a number when data are treated as being continuous. For example, the number 12 starts at 11.5 and ends at 12.4999+, its upper limit.

Validity. In general, the extent to which a test or other evaluation device does what it is supposed to do. Usually discussed by types as follows: *Concurrent validity* is a type of validity in which the criterion measures are collected at the same time that the test is administered. An instrument that separates the well-adjusted from the poorly adjusted has concurrent validity. *Construct validity* is a type of validity determined by investigating what psychological traits or factors a test measures. *Content validity* is a type of validity that is brought about by seeing that the test does an adequate job in covering both the content and the objectives of a course or unit of study. This type of validity is most commonly associated with achievement tests for which no adequate criteria are available for the computation of validity coefficients. Sometimes referred to as *curricular* or *logical validity*. *Predictive validity* is a type of validity in which the criterion measures are collected at a time later than when the test is administered. School grades obtained at the end of the semester when correlated with intelligence tests given at the beginning of the semester result in validity coefficients of this type. Also referred to as *statistical* or *empirical validity*.

Verbal Test. A test in which results depend to a great extent upon the use and comprehension of words. Most of our pencil-and-paper tests are of this type.

X (or Y). In measurement work the symbol used to designate a raw score.

x. The deviation of a score from the mean. $x = X - \bar{X}$. The sum of the deviations about the mean is always zero.

z-score. See STANDARD SCORE

INDEXES

474 INDEX

Warner, W. L., 420, 423, 427
Wechsler, D., 255, 258, 298
Weiner, M., 263-4, 298
Weisbrodt, J., 125, 130, 221
Welsh, G. S., 370
Westie, F. R., 407, 418
White, W. F., 331, 370
Wickman, E. K., 333, 371
Wissler, C., 257

Womer, F. B., 128, 130
Wood, D. A., 194
Woods, C. G., 12, 19
Woodworth, R. S., 358, 361
Wrightstone, J. W., 167
Wrinkle, W. L., 72, 81
Wundt, W. M., 256

Yerkes, R. M., 258

SUBJECT INDEX